Adobe Illustrator® CS4 Digital Classroom

Adobe Illustrator® CS4 **Digital Classroom**

Aquent Creative Team

Wiley Publishing, Inc.

AQUENT

Adobe Illustrator® CS4 Digital Classroom

Published by
Wiley Publishing, Inc.
10475 Crosspoint Boulevard
Indianapolis, IN 46256

Published by Wiley Publishing, Inc., Indianapolis, Indiana
Published simultaneously in Canada
ISBN: **978-0-470-43635-6**
Manufactured in the United States of America
10987654321

For general information on our other products and services or to obtain technical support, please contact our Customer Care Department within the U.S. at (800) 762-2974, outside the U.S. at (317) 572-3993 or fax (317) 572-4002.

Please report any errors by sending a message to errata@aquent.com

Library of Congress Control Number: 2008936130

Wiley also publishes its books in a variety of electronic formats. Some content that appears in print may not be available in electronic books.

About the Authors

Aquent Creative Team is composed of Adobe Certified Experts and Adobe Certified Instructors from Aquent Graphics Institute (AGI). The Aquent Creative Team has authored many of Adobe's official training guides, and works with many of the world's most prominent companies helping them to use creative software to communicate more effectively and creatively. They work with marketing, creative, and communications teams around the world, and teach regularly scheduled classes at AGI's locations. More information at ***agitraining.com***.

Acknowledgments

Thanks to our many friends at Adobe Systems, Inc. who made this book possible and assisted with questions and feedback during the writing process. Thanks also to the many clients of AGI who have helped us better understand how they use Photoshop and provided us with many of the tips and suggestions found in this book. A special thanks to the instructional team at AGI for their input and assistance in the review process and for making this book such a team effort.

Credits

Writing
Sean Mcknight, Jerron Smith,
Caitlin Smith, Robert Underwood

Series Editor
Christopher Smith

Senior Acquisitions Editor
Jody Lefevere

Technical Editors
Chad Chelius, Larry Happy, Cathy Palmer

Editor
Marylouise Wiack

Editorial Manager
Robyn Siesky

Business Manager
Amy Knies

Senior Marketing Manager
Sandy Smith

Vice President and Executive Group Publisher
Richard Swadley

Vice President and Publisher
Barry Pruett

Project Coordinator
Lynsey Stanford

Graphics and Production Specialist
Lauren Mickol

Media Development Project Supervisor
Jeremy Osborn

Proofreading
Jay Donahue

Indexing
Broccoli Information Management

Stock Photography
iStockPhoto.com

Contents

Starting Up

Lesson 1: Adobe Illustrator CS4 Jumpstart

Lesson 2: Getting to Know the Workspace

Lesson 3: Illustrator CS4 Essentials

Lesson 4: Adding Color

Lesson 5: Working with the Drawing Tools

Lesson 6: Working with and Formatting Text

Lesson 7: Organizing your Illustrations with Layers

Lesson 8: Working with Symbols

Lesson 9: Using Effects and Transparency

Lesson 10: Exporting and Saving Files

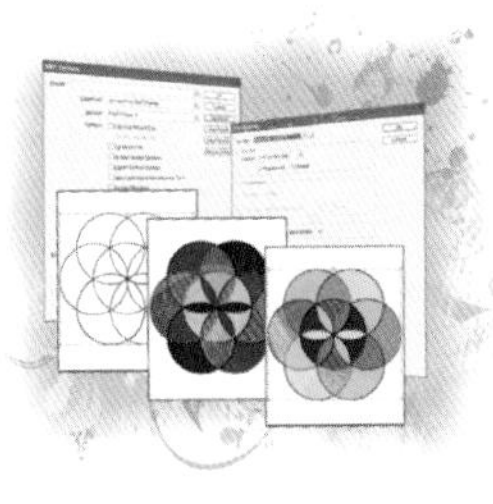

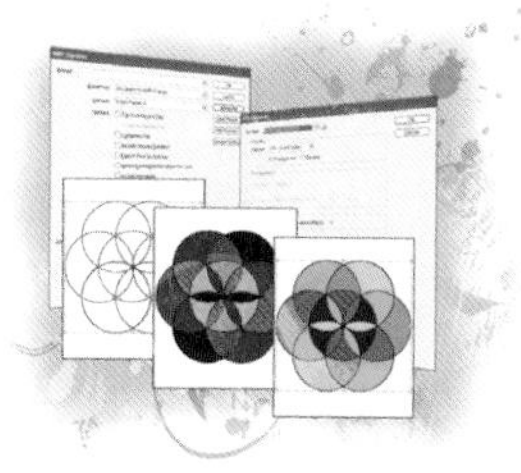

Lesson 11: Advanced Blending Techniques

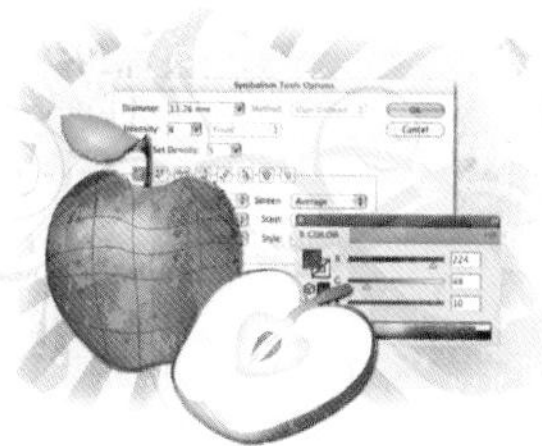

Lesson 12: Illustrator CS4 New Features

Starting up

About Digital Classroom

Adobe® Illustrator® CS4 lets you create artwork for a variety of uses. Illustrator's drawing tools let you take advantage of many ways to control color, text, and artwork in your designs. Illustrator provides you with ways to express your creative ideas and experiment with the presentation. Illustrator CS4 is also tightly integrated with other Adobe products such as Photoshop® CS4 and Flash® CS4 Professional.

Adobe Illustrator CS4 Digital Classroom is like having your own personal instructor guiding you through each lesson while you work at your own speed. This book includes 12 self-paced lessons that let you discover essential skills and explore the new features and capabilities of Illustrator CS4. Each lesson includes step-by-step instructions, lesson files, and video tutorials, all of which are available on the included DVD. This book has been developed by the same team of Adobe Certified Instructors and Illustrator experts who have created many of the official training titles for Adobe Systems.

Prerequisites

Before you start the lessons in *Illustrator CS4 Digital Classroom,* you should have a working knowledge of your computer and its operating system. You should know how to use the directory system of your computer so that you can navigate through folders. You need to understand how to locate, save, and open files. You should also know how to use your mouse to access menus and commands.

Before starting the lessons files in *Illustrator CS4 Digital Classroom*, make sure that you have installed Adobe Illustrator CS4. The software is sold separately, and not included with this book. You may use the 30-day trial version of Adobe Illustrator CS4 available at the *adobe.com* web site, subject to the terms of its license agreement.

System requirements

Before starting the lessons in *Illustrator CS4 Digital Classroom*, make sure that your computer is equipped for running Adobe Illustrator CS4, which you must purchase separately. The minimum system requirements for your computer to effectively use the software are listed on the following page.

System requirements for Adobe Illustrator CS4:

Windows OS

- 2GHz or faster processor
- Microsoft® Windows® XP with Service Pack 2 (Service Pack 3 recommended) or Windows Vista® Home Premium, Business, Ultimate, or Enterprise with Service Pack 1 (certified for 32-bit Windows XP and Windows Vista)
- 512MB of RAM (1GB recommended)
- 2GB of available hard-disk space for installation; additional free space required during installation
- 1,024x768 display (1,280x800 recommended) with 16-bit video card
- DVD-ROM drive
- Internet or phone connection required for product activation

Macintosh OS

- PowerPC® G4 or G5 or Intel® processor
- Mac OS X v10.4.11–10.5.4
- 512MB of RAM (1GB recommended)
- 2GB of available hard-disk space for installation; additional free space required during installation
- 1,024x768 display (1,280x800 recommended) with 16-bit video card
- DVD-ROM drive
- QuickTime 7 software required for multimedia features
- Internet or phone connection required for product activation

Starting Adobe Illustrator CS4

As with most software, Adobe Illustrator CS4 is launched by locating the application in your Programs folder (Windows) or Applications folder (Mac OS). If necessary, follow these steps to start the Adobe Illustrator CS4 application:

Windows

1. Choose Start > All Programs > Adobe Illustrator CS4. If you have the Creative Suite installed, you may have to select Adobe Illustrator from within the Creative Suite folder.
2. Close the Welcome Screen when it appears. You are now ready to use Adobe Illustrator CS4.

Mac OS

1. Open the Applications folder, and then open the Adobe Illustrator CS4 folder. If you have the Creative Suite installed, you may have to select Adobe Illustrator from within the Creative Suite folder.
2. Double-click on the Adobe Illustrator CS4 application icon.
3. Close the Welcome Screen when it appears. You are now ready to use Adobe Illustrator CS4.

Menus and commands are identified throughout the book by using the greater-than symbol (>). For example, the command to print a document would be identified as File > Print.

Fonts used in this book

Illustrator CS4 Digital Classroom includes lessons that refer to fonts that were installed with your copy of Adobe Illustrator CS4. If you did not install the fonts, or have removed them from your computer, you may substitute different fonts for the exercises or re-install the software to access the fonts.

If you receive a Missing Font Warning, press OK and proceed with the lesson.

Resetting Adobe Illustrator CS4 preferences

When you start Adobe Illustrator, it remembers certain settings along with the configuration of the workspace from the last time you used the application. It is important that you start each lesson using the default settings so that you do not see unexpected results when working with the lessons in this book. Use the following steps to reset your Adobe Illustrator CS4 preferences.

Steps to reset Adobe Illustrator CS4 preferences

1 Quit Illustrator.

2 Locate and rename the AIPrefs (Windows) or Adobe Illustrator Preferences (Mac OS), as follows.

- In Windows: Rename the AIPrefs file (for example, to AIPrefs.old) in the Documents and Settings/*(user)*/Application Data/Adobe/Adobe Illustrator CS4 Settings folder.
- In Windows Vista: Rename the AIPrefs file (for example, to AIPrefs.old) in the Users/*(user)*/AppData/Roaming/Adobe/Adobe Illustrator CS3 Settings/*(language_location)* folder.
- In Mac OS: Rename the Adobe Illustrator Preferences file in the Users/*(user)*/Library/Preferences/Adobe Illustrator CS4 Settings folder.

3 Start Illustrator. Illustrator creates a new preferences file.

To restore custom settings, delete the new AIPrefs file and restore the original name of the previous AIPrefs file.

Loading lesson files

The *Illustrator CS4 Digital Classroom* DVD includes files that accompany the exercises for each of the lessons. You may copy the entire lessons folder from the supplied DVD to your hard drive, or copy only the lesson folders for the individual lessons you wish to complete.

For each lesson in the book, the files are referenced by the file name of each file. The exact location of each file on your computer is not used, as you may have placed the files in a unique location on your hard drive. We suggest placing the lesson files in the My Documents folder (Windows) or at the top level of your hard drive (Mac OS).

Copying the lesson files to your hard drive:

1 Insert the *Illustrator CS4 Digital Classroom* DVD supplied with this book.

2 On your computer desktop, navigate to the DVD and locate the folder named ailessons.

3 You can install all the files, or just specific lesson files. Do one of the following:

- Install all lesson files by dragging the ailessons folder to your hard drive.
- Install only some of the files by creating a new folder on your hard drive named ailessons. Open the ailessons folder on the supplied DVD, select the lesson you wish to complete, and drag the folder(s) to the ailessons folder you created on your hard drive.

Macintosh users may need to unlock the files after they are downloaded. This only applies to MacOS computers. After downloading the files to your computer, select the ailessons folder, then choose File > Get Info. In the ailessons info window, click the You can drop-down menu labeled Read Only, which is located in the Ownership section of this window. From the You can drop-down menu, choose Read & Write. Click the arrow to the left of Details, then click the Apply to enclosed items... button at the bottom of the window. You may need to click the padlock icon before the Mac OS allows you to change these permissions. After making these changes, close the window.

Working with the video tutorials

Your *Illustrator CS4 Digital Classroom* DVD comes with video tutorials developed by the authors to help you understand the concepts explored in each lesson. Each tutorial is approximately five minutes long and demonstrates and explains the concepts and features covered in the lesson.

The videos are designed to supplement your understanding of the material in the chapter. We have selected exercises and examples that we feel will be most useful to you. You may want to view the entire video for each lesson before you begin that lesson. Additionally, at certain points in a lesson, you will encounter the DVD icon. The icon, with appropriate lesson number, indicates that an overview of the exercise being described can be found in the accompanying video.

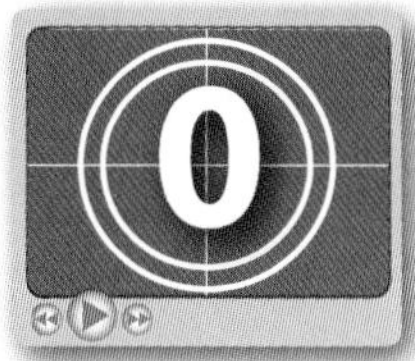

DVD video icon.

Setting up for viewing the video tutorials

The DVD included with this book includes video tutorials for each lesson. Although you can view the lessons on your computer directly from the DVD, we recommend copying the folder labeled *Videos* from the *Illustrator CS4 Digital Classroom* DVD to your hard drive.

Copying the video tutorials to your hard drive:

1 Insert the *Illustrator CS4 Digital Classroom* DVD supplied with this book.

2 On your computer desktop, navigate to the DVD and locate the folder named Videos.

3 Drag the Videos folder to a location onto your hard drive.

Viewing the video tutorials with the Adobe Flash Player

The videos on the *Illustrator CS4 Digital Classroom* DVD are saved in the Flash projector format. A Flash projector file wraps the Digital Classroom video player and the Adobe Flash Player in an executable file (.exe for Windows or .app for Mac OS). However, please note that the extension (on both platforms) may not always be visible. Projector files allow the Flash content to be deployed on your system without the need for a browser or prior standalone player installation.

The accompanying video files on the DVD use the Adobe Flash Video format to make universal viewing possible for users on both Windows and Mac OS computers.

Playing the video tutorials:

1 On your computer, navigate to the Videos folder you copied to your hard drive from the DVD. Playing the videos directly from the DVD may result in poor quality playback.

2 Open the Videos folder and double-click the AIvideos_PC.exe (Windows) or AIvideos_Mac.app (Mac OS) to view the video tutorial.

3 Press the Play button to view the videos.

The Flash Player has a simple user interface that allows you to control the viewing experience, including stopping, pausing, playing, and restarting the video. You can also rewind or fast-forward, and adjust the playback volume.

***A**. Go to beginning. **B**. Play/Pause. **C**. Fast-forward/rewind. **D**. Stop. **E**. Volume Off/On. **F**. Volume control.*

Playback volume is also affected by the settings in your operating system. Be certain to adjust the sound volume for your computer, in addition to the sound controls in the Player window.

Additional resources

The Digital Classroom series goes beyond the training books. You can continue your learning online, with training videos, at seminars and conferences, and in-person training events.

Book series

Expand your knowledge of creative software applications with the Digital Classroom series of books. Additional titles covering topics such as Flash, Dreamweaver, Photoshop, and InDesign are available. Learn more at *digitalclassroombooks.com*.

Seminars and conferences

The authors of the Digital Classroom seminar series frequently conduct in-person seminars and speak at conferences, including the annual CRE8 Conference. Learn more at *agitraining.com* and *CRE8summit.com*.

Resources for educators

Visit *digitalclassroombooks.com* to access resources for educators, including instructors' guides for incorporating Digital Classroom into your curriculum or to contact the authors.

Adobe Illustrator CS4 Jumpstart

What you'll learn in this lesson:

- Working with graphic styles
- Warping text
- Adding a symbol to the Symbols panel
- Using the Color Guide
- Converting artwork
- Erasing paths
- Creating a 3-D object

In this lesson, you will complete several exercises and receive an introduction to some of the important capabilities of Adobe Illustrator. Have fun with this lesson—these features are covered in more detail in later lessons. If you feel uncomfortable jumping right in to creating a project, you can skip to Lesson 2, "Getting to Know the Workspace" and come back to this lesson later.

Starting up

Before starting, make sure that your tools and panels are consistent by resetting your workspace. See "Resetting Adobe Illustrator CS4 Preferences" on page 3.

You will work with several files from the ai01lessons folder in this lesson. Make sure that you have loaded the ailessons folder onto your hard drive from the supplied DVD. See "Loading lesson files" on page 4.

See Lesson 1 in action!

Use the accompanying video to gain a better understanding of how to use some of the features shown in this lesson. The video tutorial for this lesson can be found on the included DVD.

The project

In this lesson, you will create artwork for a CD case and map it to a 3-D object.

1 Launch Adobe Illustrator CS4.

2 Choose File > Browse in Bridge or press the Go to Bridge button (Br) in the application bar at the top of the workspace.

By pressing the Go to Bridge button within Illustrator, you launch a separate application called Adobe Bridge. Bridge is an indispensable application that acts as the central command center for all your CS4 Suite applications and helps you organize your Adobe Illustrator projects. You can use Bridge to help you easily locate files. With Adobe Bridge, you can see a preview of every file within any folder.

3 Once Bridge opens, navigate to the ai01lessons folder within the ailessons folder that you copied to your computer and double-click ai0101_done.ai to open it. The artwork for a CD cover appears. The CD artwork contains objects created in Adobe Illustrator CS4 using auto trace, symbols, the Eraser tool, and Live Color feature. In the following exercises, you will create this file. You can keep this completed file open for reference, or choose File > Close to close it.

The completed CD artwork.

4 The Illustrator CS4 workspace is consistent with the other applications in the Creative Suite 4, which helps you to find the tools you need faster, no matter which application you are using.

Click on the gray bar above the Tools panel to toggle between a one-column and two-column view. The images in this lesson display the two-column Tools panel, but you can choose whichever format you prefer, as both options allow you to access all the tools.

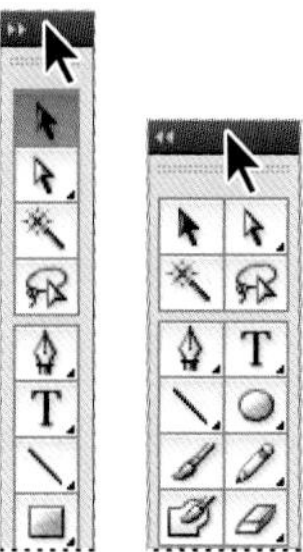

The Tools panel can be viewed as one column or two.

5 For this lesson, you want to have multiple panels showing at the same time. To make sure that you can follow the lesson more easily, choose Window > Workspace > Essentials.

Creating the background

For this artwork, you will create a simple, solid-colored background and then build additional graphics using the Live Trace, Symbols, and Live Color features.

1 Choose File > New. The New Document dialog box appears. Type **ai0101** into the Name text field.

2 Choose Print from the New Document Profile drop-down menu. By choosing the Print preset your default colors, patterns, and gradients are built from CMYK (Cyan, Magenta, Yellow, Black) colors.

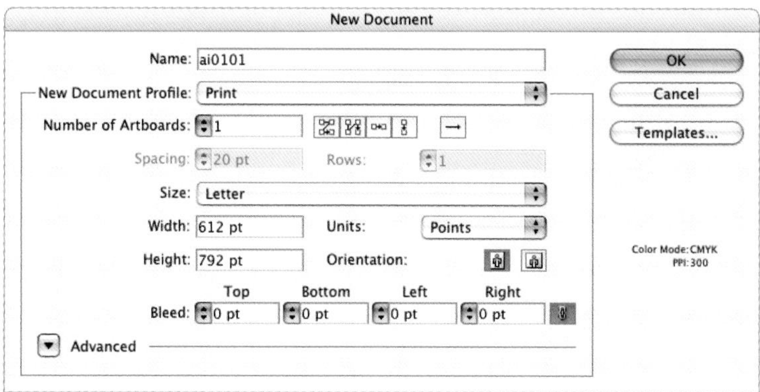

Choose Print from the New Document Profile drop-down menu.

3 Make certain that Letter is chosen from the Size drop-down menu, and choose Inches from the Units drop-down menu. Note that the New Document Profile categorization changes to Custom. Press OK; the new document is created. The document window contains a blank artboard, which represents the entire region that can contain printable artwork.

4 Select the Rectangle tool (▭) from the Tools panel. You will use this shape tool to create the initial background for your artwork. Click once on the artboard to prompt the Rectangle dialog box.

5 Type **5** in the Width text field, then click on the word *Height*; the amount of 5 is automatically entered into the Height text field as well. Press OK and a 5-inch square is created.

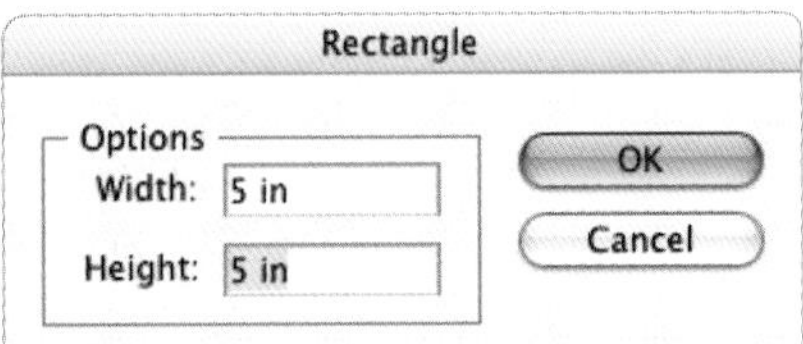

*Enter **5** in the Width text field, then click on the word Height to enter the same value in its text field.*

6 Select the square with the Selection tool (↖), then click the Fill color swatch in the Control panel to reveal the Fill Swatches panel. Select an orange color. This example uses the orange color with values C=0 M=50 Y=100 K=0. To find this exact shade, place your cursor over the different orange swatches without clicking and a tool tip containing each color's respective CMYK values appears.

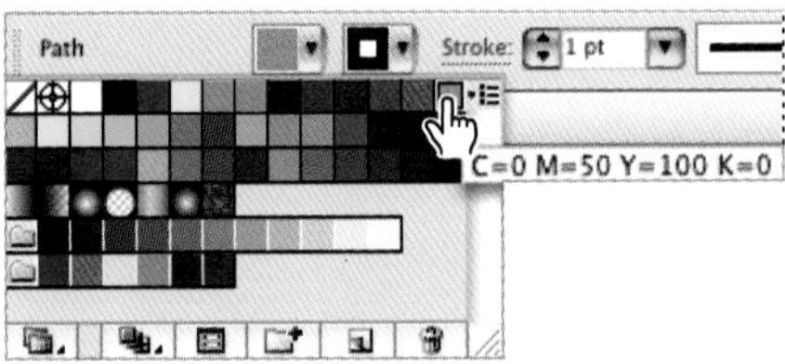

Select an orange fill color from the Control panel.

7 With the square still selected, click the Stroke color swatch in the Control panel and choose None (⧄).

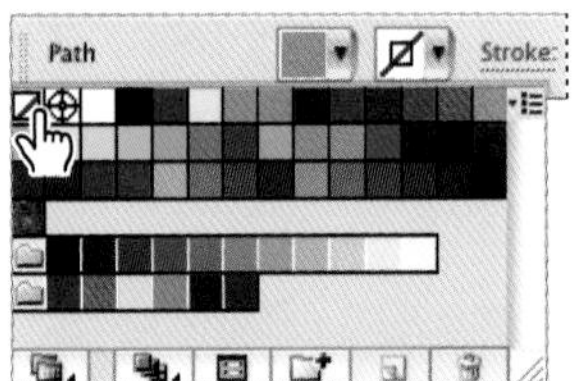

Choose to have no color on the stroke.

8 Choose Object > Lock > Selection or press Ctrl+2 (Windows) or Command+2 (Mac OS) to keep the orange rectangle visible and lock it in its current position.

If you need to reposition a shape, choose Object > Unlock, or use the keyboard shortcut Ctrl+Alt+2 (Windows) or Command+Option+2 (Mac OS).

9 Choose File > Save. In the Save As dialog box, navigate to the ai01lessons folder. Since you named the document ai0101 when you created the new file, *ai0101.ai* automatically appears in the Save As text field. Press Save.

10 When the Illustrator Options dialog box appears, press OK. Keep the file open for the rest of the lesson.

Taking advantage of graphic styles

Adobe Illustrator CS4 gives you the ability to save combinations of attributes such as fills, strokes, and special effects collectively as a graphic style. Graphic styles save you time and help keep your styles and colors consistent across a document or series of documents. When using a graphic style, you can apply interesting effects to multiple objects at once. In this example, you will create a graphic style using the Effects menu and the Appearance panel.

1 Press the letter **D** on your keyboard. This reverts you to the default colors—a white fill and a black stroke.

2 Click and hold on the Rectangle tool (□) in the Tools panel and select the hidden Ellipse tool (○).

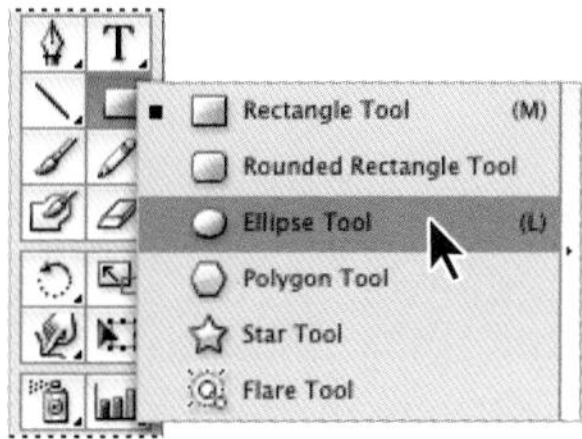

Select the hidden Ellipse tool.

3 Hold down the Shift key while you click and drag on the artboard. This creates a perfect circle. Release the mouse before releasing the Shift key; don't worry about the circle's size.

4 Choose Window > Transform or use the keyboard shortcut Shift+F8. When the Transform Panel appears, click the Constrain Width and Height Proportions button (🔗) and type **.25** in the W text field, then press the Tab key. The width and height are changed to a quarter of an inch.

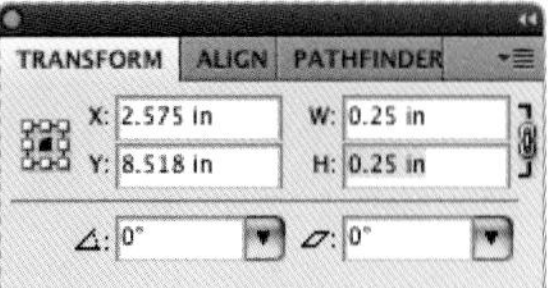

Change the size of your shape after creating it.

5 Press the Appearance button (◉) in the dock on the right side of the workspace to reveal the Appearance panel. The Appearance panel displays the attributes that have been applied to the selected object. In this example, the only color attributes that are visible are a fill, a stroke, and the default opacity, but you will see more attributes added to the list as you work in this lesson.

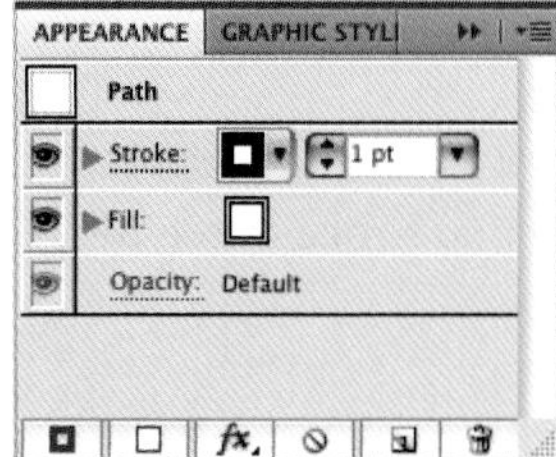

The Appearance panel.

6 Choose File > Save. Keep this file open for the next part of this lesson.

One object, multiple fills and strokes

Illustrator objects can have more than one fill and stroke. In this part of the lesson, you will use this feature to add multiple strokes and make one object appear as though it's made of multiple shapes.

1 With the circle selected, select the Stroke listing in the Appearance panel, then press the Duplicate Selected Item button (⧉) at the bottom of the Appearance panel. You now have two strokes. You can't see the second stroke around the object, since it was created on top of the initial stroke.

2 Now you will duplicate the stroke, creating a total of three strokes, using a different method. With the topmost stroke still selected, drag it to the Duplicate Selected Item button at the bottom of the Appearance panel. You now have three identical strokes listed in the Appearance panel.

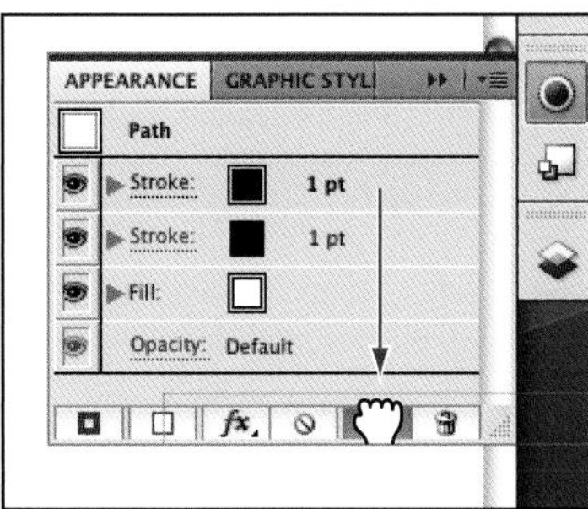

Duplicate a stroke by clicking or dragging to the Duplicate Selected Item button.

3 Select the second stroke in the Appearance panel and choose Effect > Path > Offset Path. The Offset Path dialog box appears. Check the Preview checkbox and see that this effect offsets the selected path from its original location.

4 Type **.1** into the Offset text field and press OK. The stroke is offset by .1 inches. In the Appearance panel, press the arrow to the left of the second stroke to see the effect applied.

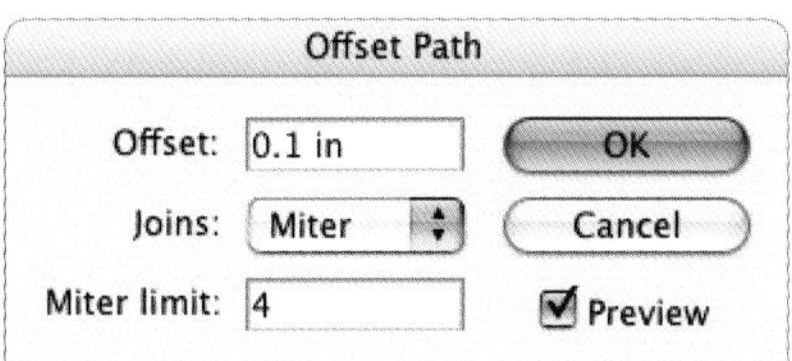

Change the offset path to .1 inches.

5 Select the second stroke again in the Appearance panel, and click the Stroke color swatch to reveal the Stroke Swatches panel. Choose CMYK Yellow. The offset stroke is now a different color from the original black stroke.

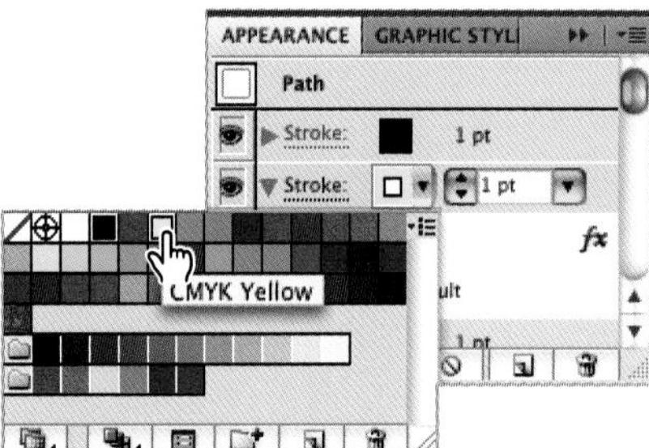

The Appearance panel allows you to change the stroke and color directly in the panel.

6 With the second stroke still selected, choose 4 pt from the Stroke Weight drop-down menu that is built right into the Appearance panel; the second stroke's width changes to 4 points. Notice that the attributes of the stroke are now listed in the Appearance panel.

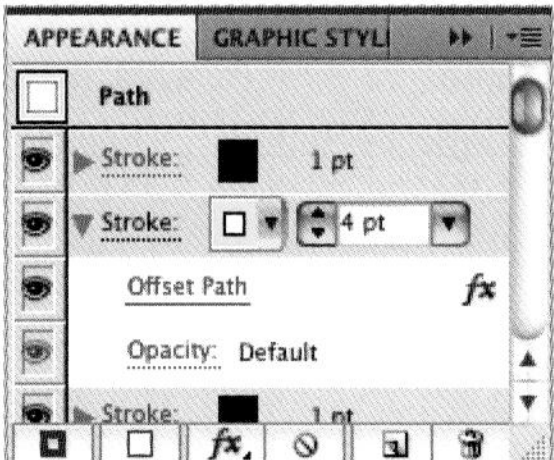

The Appearance panel lists the stroke's adjusted attributes.

The 4-point, CMYK Yellow offset path.

7 Now select the topmost stroke in the Appearance panel and choose Effect > Path > Offset Path. In the resulting Offset Path dialog box, type **.15** in the Offset Path text field and press OK.

8 Select the topmost stroke in the Appearance panel again to make sure that it is selected, then choose 2 pt from the Stroke drop-down menu next to the Stroke listing in the Appearance panel. The outside stroke changes to 2 points.

9 Press the Stroke box in the Appearance panel and choose the blue color that displays the combination of C=85 M=50 Y=0 K=0. The outer stroke is now blue.

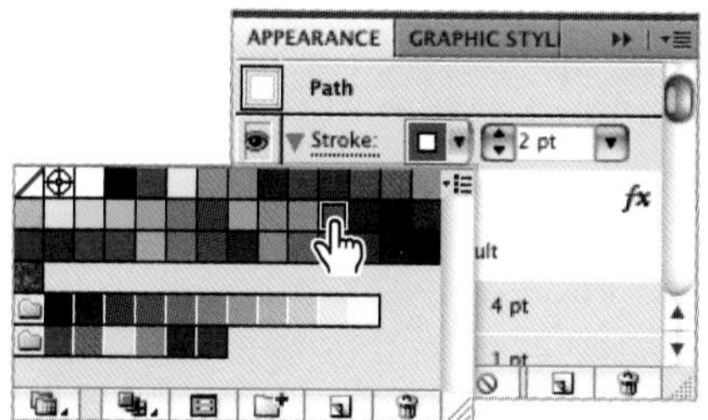

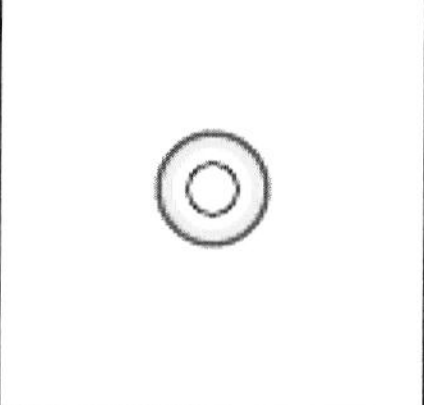

The object with multiple strokes.

Saving a graphic style

You will save the combination of effects that you've implemented as a graphic style, allowing you to easily apply these collective effects to other objects. Using a graphic style makes it easier to convey any changes you make to the graphic style to all objects to which that style is applied.

1 Make sure that the circle with the offset strokes is still selected and click on the Graphic Styles tab at the top of the Appearance panel to reveal the Graphic Styles panel. Press Alt (Windows) or Option (Mac OS) and click on the New Graphic Style button (▫) at the bottom of the Graphic Styles panel. The Graphic Style Options dialog box appears.

2 Type **circle** in the Style Name text field, then press OK.

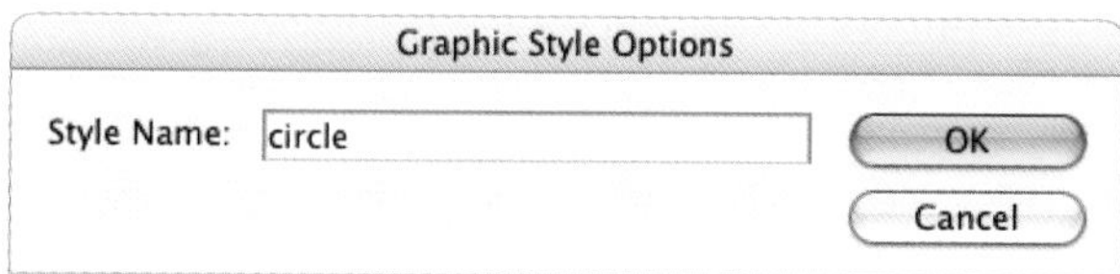

Name the new graphic style.

The strokes become a style added to the Graphic Styles panel.

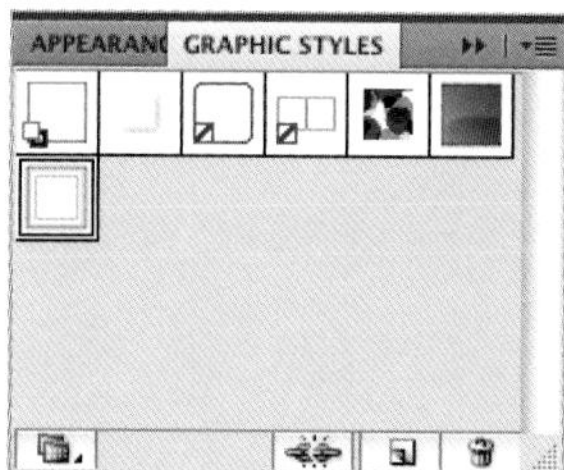

The circle style is added to the Graphic Styles panel.

3 Choose File > Save. Keep this file open.

Creating a symbol from the circle art

By creating a symbol, you can add multiple occurrences of an object to your artwork. A symbol can be created from vector art and raster art that is embedded in an Illustrator file. In this lesson you will use a symbol to create artwork directly in Illustrator, which you will learn more about in Lesson 8, "Working with Symbols." You can also create movie clip symbols right in Adobe Illustrator CS4 that can be imported directly into Flash CS4.

1 Choose Window > Symbols or press the Symbols button (♣) in the dock to open the Symbols panel.

2 Using the Selection tool (↖), select the circle with the offset strokes on the artboard and drag it into the Symbols panel. When the circle is over the Symbols panel, release the mouse to drop the circle.

3 In the resulting Symbols Options dialog box, type **circle** into the Name text field and select the Graphic radio button. Press OK. The circle is added to the Symbols panel.

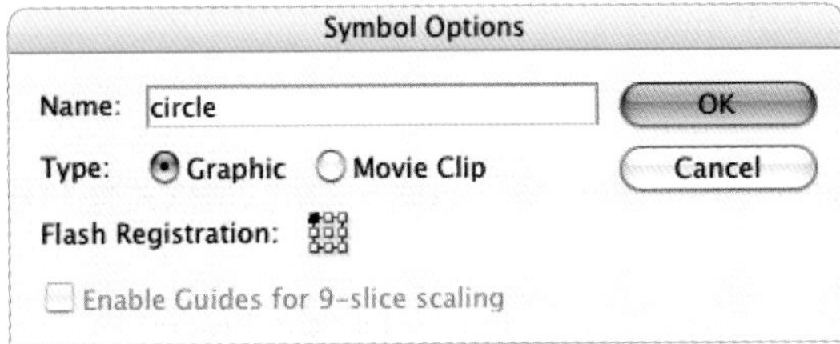

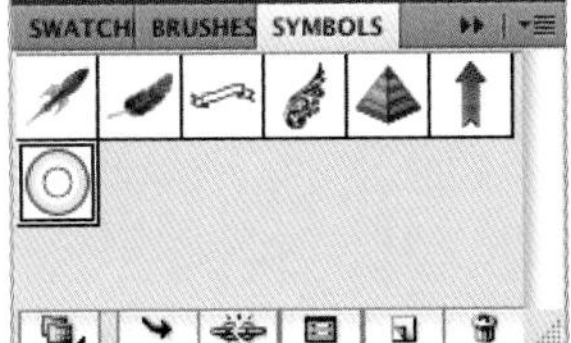

Add your circle to the Symbols panel.

4 Using the Selection tool, select the original circle and choose Edit > Clear. Now that you created a symbol, you no longer need the original. Now you will use the symbol feature to populate your background with the circle artwork.

5 Select the Symbol Sprayer tool from the Tools panel. Your cursor becomes a small spray paint can with a circle around it, indicating the size of the spray area. Adjust its size by pressing the Left bracket key ([ )on your keyboard to make it smaller or the Right bracket key ( ]) to make it larger.

6 Click and drag with the mouse in a quick, steady motion throughout the orange square that you created earlier. The circle symbols are sprayed over the square. Stop when you have between 10 and 20 circles on your artboard. If you want to redo the spray of the circles, press Ctrl+Z (Windows) or Command+Z (Mac OS) and start spraying again. The circles that you sprayed onto your artwork are symbol instances.

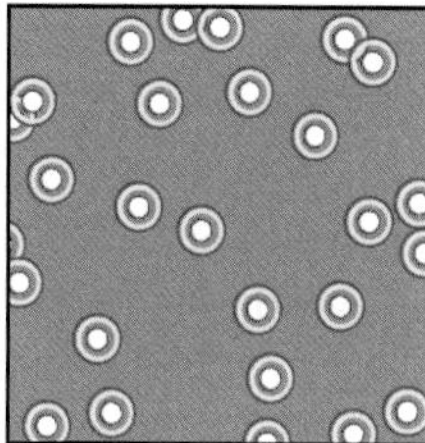

Use the Symbol Sprayer tool to add circles to your artwork.

Now you will apply transparency to the symbol instances using the Symbol Screener tool.

7 Press the Swatches button (▦) in the dock and choose a yellow color from the color options so that Yellow becomes the selected fill color. In this example, CMYK Yellow is used.

8 Click and hold on the Symbol Sprayer in the Tools panel to select the hidden Symbol Screener Tool ().

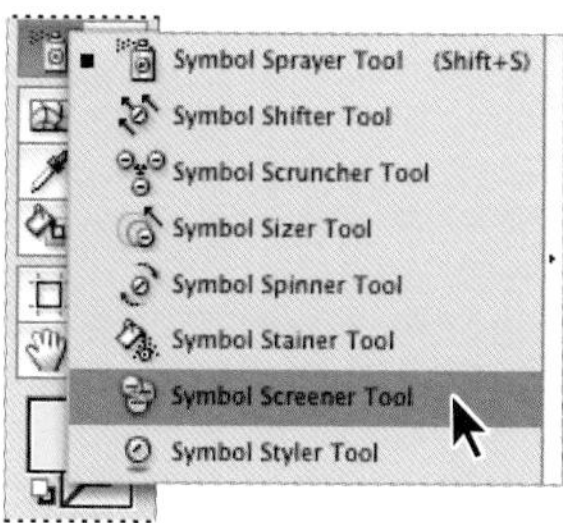

Use the Symbol Screener tool to change opacity.

9 Double-click on the Symbol Screener tool in the Tools panel; the Symbolism Tools Options dialog box appears. Using the Symbolism Tools Options dialog box you can change attributes of each of the Symbolism tools. The Symbol Screener tool controls a symbol instance's opacity. You will adjust a setting in the Symbolism Tools Options dialog box so that the opacity change is more subtle.

10 In the Symbolism Tools Options dialog box, type **3** into the Intensity text field, or drag the Intensity slider to 3, then press OK.

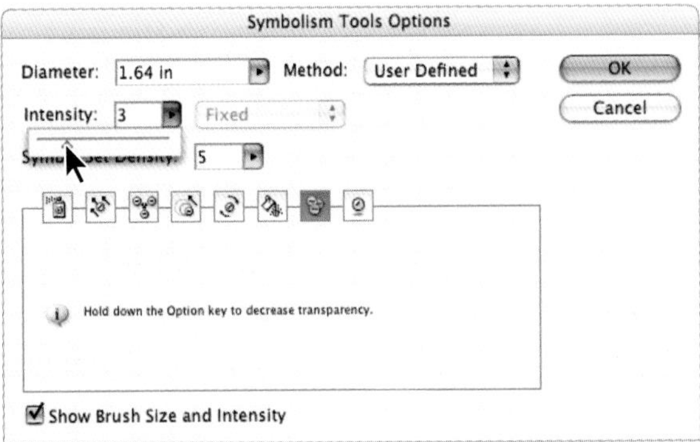

Reduce the intensity to 3.

11 Position your cursor over one of the circle symbol instances on the artboard and click on it. All the symbol instances covered by the radius around the Symbol Sprayer tool fade slightly. The longer you hold down the mouse, the more drastic the change in opacity.

12 Now hold down the Alt (Window) or Option (Mac OS) key and click on one of the symbol instances that you used the Symbol Screener tool on. By holding down the Alt/Option key, you can undo the Symbols Screen effects and bring the opacity back up to 100%.

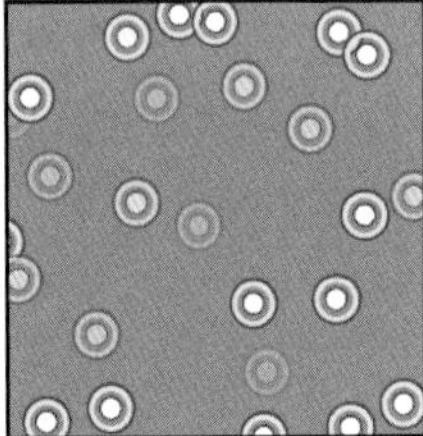

The symbols after using the Symbol Screener tool.

There is no exact effect you are trying to achieve with this tool, so experiment with the Symbol Screener tool until you have the effect that you like.

13 Choose File > Save. Keep this file open for the next part of this lesson.

Creating the text logo

Now that you have saved the attributes of your object, you will add some text, to which you will apply your graphic style.

Before starting, you will create a new layer so that you can easily lock down the artwork you have already created.

1 Choose Window > Layers or press the Layers button (◈) in the dock to open the Layers panel.

2 Click in the empty area to the right of the visibility icon (👁); a padlock icon (🔒) appears and the artwork on Layer 1 is now locked.

3 Hold down the Alt (Window) or Option (Mac OS) key and click on the Create New Layer button (◘) in the Layers panel.

4 In the resulting Layer Options dialog box, type **text logo** in the Name text field. Press OK.

   The new layer appears in the Layers panel.

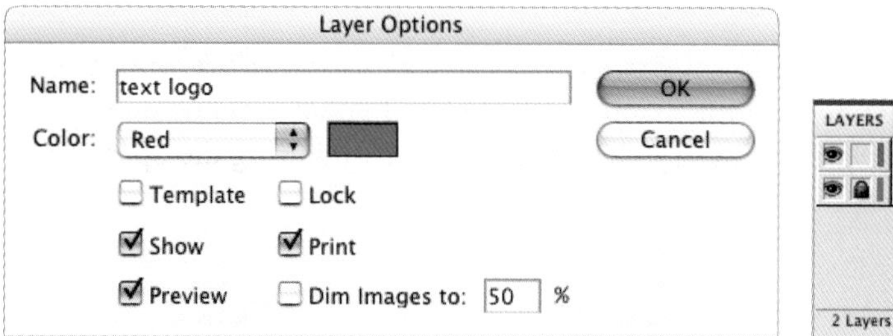

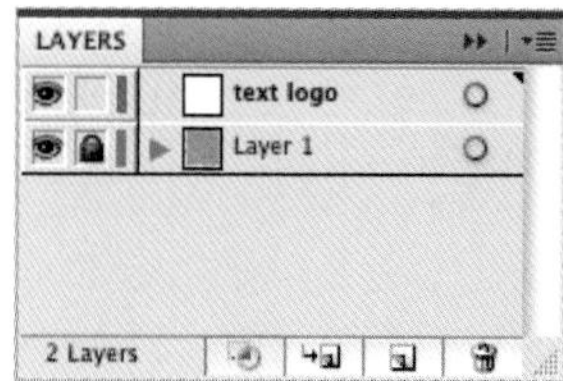

The new text logo layer appears above the locked Layer 1.

5 Select the Type tool (T) from the Tools panel, and the type attributes and options appear in the Control panel.

6 Click on the Character link in the Control panel select Minion Pro from the Font drop-down menu and choose Bold from the Font Style drop-down menu. Type **70** into the Size text field and press Enter (Windows) or Return (Mac OS).

7 Click on the Fill color swatch in the Control panel and choose the black swatch, then click the Stroke color swatch and choose None (⊠).

8 Click once anywhere on your artboard. Type **Sound Art**.

9 Activate the Selection tool. Click and drag on the text you created and position it in the center, toward the top of the orange square.

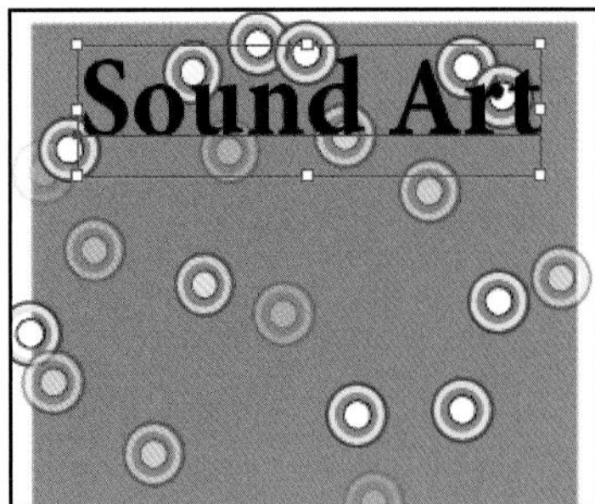

Type on the artboard.

10 Choose File > Save to save your work. Keep the file open.

Applying the graphic style to the text logo

Now that you created the text logo for the artwork, you will apply the graphic style that you saved earlier in the lesson.

1 Using the Selection tool (), click on the Sound Art text to make sure it is selected.

2 If your Graphic Styles panel is not visible, choose Window > Graphic Styles or press the Graphic Styles button () in the dock.

3 Select the circle graphic style that you created earlier. The style is applied to the text.

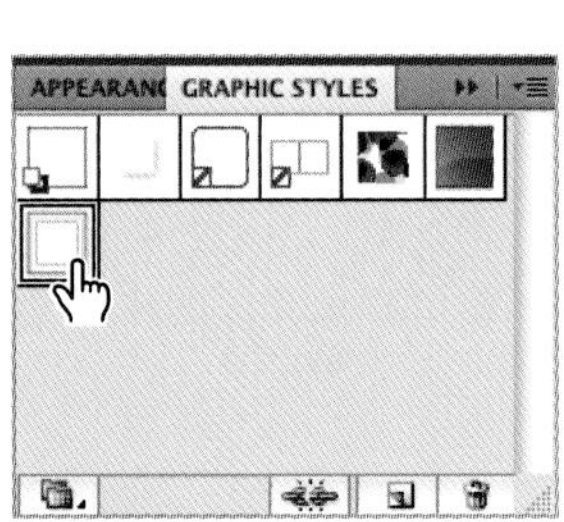

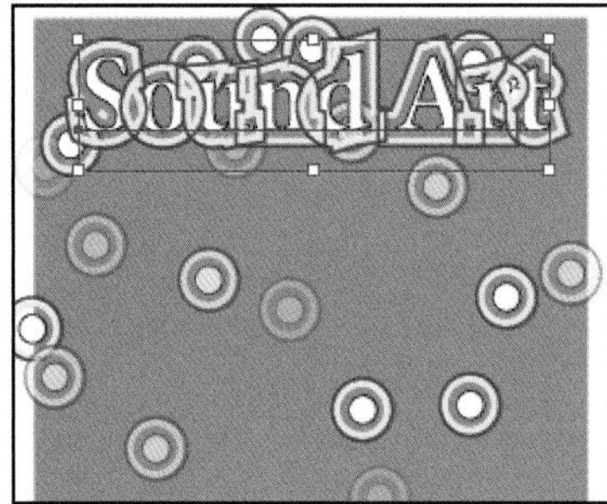

Click on the saved graphic style.

Though the correct style is applied, it doesn't work well for text. You will use the Add Effect feature to create a much better result.

4 Select the Appearance tab in the Graphics Style panel to bring forward the Appearance panel. Make sure the text is still selected with the Selection tool and click on the topmost stroke listed in the Appearance panel, then choose Effect > Pathfinder > Add. This effect adds the separate shapes together, making the effect a little more attractive.

5 Select the second stroke listed in the Appearance panel and choose Effect > Pathfinder > Add. Now the yellow stroke forms a much cleaner outline.

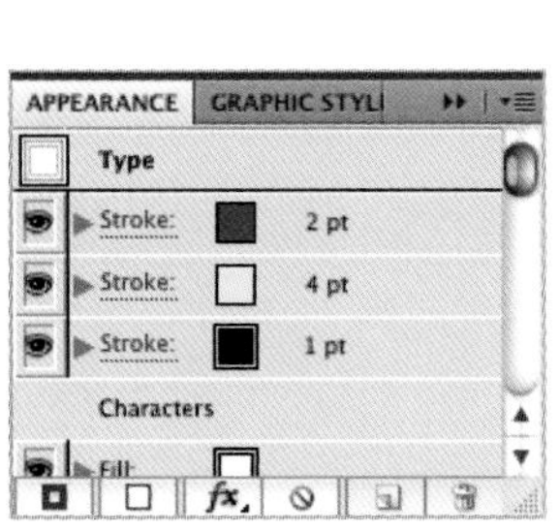

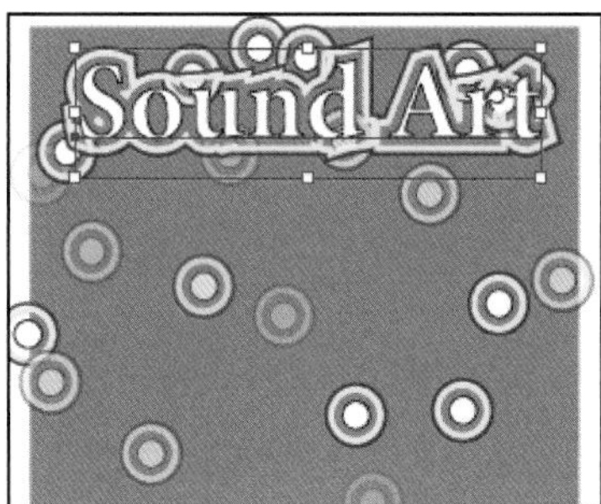

Add the strokes.

Warping the text logo

1 With the text logo still selected on the artboard, click on the word Type at the top of the Appearance panel, then choose Effect > Warp > Flag. The Warp Options dialog box appears with the Flag style already selected. Check the Preview checkbox to see how the warped text looks as you make changes in the dialog box.

2 In the Distortion section, click and drag the Horizontal slider left to –30 or type **-30** into the Horizontal percent text field and press OK.

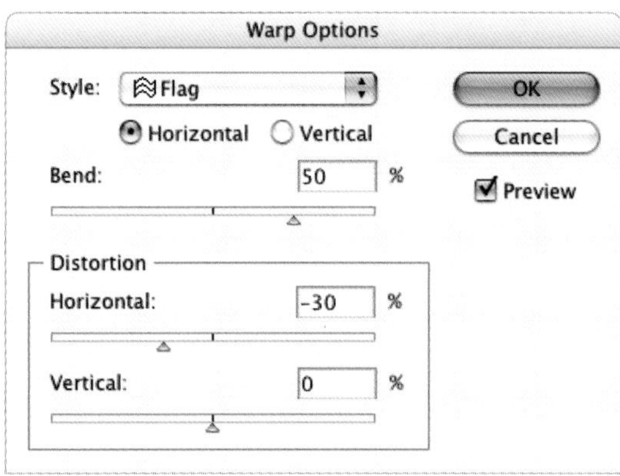

Set the warp options.

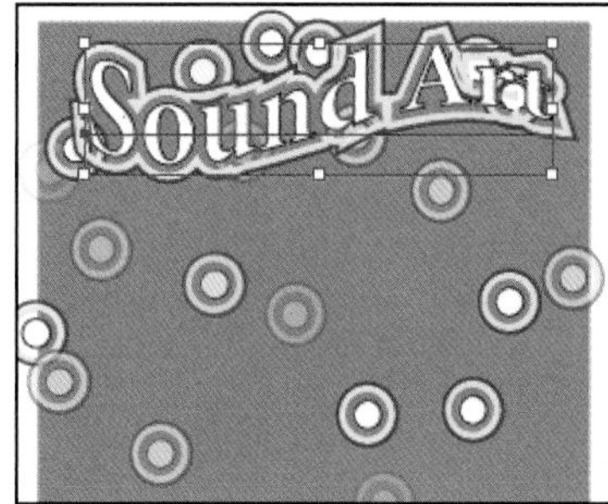

The resulting warped text.

3 Choose File > Save to save your work. Keep this file open for the next part of this lesson.

Using the Color Guide

In this exercise, you will use some of the new Live Color features. You will select a color and then use the Color Guide, which allows you to select one of Live Color's harmonious relationships for your current color, making the job of finding complements and matching colors much easier.

1 Make sure that no objects are selected on your artboard by selecting Select > Deselect, using the keyboard shortcut Shift+Ctrl+A (Windows) or Shift+Command+A (Mac OS), or by clicking anywhere on the white artboard.

2 Make sure that at the bottom of the Tools panel, the fill (◳) is the foreground color and the stroke is in the background. Click the Fill box in the Control panel to see your color options and choose CMYK Red.

3 Press the Layers button (◈) in the dock or choose Windows > Layers to reveal the Layers panel. Click the padlock icon (🔒) to the left of Layer 1 to unlock it.

4 Select Object > Unlock All in order for the large orange square to be affected by the Live Color. Activate the Selection tool, then choose Select > All. This selects all objects in the document.

5 Press the Color Guide button (◪) in the dock or choose Window > Color Guide to open the Color Guide panel. Notice that the red fill color is automatically made the base color, from which other harmonious color groups are assigned. Click on the Harmony Rules drop-down menu (to the right of the active colors) to see that you can select different harmonious colors that are related to the original red base. Choose Right Complement.

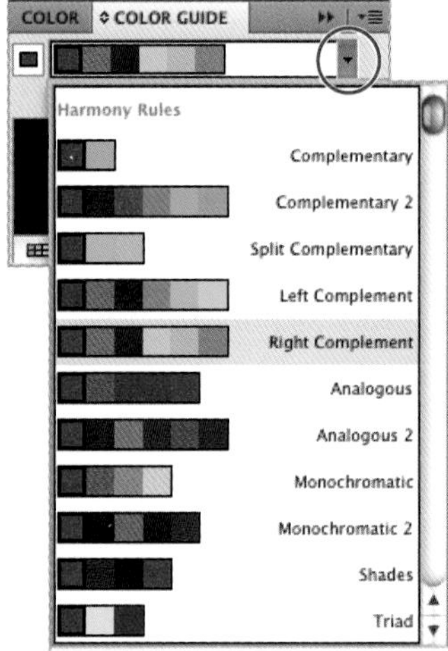

Illustrator automatically calculates harmonious color groups for you.

6 Click on the Edit or Apply Colors button (icon) at the bottom of the Color Guide panel. The Recolor Artwork dialog box appears. Leave the settings at their defaults and press OK. The Right Complementary colors are applied to your artwork.

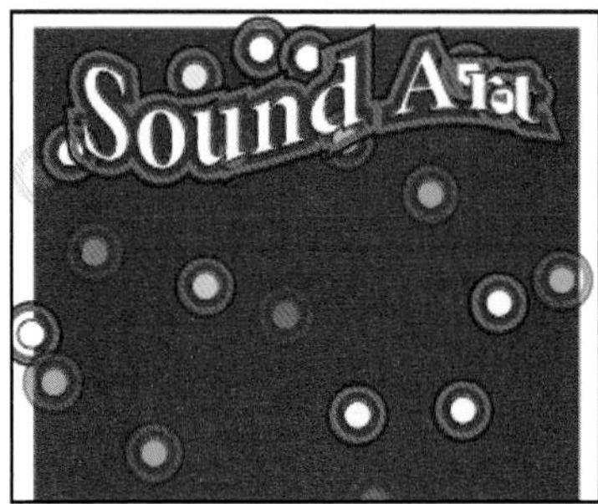

The result.

7 Repeat step 5 to try different harmonious color selections. When you are finished experimenting, return to the choice of Right Complement but do not close the dialog box.

8 Click on the New Color Group button (icon) at the top of the Recolor Artwork dialog box; your group of colors is added to the list of color groups on the right side of the dialog box.

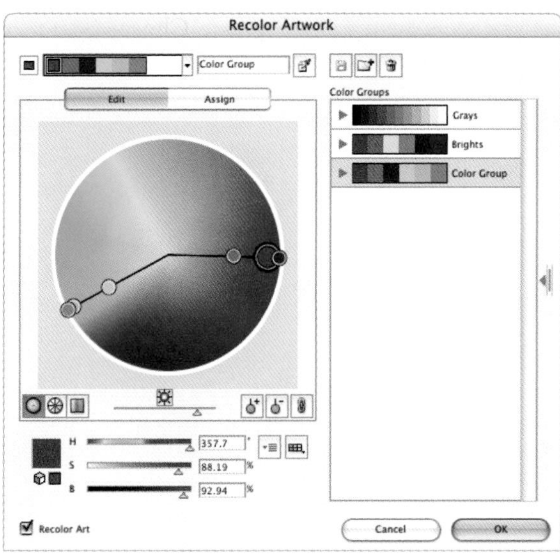

Add the colors as a new group.

9 Double-click on the words Color Group, which appear to the right of the colors you just added to the list. In the Edit Name dialog box that appears, type **cd colors** into the Name text field and press OK. Back in the Live Color dialog box, press OK again. Illustrator prompts you with a message asking if you'd like to save the changes to swatch group "cd colors" before closing. Choose Yes.

10 Click on the Swatches button (▦) in the dock to open the Swatches panel. The cd colors color group has been added to the swatch selections.

You can do much more with the Live Color feature, like convert multicolored artwork into Pantone spot colors, as well as adjust the amount of colors in your artwork. Find out more about Live Color in Lesson 4, "Adding Color."

11 Choose File > Save. Keep the file open for the next part of the lesson.

Incorporating an image into your artwork

Adobe Illustrator accepts many types of image files. In this lesson, you will place a native Photoshop file onto the artboard and trace it using the Live Trace feature. By using the Live Trace feature, you can convert your image into vector artwork.

1 Choose Window > Layers or press the Layers button (◈) in the dock. Select Layer 1 so that it is the active layer.

2 Choose File > Place. In the Place dialog box, navigate to the ai01lessons folder and select the image named ai0102.psd. Press Place. If an Embedded Profile Mismatch dialog box appears choose to Use the embedded profile and press OK. The image is placed onto the artboard.

The image, clearly, is too big. You will use the Scale tool to make the image smaller.

3 Double-click on the Scale tool (⊡) in the Tools panel; the Scale dialog box appears. In the Uniform section, type **50** into the Scale text field and press OK. The image is reduced to 50% its original size.

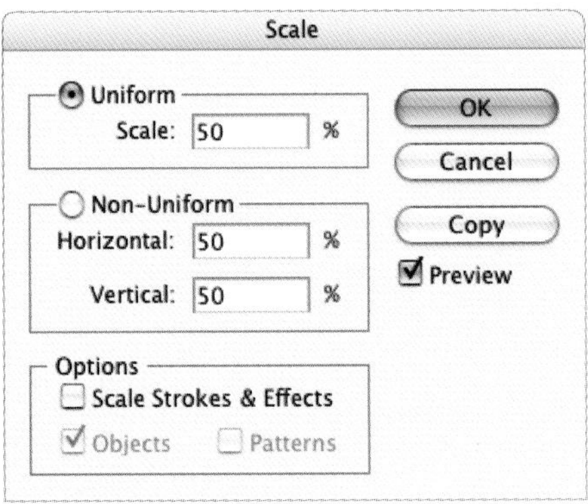

Reduce the image's size.

4 Activate the Selection tool (↖) and click and drag the image so that it is flush with the bottom of the rectangle. If necessary, reposition the text logo so that it is not hidden beneath the image.

5 Make sure the image of the man is selected, then click on the arrow to the right of the Live Trace button in the Control panel. Several options appear. Choose Tracing Options from the Live Trace drop-down menu. The Tracing Options dialog box opens.

The Tracing Options dialog box.

You will use the Tracing Options dialog box to control how Adobe Illustrator converts your placed image from a raster scanned image to vector artwork.

6 Check the Preview checkbox on the right side of the dialog box to turn the feature on.

7 From the Preset drop-down menu, choose Photo Low Fidelity. The image is now broken down into 16 shades of color, as you can see in the Max Colors text field.

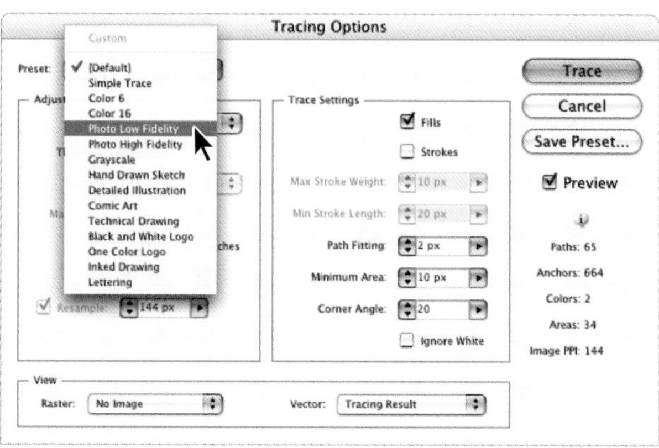

Determine the settings for converting the raster scanned image to a vector image.

8 In the Trace Setting section, type **50** into the Minimum Area text field or drag the slider to 50.

9 Click in the Ignore White checkbox at the bottom of the Trace Settings section. The image's white background becomes transparent and the cutout of the man rests on the red square. Press Trace. The image is now a vector object.

The resulting image.

10 With the traced image still selected, click the Expand button in the Control panel to expand the Live Trace object into visible vector paths.

11 Choose File > Save. Keep this file open.

Erasing vector paths and shapes

In the next part of the lesson, you'll work with the Eraser tool. The Eraser tool erases portions of your artwork. The Eraser tools erases right through vector shapes and paths. You have to experience this tool to fully appreciate its capabilities.

1 If the traced image of the man is not already selected, select it now. When an item is selected, the anchor points become visible. In artwork as complicated as the autotrace man, this is distracting, and makes it difficult to see what you are doing. In the next step, you will hide the selection edges, but still keep the artwork active.

2 Choose View > Hide Edges, or use the keyboard shortcut Ctrl+H (Windows) or Command+H (Mac OS). Hiding the edges of the selection allows you to see the results of the work you will do with the Eraser tool.

3 Select the Eraser tool ( ) in the Tools panel and position the cursor in the lower-left corner of the traced image.

Press the] (right bracket) key about 3-4 times to make your eraser tool larger. If you need to make it smaller you press the [(left bracket key). No exact size is needed for this exercise, but with a larger brush you can see the tool's effects more easily.

4 With the Eraser tool, click and drag using a rough up-and-down movement (like you might use with an actual eraser), progressing from the lower-left side to the lower-right side of the image.

Start in the lower left of the artwork.

When you release, you see that you've erased the bottom of the image of the man, but that the red square and its contents are intact. You will now soften the edges of the traced image.

5 Choose View > Show Edges. Make sure the image is selected and choose Effect > Stylize > Feather.

6 In the resulting Feather dialog box, select the Preview check box, then type **.1** into the Feather Radius text field and press OK. The edge of the image is softened.

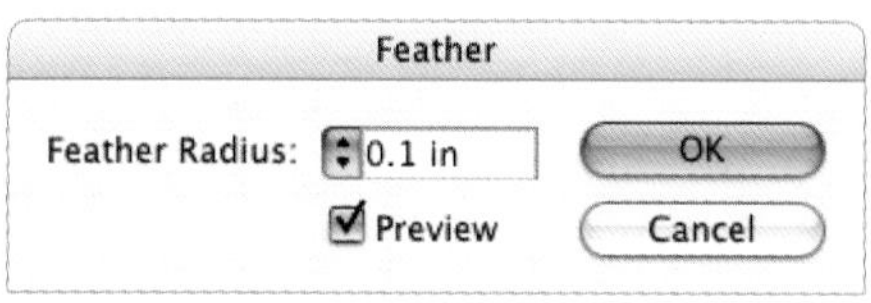

Apply the feather amount.

Result.

7 Choose View > Show Edges, or use the keyboard shortcut Ctrl+H (Windows) or Command+H (Mac OS) to turn the selection edges back on. By turning on the Show Edges feature, you can turn on the selection points' visibility, thereby making it easier to see your selected artwork. If you forget to do this, you won't be able to see what is selected.

8 Choose Select > All to make sure all your artwork is selected.

9 Open the Symbols panel by clicking on the Symbols button (♣) in the dock on the right side of the workspace, or by choosing Window > Symbols.

10 Click on the New Symbol button () at the bottom of the Symbols panel; the Symbol Options dialog box appears.

11 Type **cdart** into the Name text field and select the Graphic radio button from the Type section, then press OK.

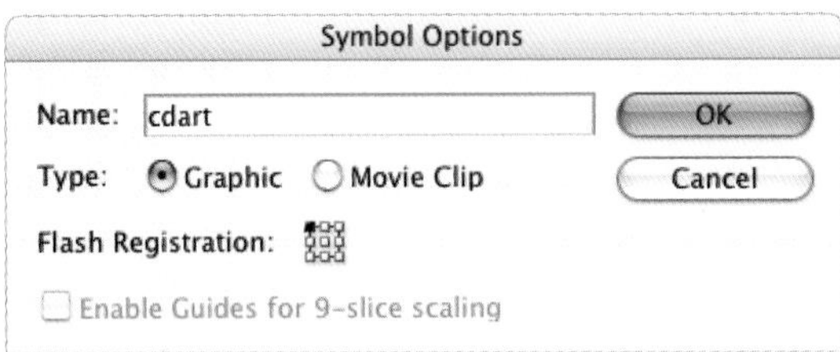

Name the new symbol.

The artwork in its entirety is now saved as a symbol.

12 Select the original artwork with the Selection tool () and press Delete. Since the artwork is now saved as a symbol, you only need the symbol instance for the remainder of the lesson.

13 Choose File > Save. Keep the file open.

Creating a 3-D object

Now you will create the CD case and map the artwork you saved as a symbol to the case.

1 Select the Rectangle tool (). You may have to click on and hold down the Ellipse tool () button in the Tools panel since you used that tool last.

2 Click once on the artboard. The Rectangle dialog box appears.

3 Type **5** into the Width text field, then click on the word Height to put the same value into the Height text field. Press OK. A 5-inch square appears on the artboard.

4 Click the Fill color swatch in the Control panel and select the CMYK Red color.

5 Choose Effect > 3D > Extrude & Bevel. The 3D Extrude & Bevel Options dialog box appears. Check the Preview check box on the right side of the dialog box.

6 Make sure the options are set at their defaults. In the Position section, the rotation around the X axis (⊖) text field should be -18°. The rotation around the Y axis (⦶) should be -26° and the rotation around the Z axis (↻) should be 8°. In the Extrude & Bevel section, the Extrude Depth value should be 50 pt and Bevel should be set to None.

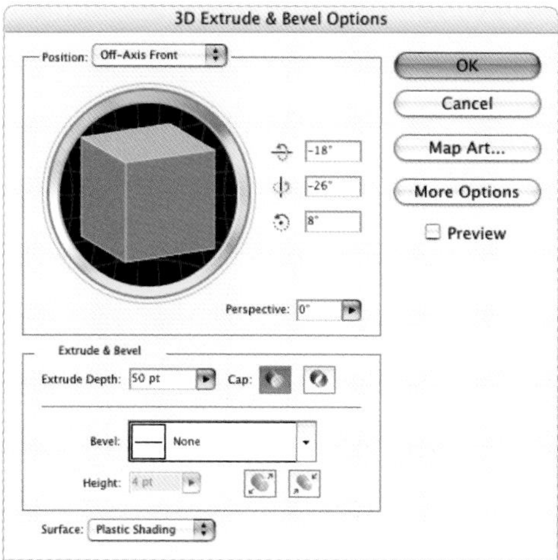

The default 3D Extrude and Bevel settings.

7 Click on the Map Art button on the right side of the dialog box. Mapping art allows you to place symbol artwork onto a 3-D object. This may take a few moments.

8 After choosing the art, the Surface selector shows 1 of 6. If it is showing anything different, click on the First Surface button (|◀). Click on the arrow to the right of the Symbol drop-down menu and choose cdart, your saved symbol.

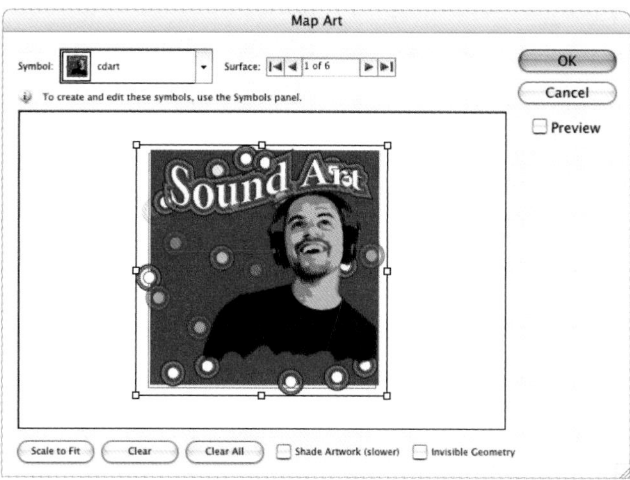

Assign the cdart symbol to Side 1 of your CD case.

9 Reposition the artwork by dragging the symbol so it aligns with the outline of the CD case in Map Art dialog box.

10 Press OK to exit the Map Art dialog box, then OK to exit the 3D Extrude & Bevel dialog box. A progress bar appears as Illustrator maps your image to the side of the 3-D object, which is a CD case.

The final result.

11 Choose File > Save to save your work, then choose File > Close.

Congratulations! You have completed Lesson 1, "Adobe Illustrator CS4 Jumpstart."

What you'll learn in this lesson:

- Opening an existing Adobe Illustrator file
- Navigating through the document window
- Zooming in and out of the document window
- Finding and using common panels
- Selecting and using tools

Getting to Know the Workspace

The Adobe Illustrator workspace includes tools, panels, and windows that you use to create and manipulate your artwork. In this lesson, you find out where all these necessary components are located and how they can be organized. You also discover how to customize the workspace for your specific needs.

Starting up

Before starting, make sure that your tools and panels are consistent by resetting your workspace. See "Resetting Adobe Illustrator CS4 Preferences" on page 3.

You will work with several files from the ai02lessons folder in this lesson. Make sure that you have loaded the ailessons folder onto your hard drive from the supplied DVD. See "Loading lesson files" on page 4.

See Lesson 2 in action!

Use the accompanying video to gain a better understanding of how to use some of the features shown in this lesson. The video tutorial for this lesson can be found on the included DVD.

Opening Illustrator

1 Launch Adobe Illustrator CS4. If you have not changed your default settings, a Welcome Screen appears. If you do not see it, choose Help > Welcome Screen.

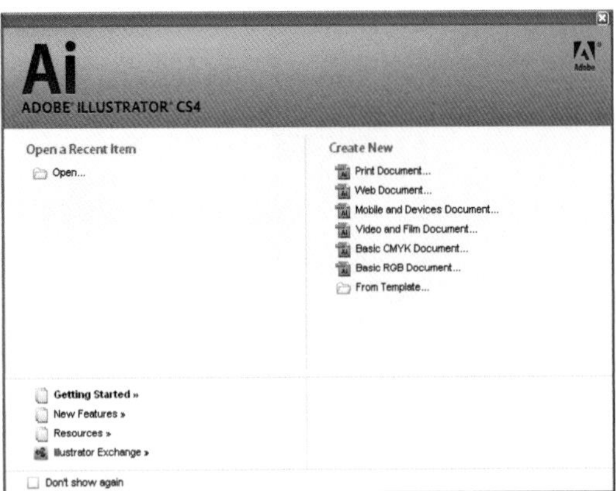

The Welcome Screen is a valuable resource.

The Welcome Screen provides you with links to important information about starting up, and a list of new features and resources that include videos and links to online support.

You can use the Welcome Screen to access recently opened projects or to create new projects using the presets on the right.

2 Check the *Don't show again* checkbox in the lower-left corner so that the Welcome Screen does not appear every time you launch Illustrator. Close the Welcome Screen by clicking the X in the upper-right corner (Windows) or the circle in the upper-left corner (Mac OS). You can access the Welcome Screen anytime by selecting Help > Welcome Screen.

Choosing a workspace

Workspaces define which panels are visible on your screen. Illustrator starts you off with a number of workspaces: Automation, Essentials, Like FreeHand, Like InDesign, Like Photoshop, Painting, Printing and Proofing, Typography, and Web. You will learn a little more about these later in the lesson.

1 Choose Window > Workspace > Essentials to display the Illustrator application bar, Tools panel, Control panel, and five panel groups that are collapsed into tabs and docked on the right side of the workspace.

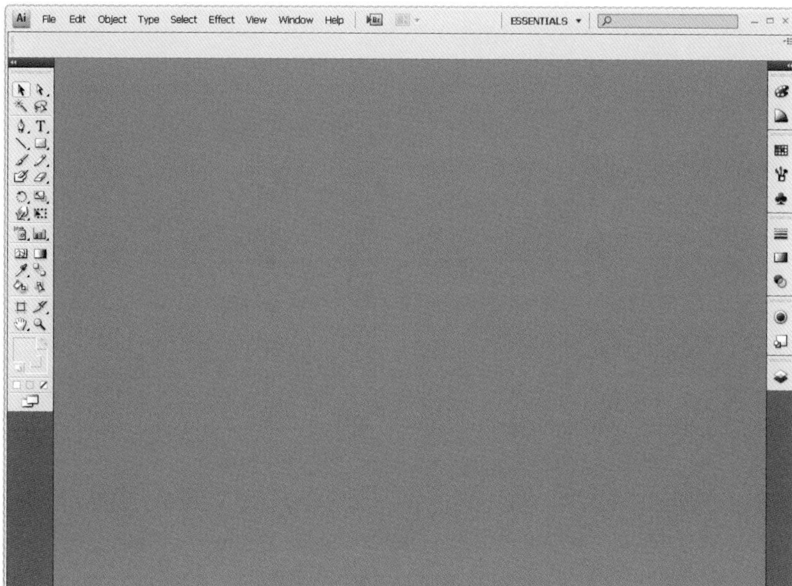

Choosing the Essentials workspace displays the most commonly used panels.

You could also have chosen the Panel workspace, which expands the default panels but keeps them docked on the right side of the screen, or the Type workspace, which gives you instant access to the docked, expanded panels you'll use most frequently for type formatting.

2 Press one of the buttons in the dock on the right side of the workspace. This expands the button to reveal its panel. Press the same button to collapse the panel.

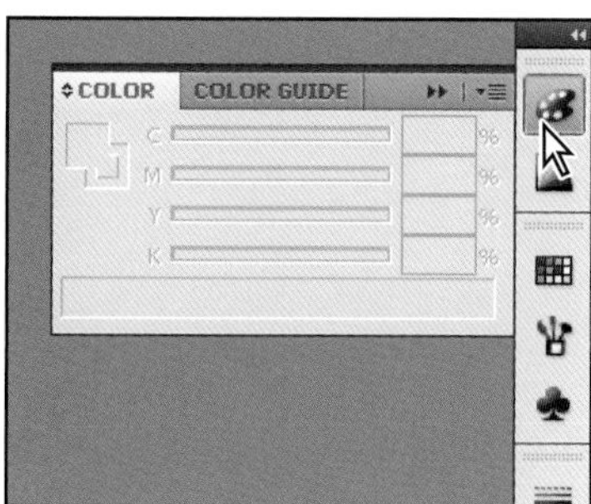

Press the button in the dock to open the button's panel.

The panels currently listed in the dock are displayed by default, but you can add any panel to the workspace by selecting it specifically from the Window menu, then dragging the panel to the dock. You can also save and manage your own custom workspaces from the Window > Workspace menu. These functions are described in more detail later in this lesson.

Opening a file

To begin this lesson, you'll open an existing file using Adobe Bridge.

1 Choose File > Browse in Bridge to open Adobe Bridge. In Bridge, if the Folders panel is not in the foreground, select its tab to bring it forward, then choose Desktop from the list.

2 In the Content panel to the right of the Folders panel, double-click the ailessons folder that you copied onto your computer, then open the ai02lessons folder.

3 Locate and double-click on the file named ai0201.ai to open it within Illustrator.

A Convert to Artboards dialog box may appear when you open certain files. Press OK to continue opening the file.

Choosing File > Browse in Bridge is one way to open an existing file in Illustrator.

4 In Illustrator, choose File > Save As. In the Save As dialog box, navigate to the ai02lessons folder. In the Name text field, type **ai0201_work.ai** and press Save.

If a dialog box appears warning you about converting spot colors in transparency to process colors outside of Illustrator, take note, then press Continue.

5 In the Illustrator Options dialog box, make sure the Version is set to Illustrator CS4, leave the other settings at their defaults, and press OK.

The document window

The document window displays the entire contents of your file. In this example, it shows a design for the liner notes (front and back) for a CD. In addition to the artwork, the document window also displays the following:

- **Artboard:** The artboard represents the printable page containing your artwork. It's bounded by solid lines and can be enlarged or reduced to accommodate larger or smaller artwork. The default artboard size is U.S. Letter (8.5 inches wide by 11 inches tall), but it can be set as large as 227 inches by 227 inches, or almost 19 feet by 19 feet.
- **Scratch Area:** The scratch area is a space for experimenting with and storing elements of your design before moving them onto the artboard. It consists of the blank white area outside of the artboard, and extends to 227 inches in each dimension. Although visible on screen, elements placed on the scratch area will not print, and should be removed before printing to reduce file complexity.
- **Imageable and Non-imageable Areas:** The imageable and non-imageable (or printable and non-printable) areas of a page can also be displayed on the Illustrator artboard, and are delineated by a series of dotted lines. Because this file contains crop marks that were placed manually, the guidelines for imageable and non-imageable areas aren't necessary.

Switching screen modes

For easier viewing of artwork, the display properties of the document window and accompanying menu bar can be changed by switching screen modes. By switching screen modes you can open up your workspace.

1 With the ai0201_work file open, press the Change Screen Mode button (⊡) at the bottom of the Tools panel to expand the Screen Mode drop-down menu, and cycle through the options.

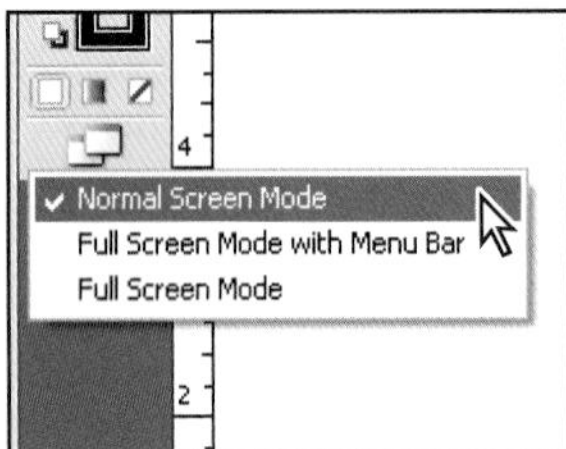

Switching screen modes allows easier viewing of artwork.

2 If necessary, choose Normal Screen Mode to show the artwork in a standard document window that contains a menu bar, scroll bars, and a title bar.

3 Choose Full Screen Mode with Menu Bar to show the artwork in a full-screen document window with only a menu bar (and no scroll bars or title bars).

4 Choose Full Screen Mode to show the artwork in a full-screen document window with no menu bars, scroll bars, or title bars.

   You might think that you cannot do much work without any tools present, but this is not true. You can use keyboard shortcuts to access your tools anytime that you need them.

5 Press **Z**. The cursor turns into the Zoom Curser (🔍). Click to zoom into the image.

6 Now press **V**. By pressing V, you have switched to the Selection tool. Each tool has a keyboard shortcut to access it. You will find out all the shortcuts later in this lesson in the section covering the Tools panel.

7 Press the Escape key to return to Normal Screen mode to continue this lesson.

Changing your view

Because you'll be creating artwork visually in Illustrator, the way in which that artwork is displayed on-screen (the size, color, and location of objects) is a primary concern. Illustrator provides the flexibility with which you can change the view of your artwork to best suit your needs.

Preview versus Outlines

By default, Illustrator displays artwork colors, gradients, meshes, and complex paths. The more complex the elements are, the more time it takes Illustrator to redraw the screen when you make changes to the artwork.

You may also discover that attributes of the objects that you are creating, such as strokes and colors, can make it difficult to make precision adjustments to detailed artwork. To help you, Illustrator provides you with several view modes, the most commonly used modes being the Preview (default) and Outline modes.

1 To toggle between view modes, choose View > Outline, or use the keyboard shortcut Ctrl+Y (Windows) or Command+Y (Mac OS). In Outline mode, Illustrator displays artwork so that only its outlines (or paths) are visible.

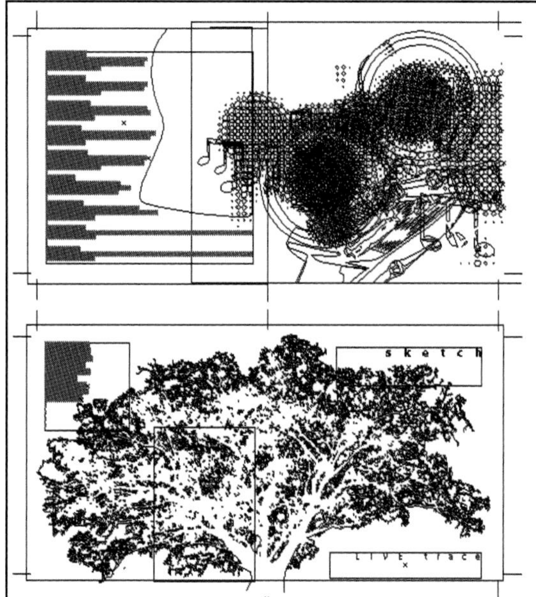

Viewing artwork in Outline mode displays only the paths used to build it.

2 Choose View > Preview. In Preview mode, the paint attributes of the artwork are displayed.

Zooming and scrolling

It is amazing how details seem different when you zoom in and out of artwork. Usually you discover that the artwork isn't as precise as you think it should be. Fortunately you have the opportunity to zoom in to 6400 percent in Adobe Illustrator CS4. Just in case you don't have a general understanding of what zooming in and out of an image does, understand that changing the view of a file changes only the on-screen display, and not the actual size of your artwork. There are many ways to change the view of your artwork in Illustrator:

Zooming with the View commands

The easiest, but most time-consuming method for zooming in and out is using the View menu item. You will be using keyboard shortcuts throughout the lessons in this book, but it is helpful to know where you can find the zoom menu items in case you have a lapse in keyboard shortcut memory.

1 Choose View > Zoom In to enlarge the display of the CD artwork. The view depth increases incrementally each time you choose View > Zoom In from this menu, and allows you to closely examine portions of the design that were not otherwise visible.

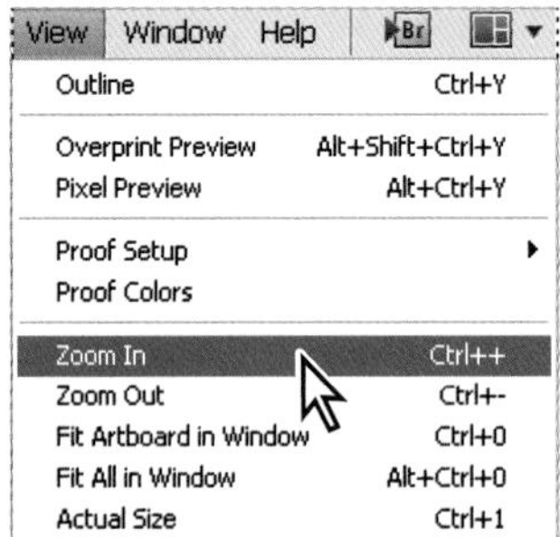

Commands under the View menu allow you to change the magnification of your artwork.

2 Choose View > Zoom Out to reduce the display of the CD artwork. The view depth decreases incrementally each time you choose View > Zoom Out from this menu, and allows you to view the artwork from a distance to see how the elements work together.

By default, Illustrator zooms in or out on the center of your document window when the View commands are used. You can then scroll to different areas of your artwork using the scroll bars.

Keep in mind that the Illustrator Artboard can be up 227" x 227". If your artboard is much smaller, perhaps letter-sized, that remaining area becomes your scratch area. The scratch area frequently becomes "nowhere land" for new users as they accidently navigate into blank space. Once in this blank area, it can be difficult to find your artwork again.

3 Choose View > Fit All in Window to instantly center the document window into your viewing area. The keyboard shortcut is Ctrl+0 (zero) (Windows) or Command+0 (zero) (Mac OS).

4 Choose View > Fit Artboard in Window to center the artboard only in the workspace.

Zooming using the View Depth text field and drop-down menu

Whenever you zoom in or out on your artwork, the view depth percentage is displayed in a field in the lower-left corner of the document window. This field, along with an attached drop-down menu, allows you to make further changes to the view depth of your artwork.

1 In the lower-left corner of the document window, type **120%** into the View Depth text field. Typing into this field allows you to choose whatever enlargement or reduction percentage you'd like to view your artwork at. Press Enter (Windows) or Return (Mac OS) on your keyboard to enlarge the view of your artwork to 120 percent.

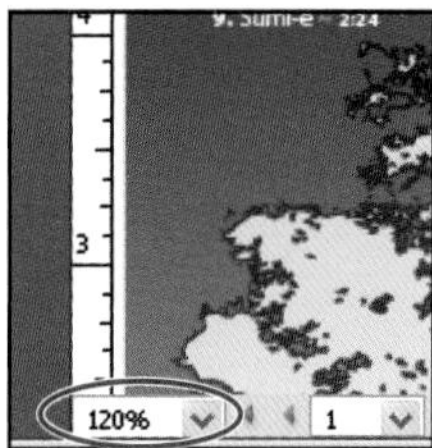

*Type **120%** in the View Depth text field to zoom in on the document.*

2 Press the arrow to the right of the View Depth text field. A drop-down menu appears that allows you to choose a preset zoom percentage, from 3.13 percent to 6400 percent, simply by selecting it.

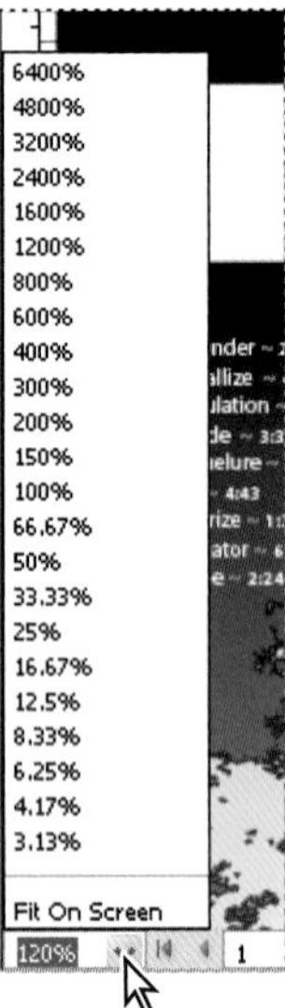

Scrolling through the preset zoom percentages allows you to choose magnifications from 3.13 percent to 6400 percent.

3 Choose 50 percent from the drop-down menu to reduce the view of your artwork to 50 percent.

4 Choose 66.67 percent from the drop-down menu to continue this lesson.

Zooming with the Zoom tool

1 Select the Zoom tool (🔍) from the Tools panel on the left of the workspace.

2 Using the Zoom tool, click the photo of the guitarist in the lower-left corner of the document window to enlarge the view. Each click enlarges the photo at a higher (preset) magnification.

3 Hold down the Alt (Windows) or Option (Mac OS) key on your keyboard, and note that the zoom cursor now contains a minus sign (🔍).

4 Click the photo of the guitarist to reduce the view of the photo. Release the Alt (Windows) or Option (Mac OS) key to return the Zoom tool to its default Zoom In function.

You may have discovered that by clicking to Zoom (with the Zoom tool) that you have very little control over the resulting zoomed in view. You can better control your zooming by simply clicking and dragging with the Zoom tool selected.

5 With the Zoom tool, drag a marquee (box) around the photo of the guitarist to zoom in on that particular area of the artwork, without the redundancy of clicking multiple times. Note that you cannot draw a marquee to reduce the display size.

Drag a marquee around selected portions of your artwork with the Zoom tool.

There may be times when you wish to access the Zoom controls without leaving the active tool.You can use keyboard shortcuts to temporarily active the zoom tool and then quickly return back to your work in progress.

6 Press **V** to switch to the Selection tool.

7 Hold down the Ctrl+Spacebar keys (Windows) or Command+Spacebar (Mac OS) to temporarily switch to the Zoom tool.

8 While keeping the Ctrl/Command+Spacebar keys pressed, click and drag in any area in the image to zoom into a specific area.

9 Release the Ctrl+Spacebar, or Command+Spacebar, and the tool is returned to the Selection tool.

10 Easily zoom back out by pressing Ctrl+0 (zero) (Windows) or Command+0 (zero) (Mac OS).

Scrolling with the Hand tool

Much like moving a piece of paper around on your desk, you can use the Hand tool to push your artboard around. This is much more time efficient than using the scroll bars, and you can even access the hand tool without leaving any other tools that you have active.

1 Select the Hand tool (✋) from the Tools panel.

2 Click and drag in the document window. The artwork moves in the direction you drag.

The Hand tool moves the artwork as if it were a piece of paper on your desk.

3 Now Press **V** to return to the Selection tool, click on any item to select it, then hold down the Spacebar. Notice that the cursor now changes into the Hand tool

4 Click and drag to reposition your artboard, then release the Spacebar. You are returned to the Selection tool. This feature is extremely handy, especially when you are working with operations that require you to be zoomed into your artwork.

The Hand tool can also be used as a Zoom tool, to fit all artwork in the document window.

5 Double-click the Hand tool in the Tools panel to return the file to Fit Artboard in Window view.

Changing views with the Navigator panel

If you prefer a more visual method for zooming in and out of an image, you can use the navigator panel.

1 Choose Window > Navigator to open the Navigator panel.

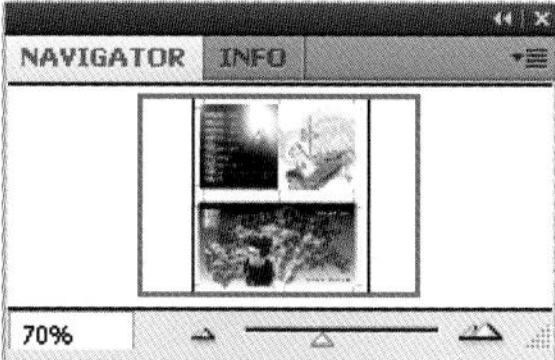

The Navigator panel.

2 In the Navigator panel, press the Zoom In button (⛰) at the bottom of the panel, or drag the slider to the right to enlarge the view percentage of your artwork. As you do so, watch the View Depth percentage change in the lower-left corner of this panel, and stop enlarging when you reach 150 percent. The current view of your artwork increases to 150 percent.

3 Note that a red box is visible in the panel, showing the content currently being displayed inside your document window. This red box shrinks as you increase the magnification of your artwork, and can also be used to scroll around your illustration. Position your cursor over the red box in the Navigator panel, and when the cursor changes to a hand, drag the red box to scroll to the lower-left corner of the artboard. This allows you to view the intricate branches of the tree illustration in closer detail.

Using the Navigator panel simplifies the process of zooming and scrolling in your artwork.

4 In the Navigator panel, drag the slider to the left to reduce the view percentage of your artwork. Note that the red box increases in size to show the increased content inside your document window.

5 Position your cursor over the red box in the Navigator panel, and when the cursor changes to a hand, drag the red box to scroll to the upper-right corner of the artboard. This enables you to view the guitar illustration from farther away and see how it interacts with the other parts of the design.

6 Control the zoom even more by holding down the Ctrl key (Windows) or Command key (Mac OS) and then dragging over an area that you want to zoom into in the Navigator panel. By essentially drawing a zoom area with the cursor you control the final zoom result in the artboard.

7 Type **100** into the View Depth text field in the Navigator panel and press Enter (Windows) or Return (Mac OS) to return to actual size.

The Tools panel

In Illustrator, you use the tools in the Tools panel to create, select, and edit portions of your Illustrator artwork.

Direct Selection Tool (A)
Group Selection Tool

Type Tool (T)
Area Type Tool
Type on a Path Tool
Vertical Type Tool
Vertical Area Type Tool
Vertical Type on a Path Tool

Pen Tool (P)
Add Anchor Point Tool (+)
Delete Anchor Point Tool (-)
Convert Anchor Point Tool (Shift+C)

Rotate Tool (R)
Reflect Tool (O)

Rectangle Tool (M)
Rounded Rectangle Tool
Ellipse Tool (L)
Polygon Tool
Star Tool
Flare Tool

Line Segment Tool (\)
Arc Tool
Spiral Tool
Rectangular Grid Tool
Polar Grid Tool

Pencil Tool (N)
Smooth Tool
Path Eraser Tool

Warp Tool (Shift+R)
Twirl Tool
Pucker Tool
Bloat Tool
Scallop Tool
Crystallize Tool
Wrinkle Tool

Eraser Tool (Shift+E)
Scissors Tool (C)
Knife Tool

Scale Tool (S)
Shear Tool
Reshape Tool

Selection Tool (V) — Direct Selection Tool (A)
Magic Wand Tool (Y) — Lasso Tool (Q)
Pen Tool (P) — Type Tool (T)
Line Segment Tool (\) — Rectangle Tool (M)
Paintbrush Tool (B) — Pencil Tool (N)
Blob Brush Tool (Shift+B) — Eraser Tool (Shift+E)
Rotate Tool (R) — Scale Tool (S)
Warp Tool (Shift+R) — Free Transform Tool (E)
Symbol Sprayer Tool (Shift+S) — Column Graph Tool (J)
Mesh Tool (U) — Gradient Tool (G)
Eyedropper Tool (I) — Blend Tool (W)
Live Paint Bucket (K) — Live Paint Selection Tool (Shift+L)
Artboard Tool (Shift+O) — Slice Tool (Shift+K)
Hand Tool (H) — Zoom Tool (Z)
Swap Fill and Stroke (Shift X)
Fill (X)
Stroke (click to activate) (X)
Default Fill and Stroke (D)
Gradient (>)
Color (<)
None (/)
Change Screen Mode (F)

Symbol Sprayer Tool (Shift+S)
Symbol Shifter Tool
Symbol Scruncher Tool
Symbol Sizer Tool
Symbol Spinner Tool
Symbol Stainer Tool
Symbol Screener Tool
Symbol Styler Tool

Column Graph Tool (J)
Stacked Column Graph Tool
Bar Graph Tool
Stacked Bar Graph Tool
Line Graph Tool
Area Graph Tool
Scatter Graph Tool
Pie Graph Tool
Radar Graph Tool

Eyedropper Tool (I)
Measure Tool

Hand Tool (H)
Print Tiling Tool

Slice Tool (Shift+K)
Slice Selection Tool

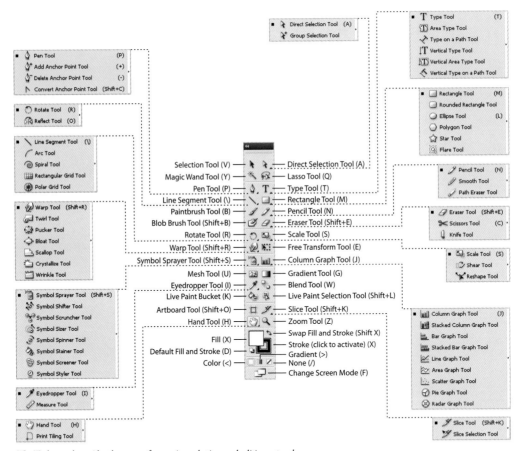

The Tools panel provides the means for creating, selecting, and editing artwork.

Nearly all the tools in the Tools panel have keyboard shortcuts that can be used to access them. Place your cursor over a tool in the panel to display its tooltip, which includes the tool's name and its shortcut (in parentheses).

Using tools and panels

To keep all the options organized, Adobe Illustrator uses panels. Some panels are displayed in the default Illustrator workspace, and all other panels can be displayed by choosing them from the Window menu. Most panels have panel menus containing options specific to that panel's functions.

By default, when you open Illustrator, you'll see the Basic workspace. The Basic workspace includes the Tools panel on the left side of your screen, the Control panel at the top of your screen (under the application bar), and five panel groups collapsed into the panel dock on the right side of your screen.

1 The Selection tool (↖) is used to identify objects in your artwork for editing. Choose the Selection tool from the Tools panel.

2 Click and hold the photo of the guitarist in the lower part of your document window, and drag with your mouse to move it slightly downward.

3 Certain tools offer additional options for selecting, drawing, painting, and repositioning objects. To access the Selection tool's options, double-click on the Selection tool in the Tools panel. In the Move dialog box that appears, type **-.025** in the Horizontal text field and press the OK button to move the photo slightly to the left.

4 To switch to another tool, you can either click on the new tool to select it, or access it using a keyboard command. Press **T** on your keyboard or press the Type tool (T) in the Tools panel to access the Type tool.

5 Using the Type tool, select the *s* in the word *sketch* in the top-right corner of the artwork's bottom panel, and type an uppercase *S* to replace it.

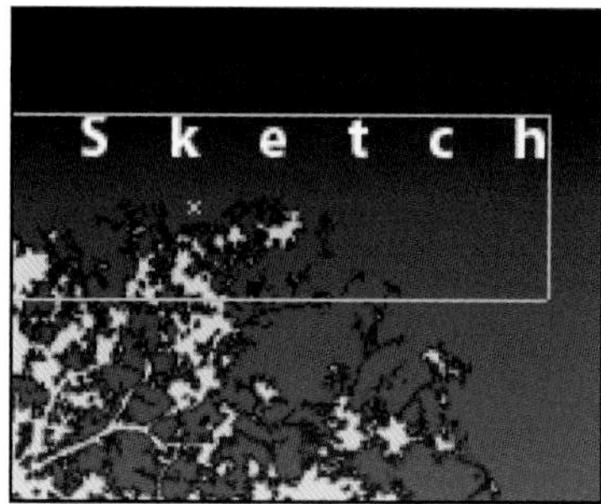

Replace the character using the Type tool.

6 Press the Esc key. This closes the text frame and returns you to the Selection tool.

Hidden tools

Some tools in the Tools panel have black triangles in the lower-right corner of their icons, which indicate that there are hidden (related) tools beneath them.

1 Choose Select > Deselect to deselect items on the artboard that may be selected, then press and hold the Type tool (T) in the Tools panel.

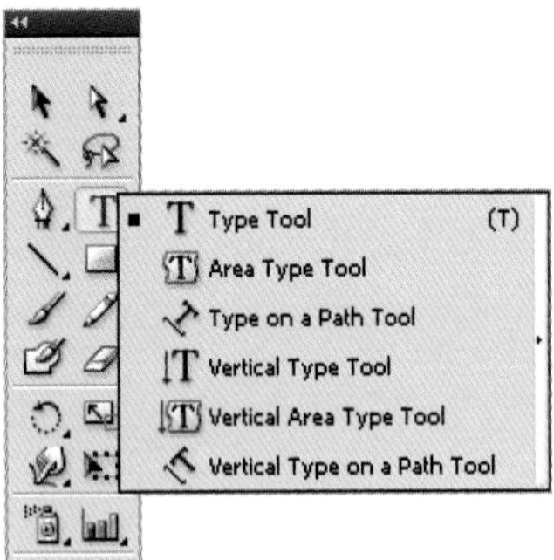

Some tools have hidden tools nested beneath them.

2 Still holding down the mouse button, move your cursor over one of the options in the Type tool's contextual menu.

If you forget the name of a certain tool, simply position your cursor over the tool. A tooltip appears, listing the name of the tool. In parentheses next to the tool's name is a keyboard shortcut that can be used to access that tool.

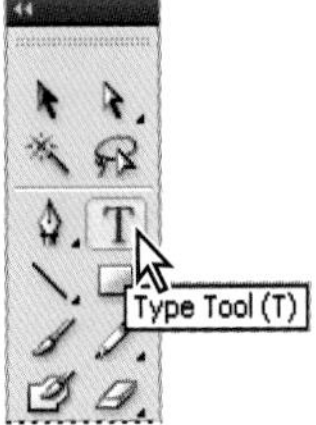

Tooltips display tools' names as you position the cursor over them.

These and other keyboard shortcuts can be changed and saved as part of a personal workspace. Techniques for creating shortcuts and saving workspaces are discussed later in this lesson.

Tearing off tools

Related tools (both default and hidden) can be separated from the Tools panel and displayed as a separate, repositionable panel.

1 Press and hold the Type tool in the Tools panel. With the mouse button held down, move the cursor to the tab marked with an arrow at the far right of the hidden tools menu.

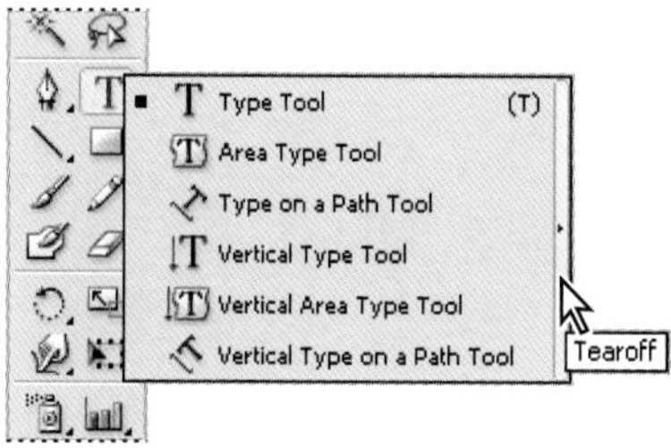

Tearoff tabs allow you to separate groups of tools from the Tools panel.

2 When the tab changes color, release your mouse button to tear off the tools into a separate panel.

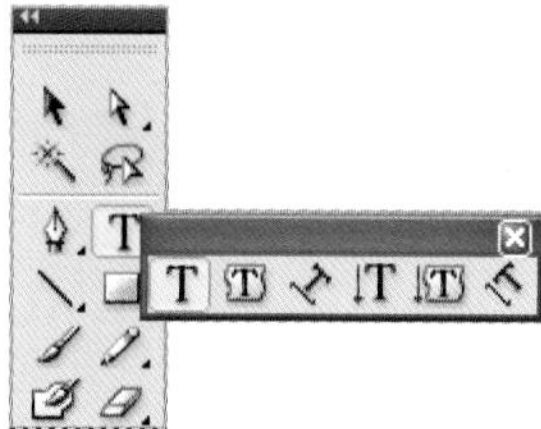

The separated tools.

Click and drag the bar at the top of the torn-off panel to reposition it on your screen.

Adjusting the Tools panel

The Tools panel can be reconfigured to different views, and repositioned to different locations on your screen.

1 To change the visual configuration of the Tools panel, click on the double arrow in the upper-left corner of the Tools panel to change it from its default two-column configuration to a one-column configuration.

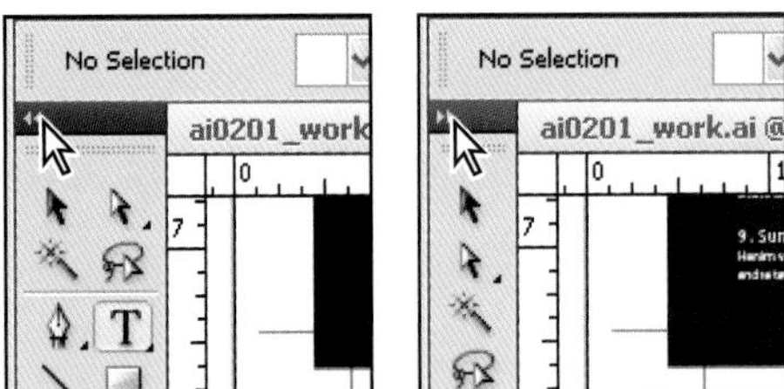

Change the column width of the Tools panel from two columns to one column by pressing the double arrows at the top of the panel.

2 Select the double arrow again to return the Tools panel to two-column view.

3 To move the Tools panel, click on the gray bar at the top of the Tools panel and drag it to a new location on your screen.

4 Release the mouse button when the Tools panel is at the desired location.

The Control panel

The Control panel provides easy access to options used to modify your artwork. It is context-sensitive, meaning that the options displayed will change depending on the type of object you select, and the tool you used to select it. For example, text-formatting settings are displayed in the Control panel when a text object is selected in your artwork.

When text is selected in your artwork, text-formatting settings are displayed in the Control panel.

When an option name is blue and underlined in the Control panel, you can click on it to display a related dialog box or panel. Click anywhere outside the panel or dialog box to close it.

You can customize the content of the Control panel at any time by making choices from its panel menu.

1 Press the Control panel menu button (▾≡) in the upper-right corner of the Control panel to show the settings that can be displayed in the Control panel. Those that are currently being displayed have check marks next to them.

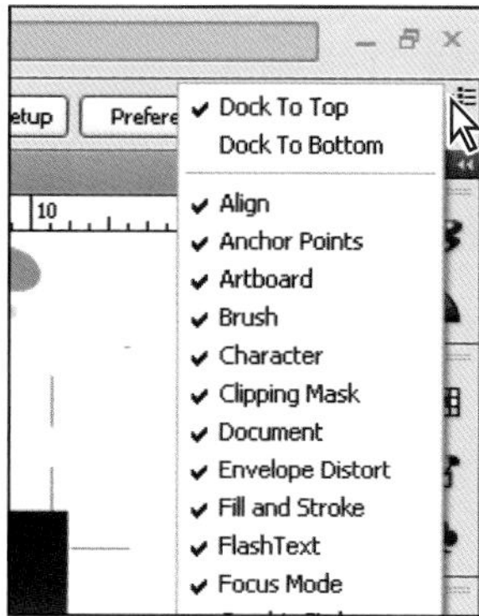

The Control panel options can be found by pressing the panel menu button.

2 Select Brush from the menu, and notice that the Brush settings disappear from the Control panel to the left.

3 Access the panel menu again, and select Brush again to turn these settings on in the panel.

Moving the Control panel

As with other panels, the Control panel can be repositioned on your screen to further customize your workspace.

1 Drag the gray bar on the left edge of the Control panel away from its default position.

2 Drag the Control panel to the top or bottom of the screen to re-dock it.

3 From the Control panel menu (▾≡), choose Dock to Top or Dock to Bottom to change the docking location of the panel.

Panel groups and the dock

The ability to arrange panels in groups, and then dock them to the Illustrator workspace, allows for both better organization and increased functionality.

Panel groups

Panels with related functions can be nested and displayed together in panel groups. An example is the Navigator panel (described earlier in this chapter), which is part of a panel group that also includes the Info panel.

1 From the Window menu, choose a panel to display within the workspace. For this exercise, choose the Align panel, which is part of a panel group that includes the Transform and Pathfinder panels.

2 Choose Window > Attributes to also display the Attributes panel in the workspace.

3 Select the Attributes tab at the top of the Attributes panel and drag it to the Align panel.

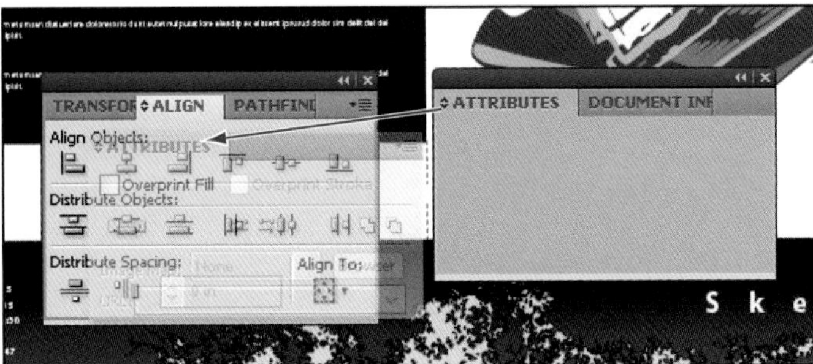

Drag the Attributes tab to the Align panel.

4 Release the mouse button to add the Attributes panel to the panel group.

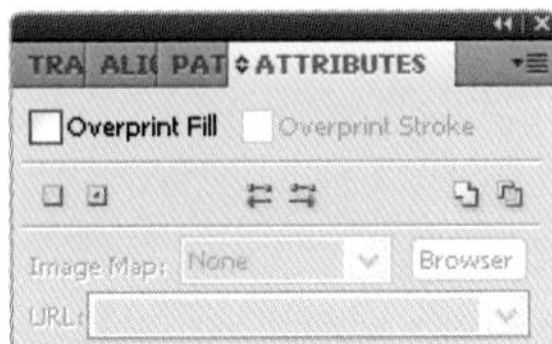

Release the mouse button to add the Attributes panel to the group.

5 To remove the Align panel from the panel group, select the Align tab at the top of the panel and drag it away from the panel group you just created.

6 Release the mouse button to separate the Align panel from the panel group.

Using the dock

If you choose, you can store panels and panel groups in the panel dock, located on the right side of your screen. In the Essentials workspace, there are five panel groups displayed by default, including panels such as Color, Swatches, Stroke, Appearance, and Layers.

1 To dock a panel, select the Align panel, which you made independent in the last exercise, and drag it to the dock at the top, bottom, left, right, or in between existing panels.

2 When you see a light-blue line marking the panel's desired position in the dock, release the mouse button and the panel becomes docked.

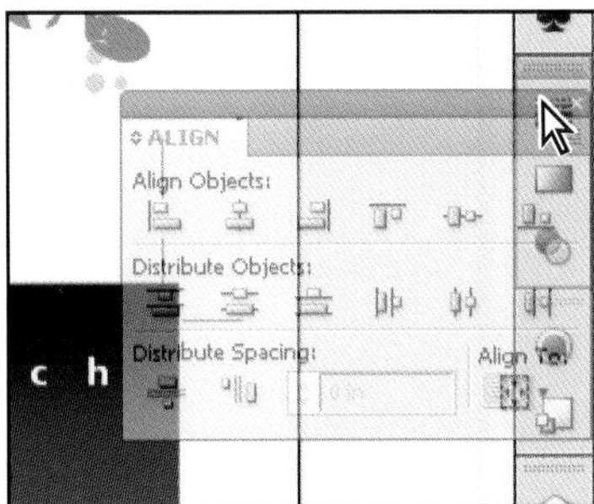

Drag a panel by its tab, and position it over the dock to store it there.

Docking a panel group

To dock a panel group, you'll need to drag the group by its title bar (not individual panel tabs) into the dock.

1 Select the bar at the top of the Attributes panel and drag it into the dock.

2 Release the mouse button when a light-blue line marks the panel's desired position, and it becomes docked.

Removing a panel or panel group from the dock

To remove a panel or panel group, drag it out of the dock by its tab or title bar. You can drag it into another dock or make it free-floating.

1 To remove a panel from the dock, select the desired button and drag it away from the dock. To remove a panel group, select the gray bar at the top of the group in the dock and drag it away from the dock.

2 Release the mouse to move it into another dock or make it a floating panel group.

If you remove all panels and panel groups from the dock, the dock will disappear. It will reappear when new panels or groups are dragged into it.

Adjusting the dock

Like the Tools panel (which, incidentally, can also be docked), the panel dock can be reconfigured to further customize your workspace.

1 To change the configuration of the dock, press the double arrow ( ) in the upper-right corner of the dock to expand all the panels therein to their full width.

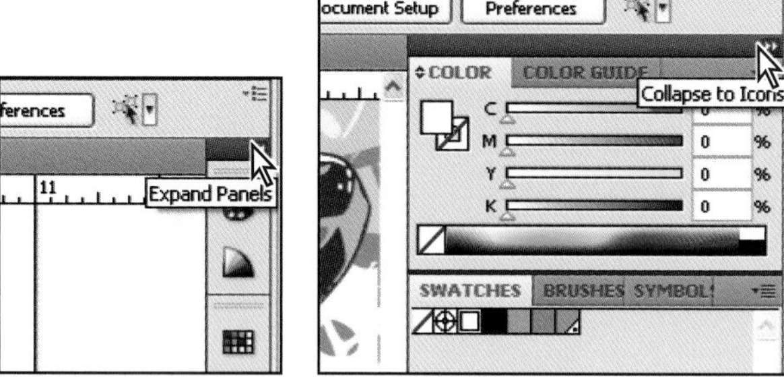

Press the double arrow at the top of the dock to change from Icon to Expanded mode.

2 Press the double arrow again to collapse the panels to icons.

3 Expand the width of panels in the panel dock by clicking and dragging the left side of the dock to the left.

4 Reduce the width of panels in the panel dock by clicking and dragging the left side of the dock to the right.

5 Alternately, click the gray bar at the top of the dock to toggle between Icon and Expanded modes.

Custom workspaces

Once you've configured, moved, and manipulated Illustrator's panels to your liking, you can save custom workspaces and switch among them.

Saving workspaces

When you save the current size and position of panels as a custom workspace, you can restore that workspace even if you've moved or closed panels in the meantime.

1 Dragging them by their name tabs, pull the Color and Swatches panels out from the dock and drop them on your artboard. Nest the Swatches panel inside the Color panel by dragging it on top of the Color panel. Drag the new panel group by its title bar and position it next to the Tools panel on the left side of your screen.

2 Collapse all other panels in the dock by clicking on the double arrow in the upper-right corner of the dock.

3 To save this customized workspace, choose Window > Workspace > Save Workspace.

4 In the Save Workspace dialog box, type **Color** in the text field to label your new workspace, and press OK.

5 Choose Window > Workspace again, and notice that your named workspace is now at the top of the list.

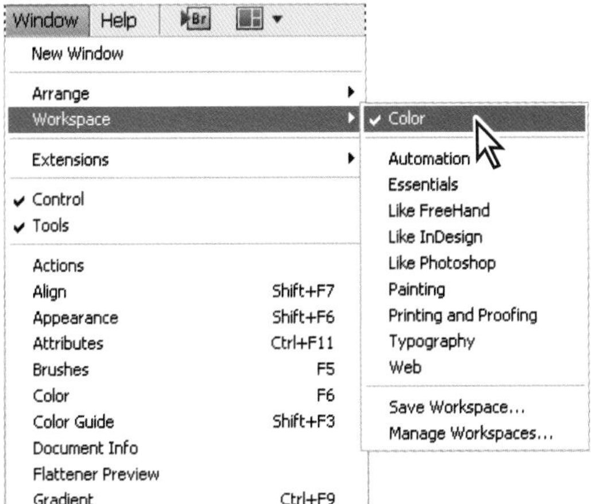

Choose Window > Workspace to save a customized workspace.

6 To restore a default workspace, choose Window > Workspace to display both the preset workspaces and the custom workspace you just saved. Choose Essentials to return to that workspace. All panels return to their original appearance.

Now you can see how Illustrator allows you to return to the custom workspace you've saved.

7 To restore your custom workspace, choose Window > Workspace, noting that your Color workspace appears at the top of the list. Choose the Color workspace from the list to return to that workspace. All panels return to the customized appearance you chose to save.

Using the Manage Workspaces dialog box

Custom workspaces can also be saved (and deleted) using the Manage Workspaces dialog box.

1 To add a new custom workspace using the Manage Workspaces feature, choose Window > Workspace > Manage Workspaces. The Manage Workspaces dialog box appears.

2 Press the New Workspace button (◲) at the bottom of this dialog box to save the current panel configuration as a custom workspace.

3 Name the new workspace **Color 2** in the field at the bottom and press OK. You are creating this replica merely to practice deleting an undesired workspace.

4 Your new workspace is added to both the list in the Manage Workspaces dialog box, and the Window > Workspace menu.

Choose Window > Manage Workspaces to add and delete custom workspaces.

Deleting a custom workspace

Using the Manage Workspaces dialog box to delete a custom workspace is just as easy as it was to add one.

1 To delete a custom workspace using the Manage Workspaces feature, choose Window > Workspace > Manage Workspaces. The Manage Workspaces dialog box appears.

2 Select the Color 2 workspace you just added from the list at the top.

3 Press the Delete button (🗑) at the bottom of the dialog box.

4 The Color 2 workspace is deleted from both the list in the Manage Workspaces dialog box and the Window > Workspace menu. Press OK.

5 Choose Window > Workspace > Essentials to revert back to the original workspace.

The default workspaces are not listed in the Manage Workspaces dialog box and cannot be deleted.

Customizing keyboard shortcuts

A keyboard shortcut is a combination of keys that, when pressed simultaneously, perform some task that ordinarily requires use of a mouse or other input device and may take longer to do. In Illustrator, keyboard shortcuts are provided for many tools and commands to save you the trouble of searching for these options in its menus and panels. You can view a list of all the shortcuts, and create or edit your own, using the Keyboard Shortcuts command.

Default shortcuts

Illustrator's set of default shortcuts can be viewed and printed from an easy-to-create plain-text file.

1 To view a list of default keyboard shortcuts, choose Edit > Keyboard Shortcuts.

2 In the Keyboard Shortcuts dialog box, choose Illustrator Defaults from the Set drop-down menu.

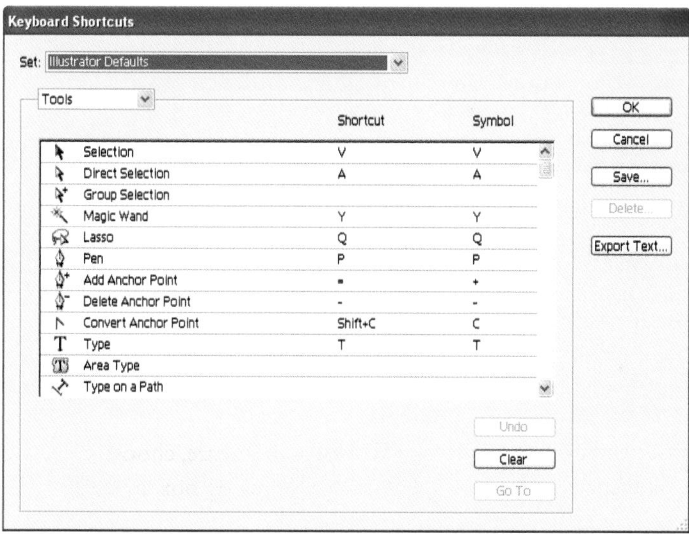

The Keyboard Shortcuts dialog box allows you to view a list of all shortcuts, and create or edit your own.

3 To create a text file containing the default shortcuts, press the Export Text button.

4 When prompted, save your Illustrator Defaults text file to the desktop, leaving the name as Illustrator Defaults.

5 Use Notepad, TextEdit, or another text editing application to open, view and print your default shortcuts file.

Custom shortcuts

For missing or hard-to-remember keyboard shortcuts, Illustrator allows you to add to or edit its list of defaults. It is highly recommended that you make a copy of the default keyboard shortcuts first before altering the original shortcut list. To do so, press the Save button and rename the new listing, then choose that new listing from the Set drop-down menu.

1 To add a custom shortcut, choose Edit > Keyboard Shortcuts.

2 In the Keyboard Shortcuts dialog box, choose the Menu Commands shortcut type from the drop-down menu above the shortcut list.

3 In the shortcut list below, click the arrow next to the File menu designation to expand that portion of the list.

4 Scroll down the menu list to the Place command, which, by default, doesn't have a keyboard shortcut.

5 Click the Shortcut column next to the Place command, and press Ctrl+E (Windows) or Command+E (Mac OS) to enter that shortcut.

6 Click the Symbol column next to the Place command, and type **E**, if there's not already one there. This is the symbol that will appear in the menu next to the Place command.

If you enter a shortcut that's already assigned to another command or tool, you'll get a warning about this at the bottom of the Keyboard Shortcuts dialog box.

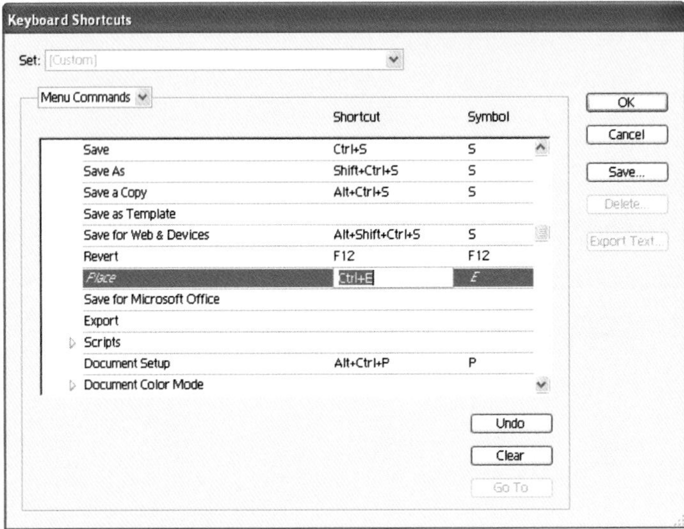

Change the keyboard shortcut of the Place command.

If this happens, do one of the following:

- Press the Undo button below to withdraw the entry.
- Press the Go To button to enter a different shortcut for the other command.
- Ignore the warning, and Illustrator will delete the shortcut for the other command in favor of your new one.

7 To edit an existing shortcut, click on the shortcut you want to change in the Shortcut column of the list, and type a new shortcut.

8 If that shortcut has already been assigned, follow the directions above to Undo or Go To the other command.

Saving shortcut sets

Saving sets of custom shortcuts in Illustrator will allow you to return to them and use them whenever you choose.

1 Make changes to an existing shortcut set in the Keyboard Shortcuts dialog box as noted in the previous section, "Custom shortcuts."

2 Press OK to save those changes to the currently selected shortcut set.

You cannot save changes to the Illustrator Defaults set.

3 To save a new set of custom shortcuts, make changes to an existing shortcut set in the Keyboard Shortcuts dialog box as noted in the previous section, "Custom shortcuts."

4 Press Save and type a name for the new set when prompted. The new set will appear in the Set drop-down menu under its new name.

Save the new set.

Deleting shortcut sets

You can delete unused or unwanted shortcut sets in the Keyboard Shortcuts dialog box.

1 Select the unwanted new set from the Set drop-down menu at the top of the dialog box.

2 Press the Delete button, then press Yes to confirm in the alert box that appears to remove that set from the list. Note that you cannot delete the Illustrator Default set.

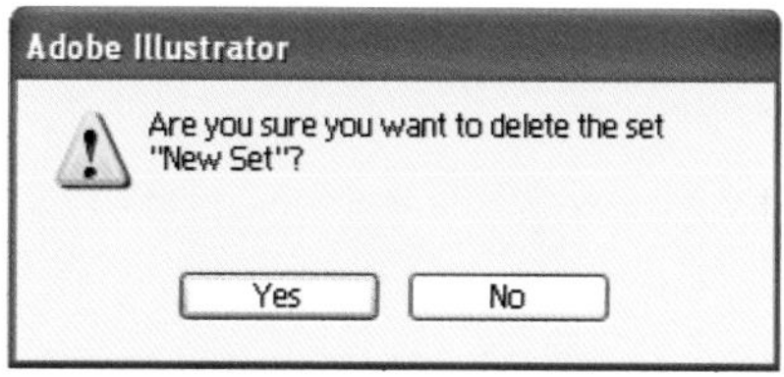

Illustrator warns you when you try to delete an existing set of keyboard shortcuts.

3 Press OK to exit the dialog box. Choose File > Save, then choose File > Close.

Now that you're familiar with the features and customization options of Illustrator workspaces, you're ready to begin creating and editing artwork in the next chapter.

Self study

Using your new knowledge of Illustrator workspaces, try some of the following tasks to build on your experience. Use the ai0201.ai file from your ai02lessons folder as an example file.

1 Choose the Selection tool (↖) from the Tools panel, and select different objects within the example artwork. Watch as the options available in the Control panel change based on what's selected, and try to make yourself familiar with how and why these options change.

2 Explore the default workspaces. Rearrange the panels in each workspace to meet your needs. Create and save your own custom workspace, and then return to the Essentials workspace, noting the differences between the workspaces.

3 Create your own set of keyboard shortcuts, changing those that you think are less intuitive than others, and adding shortcuts where there aren't any by default. Think about how these shortcuts can speed up your workflow and customize the way Illustrator creates and edits artwork.

Review

Questions

1 Describe the advantages of using the Navigator panel to change the view of your artwork.

2 How do you select hidden tools in Illustrator?

3 Describe three ways to change the configuration of the panel dock.

4 How can saving workspaces help you work more efficiently?

5 What can you do if a keyboard shortcut you've added is the same as one already in existence?

Answers

1 The Navigator panel allows you to reduce or enlarge the view of your artwork in the document window by dragging its Zoom slider. It also allows you to scroll to different locations within your artwork by dragging the box in its proxy window. These options, along with the ability to marquee-zoom in on areas of your illustration, are all available in the same panel and do not require you to switch tools or choose different commands to access them. This makes it a more efficient choice for changing the view of your artwork while you're working.

2 Tools that have other, related tools hidden beneath them are indicated by a small black triangle in the lower-right corner of the tool icon. To access these hidden tools, you position your cursor over any tool that has the black triangle displayed, and click to expose the hidden tools nested within it. Then, with the mouse button held down, you scroll to the desired tool and release the mouse button to select it.

3 The panel dock can be reconfigured by clicking on the double arrow in its upper-right corner. This toggles the dock between expanded and collapsed (◂◂) view. In addition, you can click and drag the gripper handle in the dock's upper-left corner to expand or reduce the width of the panels contained in it. You can also click on the gray bar at the top of the dock to toggle between icon and expanded modes.

4 Saving a workspace allows you to lock in the position and visibility of panels on your screen. It also allows you to return to that workspace whenever you choose, even after you've opened and closed panels or switched to other workspaces. This ability to customize your workspace ensures that you only have to work with the panels that you need the most at any given time, and streamlines your workflow in the process.

5 If you've added a keyboard shortcut in Illustrator, either to an existing set or to a new custom set, and you get a warning about another command that already uses the same shortcut, you have three choices: you can ignore the warning and forfeit the shortcut for the other command in favor of a new choice. You can click on the Undo button in the Keyboard Shortcuts dialog box to reverse the change. Or you can click on the Go To button to change the other command's shortcut so they no longer conflict.

Lesson 3

What you'll learn in this lesson:

- Creating shapes
- Selecting objects using the selection tools
- Transforming shapes
- Using layers to organize artwork

Illustrator CS4 Essentials

Illustrator can be used to create many types of artwork. In this lesson, you will use the shape tools, work with basic selection techniques, and assemble some artwork using object stacking order. Along the way, you will learn some helpful tips for creating artwork on your own.

Starting up

Before starting, make sure that your tools and panels are consistent by resetting your workspace. See "Resetting Adobe Illustrator CS4 Preferences" on page 3.

You will work with several files from the ai03lessons folder in this lesson. Make sure that you have loaded the ailessons folder onto your hard drive from the supplied DVD. See "Loading lesson files" on page 4.

See Lesson 3 in action

Use the accompanying video to gain a better understanding of how to use some of the features shown in this lesson. The video tutorial for this lesson can be found on the included DVD.

Using the shape tools

Making shapes is an important part of using Adobe Illustrator. In Lesson 5, "Working with the Drawing Tools," you learn how to make your own custom shapes and lines using the Pen tool, but many times you will work with shapes that are ready-to-go, right off the Tools panel.

Though it may seem simple if you have used Illustrator before, transferring a shape from the Tools panel to the artboard can be a little confusing for new users. To start this lesson, you'll create a new blank document; think of it as a piece of scratch paper that you can use for shape practice. You will put a number of shapes on this new document throughout the exercise; feel free to delete or reposition them as you move on to make room for new ones. You won't use this document in any other lessons.

1 In Illustrator, choose File > New; the New Document dialog box appears.

2 If they are not already selected, choose Print from the New Document Profile drop-down menu and Inches from the Units drop-down menu. When you change the units to inches, the New Document Profile setting changes to [Custom].

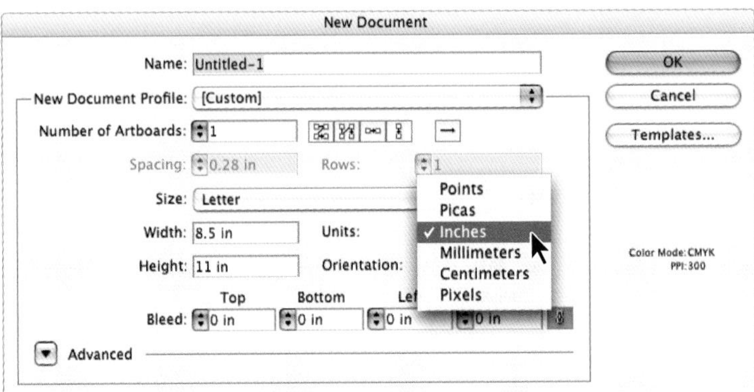

Specify the settings of your new Illustrator document.

3 Press OK. A new blank document appears.

4 Select the Rectangle tool (▭) from the Tools panel. Click and drag anywhere on the artboard. By clicking and dragging, you determine the placement and size of the rectangle. Typically, you would pull from the upper-left corner diagonally to the lower-right corner.

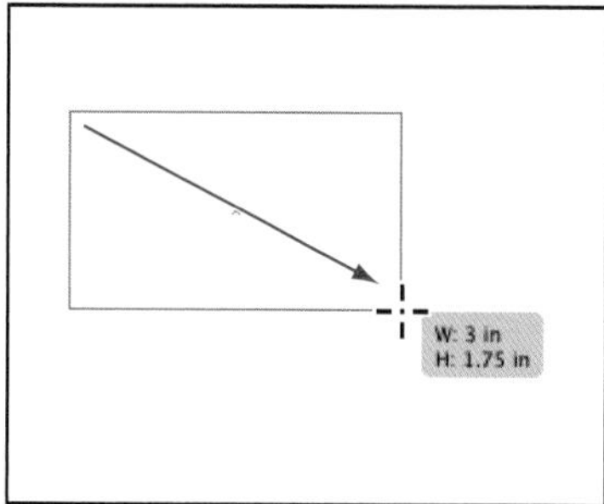

Click and drag from the upper-left to the lower-right corner.

5 It is essential that you save your files often after you start working. Choose File > Save As to save this file. The Save As dialog box appears.

6 Type **ai0301_work.ai** into the File name (Windows) or Save As (Mac OS) text field, navigate to the ai03lessons folder within the ailessons folder that you dragged onto your desktop, then press Save.

7 When the Illustrator Options dialog box appears, leave the version set to Illustrator CS4 and press OK. The file is saved.

If you are not able to save in the ai03lessons folder, the folder may be locked. See the tip on page 4 for instructions to unlock your lessons folder.

Repositioning and visually resizing the rectangle

Now that you have your first shape on the page, perhaps you want to relocate it or alter its shape or size.

1 Choose the Selection tool (↖) from the Tools panel. A bounding box with eight handles appears around the rectangle you just drew. If you do not see the eight handles, make sure you have the rectangle selected by clicking on it once. If the bounding box is still not visible, choose View > Show Bounding Box. The bounding box is a feature that can be turned on or off and that allows you to transform a shape without switching away from the Selection tool.

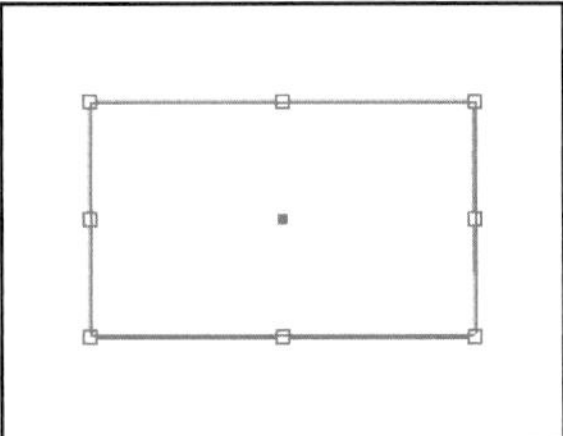

The bounding box provides handles to help transform shapes.

2 Using the Selection tool, click inside the rectangle and drag it to another location on the page (do not click on the handles, as that resizes the shape).

If you click inside a shape and it becomes unselected, it probably has no fill. Fill and stroke are discussed in Lesson 4, "Adding Color." By pressing the letter D, you revert back to the default white fill and black stroke, and you can easily select the shape.

3 Hover over the bottom-middle handle until the cursor becomes a vertical arrow and the word *path* appears. Click and drag. When you click on a middle handle and drag, you adjust the size of the selected handle's side only.

4 Click on a corner handle and drag. When you click on a corner handle, you adjust both the sides connected to the corner point.

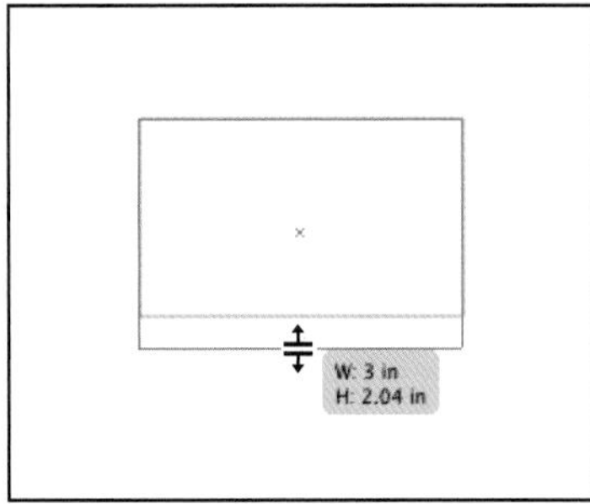

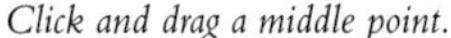

Click and drag a middle point.

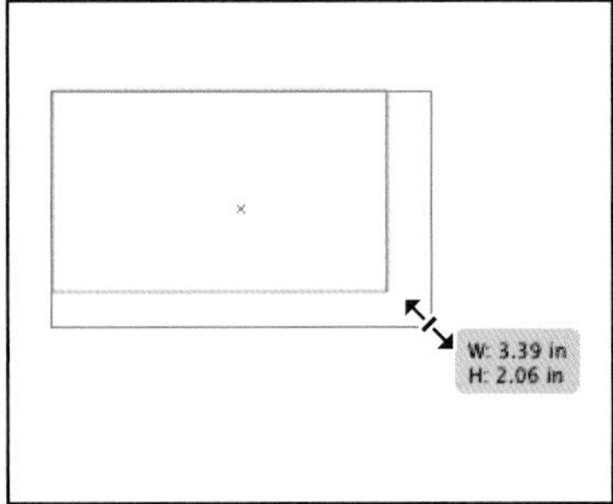

Click and drag a corner point.

5 Choose File > Save to save your work.

Finding or changing the shape's dimensions using the Transform panel

What if you need to know a shape's dimensions, or need it to be an exact size? This is when you should refer to the Transform panel.

1 Make sure the rectangle is still selected and open the Transform panel by choosing Window > Transform. The Transform panel appears. The values displayed are for the selected item, which in this case is the rectangle.

The Transform panel displays information about the rectangle's location and size. Here is something to keep in mind: the values (except for the X and Y values, which refer to the selected reference point) displayed in the Transform panel refer to the rectangle's bounding box. By default, the reference point is the center of the shape.

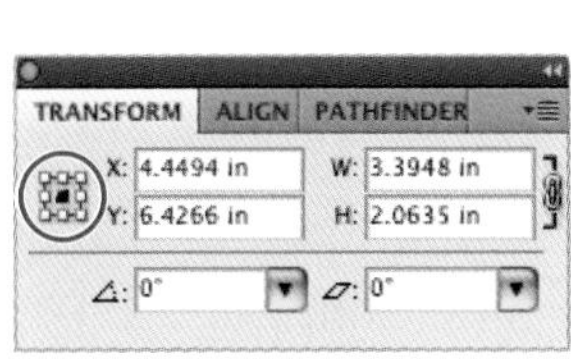

The center reference point.

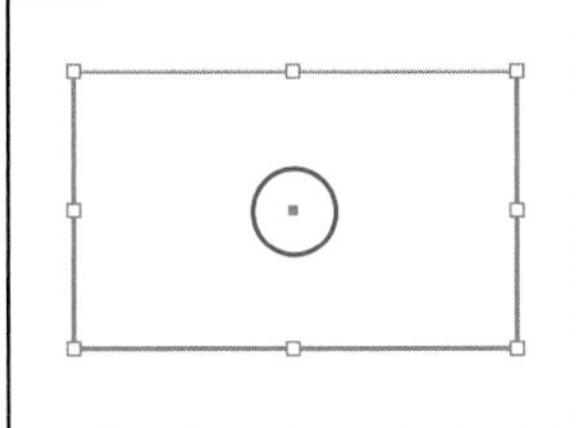

The reference point locator.

2 Click on the upper-left corner of the reference point locator to see that the X and Y values change, reflecting the shape's position based upon the upper-left corner as the reference point. Because you created your rectangle without given parameters, its values are different from those displayed in the figure below.

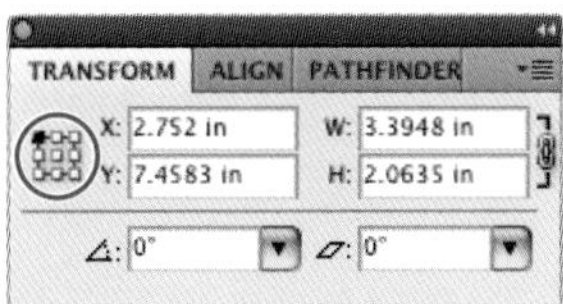

The X and Y coordinates change depending on the reference point selected.

3 Choose View > Show Rulers to display the rulers, or use the keyboard shortcut Ctrl+R (Windows) or Command+R (Mac OS).

The default ruler origin of zero is located in the lower-left corner of the artboard. This can be confusing if you are accustomed to the rulers in page layout applications, which start at zero in the upper-left corner of the page.

4 In the Transform panel, type **2** into the X text field and press the Tab key to move the cursor to the Y text field. Type **10** into the Y text field. Make sure the Constrain Width and Height proportions button (⛓) is not selected, then type **1** into the W (Width) text field and **1** into the H (Height) text field. The rectangle is now positioned and sized according to these values.

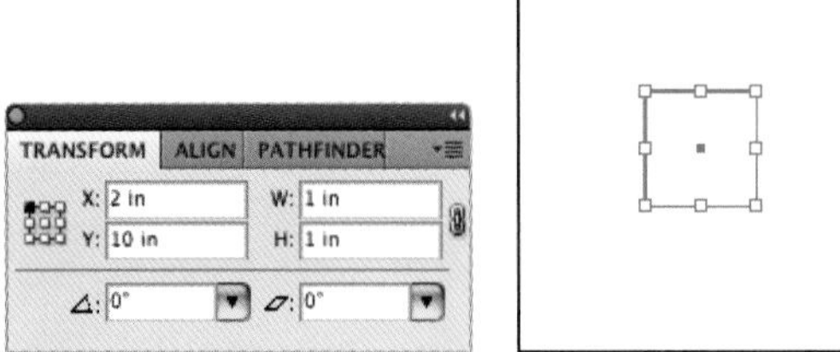

Manually enter values. *The result.*

5 Choose File > Save to save your work.

Rotating and shearing using the Transform panel

You can also use the Transform panel to enter exact rotation and shear values for the shapes on the artboard.

1 With the shape still selected, type **25** into the Rotate text field at the bottom of the Transform panel and press Enter (Windows) or Return (Mac OS). The square rotates 25 degrees counterclockwise and the dimensions in the Transform panel are updated.

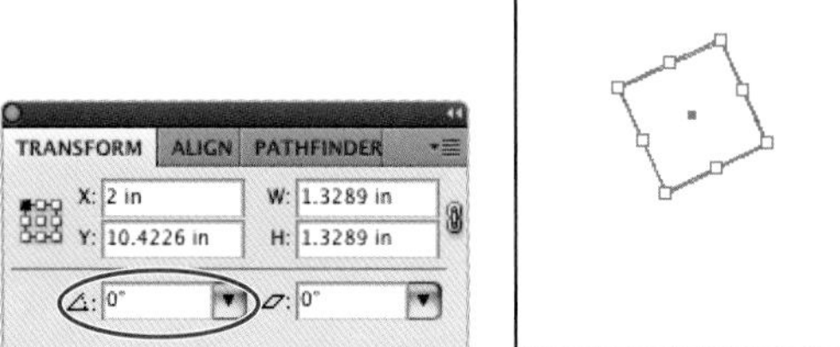

Type 25 *into the Rotate text field.* *The result.*

2 Click and hold on the arrow to the right of the Shear text field and choose 30° from the drop-down menu. Illustrator shears the shape by 30 degrees.

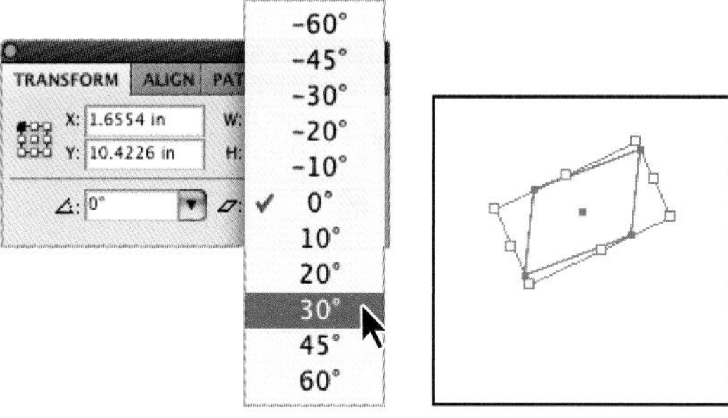

Type a value into the Shear text field. *The result.*

3 Choose File > Save.

Constraining a shape

You have created a shape visually and then used the Transform feature to make the rectangle a square. You can also use keyboard commands to create the shape that you want right from the Tools panel.

1 Select the Rectangle tool (□) from the Tools panel.

2 Hold down the Shift key and click and drag on an empty area on the artboard. Note that the shape tool is constrained to create a square. In order for the finished product to remain a square (and not become a rectangle), you must release the mouse before you release the Shift key. Now try this with the Ellipse tool.

3 The Ellipse tool (○) is hidden beneath the Rectangle tool. Click and hold on the Rectangle tool in the Tools panel to reveal and select the Ellipse tool.

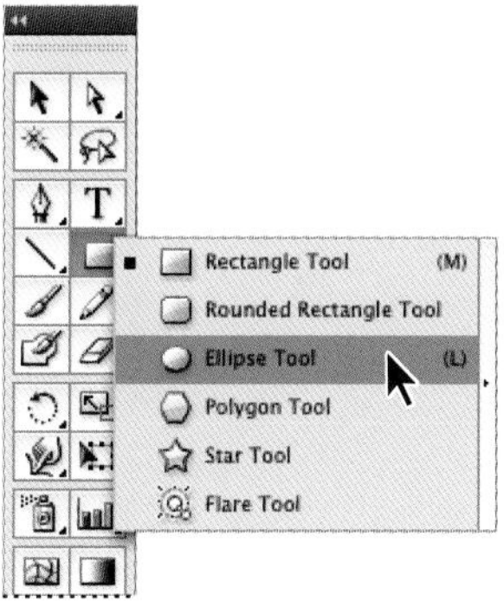

Select the hidden Ellipse tool.

4 Hold down the Shift key, click on an empty area of the artboard, and drag to create a circle. Remember to release the mouse before you release the Shift key to keep the shape a circle.

5 Choose File > Save. Keep this file open for the next part of the lesson.

Entering exact dimensions

You can also modify a shape's properties and dimensions through the shape tool's dialog box. You'll do that now using the Ellipse tool.

Before you start, you should know where to set the units of measurement. Even after indicating that you want the rulers to use inches, you may still have values recognized in points.

1 Choose Edit > Preferences > Units & Display Performance (Windows) or Illustrator > Preferences > Units & Display Performance (Mac OS). The Preferences dialog box appears.

2 Select Inches from the General drop-down menu, if it is not already selected. Leave all other measurements the same and press OK.

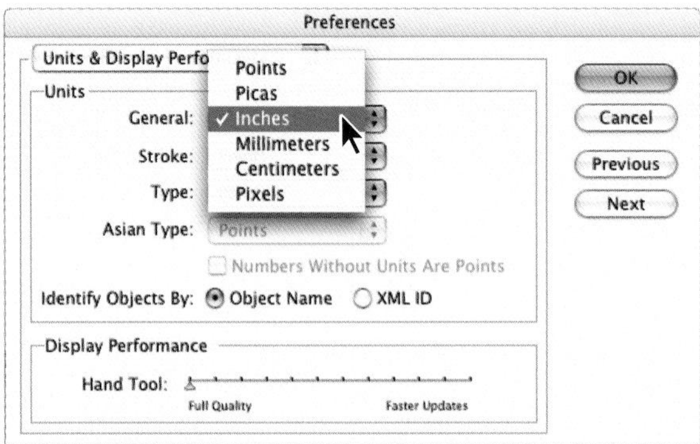

Change the general units of measurements to inches.

3 Using the Ellipse tool (○), click once on the artboard. The Ellipse dialog box appears.

If the Ellipse dialog box does not appear, you may have inadvertently clicked and dragged. Even a slight drag instructs Illustrator to create a tiny shape rather than open the dialog box. If this happens, press Ctrl+Z (Windows) or Command+Z (Mac OS) and click on the artboard again.

4 Type **4** into the Width text field, then click on the word *Height*. When you do this, the measurement is matched to the value that you entered into the Width text field. Press OK.

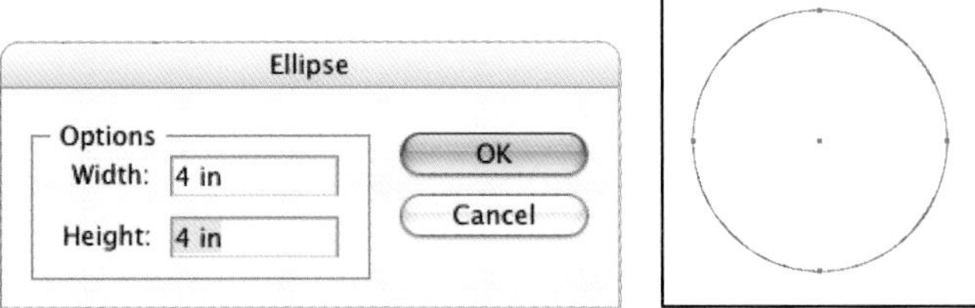

Click on Height to match the value in the Width text field.

You can use this same method to change shape options.

5 Hidden beneath the Ellipse tool in the Tools panel are a number of other shape tools. Click and hold the Ellipse tool to see the other options. Select the Star tool (☆) and click once on a blank area of the artboard. The Star dialog box appears.

6 Set the star's Radius 1 to **1.5** inches and its Radius 2 to **2** inches; then type **15** in the Points text field. Press OK.

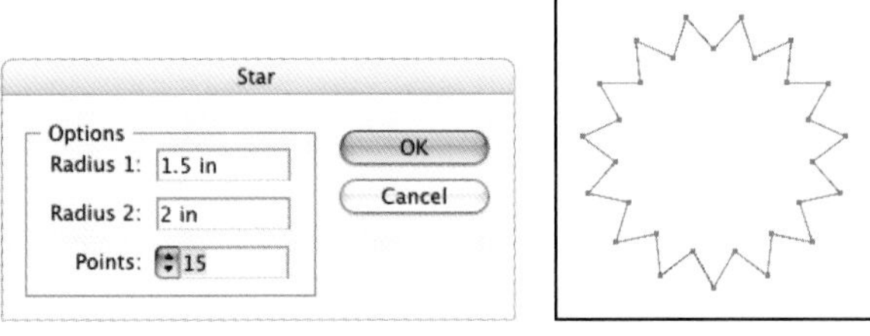

Enter star values. *The result.*

7 Choose File > Save, then File > Close. You won't be working with this file anymore.

You will now create a logo using some of these basic shapes as well as additional fundamental features.

Selecting artwork

In this part of the lesson, you will receive a quick primer on the selection tools and techniques in Adobe Illustrator. As the old saying goes, you have to select it to affect it. You need to know how to select objects in order to reposition, color, transform, and apply effects to them.

Helpful keyboard shortcuts for selections

FUNCTION	WINDOWS	MAC OS
Switch to last-used selection tool	Ctrl	Command
Switch between Direct Selection tool and Group Selection tool	Alt	Option
Add to a selection	Shift+click	Shift+click
Subtract from a selection	Shift+click	Shift+click
Change pointer to cross hair for selected tools	Caps Lock	Caps Lock

The selection tools

While there are several selection tools in Adobe Illustrator, the two main tools are the Selection tool and the Direct Selection tool. You will have an opportunity to experiment with selections in this part of the lesson.

1 Choose File > Open and navigate to the ai03lessons folder. Select the file named ai0302.ai and press Open. A file opens with a completed fish illustration on the top and the individual components of that fish at the bottom. The top fish artwork is locked and not accessible; use this for reference as you follow the exercise.

2 Choose File > Save As. The Save As dialog box appears.

3 Type **ai0302_work.ai** into the Name text field and press OK. When the Illustration Options dialog box appears, press OK.

4 Choose the Selection tool (↖) from the Tools panel and pass the cursor over the shape pieces at the bottom of the artwork. As you pass over the objects, notice that the cursor changes to reflect where there are selectable objects. Do not click to select any of these objects just yet.

Selectable object.

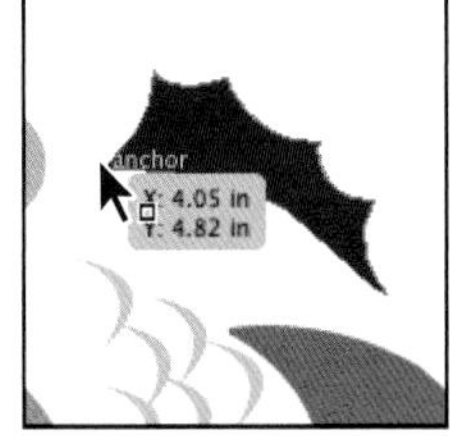

Anchor point.

No selectable object.

5 Click on the large red fin; the entire fin is selected. If you do not see the bounding box appear around the fin, choose View > Show Bounding Box.

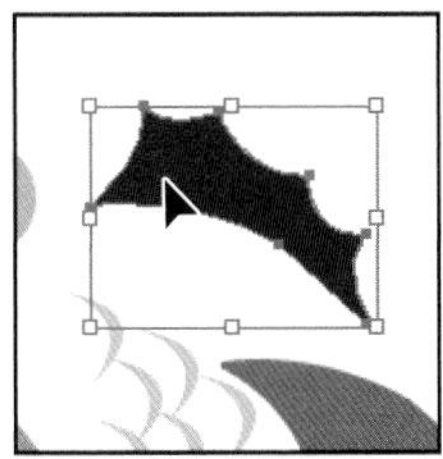

The entire shape is selected and has a bounding box surrounding it.

6 Click and drag to reposition the fin anywhere on the page. When you use the Selection tool, you select an entire object or group.

7 Choose the Direct Selection tool (↖) from the Tools panel. Using this tool allows you to select individual points or path segments of an object.

8 Without clicking on the selected large fin, reposition the cursor over one of the tips of the fin to see how the cursor changes to indicate that there is a selectable anchor beneath the cursor. A light-gray box giving the x- and y-coordinates of the anchor point also appears. Click when you see the arrow with the small white square.

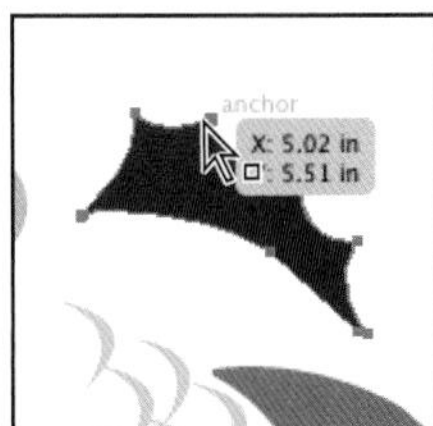

Cursor changes to show the selectable item.

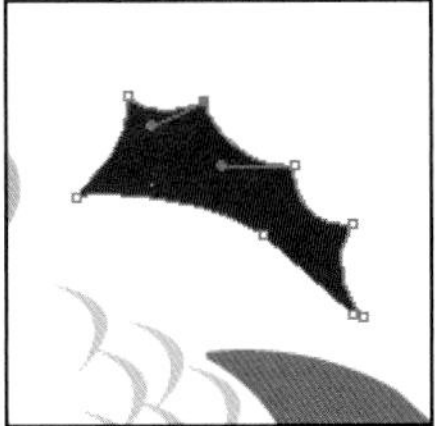

Individual anchor point selected.

9 Notice that only the anchor point that you clicked on is solid; all the other anchor points are hollow and not active.

10 Click on the solid anchor point and drag upward to reposition the anchor point and change the shape of the fin. By using the Direct Selection tool, you can alter the shape of an object.

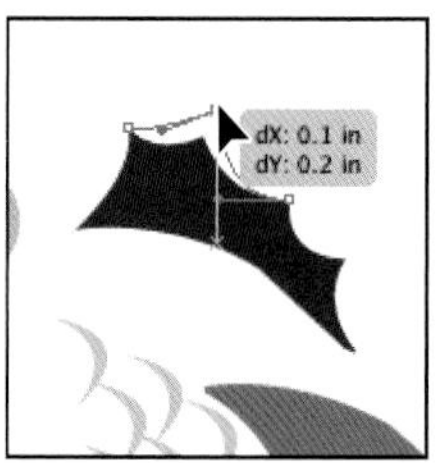

Click and drag with the Direct Selection tool to alter a shape.

11 Press Ctrl+Z (Windows) or Command+Z (Mac OS) to undo the last step, or choose Edit > Undo Move.

12 Choose File > Save. Keep this file open for the next part of this lesson.

Grouping the scales

You will now turn the individual scales in the artwork into a group that you can move and modify as a collective unit.

1 Activate the Selection tool (↖). Click on one of the pale orange scales, then add to the selection by holding down the Shift key and clicking on one of the other five scales.

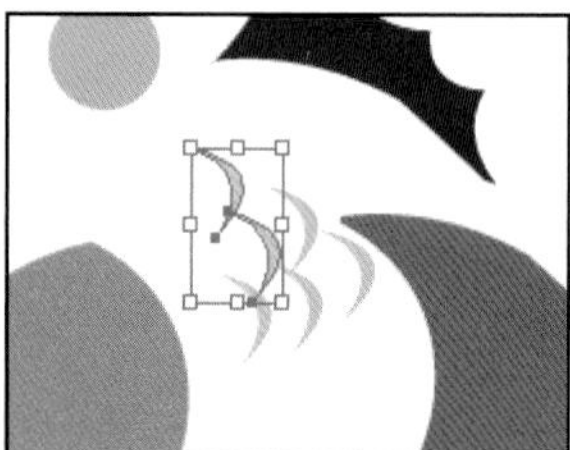

Shift+click to add to the selection.

2 With the two scales selected, choose Object > Group or use the keyboard shortcut Ctrl+G (Windows) or Command+G (Mac OS). The two scales are grouped together. When you select one with the Selection tool, the other is also selected.

3 Shift+click a third scale to add to the selection, then Shift+click the remaining scales. All the scales are now selected.

4 Press Ctrl+G (Windows) or Command+G (Mac OS) to group all the six scales together.

5 Choose Select > Deselect, or press Shift+Ctrl+A (Windows) or Shift+Command+A (Mac OS), to deselect the scales.

6 Using the Selection tool, click on one of the first scales you selected. The scales act as a collective group now, and all the scales are selected.

7 Press Shift+Ctrl (Windows) or Command+A (Mac OS) to deselect everything again.

You will now use the Group Selection tool to select individual items in a group.

8 Click and hold down on the Direct Selection tool (↖) in the Tools panel and choose the hidden Group Selection tool (↖+).

9 Click once on the top-most scale of the group; only the one scale is selected.

10 Now click on the same scale again and the second scale that you grouped back in step 1 also becomes selected.

11 Click on the same scale a third time and the entire last group of items becomes selected. By using the Group Selection tool, you can select individual items and even groups within groups.

12 With all the scales selected, click and drag the scales on top of the fish's orange body.

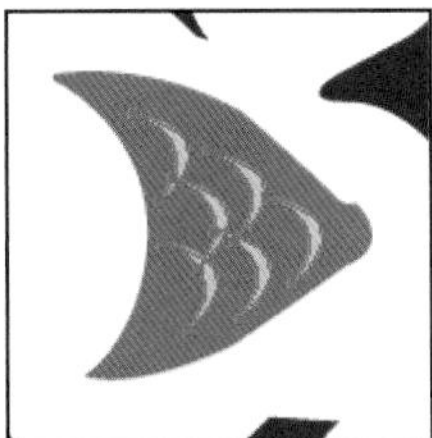

Click and drag to reposition the scales.

13 Now switch back to the Selection tool to reposition the rest of the separate components together to complete the fish. The positioning guides help you to best position and arrange the different pieces into one fish.

The completed fish.

14 Choose File > Save, then File > Close to close the document. You won't be working with this file anymore.

Isolation mode

Isolation mode is an Illustrator mode in which you can select and edit individual components or sub-layers of a grouped object. There are four ways to enter into isolation mode:

- Double-click a group using the Selection tool (↖).
- Click the Isolate Selected Group button (⁑) in the Control panel.
- Right-click (Windows) or Ctrl+click (Mac OS) a group and choose Isolate Selected Group.
- Select a group in the Layers panel and choose Enter Isolation Mode from the Layers panel menu (▾≡).

Using shape and transform tools to create artwork

You will add to the basics that you have discovered to complete some different fish artwork.

1 Choose File > Open and navigate to the ai03lessons folder. Double-click on ai0303_done.ai to open the file in Adobe Illustrator. Artwork of two swimming fish appears.

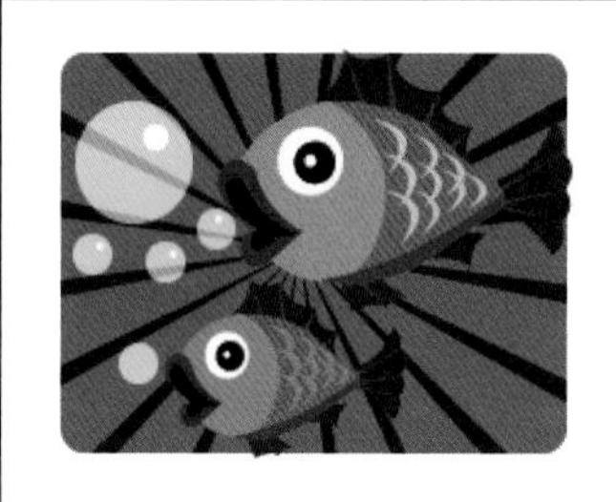

You can leave this file open for reference or choose File > Close.

2 Choose File > Open, navigate to the ai03lessons folder, and double-click on the ai0303.ai file. A document with four guides in the center of the page opens.

3 Choose File > Save As. The Save As dialog box appears.

4 Type **ai0303_work.ai** into the Save As text field and navigate to the ai03lessons folder you saved on your hard drive; then press Save.

5 When the Illustrator Options dialog box appears, press OK.

Using the transform tools

There are several transform tools. Though each performs a different task, they are essentially used in the same manner.

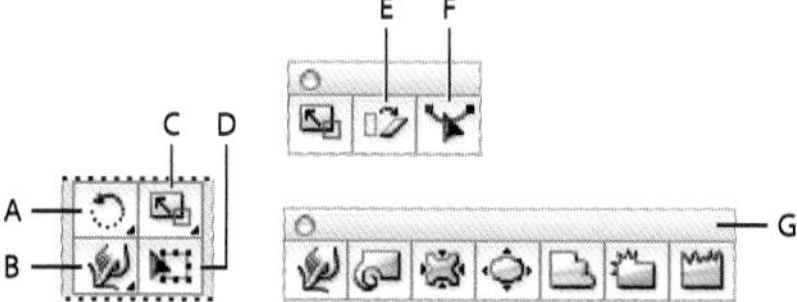

A. Rotate. B. Warp tools. C. Scale. D. Free Transform. E. Shear. F. Reshape. G. Additional Warp tools.

You used the Transform panel to rotate and shear earlier in this lesson. You will now use the transform tools to make changes by entering exact values.

1 Click and hold on the Star tool (☆) in the Tools panel to reveal the hidden tools. Select the Rounded Rectangle tool (▢).

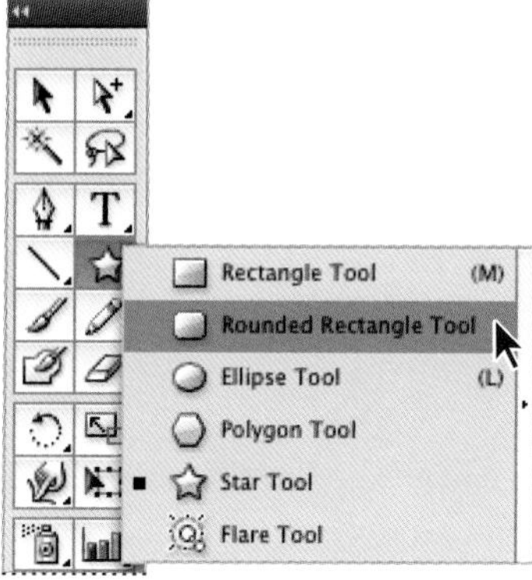

Select the Rounded Rectangle tool.

2 Click and drag to create a square with rounded corners of any size.

3 Activate the Selection tool (↖) and, using the bounding box's anchors, click and drag until the rounded rectangle fits the dimensions of the guides located in the center of the document.

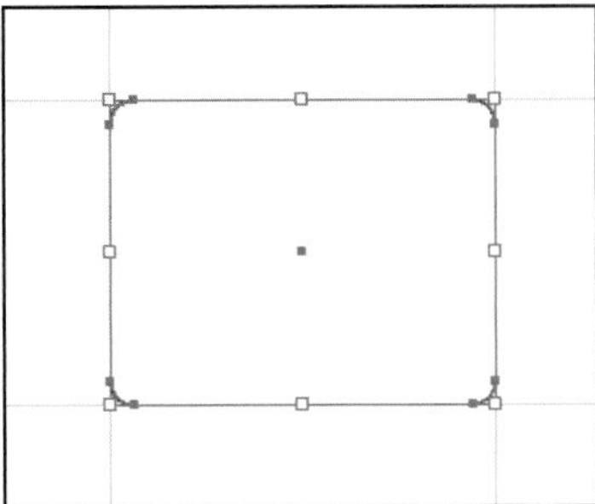

Manually drag anchors to fit the rectangle inside the guides.

Adding a fill color

You will now fill the rounded rectangle with a color.

1 Make sure the rounded rectangle is still selected. If it is not selected, click on it using the Selection tool (↖).

2 Locate the Control panel at the top of your workspace and click on the Fill box on the left side of the Control panel. Color swatches appear, from which you can choose a color. Pass your cursor over the swatches, and each color's name appears in a tooltip. Select the color named *CMYK Blue*. If the tooltip does not appear, select the color you see highlighted in the figure below. Illustrator colors the shape blue.

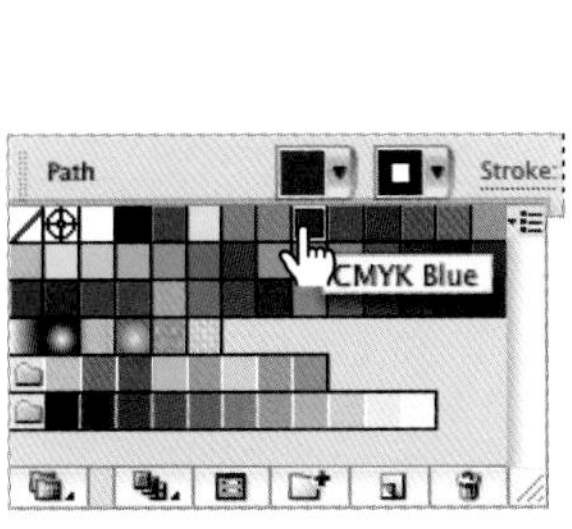

Select CMYK Blue for the fill.

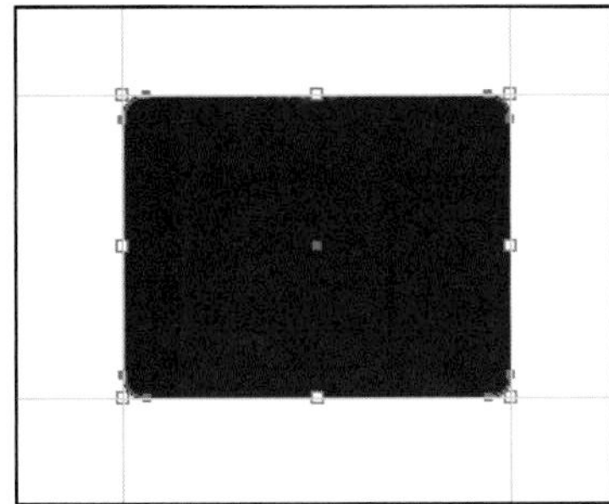

The result.

3 Lock the selected rectangle by pressing Ctrl+2 (Windows) or Command+2 (Mac OS), or by choosing Object > Lock > Selection. This makes it impossible to select the rectangle unless you unlock it. This feature is extremely helpful when you start creating more complicated artwork.

Modifying a shape

You will now use the shape tools to create and add light rays to the illustration.

1 From the list of hidden shape tools beneath the Rounded Rectangle tool in the Tools panel, select the Polygon tool (⬡) and click once on the artboard. The Polygon dialog box appears.

2 Leave the radius as it is; type **3** into the Sides text field and press OK. A triangle is drawn.

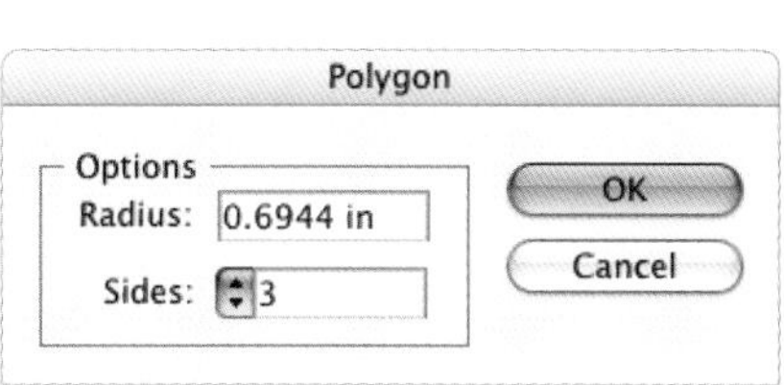

Change the amount of sides.

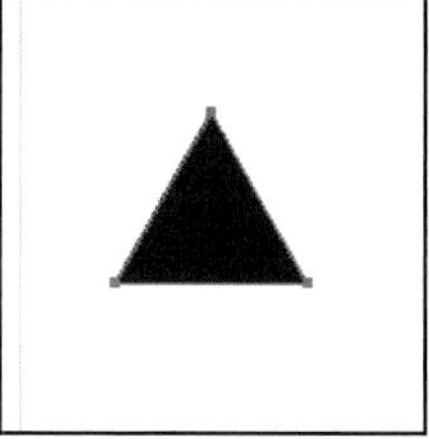

The result.

3 Choose the Selection tool (↖), and click and drag the top center anchor of the bounding box upward, to stretch the triangle.

4 Elongate the triangle more by clicking on the lower-right corner of the bounding box, pulling down, and dragging the anchor to the left.

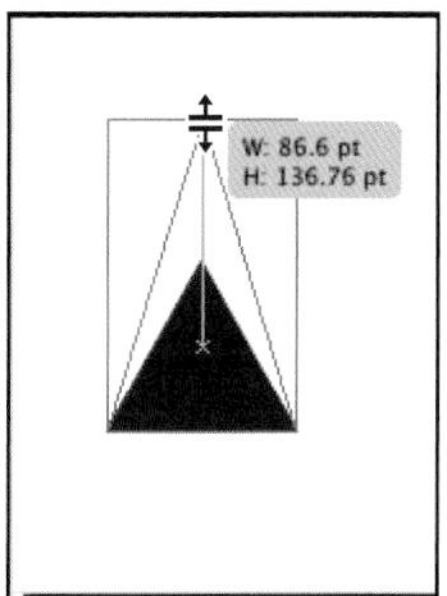

Click and drag upward.

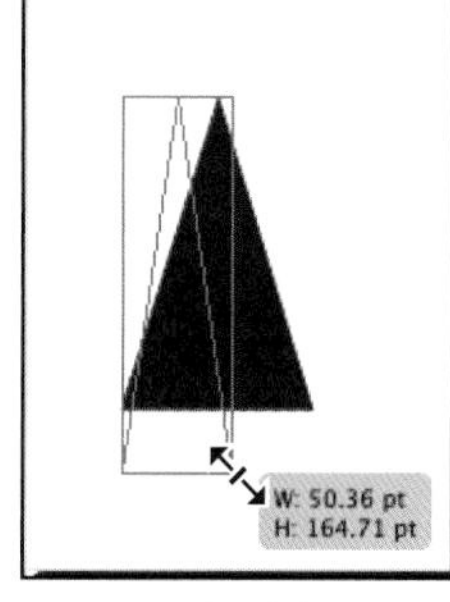

Drag inward and down.

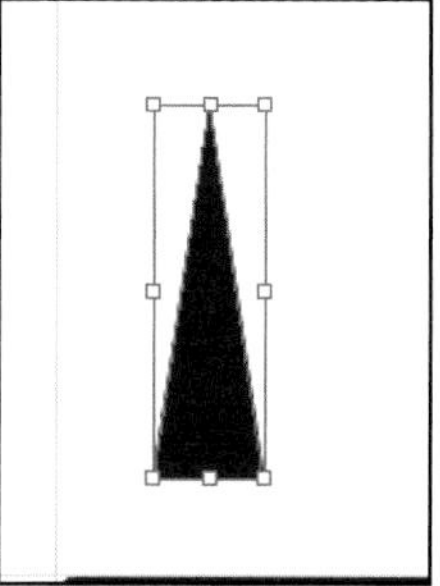

The result.

By clicking and dragging the anchor, you visually resize the shape.

Entering a shape size in the Transform panel

For the purpose of this illustration, you will use the Transform panel to make sure that the triangle is sized correctly.

1 If it is not visible, choose Window > Transform to open the Transform panel.

2 With the triangle still selected, type **.5** in the W (Width) text field, and type **2** into the H (Height) text field. Press Enter (Windows) or Return (Mac OS).

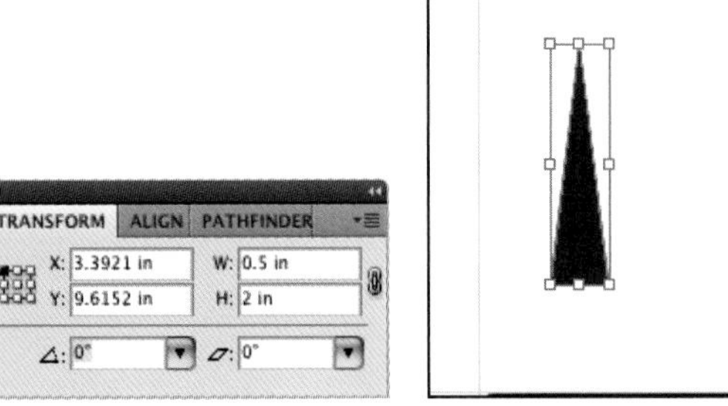

Enter values in the Transform panel. *The result.*

3 Press **D**; the triangle's color reverts to the default white fill and black stroke colors.

4 Click once on the Stroke box in the Control panel at the top of the Illustrator work area and select None from the Stroke swatches drop-down menu. The triangle is not visible at this time (as it is white on a white background), but you can still see its anchor points.

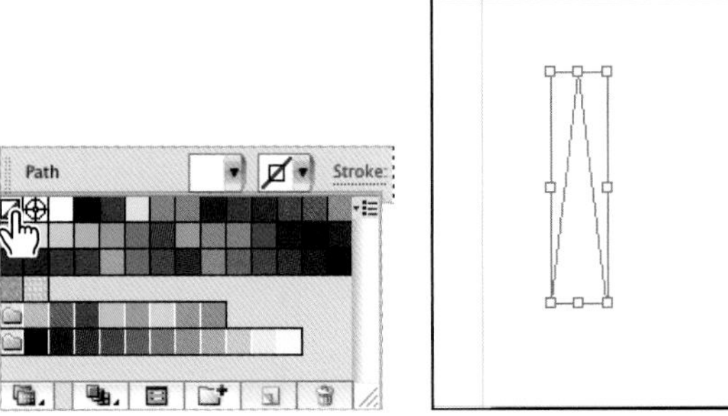

Change the stroke color to None. *The result.*

Viewing in Outline view

By default, previews of Adobe Illustrator artwork are in color. There will be times, however, when you create shapes that are white, or possibly have no fill or stroke color. Finding these items on your white artboard after you deselect them can be difficult. This is where Outline view can help.

1 With the Selection tool (↖), click somewhere on the artboard to deselect the triangle. Unless your triangle crosses over the rectangle you created earlier, you can no longer see the shape.

2 Choose View > Outline, or press Ctrl+Y (Windows) or Command+Y (Mac OS). Outline view displays artwork so that only its outlines (or paths) are visible. Viewing artwork without fill and stroke attributes speeds up the time it takes Illustrator to redraw the screen when working with complex artwork; it is also helpful when you need to locate hidden shapes.

3 With the Selection tool, click on one of the triangle's sides and reposition it so its tip touches the center (indicated by an x) of the rectangle.

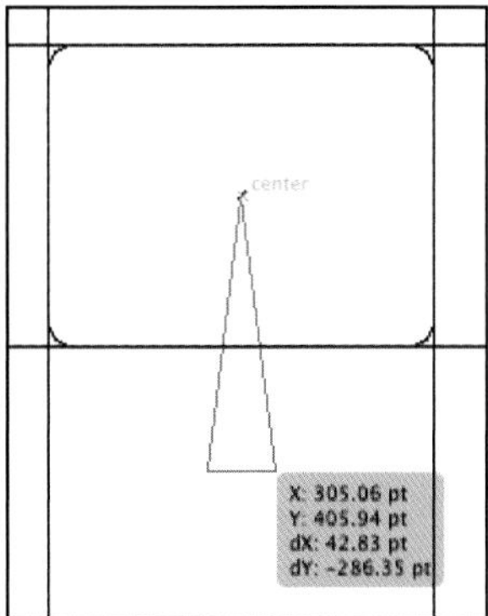

The triangle and rectangle arranged in the Outline view.

4 Choose View > Preview, or press Ctrl+Y (Windows) or Command+Y (Mac OS) once more. The color attributes are visible again.

Rotating the shape

You will now create a series of triangle shapes and rotate them 360 degrees, creating what will look like rays of light.

1 Make sure the triangle is selected.

2 Select the Rotate tool (↻) from the Tools panel. The Rotate tool allows you to visually rotate objects, as well as enter specific rotation angles. In this example, you will enter values so that the triangles are evenly spaced.

3 Alt+click (Windows) or Option+click (Mac OS) the tip of the triangle aligned with the rectangle's center. When you have a Rotate tool selected and you Alt+click (Windows) or Option+click (Mac OS) on the artboard, you define the reference point from which the selected shape is rotated. Doing this also displays the Rotate dialog box, in which you can enter an exact value for the angle.

4 Type **18** into the Angle text field and press Copy. This rotates a copy of your triangle 18 degrees and keeps the original triangle intact. The value of 18 degrees evenly divides into 360 degrees, which will make the distribution of these rays even when you circle back to the starting point.

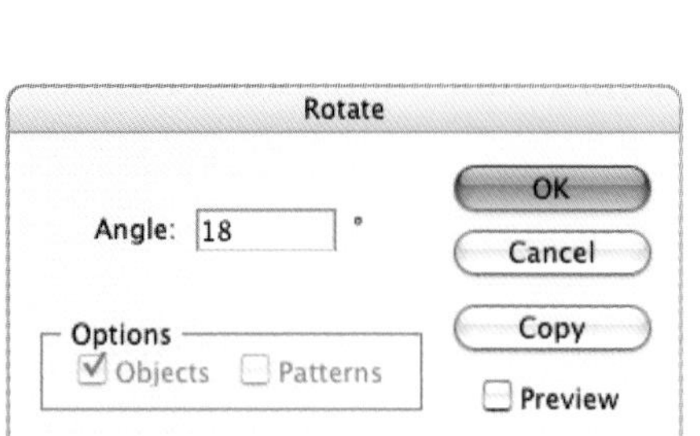

Enter rotate values and press Copy.

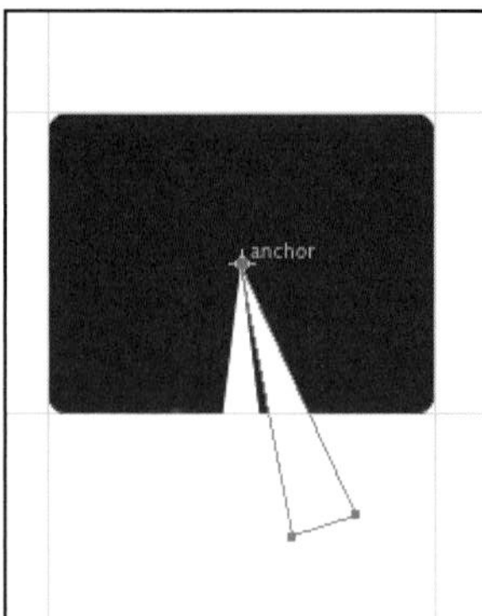

A rotated copy is created.

5 Press Ctrl+D (Windows) or Command+D (Mac OS) to repeat the transformation. The triangle shape copies, and rotates again.

6 Continue to press Ctrl+D (Windows) or Command+D (Mac OS) until you reach the original triangle.

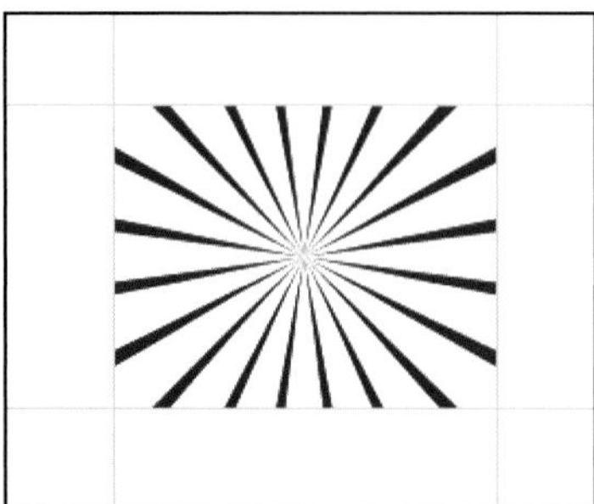

The triangle after being rotated.

Changing the color of the triangles

You will now select the triangles and change their opacity.

1 Switch to the Selection tool (↖) and select any one of the white triangles.

2 Choose Select > Same > Fill Color and all the white triangles become selected. The Select > Same feature can be helpful when selecting objects that share a common feature, including fill color, stroke color, stroke point size, and more.

3 Choose Object > Group. Grouping these shapes together makes it easier to select them later.

4 Type **50** into the Opacity text field in the Control panel and press Enter (Windows) or Return (Mac OS) to change the opacity of the white triangles to 50 percent.

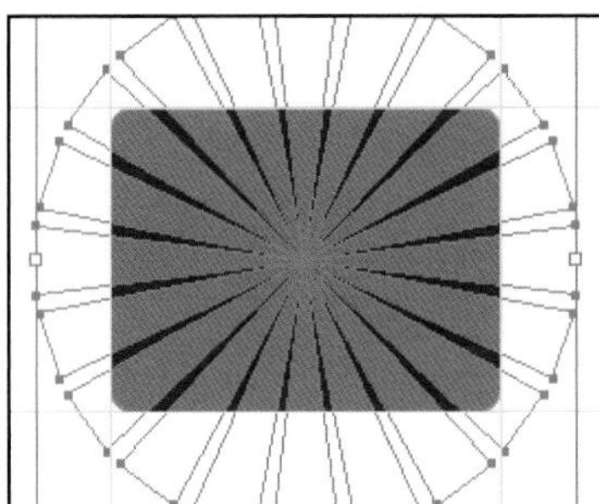

Select the triangles and change the opacity to 50 percent.

5 Choose File > Save to save your work.

Using layers when building an illustration

Layers have many uses in Adobe Illustrator. You will learn more about layers in Lesson 7, "Organizing your Illustration with Layers." In this lesson, you will find out how to use layers to lock and temporarily hide artwork that you don't want to inadvertently select while you work on other things.

1 Open the Layers panel by pressing the Layers button (◈) in the dock on the right side of the workspace. Notice that when you start to work in Illustrator, you begin with a layer named Layer 1. All the artwork that you have created throughout this lesson is added as a sub-layer to this layer. You will now lock a sub-layer and create a new layer onto which you can put additional artwork.

2 Click on the Toggles lock (a small empty box) to the left of Layer 1 in the Layers panel. A padlock icon (🔒) appears, indicating that this layer is locked. You cannot select or change any items on this layer.

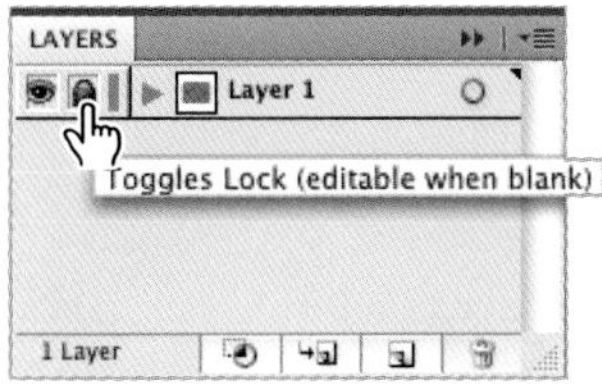

The Toggles lock area of the Layers panel.

Earlier in this lesson, you selected and locked the rectangle using the Object > Lock menu item. That method works well for individual items, especially if you don't typically work with layers. Locking a layer is different, as it locks all items on the layer at once.

3 To unlock the layer, click on the padlock icon. The layer unlocks.

4 Relock Layer 1 by clicking on the Toggles lock square again.

Creating a new blank layer

You will now create a new blank layer onto which you can paste artwork.

1 Alt+click (Windows) or Option+click (Mac OS) the Create New Layer button (◘) at the bottom of the Layers panel. The Layer Options dialog box appears. By holding down the Alt/Option key, you can name the layer before its creation.

2 Type **Fish** into the Name text field and press OK. A new empty layer appears on top of the original (Layer 1) displayed in the Layers panel. You are now ready to copy and paste artwork from another Illustrator file into this one.

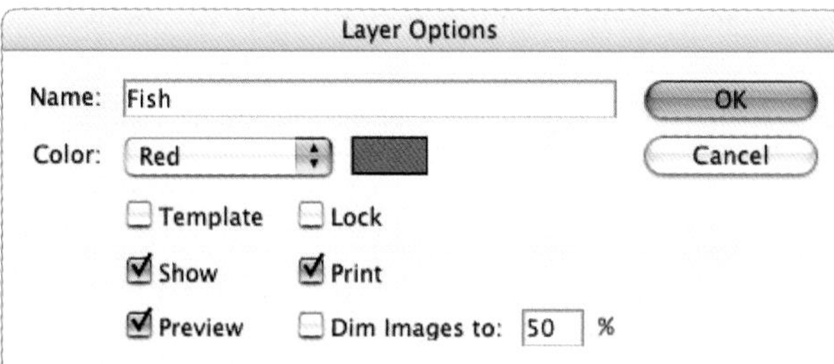

Name the new layer.

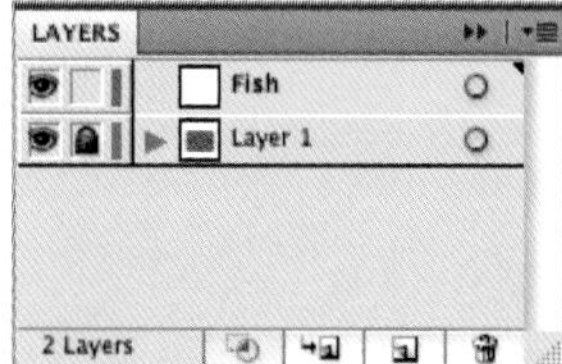

The layer in the Layers panel.

Cutting and pasting objects

You will now open another document and cut and paste artwork from one Illustrator file to another.

1 Choose File > Open. In the Open dialog box, navigate to the ai03lessons folder and double-click on the file named ai0304.ai. Artwork of two fish appears.

The fish artwork.

2 Use the Selection tool (↖) to click once on the larger of the two fish, then Shift+click on the second fish to add it to the selection.

3 Choose Edit > Cut, or press Ctrl+X (Windows) or Command+X (Mac OS), to cut the fish.

4 Return to the work file by choosing Window > ai0303_work.ai. Choose Edit > Paste, or press Ctrl+V (Windows) or Command+V (Mac OS), to paste the fish onto the artboard. The fish are pasted onto the Fish layer, which is the active layer.

5 Press Shift+Ctrl+A (Windows) or Shift+Command+A (Mac OS), or click on a blank area of the artboard, to deselect the fish.

6 Activate the Selection tool; click on the smaller of the two fish and drag it to a spot on top of the larger fish. Notice that the smaller fish disappears behind the larger fish. The order in which artwork appears is based on the order in which artwork is created. Newer artwork is placed higher in the object stacking order, which can be changed using the Arrange feature.

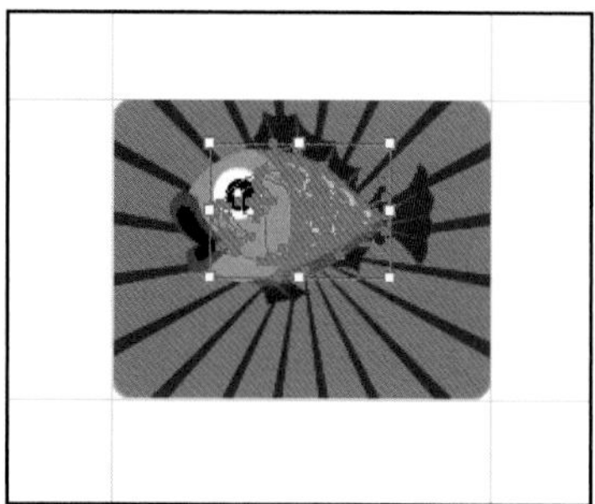

The smaller fish falls behind the larger fish in the stacking order.

7 With the smaller fish still selected, choose Object > Arrange > Bring to Front.

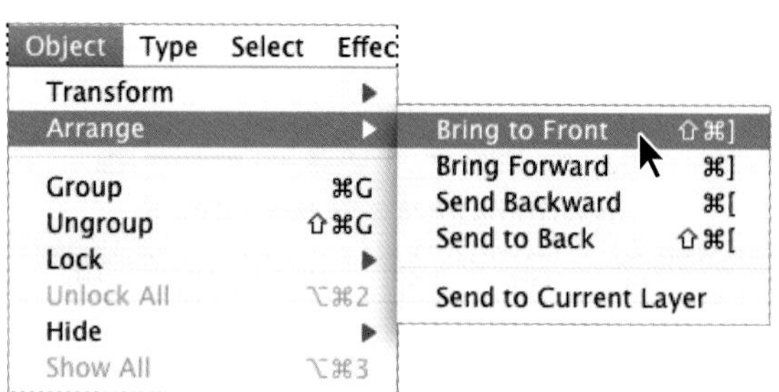

Choose to bring the small fish to the front.

The result.

8 Select the smaller fish and reposition it so that it slightly overlaps the bottom of the larger fish.

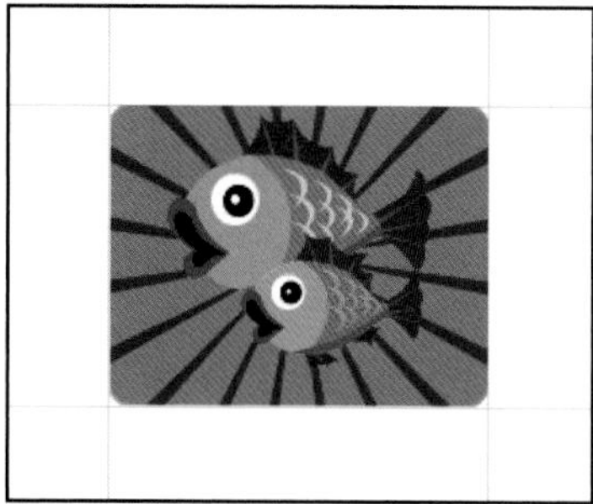

Reposition the smaller fish to overlap the larger fish slightly.

9 Choose File > Save. Keep this file open for the next part of this lesson, but close ai0304.ai. When asked if you'd like to save the changes made to the document, choose No (Windows) or Don't Save (Mac OS).

Creating bubbles

You will now create a bubble, and then clone it several times to finish the illustration.

1. Click and hold down on the last-used shape tool (the Polygon tool) in the Tools panel and select the hidden Ellipse tool (○).
2. Click once on the artboard to display the Ellipse dialog box.
3. Type .5 into the Width text field, then click on the word *Height*. This enters the **.5** value into the height text field as well. Press OK. A small circle is created.
4. Click the Fill color swatch in the Control panel and choose the color CMYK Cyan from the drop-down swatches menu.

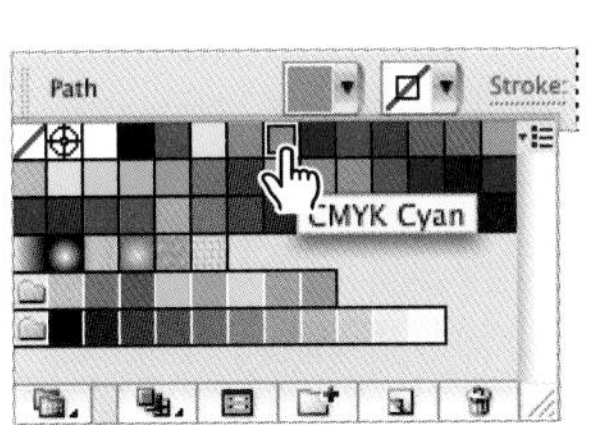

Change the fill color to CMYK Cyan.

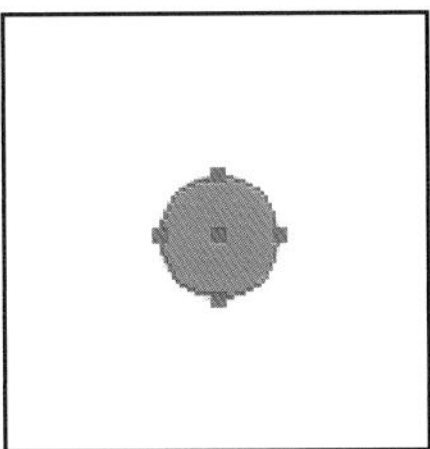

The result.

5. If the Stroke is not set to none (☒), choose the Stroke box in the Control panel and choose None from the drop-down swatches menu.

   Now you will create a smaller circle to use as a reflection in the circle you already created.
6. With the Ellipse tool still active, click once on the artboard.
7. In the resulting Ellipse dialog box, type **.1** into the Width text field then click on the word *Height* to match values. Press OK.

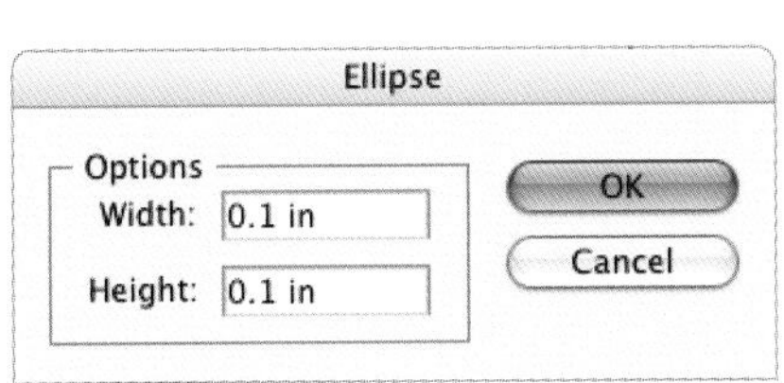

Create a smaller circle.

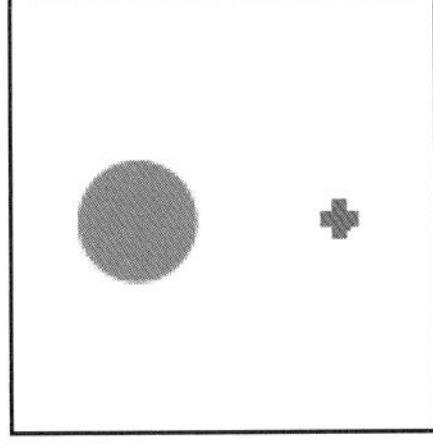

The result.

8. Use the Fill box in the Control panel to select White for the small circle's fill.

9 Activate the Selection tool (), then click and drag the smaller circle on top of the larger cyan (blue) circle. Position it anywhere you want on the circle, as long as it looks like a light reflection on the bubble.

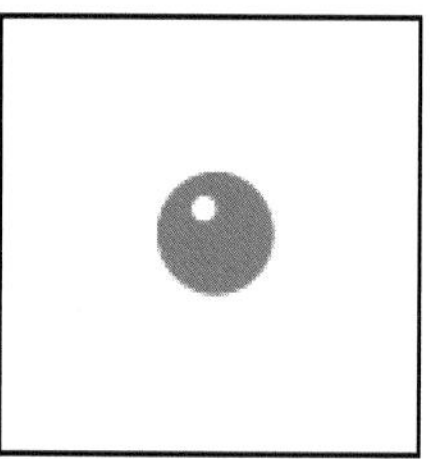

Position the smaller white circle on top of the cyan circle.

10 Shift+click the larger and smaller circles to select them both. Choose Object > Group, or press Ctrl+G (Windows) or Command+G (Mac OS), to group the circles.

11 Choose File > Save to save your work.

Cloning the bubble group

You will now clone, or duplicate, the bubble several times.

1 Make sure the bubble group is selected.

2 Hover your cursor over the bubble and hold down the Alt (Windows) or Option (Mac OS) key. Note that the icon becomes a double cursor ().

3 While holding down on the Alt/Option key, click and drag to the right. Notice that as you drag, the original group of circles remains intact and you create a second group. Release the mouse when you are off to the right and the cloned bubble no longer touches the original.

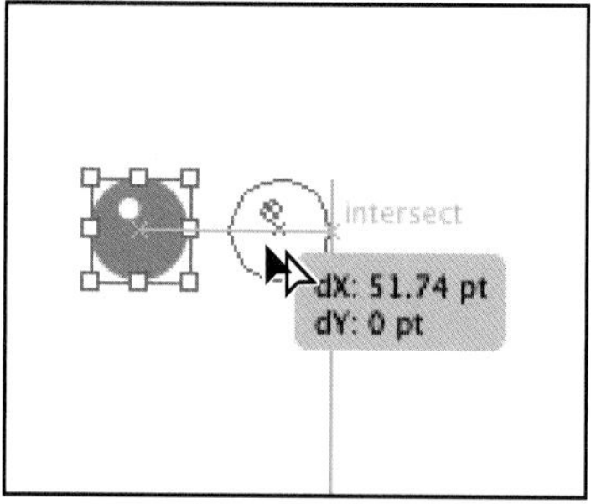

Hold down the Alt (Windows) or Option (Mac OS) key, then click and drag.

4 Press Ctrl+D (Windows) or Command+D (Mac OS) to repeat the duplication. Illustrator remembers the distance and angle of the last movement. You can also perform this function by selecting Object > Transform > Transform Again.

5 Press Ctrl+D (Windows) or Command+D (Mac OS) once more to create a total of four circle groups.

If you hold down the Shift key while cloning, you can constrain the cloned objects to move on a straight path, or a 45- or 90-degree angle.

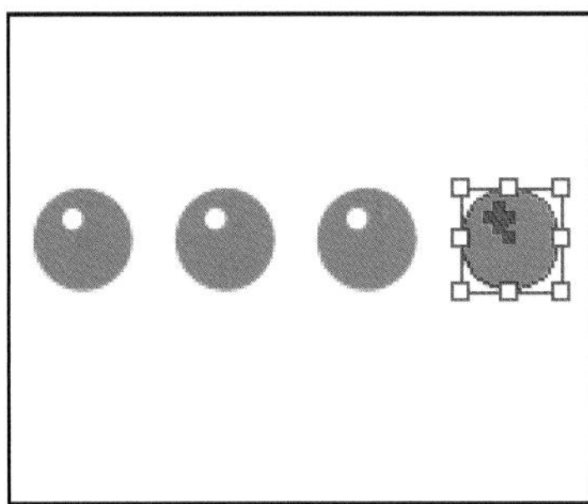

Clone the circle group three times.

6 Choose File > Save to save your work. Keep the file open for the next part of the lesson.

Repeating a resize transform

You will now use the Transform Again keyboard shortcut to transform the bubbles so they are varying sizes.

1 Select the second bubble. You will leave the original bubble at its present size.

2 Hold down the Shift key (to constrain the proportions as you resize), and click and drag a corner anchor point to resize the bubble only slightly. An exact amount is not important for this. Once you resize, do not perform any other actions, such as repositioning. The resizing has to be the last action that you performed for the Transform Again feature to work properly.

3 Select the third bubble group and press Ctrl+D (Windows) or Command+D (Mac OS). This applies the same transformation to the third bubble. With the same bubble still selected, press Ctrl +D (Windows) or Command+D (Mac OS) again and the resize transformation is applied, making it even smaller.

4 Select the last (fourth) bubble and press Ctrl+D (Windows) or Command+D (Mac OS) three times, making this the smallest bubble.

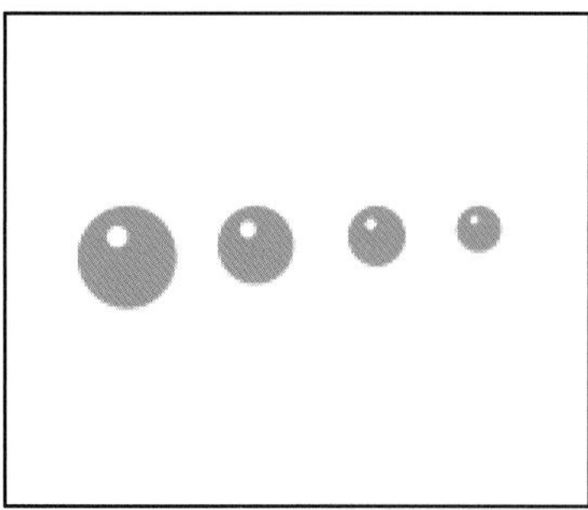

The bubbles after they have been transformed into differently sized bubbles.

Remember that the Transform Again feature (Ctrl+D [Windows] or Command+D [Mac OS]) repeats the most recent transformation, including positioning, that you performed. If you resize and then move an object, the repositioning, not the resizing, is repeated. If this occurs, press Ctrl+Z (Windows) or Command+Z (Mac OS) until you return to the point where all the bubbles are the same size. Then restart at step 1.

5 Using the Selection tool (↖), click and drag each bubble down and position them around the fish, on top of the rectangle. No exact position is necessary.

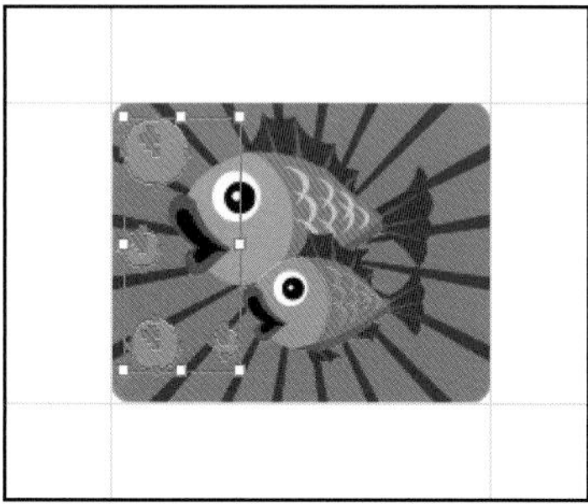

Click and drag the bubbles to reposition them in the artwork.

6 Choose File > Save to save your work. Keep the file open for the next part of the lesson.

Moving objects from one layer to another

You will now move the bubbles onto Layer 1, under the rays of light.

1 Select one of the bubble groups, then Shift+click the remaining three so that all four bubble groups are selected.

2 If the Layers panel is not visible, open it by clicking the Layers button (◈) in the dock or by choosing Windows > Layers.

   A colored dot appears to the right of the Fish layer in the Layers panel. This colored dot is called the selection indicator. If Illustrator's settings are at their defaults, the indicator is red, matching the layer selection color.

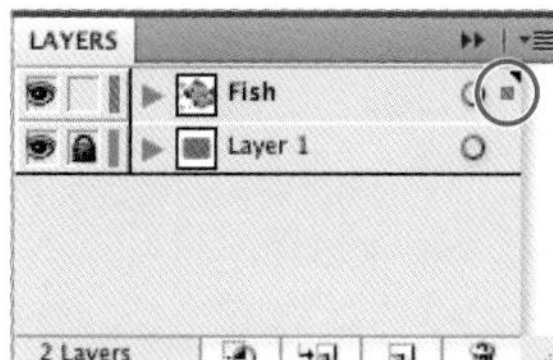

When something on a layer is selected, the selection indicator appears.

3 Click the padlock icon (🔒) to the left of Layer 1 to unlock the layer.

4 Click and drag the selection indicator from the Fish layer down to Layer 1. The bubbles are now on Layer 1 instead of on the Fish layer.

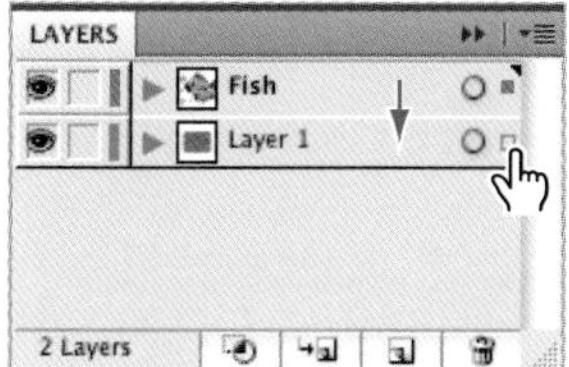

Click and drag the selection indicator to the layer beneath.

5 Click on any one of the triangles that you used to create the rays of light. Because they were grouped earlier, selecting one selects the entire group.

6 Choose Object > Arrange > Bring to Front; the triangles are now on top of the bubbles, but not on top of the fish. This is because the Fish layer is higher in the stacking order than anything on Layer 1. You will find out more about layers and the order in which objects appear in Lesson 7, "Organizing your Illustrations with Layers."

7 Choose File > Save, then File > Close.

   Congratulations! You have completed Lesson 3, "Illustrator CS4 Essentials."

Self study

Practice will help you to create the shapes that you want. To practice on your own, open the file named ai0305.ai and create the shapes that are locked on the base layer.

Review

Questions

1 Which selection tool allows you to select an individual anchor point or path segment?

2 What key modifier do you hold down to constrain a shape to equal width and height values?

3 What are two methods of inputting exact height and width values for shapes?

Answers

1 The Direct Selection tool allows you to select an individual anchor point or path segment.

2 Constrain a shape's proportions by pressing the Shift key while dragging the shape.

3 You can enter values for shapes by doing either of the following:

a. Select a shape tool and click once on the artboard. This opens the shape options dialog box, in which you can enter width and height values.

b. After a shape has been created, choose Window > Transform and enter values into the Width and Height text fields.

What you'll learn in this lesson:

- Using the Appearance panel
- Applying and adjusting fills and strokes
- Using the Live Paint Bucket tool
- Creating and applying a gradient
- Creating and updating a pattern swatch

Adding Color

Adobe Illustrator CS4 provides a number of methods to help add color to your artwork. In this lesson, you discover how to enhance your artwork with color, gradients, and patterns.

Starting up

Before starting, make sure that your tools and panels are consistent by resetting your workspace. See "Resetting Adobe Illustrator CS4 Preferences" on page 3.

You will work with several files from the ai04lessons folder in this lesson. Make sure that you have loaded the ailessons folder onto your hard drive from the supplied DVD. See "Loading lesson files" on page 4.

See Lesson 4 in action!

Use the accompanying video to gain a better understanding of how to use some of the features shown in this lesson. The video tutorial for this lesson can be found on the included DVD.

Basics of the Appearance panel

The Appearance panel in Illustrator allows you to adjust an object's fill and stroke, in addition to any effects that have been applied to the object. The Appearance panel is also an indispensable tool for determining the structure of an object. Fills and strokes are shown in the order that they are applied to an object, the same way that other effects are ordered chronologically. As your Illustrator artwork increases in complexity, the Appearance panel becomes more important, as it makes the process of editing and adjusting your document much easier. Let's explore the Appearance panel.

1 With Adobe Illustrator CS4 open, select the Go to Bridge button (Br) in the Control panel.

2 Once Bridge opens, navigate to the ai04lessons folder and open the ai0401.ai file by double-clicking on it.

3 The file opens in Illustrator. Activate the Selection tool in the Tools panel and select the orange oval behind the *ATOMIC REGION* text by clicking to the left or the right of the letters.

4 Open the Appearance panel by choosing Window > Appearance or by pressing the Appearance button (◉) in the dock on the right side of your workspace.

The Appearance panel displays the attributes of the currently selected object. In this example, the object that is selected is filled with an orange color, has no stroke, and has two effects applied to it. Without the Appearance panel, it would take you a while to determine the attributes of this object.

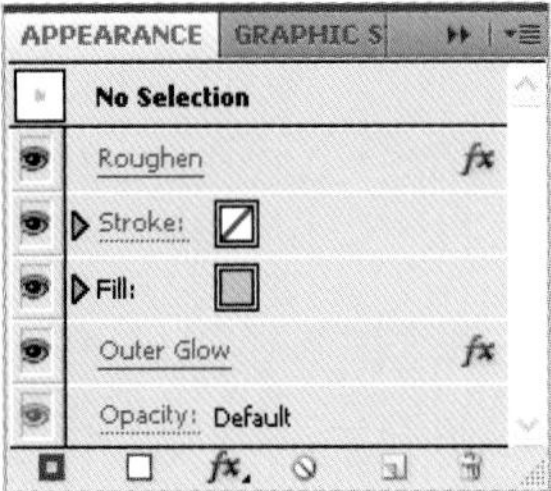

The Appearance panel shows you all the attributes associated with the selected object on your page.

5 In the Appearance panel, select the Stroke listing. Upon clicking the listing, a stroke color swatches panel and a Stroke Weight drop-down menu and slider appear, built directly into the panel.

6 Choose 3 pt from the Stroke Weigh drop-down menu. This applies a 3-point stroke to the orange background object.

7 Press the arrow next to the Stroke Color drop-down menu and choose White from the Swatches panel that appears.

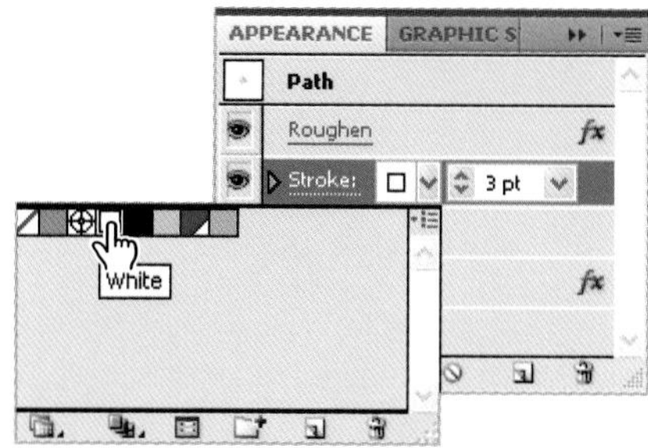

The Stroke Color option in the Control panel makes it easy to apply a color to the stroke of a selected object.

Now that you have applied a white stroke to your object, the Appearance panel updates to reflect this change.

8 Choose File > Save As. In the Save As dialog box, navigate to the ai04lessons folder and type **ai0401_work.ai** in the Name (Windows) or Save As (Mac OS) text field. Choose Adobe Illustrator from the Save as type (Windows) or Format (Mac OS) drop-down menu and press Save. When the Illustrator Options dialog box appears, press OK. Keep the file open for the next part of the lesson.

Fills and strokes

In Illustrator, an object has two basic attributes: a fill and a stroke. Fills and strokes can be customized with solid colors, tints of a color, patterns, or gradients. You can further customize strokes so that their weight is any size you want. In the following steps, you'll make some adjustments to the fill and stroke of the type at the top of the page.

1 Using the Selection tool (↖), select the *ATOMIC REGION* text frame.

2 In the Control panel, click and hold on the Stroke Color swatch, choose purple from the Stroke Swatches panel that appears. The purple is applied to the stroke of the selected text.

3 Change the weight of the selected text's stroke to 5 points by choosing 5 pt from the Stroke Weight drop-down menu in the Control panel, or by typing **5 pt** into the Stroke Weight text field.

4 Click the Fill color swatch in the Control panel. When the Fill Swatches panel appears, choose the tan color. This changes the selected type's fill color to tan.

To make the heading type really stand out, you will add a few effects to it.

5 Choose Effect > Brush Strokes > Spatter. In the resulting Effects dialog box, set the Spray Radius to **5** and the Smoothness to **3** by typing these values in their respective text fields or by dragging the sliders for each setting. Press OK.

6 Choose Effect > Warp > Bulge. In the Warp Options dialog box, type **11** in the Bend text field to set the bend to 11 percent, and press OK.

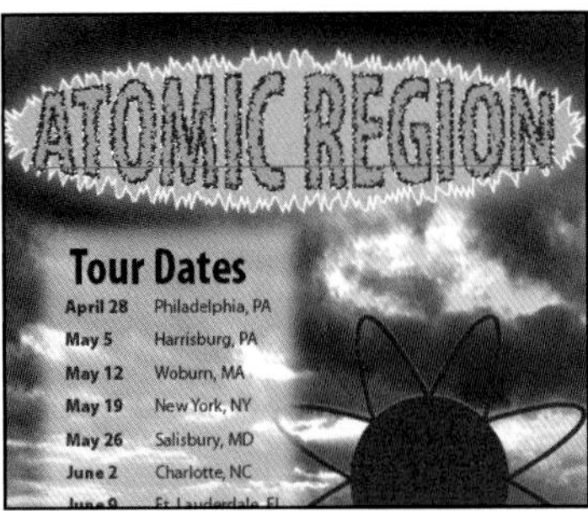

The headline type, after applying a fill, stroke, and some other effects.

If you look in your Appearance panel, you see that the Spatter and Warp: Bulge effects have been added to your type to create a more dynamic look.

Saving swatches

Adobe Illustrator CS4 contains a Swatches panel that allows you to store colors for multiple uses in your document. You can create colors using several different methods in Illustrator, and by adding them to the Swatches panel, you can store them for frequent and consistent use. Storing a swatch of a color that you plan to reuse guarantees that the color is exactly the same each time it is used. Let's create a new swatch for your document.

1 Click on the artboard (the white area surrounding the page) to deselect any objects in your document. You can also use the keyboard shortcut, Shift+Ctrl+A (Windows) or Shift+Command+A (Mac OS).

2 Click the Fill color swatch in the Control panel; the swatch expands to reveal the Fill Swatches panel. Press the panel menu button (▾≡) in the upper-right corner of the panel and choose New Swatch.

If the New Swatch option is grayed out, select a swatch in the Swatches panel first.

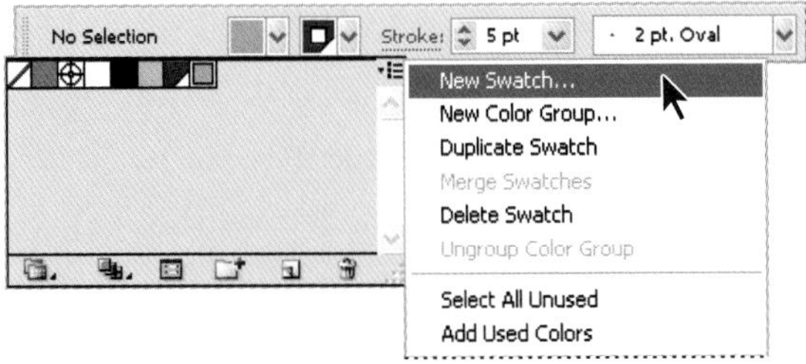

Choose New Swatch from the panel menu to define a new swatch color.

3 In the resulting New Swatch dialog box, pick a slate gray color by dragging the sliders at the bottom of the dialog box until you achieve the desired color. In this example, the combination of CMYK, C=30, M=25,Y=18, K=75, was used.

Notice that as you adjust the colors at the bottom of the New Swatch dialog box, the name changes to reflect the color values that you have chosen. This is the default behavior in Illustrator, but you aren't limited to this naming convention. To choose your own name, simply highlight the CMYK values in the Swatch Name text field and type **Slate Gray**. Press OK.

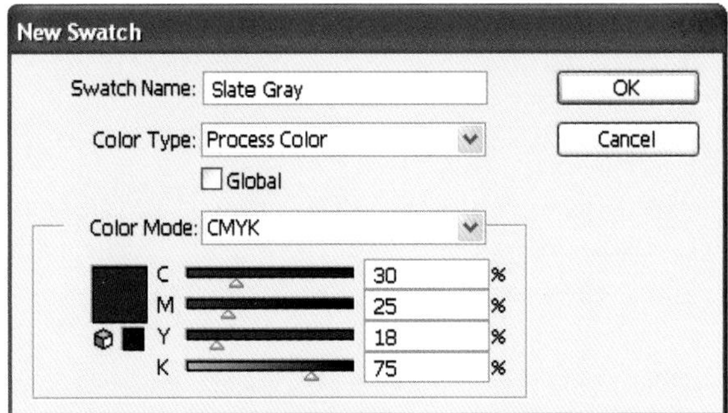

Create a custom color that will always appear in the Swatches panel of this document.

The swatch that you created is now available whenever you open this document, and can be applied to any additional objects that you create in the future.

4 Select the Type tool (T), then drag to select the *Tour Dates* text. You can also select the entire line by triple-clicking anywhere within the line of text.

5 Click the Fill color swatch in the Control panel and select the Slate Gray swatch that you created in step 3.

6 Use the keyboard shortcut Shift+Ctrl+A (Windows) or Shift+Command+A (Mac OS) to deselect all objects in the document.

7 Choose File > Save to save the document.

Reusing swatches

When you create swatches in an Illustrator document, those swatches are available only in that document by default. However, users commonly repurpose those swatches in other Illustrator documents. For example, maybe you created a poster like the one in this lesson, but then need to create a brochure that will be sent out to prospective customers. Instead of recreating all those swatches for the brochure, you can choose Save Swatch Library as AI from the Swatches panel menu, which creates a new file containing all the swatches in your current document. To reuse the swatches in another document, simply choose Open Swatch Library > Other Library from the Swatches panel menu. Now all those swatches are available to apply to objects in your new document.

There is also an option called Save Swatch Library as ASE (Adobe Swatch Exchange) in the Swatches panel menu. This performs a very similar task to Save Swatch Library as AI, except that the ASE format is interchangeable with other CS4 applications. These swatch libraries can be opened within Adobe Photoshop and Adobe InDesign, making it very easy to share colors between multiple applications. Unfortunately, any swatch patterns that have been added to the swatch library will not be accessible inside programs other than Illustrator.

Global colors

Simplifying your color and swatch options even further is an additional option available within each swatch that makes changing colors that have been used within your document a simple, hassle-free process. This option is the *Global* checkbox, found within the Swatch Options of each color. What makes this checkbox so useful is that every object that has a global swatch applied updates dynamically when that swatch is modified. Let's see how global colors can save you time when working in Illustrator.

1 Choose the Selection tool (↖) from the Tools panel, then press the Swatches button (▦) in the dock on the right side of your workspace to open the Swatches panel.

   Notice that there is one swatch in the Swatches panel that looks slightly different from the rest of the swatches, in that it contains a small, white triangle in its lower-right corner. This icon indicates that this swatch is a global color.

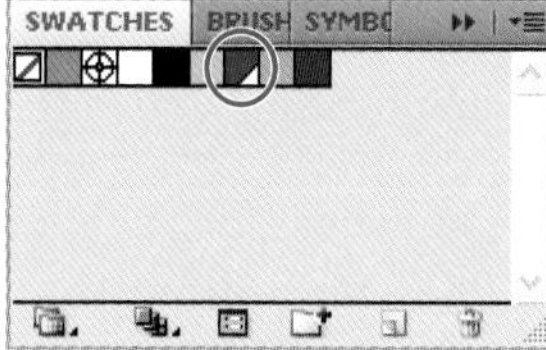

The white triangle icon on a swatch represents a global color.

2 Double-click on the global swatch to display the Swatch Options dialog box. You'll notice that the *Global* checkbox is checked, indicating that this color is a global color. Any object in the document that has this color applied to it updates when the swatch is modified.

3 Turn on the Preview option by clicking in the *Preview* checkbox. This allows you to see any changes to your file as you try out options in the Swatches panel.

4 Adjust the CMYK values of the swatch to create a darker purple color. For this example, you set the values to: C=72 M=87 Y=20 K=22. As you adjust the values, notice that all the purple elements in the document update immediately to reflect the new color. Press OK and choose File > Save.

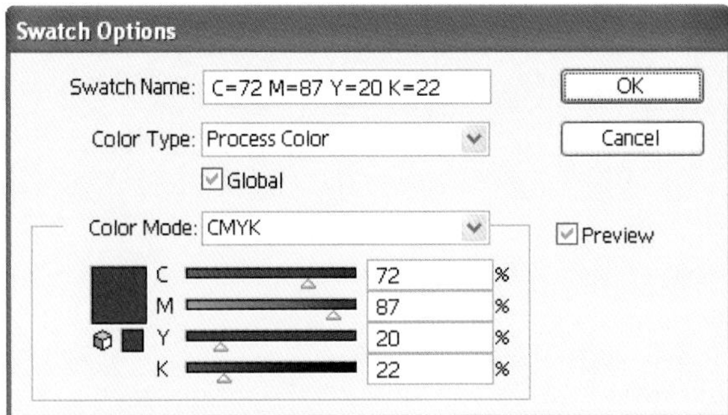

By turning on the Preview checkbox, you can see any changes to objects that have been colored using the global swatch.

You've just experienced the power of global swatches, a great feature that you can use in your day-to-day Illustrator work. If you apply a non-global color to several objects on your page, the process of updating those objects is much more cumbersome than if you use a global swatch.

Saving a set of colors as a group

When working in Illustrator, you'll often end up with quite a few swatches in your Swatches panel. As you experiment with colors and make adjustments, the number of swatches can increase to a point that makes it difficult to find a particular color. Fortunately, Illustrator simplifies the process of locating specific swatches by allowing you to create color groups to organize swatches into logical categories. Let's organize the swatches in the Swatches panel into color groups.

1 In the Swatches panel, hold down the Ctrl key (Windows) or the Command key (Mac OS) and select the six color swatches that follow the registration swatch ( ) in the Swatches panel to highlight them.

2 Press the New Color Group button ( ) at the bottom of the panel. The New Color Group dialog box appears.

3 In the New Color Group dialog box, type **Atomic Region Colors** in the Name text field. Press OK.

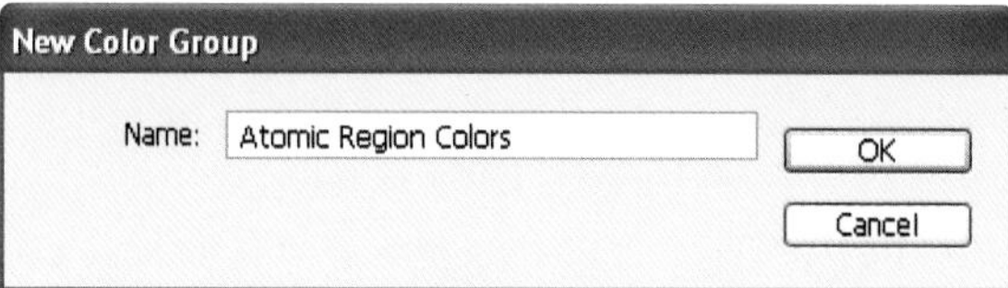

The New Color Group dialog box allows you to name the group that contains your swatches.

4 Choose File > Save to save your work. Keep the file open.

After creating the new color group, you can see that the swatches you selected in step 2 have been moved inside a color group. This is indicated by a small folder icon to the left of the swatches, which are grouped together inside a slim, white border. You can still select and apply each swatch as you did before, but now the colors are organized logically. If you hover your cursor over the color group folder icon, *Atomic Region Colors* appears in a tooltip.

If you do not see the tooltip as you hover over the color group folder icon, press Ctrl+K (Windows) or Command+K (Mac OS) to open the General Preferences. Make sure the Show Tool Tips checkbox is turned on and press OK.

Using the Color Guide panel

The Color Guide, which made its debut in Illustrator CS3, provides you with inspiration as you apply color to your artwork. The Color Guide panel suggests harmonious colors based on the color that is active in the Tools panel. You can change the suggested colors by changing the harmony rule, which is the method by which the Color Guide panel makes its color suggestions. Let's see how you can use the Color Guide panel to add a group of colors to your Swatches panel.

1 Open the Color panel by pressing the Color button ( ) in the dock on the right side of the workspace, or choose Window > Color.

2 With the Fill icon ( ) selected, click in the red area of the CMYK Spectrum at the bottom of the Color panel to choose a red color as a base to work with.

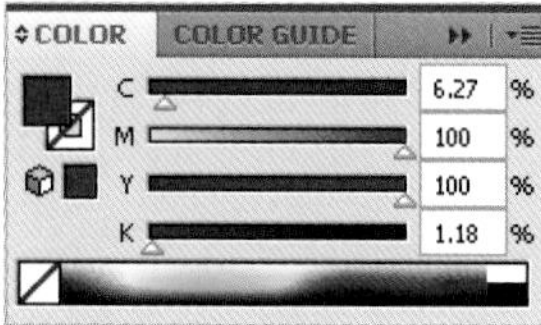

By clicking on the CMYK Spectrum at the bottom of the Color panel, you can set a new color as the base color.

3 To the right of the tab at the top of the Color panel is a tab that says Color Guide. Click on the Color Guide tab to reveal the Color Guide panel.

Notice that the color that you chose in step 2 is located in the upper-left corner of the Color Guide panel and is set as the base color. Next, you'll change the harmony rule, which dictates what colors the Color Guide suggests as harmonious colors with the base color.

4 From the Harmony Rules drop-down menu in the Color Guide panel, take a look at the different color schemes that the Color Guide suggests for each option. Choose High Contrast 2.

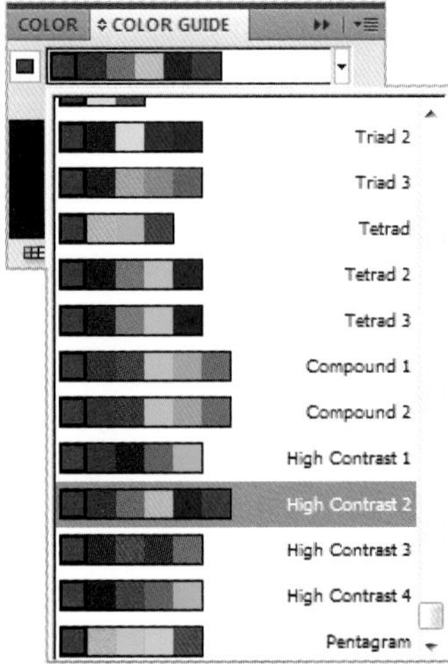

The Harmony Rules drop-down menu allows you to choose different schemes that Illustrator uses to suggest harmonious colors relative to the base color.

5 Click the Save color group to Swatches panel button (▣) in the lower-right corner of the Color Guide panel to save the color scheme as a separate group in the Swatches panel.

As you are working in the Color Guide panel, you may notice that there are many swatches that appear in the large area of the Color Guide panel. These swatches are variations of the colors that appear in the Color Harmony menu at the top of the panel. You can add any of these swatches to the Swatches panel by dragging the swatch from the Color Guide panel to the Swatches panel.

6 Press the Swatches button (▦) in the dock to open the Swatches panel and see that the new color group from the Color Guide panel has been added to the Swatches panel. You'll use this color group later in this lesson.

7 Choose File > Save to save your work. Keep the file open.

Coloring objects

When working in Illustrator, the standard method of applying color to objects has always been to select an object with either the Selection or Direct Selection tool, then click on a color or swatch to change the color of the object. Illustrator also provides some advanced methods that allow you to apply color to objects more efficiently. In the following steps, you'll use the Live Paint feature to apply color to objects in Illustrator that would normally require you to perform various Pathfinder operations. You'll then make adjustments to the colors of a Live Paint object using a feature called Live Color.

Live Paint

With Live Paint, you can apply color to an object that has been converted into a Live Paint group. A Live Paint group is broken down into components in which objects overlap each other. Once an object is a Live Paint group, you can easily apply colors to different areas of that group. Let's begin!

1 Using the Selection tool (), click on the atom graphic to select it. You can see that this graphic is a group of several separate items.

2 Click on the Live Paint Bucket tool () in the Tools panel, or press **K** on your keyboard.

3 In the Swatches panel, click on the red swatch that is inside the color group that you added to the Swatches panel from the Color Guide.

4 Your cursor now looks like this (), and if you hover your cursor over the selected atom graphic, the atom's paths are highlighted, and text reading, *Click to make a Live Paint Group,* appears to the right of the cursor. Click on the graphic to do just this.

5 Now when you hover your cursor over the atom graphic that has been converted to a Live Paint group, you see that different regions of the graphic become highlighted. If you click on an area, Illustrator colors it with the currently selected colors. Fill one of the rings with the red swatch that is currently selected, but only part of the ring. You want to create the illusion of the ring going around the sphere in the middle of the graphic.

You may want to zoom in on the atom graphic to make it easier to apply color to the smaller areas of the graphic. Zoom in to the graphic using the Zoom tool () in the Tools panel.

6 Use the right arrow key on your keyboard to toggle over to the first green color in the middle swatch above your cursor and apply that color to a different ring.

The three swatches that appear above your Live Paint Bucket cursor represent the previous, current, and next swatches within the current color group in the Swatches panel. It may help to understand this if you have the Swatches panel open as you key through the swatches. With the Swatches panel open, you can see how the active color changes in the Swatches panel, which also correlates to the swatches shown above your cursor.

7 Continue applying colors until all the rings have a different color, then select an orange color from the Swatches panel and apply the color to the sphere in the middle of the graphic.

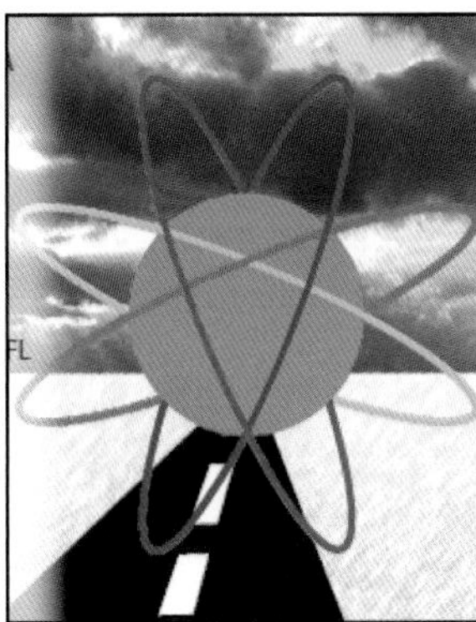

The atom graphic after applying color using the Live Paint Bucket tool.

8 Use the keyboard shortcut Ctrl+Shift+A (Windows) or Command+Shift+A (Mac OS) to deselect the atom graphic and see your work more clearly.

If you want to adjust colors using the Live Paint Bucket tool, hold down the Alt (Windows) or Option (Mac OS) key to pick a color that is already applied to your graphic instead of searching for the correct swatch in the Swatches panel.

9 Choose File > Save to save your work.

Live Color

The Live Color feature in Illustrator CS4 allows you to edit existing color groups and reassign or reduce colors in your document. This is a great feature that allows you to globally adjust several colors at once within your artwork. In the following steps, you'll adjust the atom's colors.

1 Using the Selection tool (), select the atom graphic.

2 Press the Recolor Artwork button () in the Control panel to open the Live Color dialog box.

3 Click the Edit button (near the top of the Live Color dialog box) to edit the active colors of the selected object.

4 Select the Atomic Region Colors color group from the Color Groups list on the right side of the Live Color dialog box. This applies the Atomic Region Colors to the selected object. Notice how the colors change.

On the left side of the Live Color dialog box is a color wheel that displays the current active colors from the chosen color group. Each color is represented by a marker on the color wheel.

5 Click on and drag the largest marker—representing the color group's base color—in the color group. Experiment by spinning the colors around on the color wheel and dragging the markers toward and away from the center of the color wheel. Once you have a combination of colors that you like, press OK.

6 A dialog box may appear, asking if you want to save the changes to the color group named *Atomic Region Colors*. Choose No. This applies the colors that you chose from the color wheel to the selected atom graphic without changing the appearance of the saved color group.

7 Press Shift+Ctrl+A (Windows) or Shift+Command+A (Mac OS) to deselect the atom. Choose File > Save to save your work. Keep the file open.

Using Live Color, you were able to adjust multiple colors at a time while still retaining their relationship to each other. Live Color gives you great flexibility when you need to alter the appearance of multiple objects in your artwork.

Creating a gradient swatch

Earlier in this lesson, you learned how to create and edit swatches in your artwork. Now you will learn how to add and edit a gradient swatch to apply to the atom artwork in your document. Let's begin.

1 Press the Gradient button (▪) in the dock on the right side of the workspace, or choose Window > Gradient, to open the Gradient panel.

Press the Gradient panel menu button (▾≡) and choose Show Options to display the entire Gradient panel with all its options.

2 Click once on the gradient slider in the middle of the Gradient panel to activate it. Once activated, two gradient stops appear below the gradient slider. Double-click on the black gradient stop to activate it.

3 Choose one of the orange swatches to apply it to the color stop. You should now have a white-to-orange gradient in the Gradient panel. If you don't, double-click the other color stop and apply the white swatch to it.

Transparent color stops

Illustrator includes the ability for gradient color stops to be transparent. To try this, double-click on one of the color stops in the active gradient and set its opacity level at the top of the Swatches panel.

4 From the Type drop-down menu in the Gradient panel, change the gradient type to Radial.

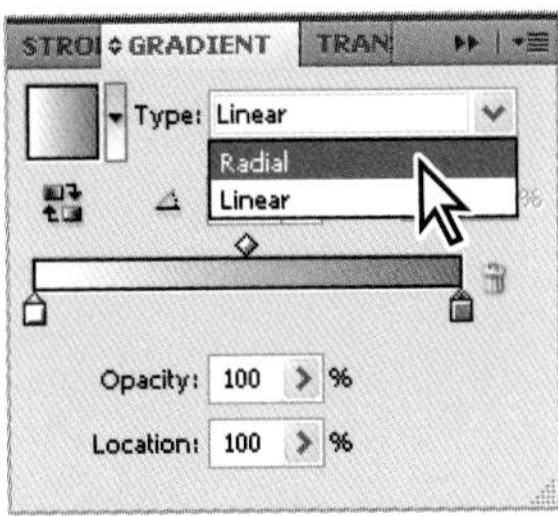

The Gradient panel allows you to specify all the attributes of your gradient.

5 Switch to the Swatches panel. To make the white-to-orange gradient a swatch, press the New Swatch button (▫) at the bottom of the Swatches panel. In the resulting New Swatch dialog box, name the gradient Orange Gradient and press OK. The gradient has been added to the Swatches panel.

Now that you've created a new gradient swatch, you can apply it to the center portion of the atom graphic in your artwork. Remember that this atom graphic is still a Live Paint object. In the next steps, you'll use the Live Paint Selection tool to select all the elements that make up the center portion of the atom graphic.

6 Select the Live Paint Selection tool (▫) from the Tools panel.

7 Click on one of the sections that make up the sphere in the center of the atom graphic and choose Select > Same > Fill Color from the menu at the top of the screen. This selects all the sections that make up that area of the graphic.

8 Click on the Orange Gradient swatch in the Swatches panel to apply it to the selected elements. This applies the gradient to each individual element within the selection.

After creating a gradient swatch, you may need to alter the gradient or perhaps the colors used within the gradient swatch. This is easily accomplished in Illustrator.

9 Press Shift+Ctrl+A (Windows) or Shift+Command+A (Mac OS) to deselect the sphere, then select the Orange Gradient swatch in the Swatches panel.

10 In the Gradient panel, replace the orange color with a color of your choosing.

11 In order to see both panels at the same time, click the Expand Panels button (◂◂) at the top-right corner of the dock. Hold down the Alt (Windows) or Option (Mac OS) key, and click and drag the Gradient Fill icon in the Gradient panel and drop it on top of the existing Orange Gradient swatch in the Swatches panel. This replaces the old gradient swatch with the new one, but keeps the same name.

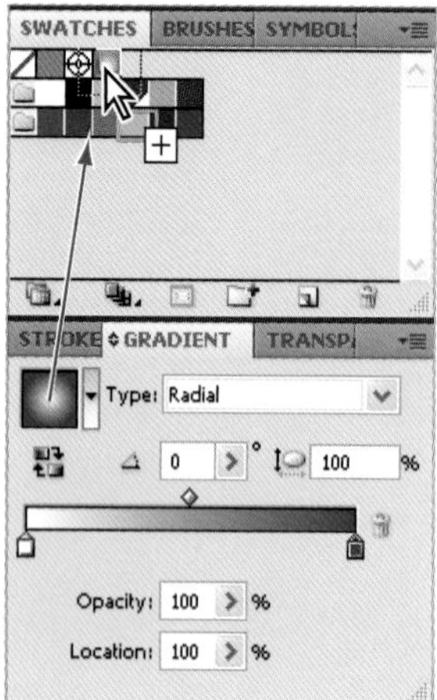

Replace the gradient in the Swatches panel with the new gradient in the Gradient panel.

Notice that when you replace the old gradient swatch with the new one, all objects in your artwork that were based on the original gradient swatch update to reflect the appearance of the new gradient swatch. If you want to change the name of your swatch, double-click it in the Swatches panel and type in a new name.

Creating a pattern swatch

Adobe Illustrator CS4 allows you to fill objects with patterns that repeat automatically. Patterns can be used in several ways and can be scaled and rotated as needed. In this example, you'll create a pattern that will appear over the cloud area of your artwork.

1 Using the Type tool, highlight the word *atomic* at the top of your artwork. Press Ctrl+C (Windows) or Command+C (Mac OS) to copy the selected text.

2 Press Ctrl+Shift+A (Windows) or Command+Shift+A (Mac OS) to deselect the type. Click somewhere on the artboard of your document to create a new line of text and press Ctrl+V (Windows) or Command+V (Mac OS), or choose Edit > Paste, to paste the word in the new location.

Notice that the pasted text only retains the general appearance of the copied text; no extra effects are included.

3 Double-click on the Scale tool (▫) in the Tools panel. In the resulting Scale dialog box, set the Uniform Scale to 40 percent and make sure that the *Scale Strokes & Effects* checkbox is checked. Press OK.

4 Switch to the Selection tool (↖) and drag the frame containing the word *atomic* into the Swatches panel to add it as a pattern swatch. Delete the text from the artboard.

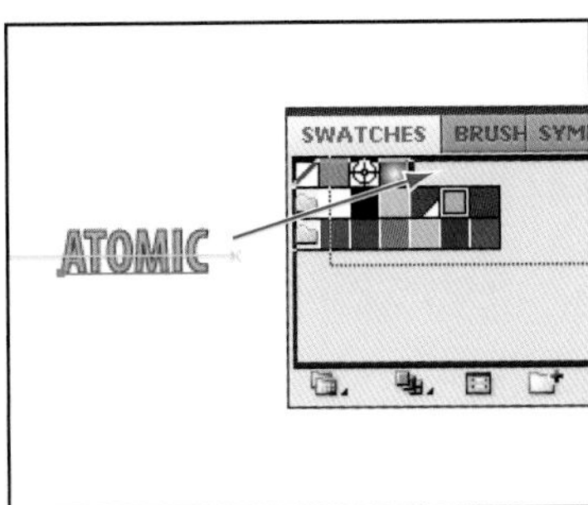

Illustrator makes the process of creating a pattern swatch very easy by simply dragging your item into the Swatches panel.

Now you need to create an object to fill with your pattern swatch.

5 Using the Rectangle tool (□), which may be hidden beneath another shape tool, draw a rectangle around the top portion of your artwork, from the horizon to the top of the document.

6 With the rectangle still selected, make sure the Fill box at the bottom of the Tools panel is in the foreground. Click on the atomic swatch that you just dragged to the Swatches panel.

The word *atomic* now fills the rectangle in a repeating pattern. Notice that the instances of the word *atomic* have no spaces between them, causing the pattern to look like one long word that is difficult to read. When you create a pattern, the outermost bounds of the object that you use as a pattern become the repeating pattern. Let's fix this to make it more readable.

7 Press Shift+Ctrl+A (Windows) or Shift+Command+A (Mac OS) to deselect the rectangle. Drag the pattern swatch from the Swatches panel to the artboard of your document. The text that was used to create the swatch appears on the artboard exactly as it was originally.

8 Using the Rectangle tool, draw a rectangle around the word *atomic*, making sure that the fill and stroke of the rectangle are set to none. Make the rectangle slightly larger than the text, especially on the sides of the word. Send the rectangle behind the type by choosing Object > Arrange > Send to Back from the menu.

9 Activate the Selection tool, and Shift+click the rectangle and the text to select both. In the Control panel, click the Horizontal Align Center (icon) and the Vertical Align Center (icon) buttons to align the two objects to each other.

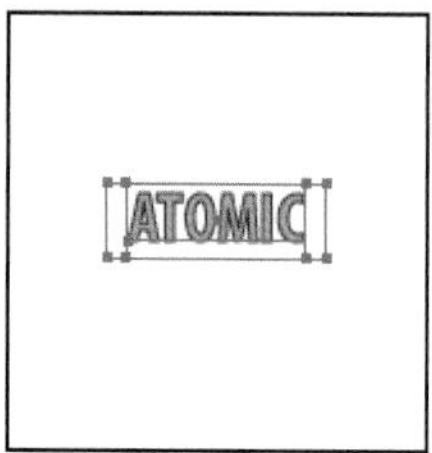

Align the rectangle and the text.

10 With the type and the rectangle still selected, hold down the Alt (Windows) or Option (Mac OS) key and drag the objects on top of the original pattern swatch in the Swatches panel to replace the old pattern swatch with the new one. Notice that the pattern instantly updates in the rectangle that contained the pattern fill.

Now you will transform only the pattern fill inside the rectangle to change how the pattern fills the object.

11 Use the Selection tool to select the rectangle containing the pattern fill, and double-click on the Scale tool (icon) to open the Scale dialog box. Turn the *Preview* and *Patterns* checkboxes on and the *Objects* checkbox off, and experiment with different scaling values to see the effects they have on your pattern. This example uses 60 percent. Press OK.

12 With the rectangle still selected, double-click on the Rotate tool (icon) to open the Rotate dialog box. Once again, turn the *Preview* and *Patterns* checkboxes on and the *Objects* checkbox off, and experiment with different rotation values. This example uses 30 degrees.

13 With the rectangle still selected, press Ctrl+[(Windows) or Command+[(Mac OS) several times until the rectangle appears behind all the objects in the artwork except for the sky.

14 As a finishing touch, open the Transparency panel from the dock by pressing the Transparency button (icon), and choose Darken from the blending mode drop-down menu.

15 Choose File > Save to save your work, then choose File > Close.

If you want to move your pattern around inside your shape to get the ideal tile pattern, hold down the tilde key (~). It's the key just under the Escape key at the top left corner of the keyboard. Take the Selection tool and click on the art that has the pattern fill. Then hold down the tilde key and click and drag inside the shape. Then let go of the mouse. The shape will not have moved at all, but the pattern will be in a different location. The same thing can be done with the keyboard arrow keys. Click on the shape with the Selection tool and then hold down the down arrow key. The pattern will move down.

Spot colors

When designing a product that will be reproduced on a printing press, some decisions need to be made regarding what colors will be used in the document. So far in this lesson, you have created all your swatches based on the CMYK color space. CMYK colors—Cyan, Magenta, Yellow, and Black—are referred to in the printing industry as *process colors*. Using these four inks printed in succession, it is possible to create a wide range of colors on a printed piece. Photographs, for example, are printed using process colors. However, process colors do have limitations. Certain colors are simply not achievable using CMYK due to the somewhat limited gamut of the CMYK color space. To more accurately achieve a specific color on a printed piece, spot colors come in handy.

Spot colors are colored inks that are specifically mixed to produce a desired color. The most common spot colors in the printing industry are made by a company called Pantone, Inc. *Pantone* and *spot color* are used almost synonymously in the printing industry, as Pantone colors are the primary inks used to specify spot colors for a printing job.

Spot colors can be used in many ways, but the primary reasons for using a spot color are:

- When color matching is critical. If a company logo is required to appear in the exact same color each time it is printed, a spot color may be used to reproduce the color consistently. In this example, adding a spot color to an existing process color job increases the costs of the project.
- To save money, instead of printing a product, such as a business card, using four process colors, you may choose to print the card in two spot colors or one spot color and black to reduce the cost of the printed product.
- To produce very rich, vibrant colors. These may be colors that process printing cannot recreate. This type of print job is often very expensive to produce.

In the following exercise, you will finish a business card that was started by using the atom logo from the poster you created earlier. You will then load Pantone colors into Illustrator CS4 that will be used to colorize the atom logo and some other elements within the business card.

1 Choose File > Browse in Bridge or press the Go to Bridge button (Br) in the menu bar.

2 Navigate to the ai04lessons folder within Bridge and open the file ai0402.ai by double-clicking on it.

3 Back in Illustrator, choose File > Save As. In the Save As dialog box, navigate to the ai04lessons folder and type **ai0402_work.ai** in the File name field. Choose Adobe Illustrator from the Save as type drop-down menu and choose Save. Press OK when the Illustrator Options dialog box appears.

4 Open the completed poster file (ai0401_done.ai) using the same method outlined in steps 2 and 3.

5 Using the Selection tool (), select the atom logo in the poster file and choose Edit > Copy. Close the poster file. If asked if you want to save changes to the file, choose No (Windows) or Don't Save (Mac OS).

6 With the business card file open, choose Edit > Paste.

The atom logo is clearly way too big for your business card, so let's scale it down to fit a little better.

7 Double-click on the Scale tool () in the Tools panel to open the Scale dialog box. Select the *Uniform* radio button and type **20** in the Scale text field. To see the change in scaling before you apply it, ensure that the *Preview* checkbox is checked. Press OK.

8 Using the Selection tool, position the atom logo beneath the *Atomic Region* text on the business card.

9 Choose File > Save to save your work.

Loading Pantone colors

Now you will load some Pantone colors into your document to color the card's elements.

1 In the application bar, choose Window > Swatch Libraries > Color Books > PANTONE solid coated. This opens a new panel on your screen that lists all the colors in the PANTONE solid coated library.

2 From the panel menu of the PANTONE solid coated panel, choose Small List View to make it easier to identify the swatches; then, from the same panel menu, choose Show Find Field.

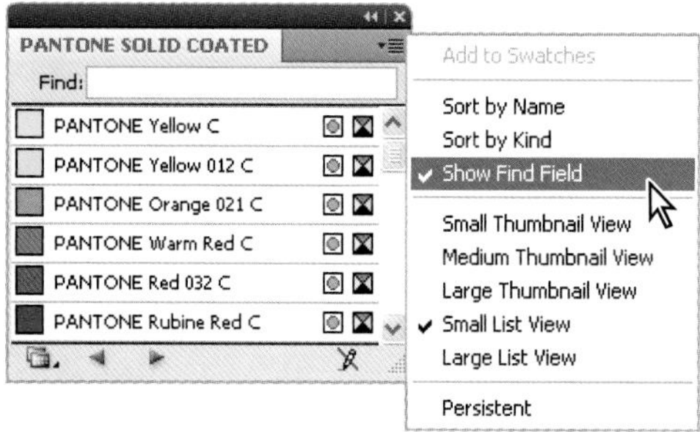

Change the view of and add a find field to the Pantone solid coated panel.

3 In the Find field of the PANTONE solid coated panel, type **7409**. Illustrator highlights the color in the panel that matches the number that you entered. Select the highlighted number and drag it into your Swatches panel to add it to your list of swatches. Repeat this step for color 512, and then close the PANTONE solid coated panel.

Notice that the icons you dragged into the Swatches panel have a different icon from the rest (◙). The white, lower-right corner with the black dot indicates that the swatches are spot colors.

4 Using the Selection tool (↖), select the text box containing the text on the right side of the business card. Click on the Fill button in the Control panel and choose the swatch named 7409 from the swatches. The text fills with the 7409 color.

Do the same to the yellow oval graphic behind the Atomic Region text.

5 Use the Selection tool to select the *Atomic Region* text, and change the stroke by clicking on the stroke button in the Control panel and selecting the purple 512 color. Change the text's fill by clicking on the Fill button in the Control panel and selecting the same purple 512 color that you applied to the stroke.

6 Click on the Color button in the dock to open the Color panel. Reduce the fill's tint value by dragging the tint slider at the top of the panel to 60 percent to create a contrast between the text's fill and stroke.

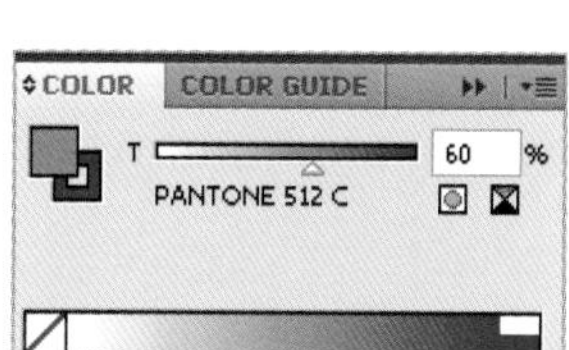

Drag the tint slider of the Color panel to change the value of the Pantone color in the fill of the text.

Applying spot colors to the logo

You will now apply spot colors to the atom logo. To do this, you will use the Live Color feature to remap the colors in the atom logo to a Pantone color. First, you will create a new color group that contains the two Pantone colors in your job.

1 Make sure that nothing is selected in your document by clicking on a white area outside the business card or by using the keyboard shortcut Shift+Ctrl+A (Windows) or Shift+Command+A (Mac OS).

2 Open the Swatches panel from the dock. Select both Pantone colors—7409 and 512—by holding down the Shift key while clicking on them. Press the New Color Group button (◘) at the bottom of the Swatches panel.

3 In the resulting New Color Group dialog box, type **Pantone group** in the Name text field and press OK.

4 Activate the Selection tool (↖) and select the atom logo. Select the Recolor Artwork button (◈) in the Control panel.

5 In the Recolor Artwork dialog box, press the Assign button to activate that portion of the dialog box. Click on Pantone group in the Color Groups section on the right side of the Recolor Artwork dialog box.

6 In the Colors drop-down menu to the left of the Color Groups list, change the value from Auto to 1 to tell Illustrator to remap all the colors in the logo to one color.

7 Press OK. If asked if you would like to save the changes to the color group, choose No.

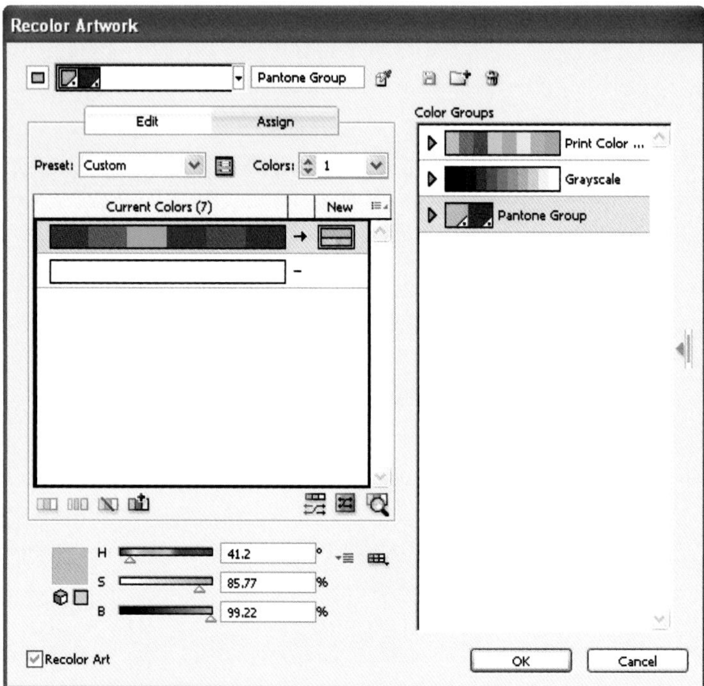

The Recolor Artwork dialog box allows you to remap a group of colors to a different group of colors in the selected artwork.

You can now see that all the colors that were in the atom logo have been remapped to one Pantone color on the business card.

8 To finish the business card, draw a rectangle the size of the business card using the Rectangle tool (▭). Click and drag from the upper-left corner of the document to the lower-right corner. Fill the rectangle with the Pantone 512 purple color by clicking on the Fill button in the Control panel and choosing the Pantone 512 swatch. If your color is still using the 60 percent tint that was previously set in the Color panel, change it back to 100 percent.

9 Choose Object > Arrange > Send to Back to put the purple rectangle behind the text, creating a purple background for the business card.

10 Choose File > Save to save your work, then File > Close.

Congratulations! You have completed Lesson 4, "Adding Color."

Self study

In this lesson, you were introduced to several great new features of Adobe Illustrator CS4, as well as some features that aren't so new, but deserve further investigation nonetheless.

The Appearance panel is a highly underused feature of Adobe Illustrator; practice on your own by exploring the capabilities harnessed within the Appearance panel. Start by drawing a line with the Line Segment tool then expanding the weight of the stroke. Add another stroke to it from within the Appearance panel, setting it to a different weight and color; you'll see that you can apply more than one stroke to a single object!

Explore Live Paint and Live Color in more detail. See Lesson 5, "Working with the Drawing Tools," for information about converting a picture into a vector-based piece of art using the Live Trace feature and then coloring it using Live Paint. Furthermore, you can experiment with Color Groups and the Recolor Artwork dialog box to change how your artwork is colorized in Illustrator.

You've worked with the Color Guide and its color harmony rules, which allow you to look at variations of the selected color group. Go to *kuler.adobe.com* to check out different color themes that people have created to share with other users. You can even post your own themes to this web site. Even better: you can download these themes to your computer and import them into the Creative Suite applications to apply to objects within your documents.

Review

Questions

1 What does the appearance of this swatch icon (◉) in the Swatches panel indicate?

2 Where in Adobe Illustrator CS4 would you look to identify the attributes of a selected object?

3 True or false: You can share swatches that you created in Adobe Illustrator CS4 with other Adobe CS4 programs.

4 When you see this swatch icon (◪) in the Swatches panel, what does it indicate?

5 How do you edit a pattern swatch?

Answers

1 This swatch icon (◉) indicates that the color is a spot color.

2 You can locate the attributes of a selected object in the Appearance panel.

3 True. You can choose the Save Swatch Library as ASE command from the panel menu of the Swatches panel. This saves all your swatches as a separate Swatch Library file (.ase) that can be imported into other CS4 applications.

4 This swatch icon (◪) indicates that the color is a global color.

5 To edit a pattern swatch, drag the swatch icon from the Swatches panel onto your Illustrator artboard. Make the necessary changes, then select the pattern art and drag it back into the Swatches panel. If you want to replace the old pattern swatch, simply hold down the Alt (Windows) or Option (Mac OS) key on your keyboard as you drag the pattern artwork on top of the old pattern swatch in the Swatches panel.

What you'll learn in this lesson:

- Using the Pen tool
- Editing existing paths
- Working with Tracing Presets
- Creating and expanding Live Trace artwork
- Adding color using Live Paint

Working with the Drawing Tools

Adobe Illustrator includes a number of impressive drawing tools that allow you to create a wide variety of artwork with speed and precision.

Starting up

Before starting, make sure that your tools and panels are consistent by resetting your workspace. See "Resetting Adobe Illustrator CS4 Preferences" on page 3.

You will work with several files from the ai05lessons folder in this lesson. Make sure that you have loaded the ailessons folder onto your hard drive from the supplied DVD. See "Loading lesson files" on page 4.

See Lesson 5 in action!

Use the accompanying video to gain a better understanding of how to use some of the features shown in this lesson. The video tutorial for this lesson can be found on the included DVD.

Working with the Pen tool

The Pen tool is the most powerful tool in Illustrator and it allows you to create any line or shape that you need. The Pen tool creates anchor points. These points can be either rounded and smooth, or, sharp and angular, and can create any line or shape that you can conceive. Using the Pen tool and mastering line construction is all about understanding the nature of anchor points and how to create and work with them.

There are two kinds of anchor points that you can create in Illustrator: corner points and smooth points. Corner points are usually seen on linear, hard-edged shapes such as polygons and squares, while smooth points are used to construct sinuous, curved lines. There are two mouse actions that are repeated over and over again when creating anchor points: click and release, which creates corner points; and click and drag, which creates smooth points.

The Pen tool has a versatile feature that allows you to create new anchor points, add anchor points to existing paths, and remove anchor points from existing paths. The tool's appearance changes, based on what your cursor is hovering over in the artboard. Pay attention to what the tool looks like, as it will assist you in using all the Pen tool's functions.

PEN TOOL VARIATION	DESCRIPTION
	Only appears as you are in the process of creating a line; it signals that the next anchor point created will continue that line.
	Indicates that the Pen tool will create a new line.
	Indicates that the Pen tool can be used to convert the anchor point it is currently hovering over. This icon only appears when the Pen tool is hovering over the last anchor point that was created in a selected path.
	Indicates that the Pen tool will pick up a path and continue from the end point you are hovering over. This icon only appears next to the Pen tool when it is hovering over the endpoint of a path that you are not currently creating.
	Indicates that the Pen tool will connect the path that is currently being created to the end point of a different path.
	Indicates that the Pen tool will close the path that you are currently creating.
	Indicates that the Pen tool will remove the anchor point that it is currently hovering over. This icon only appears when the Pen tool is hovering over an anchor point on a selected path.
	Indicates that the Pen tool will add an anchor point to the line segment that it is currently hovering over. This icon only appears when the Pen tool is hovering over a line segment on a selected path.

Drawing straight lines

The first skill you need to master when working with the Pen tool is creating a straight line. To do this, you make corner anchor points with the Pen tool. Straight lines are automatically generated as a result.

1 In Illustrator, choose File > Open. When the Open dialog box appears, navigate to the ai05lessons folder and select the ai0501.ai file. Press OK. This is a practice file containing several different line templates that you will work through in the following exercises.

2 Choose File > Save As. In the Save As dialog box, navigate to the ai05lessons folder and type **ai0501_work.ai** into the Name text field; then press Save. In the resulting Illustrator Options dialog box, press OK to accept the default settings.

3 In the Control panel at the top of the workspace, select None (⧄) from the Fill color drop-down menu. Select the color black from the Stroke color drop-down menu and select 2 pt from the Stroke Weight drop-down menu.

4 Select the Pen tool (✒) from the Tools panel and locate the template labeled Exercise 1 on the artboard. Click and release your left mouse button while hovering over label 1. This starts the line by creating the first anchor point.

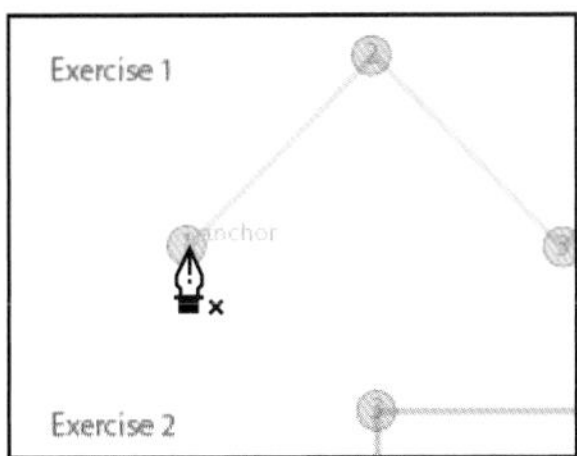

Use the Pen tool to create the first anchor point.

5 Move your cursor to the part of the line labeled 2, and click and release your mouse. The second point of the line is created. The Pen tool automatically draws a straight line between the two points you have established.

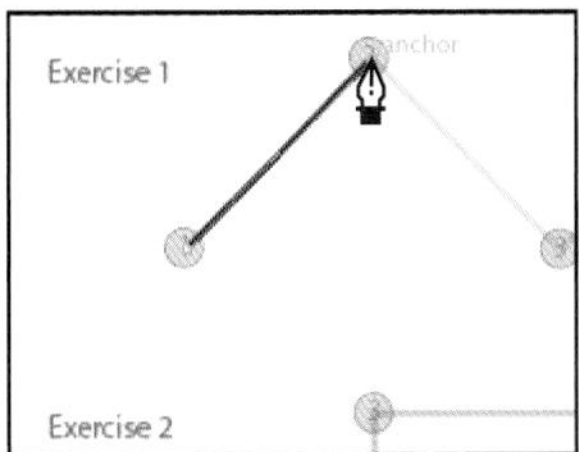

Create the second anchor point.

6 Continue to click and release to complete the line through labels 3, 4, 5, 6, and 7. Notice how the Pen tool automatically continues the line to include each new anchor point that you designate.

7 After you have set a final anchor point at label 7, press and hold Ctrl (Windows) or Command (Mac OS) and click on any empty area of the page. This deselects and ends the line. If you don't deselect and end the line, the Pen tool continues to link the line you just created to any anchor points that you create from here on.

8 Position the cursor over label 1 of Exercise 2. Click and release the left mouse button to create the first anchor point of the new line.

9 Position the cursor over label 2. Hold down the Shift key, then click and release to create the second point of the line; the Pen tool automatically connects the two points with a straight line. Because you were holding the Shift key when the second point was created, Illustrator automatically draws a perfectly horizontal line.

10 Position the cursor over label 3. Again hold the Shift key and click and release the left mouse button to set a third anchor point. This time, the line created is a perfect vertical line.

11 Continue holding down the Shift key while clicking at labels 4, 5, and 6. Doing this draws the line between points 4 and 5 at a perfect 135-degree angle, as the Shift key constrains the angle to 45-degree increments.

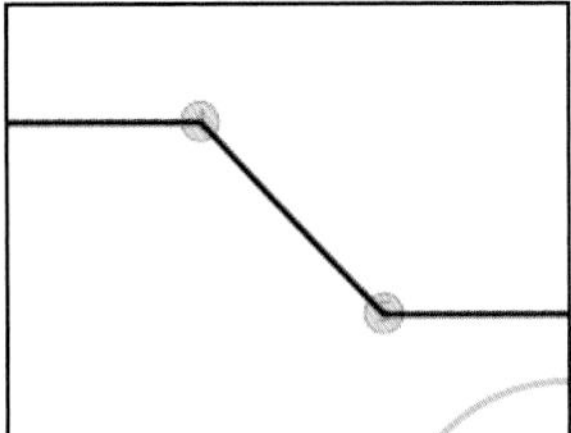

Pressing Shift while clicking allows you to create 90- and 45-degree angles with the Pen tool.

12 With a final anchor point at label 6, hold down the Ctrl key (Windows) or Command key (Mac OS) and click on the artboard to deselect and end the line.

13 Choose File > Save to save your work.

Drawing curved lines

Straight lines can only take you so far; more organic and complex compositions require you to use curved lines to render subjects. You will now complete Exercise 3.

1 Position your cursor over label 1 at the beginning of the curved line. Click and, without releasing the mouse, drag your cursor up slightly above the hump of the line to create your first anchor point. As you drag your cursor up, it looks like you are dragging a line away from the point. You are, in fact, creating a direction handle for the anchor point.

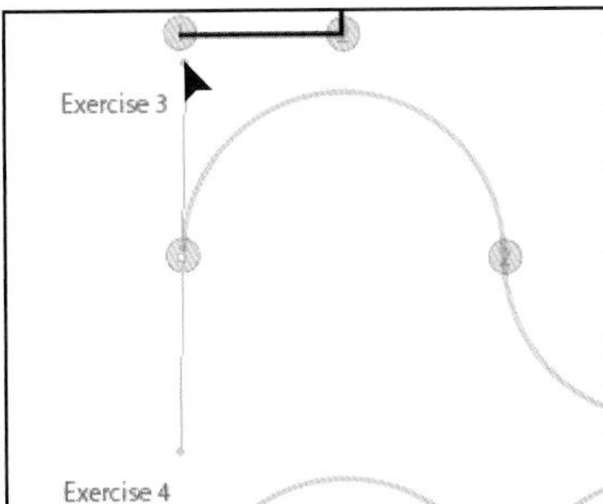

Dragging while clicking with the Pen tool allows you to create direction handles.

What are direction handles?

When you select or create a smooth point, you can see the direction handles of that point. Direction handles control the angle and length of curves. Direction handles comprise two parts: direction lines and the direction points at the ends of the lines. An anchor point can have zero, one, or two direction handles, depending on the kind of point it is. Direction handles serve as a kind of road map for the line, controlling how the lines approach and leave each anchor point. If the exiting handle is downward-facing, the line leaves the anchor point and goes down. Similarly, the line faces upwards if the direction handle is pointing upwards.

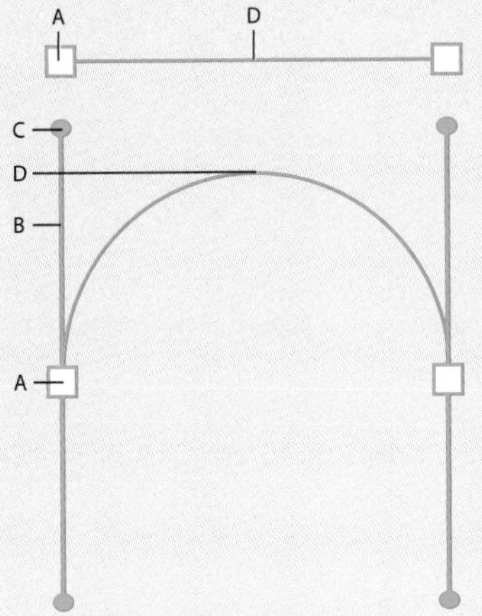

***A.** Anchor point. **B.** Direction Line. **C.** Direction Handle. **D.** Line Segment.*

2 Place your cursor over label 2, located at the end of the first curve in Exercise 3. Click and drag straight down to create the second anchor point. Continue to drag the mouse until you form the curve in the template. As you drag your cursor down, you will notice that a curve is being formed between the two anchor points in real time. As long as you do not release the mouse button, you can reshape this line by dragging the mouse in different directions.

If you need to modify any of the previous points, choose Edit > Undo or use the keyboard shortcut, Ctrl + Z (Windows) or Command + Z (Mac OS). Do not worry if the curves do not follow the template perfectly, they can be adjusted in future steps.

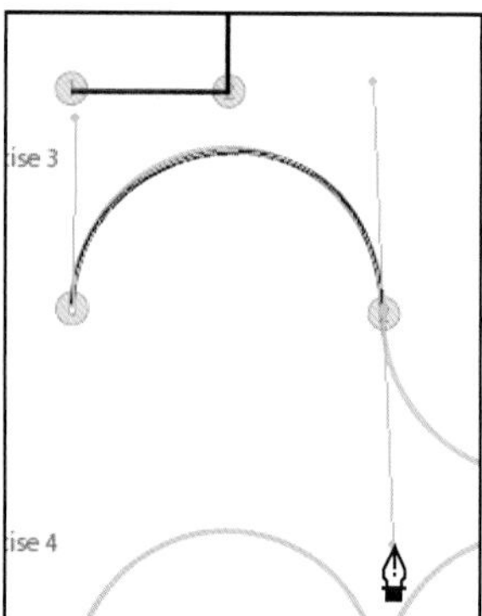

Dragging while creating the second anchor point allows you to curve the path.

3 Place your cursor over label 3, located at the end of the second curve. Click and drag up to create the third anchor point of the line. Continue to drag the mouse until you form the curve indicated by the template. Again, as long as you do not release the mouse button, you can reshape this line depending on the direction in which you drag the mouse.

4 Place your cursor over label 4, located at the end of the second curve. As in step 3, click and drag down to create the fourth and final anchor point of the line. Continue to drag the mouse until you form the curve indicated by the template.

5 As in the previous exercise, after you have created your final anchor point at label 4, hold down Ctrl (Windows) or Command (Mac OS) and click on the artboard.

6 If necessary, use the Direct Select tool (↖) to reposition the handles and points so the curves follow the path more closely, then choose File > Save to save your work.

Drawing hinged curves

In the previous exercise, you created S-curves, lines curved in the opposite direction from the previous one. In this exercise, you will create hinged curves, lines that curve in the same direction; in this case, they will all curve up like a scallop. You will now complete Exercise 4.

1 Position your cursor over label 1 at the beginning of the curved line in Exercise 4. As you did in the previous exercise, click and drag your cursor up slightly above the hump of the line to create your first anchor point.

2 Place your cursor over label 2, located at the end of the first curve. Click and drag straight down to create the second anchor point. Continue to drag the mouse until you form the curve in the template.

3 Press and hold the Alt (Windows) or Option (Mac OS) key on the keyboard. This temporarily changes the Pen tool into the Convert Anchor Point tool, which is a separate tool in the Pen tool grouping. Among other things (covered later in this chapter), this tool is used to edit direction handles. Position the Convert Anchor Point tool over the direction point for the exiting direction line, and click and drag this point so that it points upward. The two direction lines now form a V.

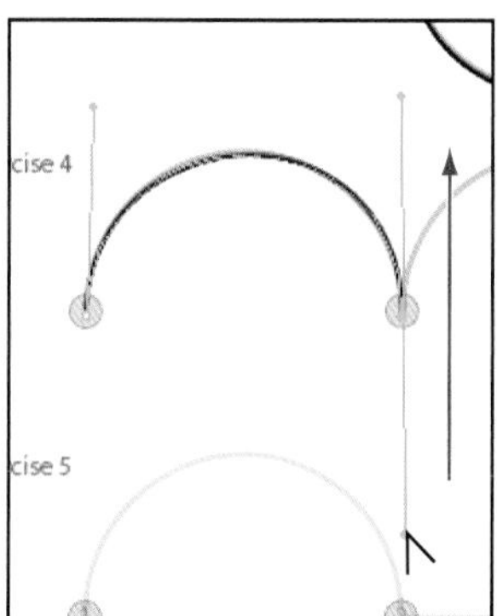

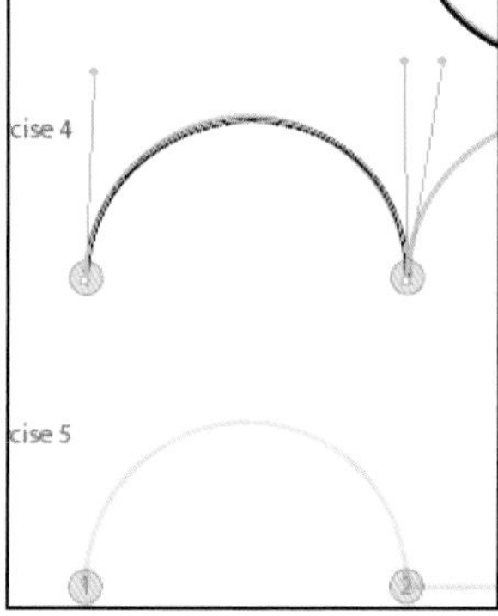

Move the direction handle to change the direction of the next path.

Direction handles control the curvature of the lines in a path. Because the exiting direction handle created in step 3 is pointing down, the line will want to go down. To draw the hinged curve, you must change the angle of this direction handle so that it points upward.

4 Place your cursor over label 3, located at the end of the second curve. Click and drag straight down to create the third anchor point. Continue to drag the mouse until you form the curve in the template.

5 Again, press and hold Alt (Windows) or Option (Mac OS) to temporarily switch the Pen tool to the Convert Anchor Point tool. Once again, position the Convert Anchor Point tool over the direction point for the exiting direction line, and click and drag this point so that it points upward and the direction lines form a V.

6 Repeat step 4 for the final curve at label 4. After you have created this final anchor point, hold down the Ctrl (Windows) or Command (Mac OS) key and click on the artboard.

7 Choose File > Save to save your work.

Drawing curved lines to straight lines

While some compositions you create in Adobe Illustrator are composed of only straight or curved lines, most are probably some combination of the two. The following two exercises cover how to draw straight and curved lines together as part of the same path. You will now complete Exercise 5.

1 Position your cursor over label 1 at the beginning of the curved line in Exercise 5. Hold the Shift key, and click and drag your cursor up slightly above the hump of the line to create your first anchor point. As you drag your cursor upwards, your movement is constrained to a perfectly vertical line. Release the mouse before releasing the Shift key.

2 Place your cursor over label 2, located at the end of the first curve. Again, while holding the Shift key, click and drag straight down to create the second anchor point. Continue to drag the mouse until you form the curve in the template.

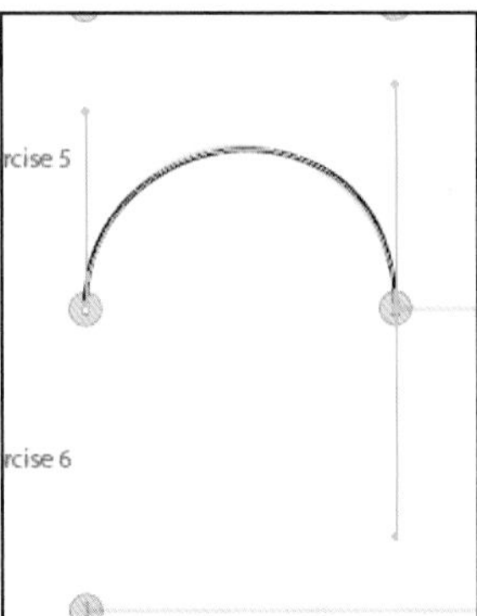

Create another curved path.

Direction handles control the curvature of the lines in a path. Because the exiting direction handle created in step 2 is pointing down, the line will want to go down. If you drag the direction point so that the line points up as in the previous exercise, it will want to curve up. To form a straight line, however, you want to remove this directional handle entirely, thus converting the anchor point into a corner point.

3 Position your cursor over the anchor point you created in step 2. The Pen tool cursor changes, giving you the ability to convert the anchor point you just created.

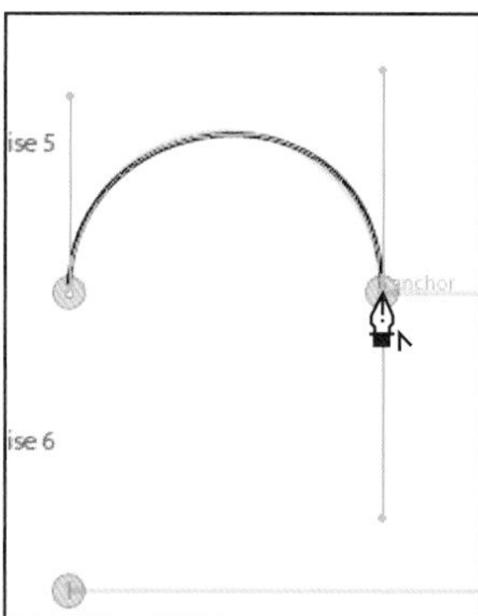

The Pen tool cursor changes, allowing you to modify the anchor point.

4 While hovering over the anchor point, click the mouse. This collapses the anchor's outgoing direction handle, allowing you to create a straight line.

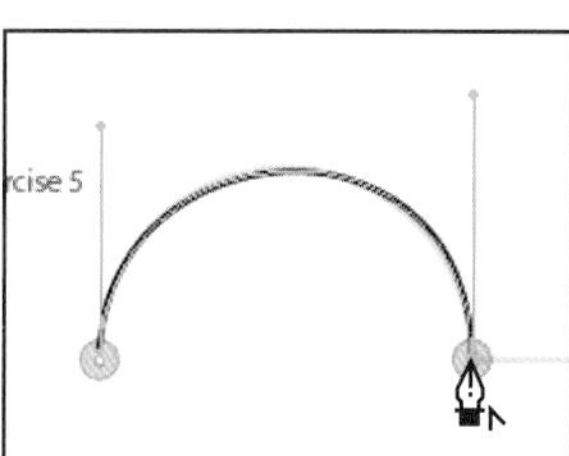

Collapse the direction handle.

5 Place the cursor over label 3. Hold the Shift key on the keyboard, and click at label 3 to create a straight line to finish the path.

6 After you have created your final anchor point at label 3, hold down Ctrl (Windows) or Command (Mac OS) and click on the artboard to deselect and end the line.

7 Choose File > Save to save your work.

Drawing straight lines to curved lines

Now, you will work from the opposite direction and connect straight lines to curved lines. Practice with Exercise 6.

1 Locate the template labeled Exercise 6. Hold the Pen tool over the start of the line (labeled 1). The cursor changes (✎ₓ), indicating that you will start a new line. Click and release your left mouse button while hovering over label 1. This starts the line by creating the first anchor point.

2 Place the cursor over label 2. Hold the Shift key and click at label 2 to create a perfectly straight line between points 1 and 2 on the path.

3 Position your cursor over the anchor point you created in step 2. The Pen tool cursor changes (✎), indicating that you can change the direction of the direction handle.

4 While hovering over the anchor point, click and drag upwards in the direction of the curve you want to draw. This creates a new direction handle.

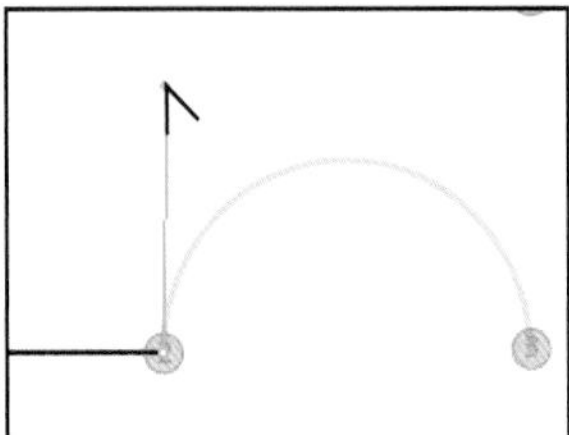

Change the direction of the direction handle.

5 Position the Pen tool over label 3. Click and drag down to create the curve seen in the template.

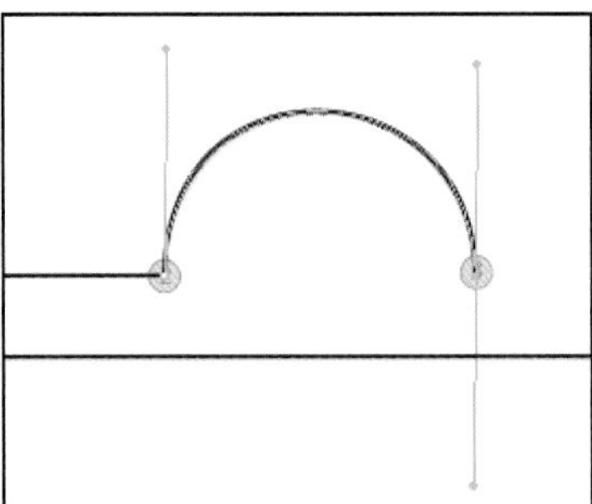

Finish the path by creating a curve.

6 After you have created your final anchor point at label 3, hold down the Ctrl (Windows) or Command (Mac OS) key and click on the artboard to deselect and end the line.

7 Choose File > Save, then choose File > Close.

Tracing images

Illustrator is often used to convert artwork that has been scanned or rendered in a pixel-based painting program, like Adobe Photoshop, into crisp vector line art.

Placing an image as a template

1 Create a new Illustrator document by choosing File > New. In the New Document dialog box, type **ai0502** in the Name text field. Choose Print from the New Document Profile drop-down menu. Choose Letter from the Size drop-down menu, if it is not already selected. Press OK.

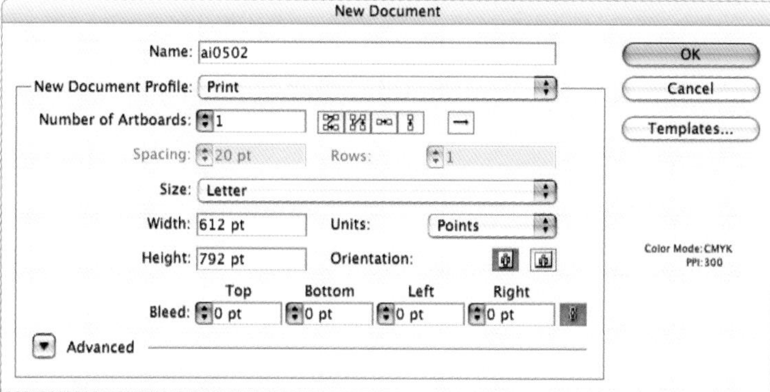

The New Document dialog box.

2 Choose File > Save As. In the Save As dialog box, navigate to the ai05lessons folder, then type **ai0502_work.ai** in the Name text field. Press Save.

3 The Illustrator Options dialog box appears. Leave all settings at their defaults and press OK.

4 Choose File > Place. In the Place dialog box, navigate to the ai05lessons folder and select the ai0502.tif file. Select the *Template* checkbox at the bottom of the Place dialog box to import the selected artwork as a template layer. Press Place. A faint outline of a truck appears in your document.

5 Click anywhere on the artboard to deselect the template. In the Control panel, choose None (⧄) from the Fill Color drop-down menu and choose the color black from the Stroke Color drop-down menu. Choose 2 pt from the Stroke Weight drop-down menu.

6 Select the Pen tool (✒) from the Tools panel. Position the cursor near label 1, then click and release to create the first anchor point of the path along the tracing template for the truck. If necessary, increase the magnification to see the template more clearly.

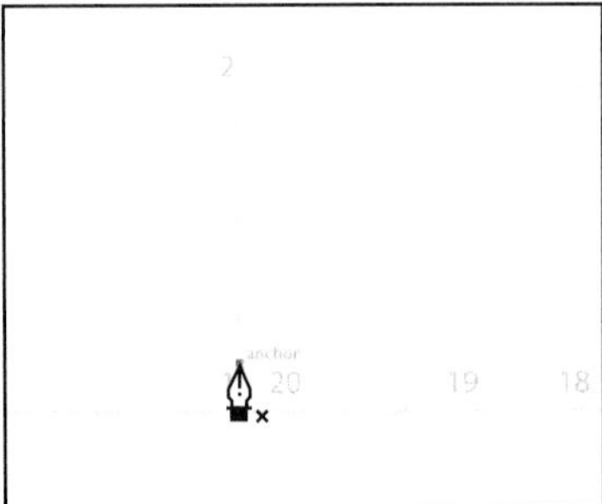

Create the first anchor point of the truck.

7 Press and hold the Shift key and click along the truck outline near label 2. This creates a second anchor point, and Illustrator automatically draws a straight line between them.

8 Press and hold the Shift key, and click at label 3 to continue tracing the truck's outline.

9 Continue to hold down the Shift key, and click along the truck body at labels 4, 5, 6, and 7.

10 The line between labels 7 and 8 is diagonal, so release the Shift key and click at label 8.

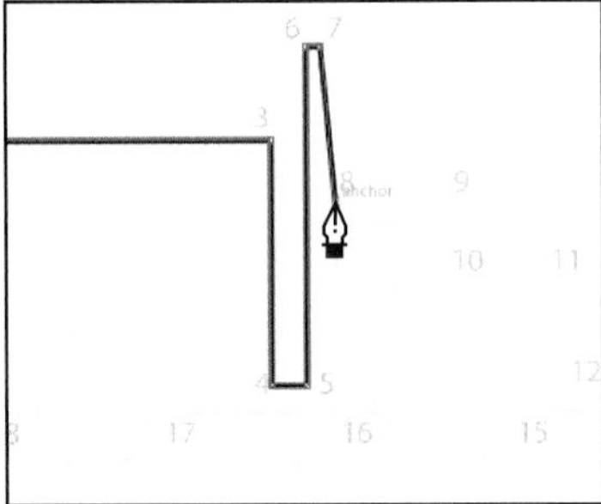

Continue outlining the truck.

11 Again press and hold the Shift key, and click at labels 9 and 10.

12 Release the Shift key on the keyboard and click at label 11. Up to this point, the exercise has dealt entirely with creating straight lines and corner points; for the line between labels 11 and 12, you need to create a curved line.

13 Because the point created at label 11 is a corner point, the Pen tool automatically attempts to create a straight line between this anchor and the next one. You can override this tendency by converting the anchor point you just created, as you did in a previous exercise. Hover the Pen tool over the anchor point created at label 11, and look for the Convert Anchor Point symbol (ꜛ) to appear next to the tool. Click and drag with the tool in the direction of the curve to create a new directional handle.

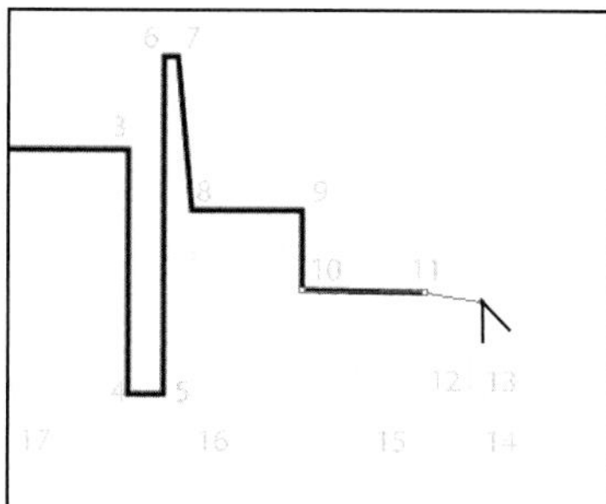

As you drag to create the directional handle, the cursor has the appearance of an arrowhead without a stem.

14 Click with the Pen tool at label 12 to create a smooth point and complete the line.

15 Hold the Shift key on the keyboard, and click labels 13, 14, then 15.

16 The half circle between labels 15 and 16 presents the same challenge that you faced previously. Again, hover the Pen tool over the anchor point you just created. While holding the Shift key, click and drag upward to create a constrained directional handle.

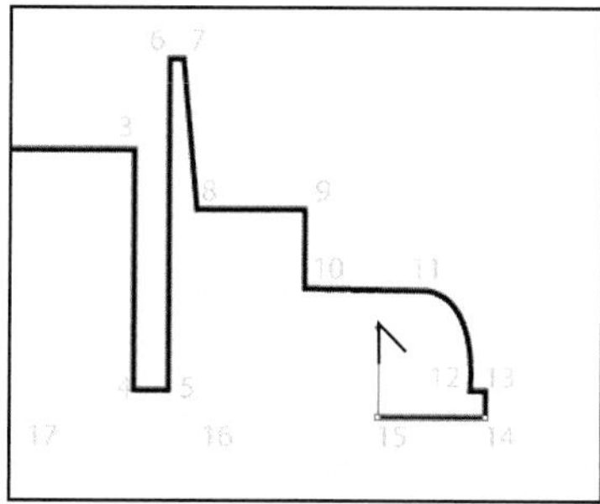

Move the direction handle up to start another curve.

17 At label 16, click and drag the cursor down to create a new smooth point and continue the line.

18 Position the cursor over the anchor point that you just created at label 16, and click on it when you see the Convert Anchor Point symbol (ꜛ) appear next to the Pen tool. Hold down the Shift key and click at label 17.

19 Repeat steps 16 to 18 until you reach the anchor point numbered 20. After you have collapsed the anchor point at label 20, position your cursor over label 1. A circle appears next to the Pen tool (✒), indicating that this action will close the path you have just drawn. Click on the anchor point to complete the line and close the path.

20 Choose File > Save, then choose File > Close.

Other drawing tools

While the Pen tool is definitely the most versatile drawing tool in the application, there are several other drawing tools that exist to fulfill specific functions.

Using the Line Segment and Arc tools

As the tool names imply, the Line Segment and Arc tools create line segments and arcs. As you learned in the previous exercises, the Pen tool can also create lines and arcs; however, unlike line segments and arcs that can be created with the Pen tool, each new line or arc is separate and unique from the previous one.

1 Choose File > Open. In the Open dialog box, navigate to the ai05lessons folder and select the ai0503.ai file. Press Open.

This is a practice file containing several different line templates that you will work through in the following exercises. Choose File > Save As. In the Save As dialog box, navigate to the ai05lessons folder, and type **ai0503_work.ai** in the Name text field. Press Save.

2 In the Control panel, choose None (☒) from the Fill Color drop-down menu and choose the color black from the Stroke Color drop-down menu. Choose 2 pt from the Stroke Weight drop-down menu.

3 Select the Line Segment tool (\) from the Tools panel on the left, and locate the template labeled Exercise 1. Hold the Line Segment tool over the start of the first line (labeled 1). Click and drag with your mouse from label 1 to label 2 to create a line segment.

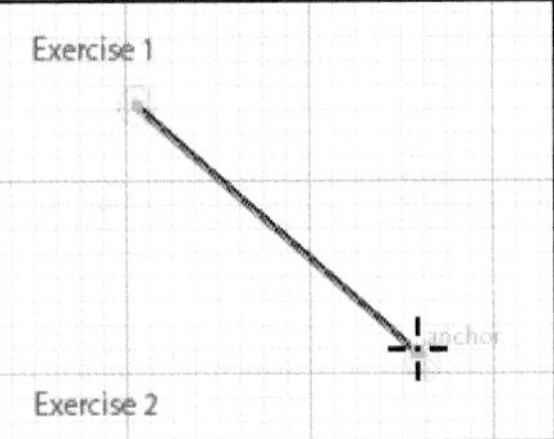

Using the Line Segment tool.

4 Position the cursor over label 3. While holding the Shift key, click and drag the mouse from label 3 to label 4. The Shift key is used to constrain the Line Segment tool to perfectly horizontal, vertical, or diagonal (45-degree) lines.

5 Position the cursor over label 5. While holding the Shift key, click and drag the mouse from label 5 to label 6.

6 Press and hold the Line Segment tool to view the hidden tools. Select the Arc tool (⌒) and locate the template labeled Exercise 2. Hold the Arc tool over the start of the first line (labeled 1). Click and drag with your mouse from label 1 to label 2. This creates an arc.

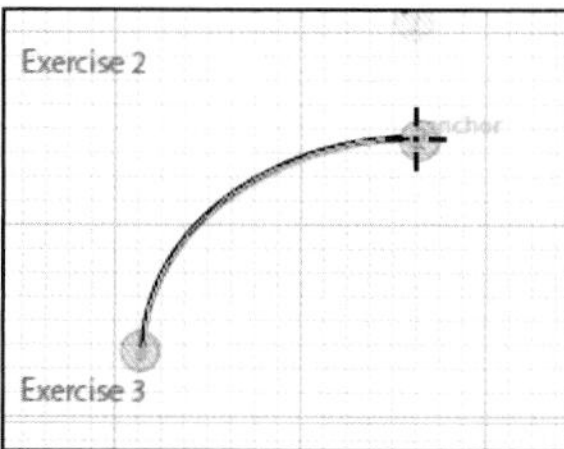

Create an arc path.

7 Position the cursor over label 3. While holding the Shift key, click and drag the mouse from label 3 to label 4. The Shift key constrains the created arc.

8 Position the cursor over label 5. Click and drag to label 6. Continue pressing down the mouse button, and notice that the arc is very similar to the others you have previously created. While still holding the mouse button, press **F** on the keyboard and release it to reverse the direction of the arc.

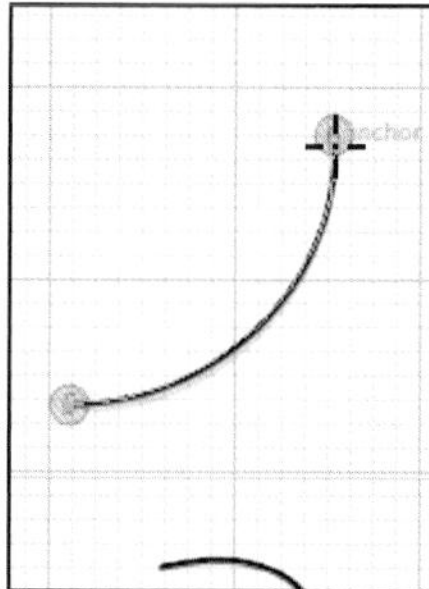

Press F while creating an arc to reverse the curve's direction.

While drawing an arc, press the up and down arrow keys on the keyboard to change the angle of the arc.

9 Choose File > Save to save your work.

Using the Pencil, Smooth, and Path Eraser tools

While the Pen tool exists for precise line work, the Pencil tool creates freeform lines. In addition to being able to draw lines, the Pencil tool can also be used to refine existing lines. You will now complete Exercise 3.

1 Select the Pencil tool (✐) from the Tools panel and locate the template labeled Exercise 3. Hold the Pencil tool over the start of the first line (labeled 1). Click and drag with your mouse from label 1 to label 2 to replicate the looping line shown in the template.

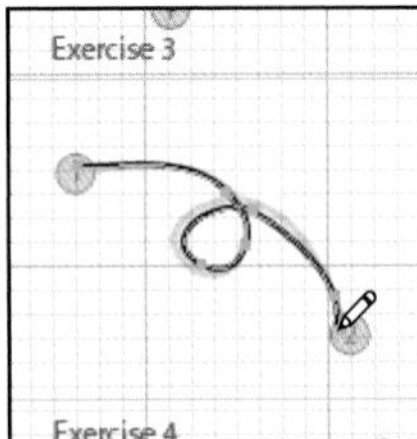

Create a line using the Pencil tool.

2 Choose the Selection tool (↖) and highlight the line between labels 3 and 4. Select the Pencil tool, then click and drag along the guideline between labels 3 and 4. The line adjusts to fit the new path you have created.

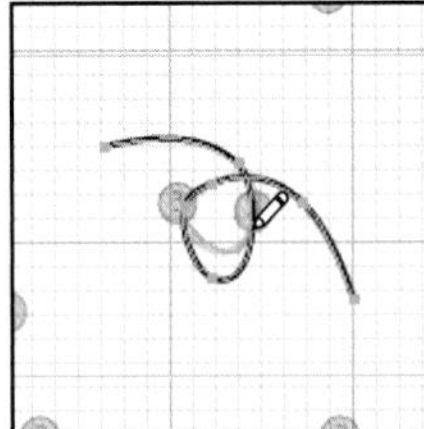

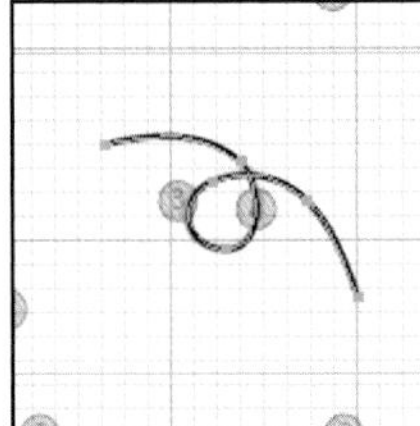

Select, then redraw a part of the path.

3 Choose the Selection tool again and highlight the line between labels 5 and 6. Press and hold the Pencil tool in the Tools panel, and choose the Smooth tool (✐).

4 Beginning at label 6, click and drag the Smooth tool back and forth across the jagged part of the line to label 7. This smooths out the jagged line. Depending upon the magnification at which you are viewing the page, you may have to repeat this process several times to match the example. When viewing the page at a higher magnification level, you will need more passes across the artwork with the Smooth tool.

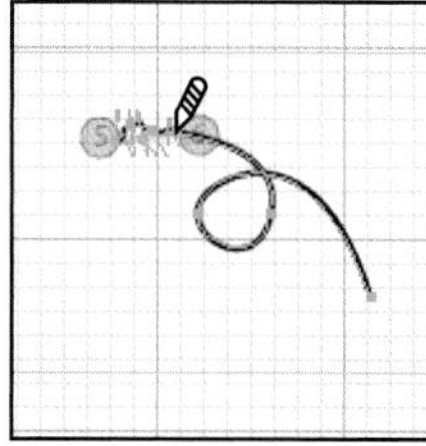
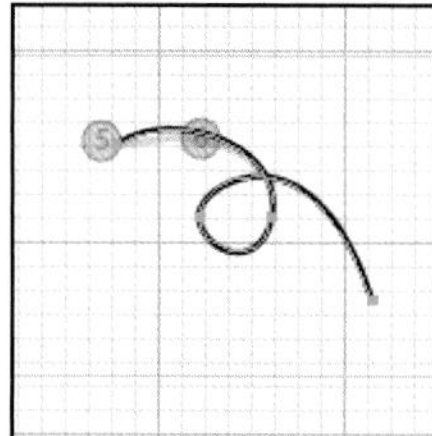

Smooth the path using the Smooth tool.

5 With the Selection tool, highlight the line between labels 7 and 8. Press and hold the Smooth tool in the Tools panel and choose the Path Eraser tool (✐).

6 Beginning at label 7, click and drag the Path Eraser tool back and forth across the selected line to erase it. Be sure to thoroughly overlap the line or you may leave stray segments intact.

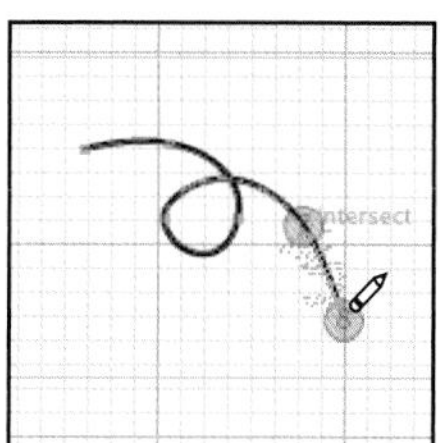
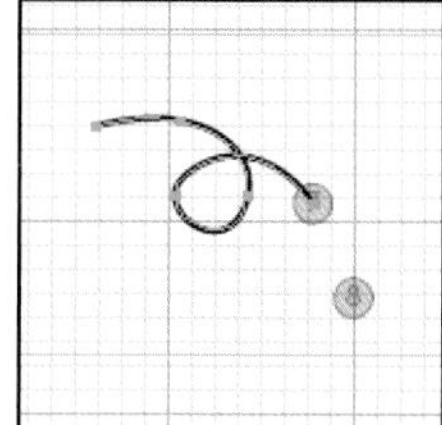

Using the Path Eraser tool, erase the path between labels 7 and 8.

7 Choose File > Save to save your work.

Using the Eraser tool

Introduced in Illustrator CS3, the Eraser tool was a welcome addition to the application's wide range of drawing and editing tools. It can erase vector objects in much the same fashion as a real-world eraser. This opens the door to the creation of a wide range of organic shapes in a very intuitive way.

1 Using the Selection tool (↖), highlight the black circle in Exercise 4, then choose the Eraser tool (⌀) in the Tools panel.

2 Click and drag from label 1 to label 2 in a pattern similar to the one in the template to the left of it. The Eraser tool bisects the circle, forming two separate shapes. Be certain to start outside the shape before clicking and dragging.

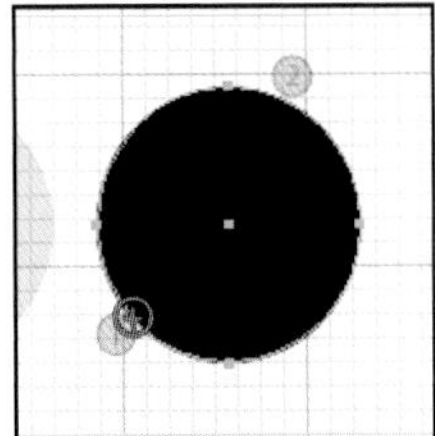
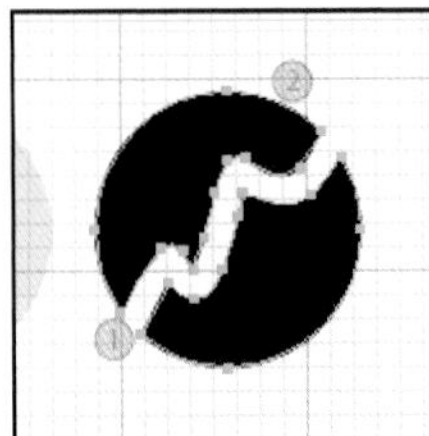

Use the Eraser tool to bisect the circle.

3 Choose the Selection tool and highlight the black line located between labels 3 and 4. Choose the Eraser tool and drag over the line between labels 3 and 4 to sever it.

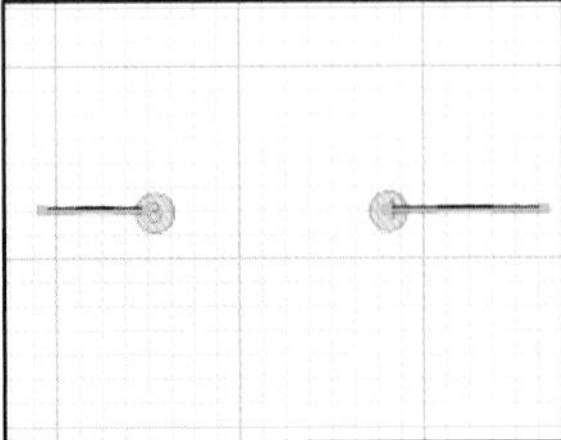

Use the Eraser tool to remove a section of the path.

4 Choose File > Save to save your work.

Editing existing paths

In addition to creating lines and shapes, the tools in Illustrator provide the ability to modify paths that you have already created. The two main ways to do this are by adding or removing anchor points to a path, and converting anchor points from smooth to corner points, or vice versa.

Adding and removing points

The best way to modify paths in your artwork is to add or remove anchor points from an existing path. Both the Pen tool and the Control panel can be used to modify the anchor points. You will now complete Exercise 5.

1 Using the Selection tool (), select the first path in Exercise 5 to highlight it, then choose the Pen tool () from the Tools panel.

2 Place the Pen tool over the portion of the path at label 1. The new cursor () indicates that clicking with the Pen tool will create an anchor point on the line segment. Click on the line segment to create a new anchor point.

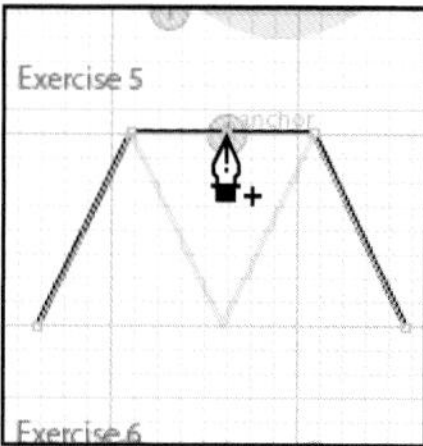

Create a new anchor point.

3 The anchor point that was just created is automatically highlighted. Use the arrow keys on your keyboard to move this anchor point into position to match the template.

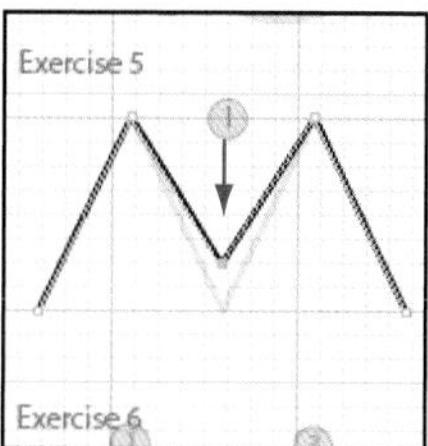

Move the anchor point using the arrow keys on the keyboard.

4 Now you'll move to the next template. Choose the Direct Selection tool () from the Tools panel, and draw a selection marquee around the anchor point at label 2 to highlight it.

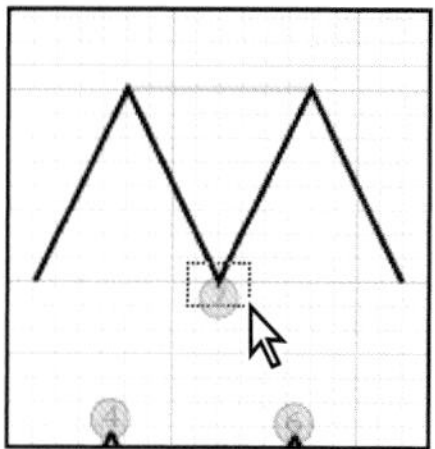

Select the anchor point.

5 Press the Remove Selected Anchor Points button (![]) in the Control panel to remove the highlighted anchor point from the line and make it match the template.

When the path is selected, you can also use the Pen tool to remove an anchor point. The only disadvantage to using the Pen tool to remove anchor points is that it cannot remove points from the beginning or end of a line.

6 Choose File > Save to save your work.

Refining a curve

You will now complete Exercise 5.

1 Locate the third and final path in Exercise 5. Using the Direct Selection tool (), draw a selection marquee around the anchor point at label 3.

2 Press the Convert Selected Anchor Point to Corner button () in the Control panel to change the smooth point into a corner point. This changes the curvature of the preceding line segment.

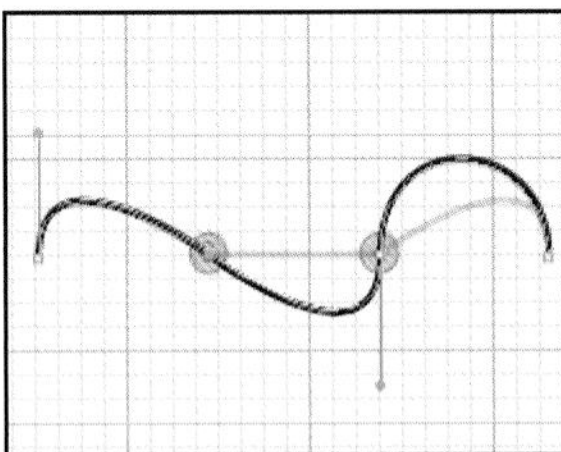

The curve changes.

3 With the line still selected, click and hold the Pen tool () in the Tools panel, then select the Convert Anchor Point tool ().

4 Select the anchor point at label 4 to convert it from a smooth point to a corner point.

If you want to convert a corner point to a smooth point, you can do so either from the Control panel or by clicking and dragging on a corner point with the Convert Anchor Point tool.

5 Press Ctrl+Shift+A (Windows) or Command+Shift+A (Mac OS) to deselect everything on the artboard. Choose File > Save to save your work.

Cutting and joining paths

One of Illustrator's very helpful features is the ability to cut and join paths. Paths can be cut either at anchor points or line segments, but they may only be joined by connecting two adjacent anchor points, called end points. You will now complete Exercise 6.

1 Locate Exercise 6. Select the Direct Selection tool (↖) from the Tools panel, and draw a selection marquee around the anchor point at label 1.

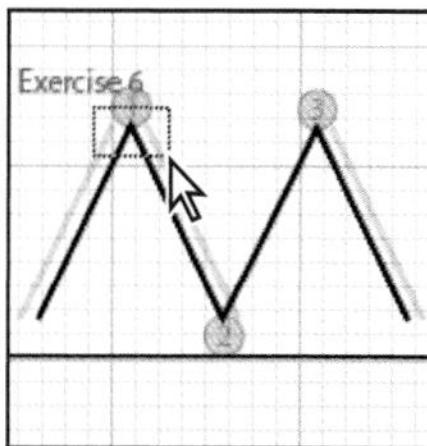

Draw a marquee around the anchor point.

2 Press the Cut Path at Selected Anchor Points button ( ) in the Control panel to sever the path at this point. Repeat this step for the anchor point at label 2.

3 Press and hold the Eraser tool ( ) in the Tools panel to reveal and select the Scissors tool (✂). Click on the anchor point at label 3. This tool performs the same function as the Cut Path at Selected Anchor Point button in the Control panel.

If you miss the anchor point even by a little, the Scissors tool displays an error message and you have to try again.

4 Choose the Selection tool (↖) in the Tools panel, and use it to move the individual line segments apart to the positions of the blue lines in the template.

5 Select the Direct Selection tool and draw a selection marquee around the two end points located at label 4. These end points are not connected.

6 Press the Connect Selected End Points button ( ) in the Control panel. When the Join dialog box appears, choose the default Corner option and press OK. This merges the two anchor points into one.

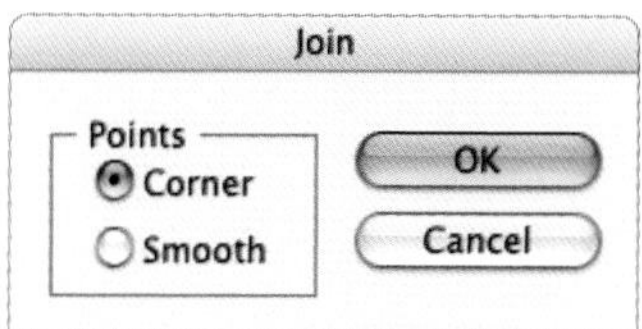

Choose Corner points in the Join dialog box.

7 Shift+click to select the two end points located at label 5, and select Object > Path > Join. When the Join dialog box appears, select Corner and press OK.

8 Select the two end points located at label 6 by clicking and dragging to create a marquees containing both points, then right-click (Windows) or Ctrl+click (Mac OS) on the page and choose Join from the contextual menu. In the Join dialog box, select Corner and press OK.

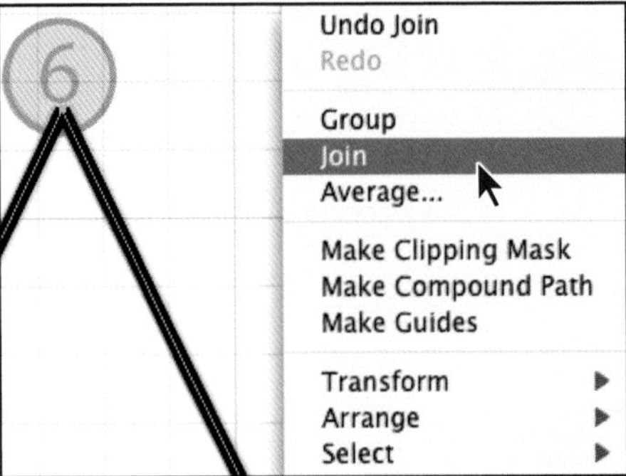

Right-click or Ctrl+click and choose Join from the contextual menu.

9 Select the two end points located at labels 7 and 8 by drawing a selection marquee using the Direct Selection tool.

10 Press the Connect Selected End Points button ( ) in the Control panel. A line connecting the two selected end points is created.

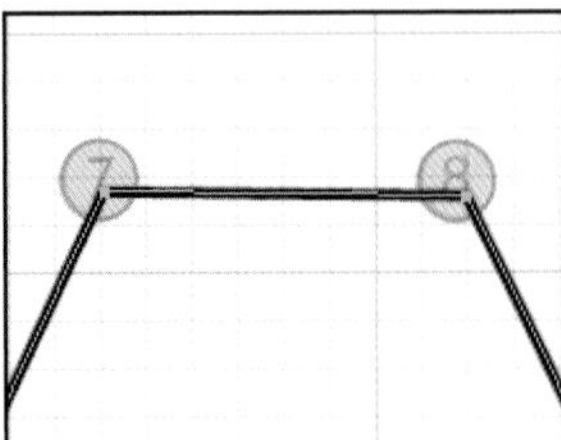

The two end points are connected.

11 Choose File > Save, then choose File > Close.

Working with Live Trace

There are times when it may be inefficient to draw complex illustrations by hand if a suitable raster version exists. At times like this, it may be better to simply scan the original artwork and use the Live Trace feature in Illustrator to have the application convert it into vector art for you.

Using the tracing presets

The Live Trace feature in Illustrator comes complete with various presets for rendering a wide variety of artwork into vector form.

1 Choose File > Open. In the Open dialog box, navigate to the ai05lessons folder and select the ai0504.ai file. This is a practice file containing an embedded JPEG graphic that you will modify in the following exercises.

   Choose File > Save As. In the Save As dialog box, navigate to the ai05lessons folder and type **ai0504_work.ai** in the Name text field. Press Save.

2 Choose the Selection tool (↖) from the Tools panel and select the butterfly image. Locate the Live Trace button in the Control panel at the top of the workspace.

3 Press the arrow next to the Live Trace button and select Hand Drawn Sketch. This option renders the entire drawing as lines and is not suitable for this image, as it would eliminate the wide range of line weights used in the original drawing.

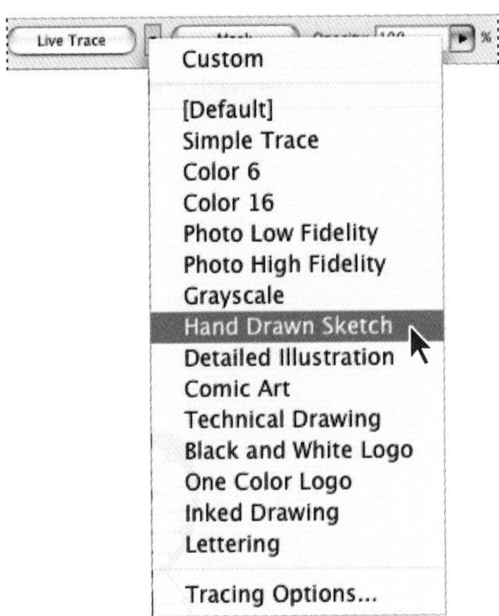

The Live Trace Preset Options.

4 Select the Inked Drawing preset from the Preset drop-down menu to have the program retrace the image with new settings. This is better, but several of the spots on the bottom wings vanish and the lines don't seem to match up with each other.

The image shown using the Inked Drawing preset.

5 With the image still selected, select the Comic Art preset from the Live Trace drop-down menu to have the program retrace the image with new settings. This preset seems to more closely match the artwork than the two previous choices.

The image shown using the Comic Art Live Trace preset.

Even the best of presets are guesses for what will probably work well with the provided type of artwork. For more control over the conversion, you can tweak the preset in the Tracing Options dialog box. Working with the Tracing Options dialog box is covered in the next section.

6 Choose File > Save to save your work.

Understanding tracing options

While the Tracing presets often produce acceptable results, the Tracing Options dialog box allows you to determine the specific settings for the tracing of a particular object.

1 With the traced image of the butterfly still selected, press the Tracing Options button (▤) next to the Preset drop-down menu in the Control panel to open the Tracing Options dialog box.

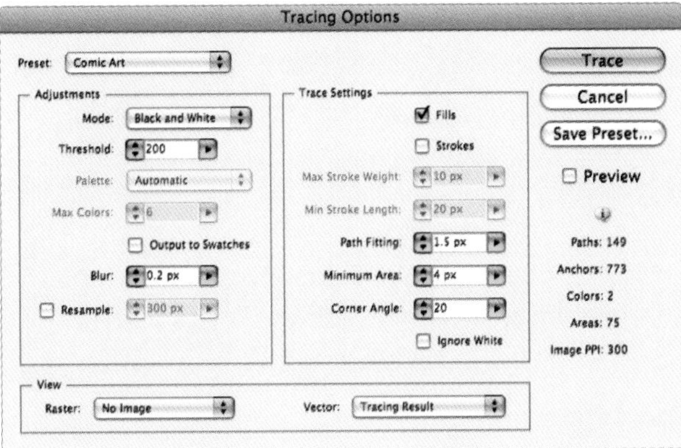

The Tracing Options dialog box.

2 The Tracing Options dialog box is divided into four different sections: Preset, Adjustments, Trace Settings, and View.

Preset: This drop-down menu is used to select which preset's options to display in the dialog box.

Adjustments: This controls the options that govern what happens to an image before the tracing operation is performed, as well as how colors are handled after the operation.

ADJUSTMENT	USE
Mode	Specifies a color mode for the tracing result. The choices in this menu are Color, Black & White, or Grayscale.
Threshold	Specifies a value for generating a black-and-white tracing result from the original image. All pixels lighter than the Threshold value are converted to white, while all pixels darker than the Threshold value are converted to black. (This option is available only when Mode is set to Black and White.)
Palette	Specifies a panel for generating a color or grayscale tracing from the original image. (This option is available only when Mode is set to Color or Grayscale.) To let Illustrator determine the colors in the tracing, select Automatic. To use a custom panel for the tracing, select a swatch library name. The swatch library must be open in order for it to appear in the panel menu.

ADJUSTMENT	USE
Max Colors	Active only when the Color or Grayscale option is selected in the mode menu and when the Palette menu is set to automatic. The Max Colors menu is used to specify the maximum number of colors that will be rendered in the tracing result.
Output To Swatches	Creates a new swatch in the Swatches panel for each color in the tracing result.
Blur	Blurs the original image before generating the tracing result. Select this option to reduce small artifacts and smooth jagged edges in the tracing result.
Resample	Resamples the original image to the specified resolution before generating the tracing result. This option is useful for speeding up the tracing process for large images but can yield degraded results.

Trace Settings: This controls the setting for the tracing operation.

SETTING	USE
Fills	Creates filled regions in the tracing result.
Strokes	Creates stroked paths in the tracing result.
Max Stroke Weight	Specifies the maximum width of features in the original image that can be stroked. Features larger than the maximum width become outlined areas in the tracing result.
Min Stroke Length	Specifies the minimum length of features in the original image that can be stroked. Features smaller than the minimum length are omitted from the tracing result.
Path Fitting	Controls the distance between the traced shape and the original pixel shape. Lower values create a path that is closer to the original pixel shapes, while higher values create looser-fitting paths.
Minimum Area	Specifies the smallest feature in the original image that will be traced. The value for this property is based on the overall area of the objects being traced.
Corner Angle	Controls the sharpness of a turn in the original image that is considered a corner anchor point in the tracing result. For more information on the difference between a corner anchor point and a smooth anchor point, you should review the sections on working with anchor points and drawing with the Pen tool earlier in this lesson.

View: This controls how the original bitmap image and vector result are displayed on the artboard.

3 In the Tracing Options dialog box, press the arrow next to the Threshold text field and change the value to 50. This changes the black and white balance of the traced image and makes the spots on the lower part of the wing more distinct.

4 Highlight the value in the Path Fitting text field and type **.5 px**.

5 Changing any setting in the dialog box, as you have done here, creates a custom tracing preset. To save this preset for later use, press the Save Preset button.

6 In the Save Tracing Preset dialog box, type **Modified Comic** into the Name text field and press OK. Press Trace to trace the butterfly image.

7 Choose File > Save to save your work.

Expanding Live Traced artwork

You may have noticed by now that even though you can change the tracing setting of the image, you don't have access to the anchor points that make up the new vector artwork. This is because the tracing is a type of intermediate stage between the original raster graphic and the fully editable vector artwork that Illustrator typically creates. To make the live traced artwork fully editable requires that you expand it.

1 With the traced image of the butterfly still selected, press the Expand button in the Control panel. The paths that make up the traced artwork are now fully editable.

2 When the original bitmap was traced, the white background became a shape. This can cause a problem, as you probably don't want a white frame around your vector artwork. Choose the Direct Selection tool (↖) from the Tools panel and click the artboard to deselect all objects, then click to select the white area behind the butterfly.

The white shape is selected.

3 Press the Backspace (Windows) or Delete (Mac OS) key on the keyboard to remove the white from the artboard, leaving only the butterfly tracing itself.

4 Choose File > Save to save your work.

Another way to avoid including white objects when you trace bitmap objects is to choose the Ignore White checkbox in the Live Trace settings window at the time you start the Live Trace.

Working with Live Paint

Traditionally Illustrator required a closed path in order to fill an area with color. Live Paint turns this working method on its head and gives the Illustrator artist the ability to fill color into any area created by overlapping lines or shapes.

Creating a Live Paint group

The Live Paint tools, the Live Paint Bucket tool, and the Live Paint Selection tool can only affect objects that are part of a Live Paint group.

1 Choose the Selection tool (↖) from the Tools panel and select the expanded image of the butterfly. Choose Object > Live Paint > Make to convert the artwork into a Live Paint group.

When you have a Live Paint group selected, a small symbol that looks like a snowflake or a star appears in each marker of the bounding box that surrounds it.

2 Choose File > Save to save your work.

Setting Gap Detection options

Earlier in this lesson, you learned that the areas that can receive color must be defined by overlapping lines. This isn't always the case though; it is possible to tell the program that two lines are close enough together to constitute an enclosed area. To do this, you must work with the Gap Detection options.

1 Choose Object > Live Paint > Gap Options.

2 In the Gap Options dialog box, make sure the *Gap Detection* checkbox is selected, and choose Medium Gaps from the Paint stops at drop-down menu. This allows paint to fill any area that has less than a 6-pt opening.

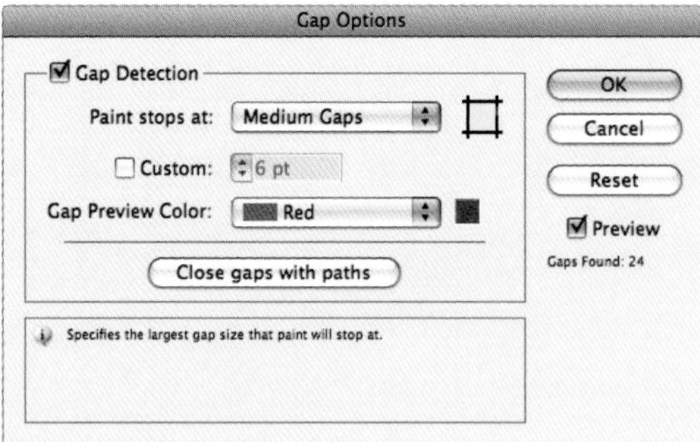

The Gap Options dialog box.

A progress bar may appear, temporarily freezing the screen while the dialogs setting are updated on your Live Paint group.

3 Press OK to close the dialog box.

4 Using the Selection tool (), click an empty area of the artboard to deselect the butterfly.

5 Choose File > Save to save your work.

Using the Live Paint Bucket tool

The Live Paint Bucket tool is used to fill enclosed areas with color. When combined with the Live Paint group's Gap Options, the Live Paint Bucket tool fills any area composed of overlapping paths or semi-overlapping paths with the currently selected fill color. The tool's options can also be set so that it can apply the active fill, the stroke color, or both.

1 Choose the Live Paint Bucket tool () in the Tools panel. Press the Swatches button () in the dock on the right side of the workspace to open the Swatches panel. One of the color groups in the Swatches panel is called *Grape blow Pop*. Select the third color in this group, a lavender, as your fill color.

2 Hover the cursor over the first open area of the left wing. The area highlights red, indicating that it can be filled with the Live Paint Bucket tool. Click on the area to fill it with the current fill color.

Fill the area with color using the Live Paint feature.

3 Fill in the rest of the top wings with the same color.

4 Press the right arrow key on the keyboard to select the next color swatch in the swatch group. Fill the remaining white area of the wings with the darker purple.

Fill the remaining areas.

Double-click on the Live Paint Bucket tool to open the Tool Options dialog box. In this dialog box, you can adjust the tool's highlighting options, as well as whether the tool can color fill, strokes, or both.

5 Choose File > Save to save your work.

Using the Live Paint Selection tool

The Live Paint Selection tool is used to select areas in a Live Paint group and assign colors to them.

1 Choose the Live Paint Selection tool from the Tools panel.

2 Select the black circle on the top-left wing to select it, then hold the Shift key on the keyboard and select the right black circle.

Select both circles.

3 Choose the white color swatch from the Fill Color drop-down menu in the Control panel to fill the circle with the new color.

4 Choose File > Save, and choose File > Close to close the file.

Congratulations! You have completed Lesson 5, "Working with the Drawing Tools."

Self study

Create a basic composition by overlapping two simple shapes within a frame. Convert the three objects (the two shapes and the frame) into a Live Paint group. Make multiple copies of this Live Paint group and then, using only black-and-white, create different color variations for these compositions with the Live Paint Bucket tool.

Another good exercise is to scan in a variety of images, black-and-white and color, and test the various Live Trace presets.

Review

Questions

1 When drawing with the Pen tool, how does creating the first point of a straight line differ from creating the first point of a curved line?

2 How do you import a bitmap image that you want to trace in Illustrator?

3 How can you set a Live Paint group to treat areas that do not have overlapping paths as areas that can be filled with color?

Answers

1 To create the first point for a straight line, you must click and release the Pen tool. When creating a curved line, you should click and drag the Pen tool in the direction of the curve you want to create.

2 Use the File > Place command and check the *Template* option in the Place dialog box. While the Template option is not required, it is helpful for tracing scanned artwork.

3 By turning on Gap Detection (Object > Live Paint > Gap Detection), you can fill areas that do not have overlapping paths.

Working with and Formatting Text

What you'll learn in this lesson:

- Importing text from an external file
- Changing text formatting
- Saving character and paragraph styles
- Setting type on a curved path
- Applying text wrap to an object

Adobe Illustrator CS4 boasts extensive text handling features. Whether you are setting type for the caption of a photo or creating text for a headline, in this lesson, you'll discover how Illustrator provides you with the tools and flexibility you need to work with text.

Starting up

Before starting, make sure that your tools and panels are consistent by resetting your workspace. See "Resetting Adobe Illustrator CS4 Preferences" on page 3.

You will work with several files from the ai06lessons folder in this lesson. Make sure that you have loaded the ailessons folder onto your hard drive from the supplied DVD. See "Loading lesson files" on page 4.

See Lesson 6 in action!

Use the accompanying video to gain a better understanding of how to use some of the features shown in this lesson. The video tutorial for this lesson can be found on the included DVD.

Formatting type

Adobe Illustrator CS4 provides several options for formatting type in your document. Depending on your desired result, you may want to set some of these options that change the overall appearance of the type. Let's explore the different options that are available to you.

1 Launch Adobe Illustrator CS4.

2 Press the Go to Bridge button (▶Br) in the upper-right corner of the Control panel.

3 Navigate to the ai06lessons folder within Bridge, and double-click the file named ai0601.ai. The file opens in Adobe Illustrator.

4 In Illustrator, choose File > Save As. In the Save As dialog box, navigate to the ai06lessons folder and type **ai0601_work.ai** in the Name text field. Press Save. If a dialog box appears stating that changing a used spot color to a process color can generate unexpected results, press Continue. In the Illustrator Options dialog box, leave the settings at their defaults and press OK.

5 To be sure that all the panels and tools are easy to find, choose Window > Workspace > Essentials. This resets your tools and panels to their default locations.

6 This document was created using layers, so before you begin working, open the Layers panel, either by pressing the Layers button (◈) in the dock on the right side of the workspace, or by choosing Window > Layers. Click on the Artwork layer, the second layer listed in the Layers panel, to make it active.

A word on legacy text

Type objects that were created in Illustrator 10 and earlier cannot be edited in Illustrator CS4 until those type objects are updated. You will encounter legacy text only if you open an Illustrator document or copy and paste text from an Illustrator document that was created in version 10 and earlier. Upon opening the file from a previous version of Illustrator, you see a dialog box asking you if you would like to convert the type. Choose No. The reason for this dialog box is that type can shift during the updating of legacy text to a new version of Illustrator, causing reflow and other physical changes. Once the document opens, select the text that needs to be converted and choose Type > Legacy Text > Update Selected Legacy Text. This allows you to see any adjustments as the text is updated. Once updated, the text can be edited and adjusted as needed.

It isn't mandatory that legacy text be updated at all. If you need to open a document that contains legacy text, you can simply choose not to update the text. You can still view the text on-screen and print your artwork as needed; you just can't edit text that hasn't been updated.

7 Activate the Type tool (T) in the Tools panel, then click once in the upper-left corner of the box's left panel, which has an image of a biker on it.

Clicking once anywhere on the artboard with the Type tool creates point type. Point type simply allows you to type text wherever you click with the cursor. Point type is generally used when setting a single line of copy or a headline. Later in this lesson, you'll learn about another method of setting text, called area type.

A blinking cursor appears where you clicked. To more closely see the cursor and the text you will type, zoom in on the document by pressing Ctrl+(plus sign) (Windows) or Command+(plus sign) (Mac OS) a few times. If you need to reposition the artboard after increasing the page magnification, use the Hand tool (✋).

8 Type **Nutz provides energy to get you through the day!**

9 With the Type tool still selected, triple-click anywhere within the type you just created to select the whole line of type.

10 Click on the Character link in the Control panel at the top of the workspace to open the Character panel. Change the font to Myriad Pro Bold Italic and set the font size to 18 pt.

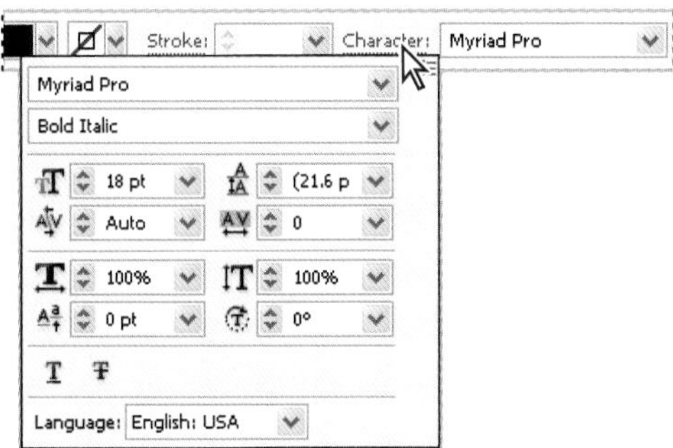

The Character panel allows you to change the attributes of the selected type.

Some character formatting options are available directly within the Control panel. Character formatting can also be accomplished by choosing Window > Type > Character.

11 To make the type more readable, change the color of the selected type to white by clicking on the Fill color swatch in the Control panel and choosing the white swatch from the Swatches panel that appears.

The word *Nutz* is the name of the fictional company that sells the box of mixed nuts you are creating. Because it is a company name, it should have an ® symbol next to it, indicating that the name is a registered trademark.

12 Click once to the immediate right of the word *Nutz* and choose Type > Glyphs to open the Glyphs panel. The Glyphs panel displays every symbol available in the currently chosen font. Scroll through the Glyphs panel, locate the ® symbol, and double-click it to insert that symbol at the location of your cursor. Close the Glyphs panel.

13 Press Shift+Ctrl+A (Windows) or Shift+Command+A (Mac OS) to deselect everything in your document. Choose File > Save to save your work.

OpenType fonts

OpenType is a relatively new font format that has a number of advantages over other formats. OpenType fonts are cross-platform, which means they can be used on the Windows and Mac OS platforms alike. In addition, OpenType fonts are composed of a single file, unlike older Postscript fonts, which require a separate screen and printer font file in order to work properly. OpenType fonts support expanded character sets and layout features that provide richer linguistic support and advanced typographic control. Most of the large font foundries are now releasing fonts in the OpenType format, and many OpenType fonts are now based upon PostScript, allowing them to be used for high-resolution imaging and printing.

Adobe Illustrator takes full advantage of the features available with OpenType fonts. In fact, Illustrator has dedicated an entire panel within the application to controlling the features of OpenType. You can open this panel by choosing Window > Type > OpenType.

Paragraph formatting

Unlike character formatting, paragraph formatting can only be applied to one or more paragraphs at a time. You can't apply a paragraph formatting attribute to a word, for instance; it's the whole paragraph or nothing. The key factor with paragraph formatting is a hidden character within a body of text that defines the end of one paragraph and the beginning of another—the paragraph return, which is created when you press Enter (Windows) or Return (Mac OS) on your keyboard. Let's apply some paragraph formatting to the text in your artwork.

1 Press Ctrl+0 (Windows) or Command+0 (Mac OS) to see the entire project, then select the Zoom tool (🔍) from the Tools panel and zoom in on the area below the nutrition facts.

The Zoom tool can also be accessed by pressing and holding Ctrl+spacebar (Windows) or Command+spacebar (Mac OS), then clicking on the area you want to magnify while still holding down the key combination.

2 Using the Type tool (T), click and drag to create a type area beneath the nutrition facts. To be certain that you create a new area for text, confirm that the cursor icon displays the I-beam with a dotted frame around the edges (⌶) before clicking and dragging. A blinking cursor appears in the upper-left corner of the frame that you just drew.

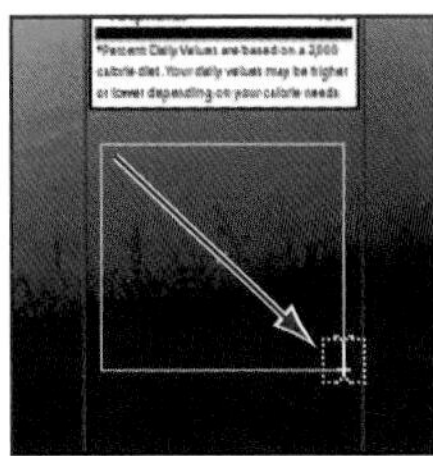

Using the Type tool, drag to create a type area.

By clicking and dragging with the Type tool, you create area type. Area type differs from point type in that it acts as a text container and allows you to resize the frame while the text reflows within it. Point type doesn't work this way; if you resize a point type frame, you scale the text within it.

3 Choose File > Place. In the Place dialog box, navigate to the Text folder inside the ai06lessons folder. Select the ingredients.txt file and press Place. In the Text Import Options dialog box that appears, leave the settings at their defaults and press OK. The contents of the ingredients.txt file are placed inside the text area.

4 Press Ctrl+A (Windows) or Command+A (Mac OS) to select all the text you just placed. In the Control panel, set the font to Myriad Pro Bold Condensed, and the size to 8 pt.

5 Click on the Fill color swatch in the Control panel and choose the White swatch from the swatch options to turn the text white. Choose Type > Change Case > UPPERCASE to make all the text uppercase.

6 Click once within the ingredients text, then click the Paragraph text in the Control panel at the top of your screen to reveal the Paragraph panel. Press the Justify with Last Line Aligned Left button at the top of the Paragraph panel to change the alignment of the text.

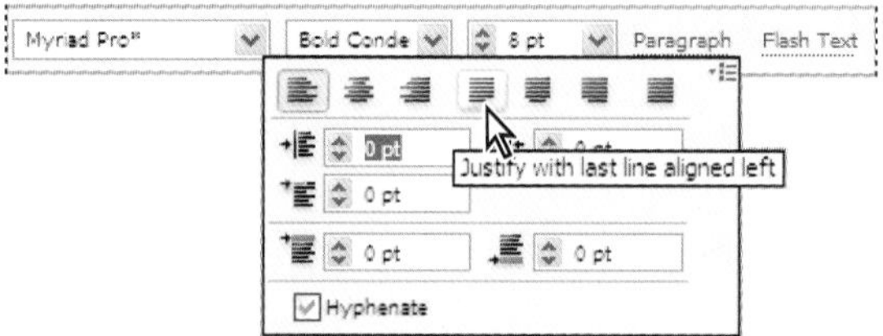

The Paragraph panel allows you to change the alignment of text for the entire paragraph as well as other paragraph-level attributes.

7 After formatting, the type may not fill the frame. To tidy things up, switch to the Selection tool (↖) and drag the center frame handle at the bottom of the frame upward to reduce the frame's size.

You can alter the size of the text frame by dragging one of the frame handles.

8 Choose File > Save to save your work. Keep the file open.

Formatting imported type

Next, you'll import some additional text that will appear on the back of the box, and apply additional paragraph formatting to the text.

1 Choose View > Fit in Window, or press Ctrl+0 (Windows)/Command+0 (Mac OS) to see the entire spread. Choose the Type tool (T) from the Tools panel, then click and drag to create a large type area on the back of the box (the box panel on the right side of your screen) package. As you did in the previous exercise, be certain that you create a new area for text by confirming that the cursor icon displays the I-beam with a dotted frame around the edges () before clicking and dragging.

2 To precisely position the text area, open the Transform panel by clicking on the Transform text on the far right side of the Control panel. Click in the center of the reference point locator () to determine that all transformations are made relative to the center of the text area. Type **1148 pt** into the X text field, **425 pt** into the Y text field, **450 pt** into the W text field, and **550 pt** into the H text field.

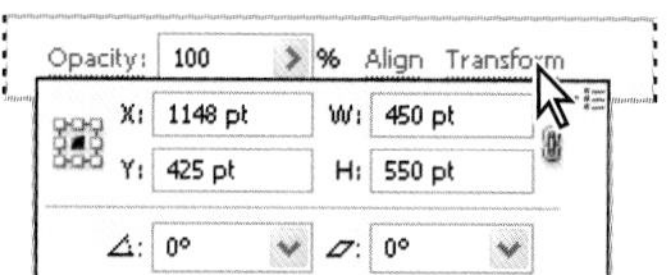

The Transform panel allows you to precisely position and size objects in your document.

3 Choose Type > Area Type Options. In Columns area of the Area Type Options dialog box, type **2** for the number of columns, **3** in the Span text field, and **.25** for the gutter. Press OK.

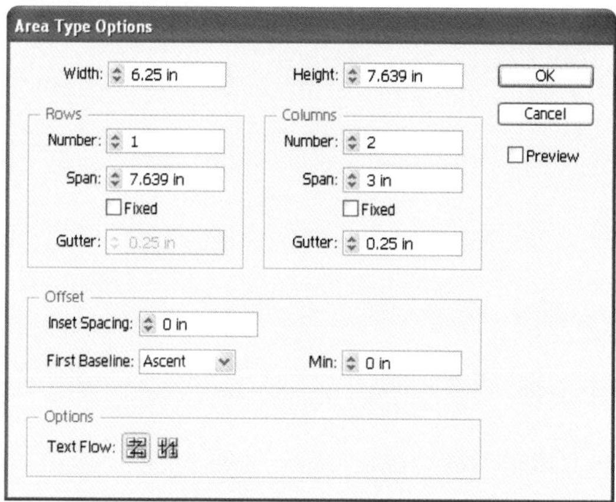

The Area Type Options dialog box allows you to customize attributes of the selected area type.

4 Click in the top-left corner of the text area with your Type tool to place the cursor within the frame. Choose File > Place. In the Place dialog box, navigate to the Text folder within the ai06lessons folder and select the nuts.txt file. Press Place. In the Text Import Options dialog box, leave the settings at their defaults and press OK. The text from the file appears within the text area, displayed in two columns.

5 Place the cursor anywhere within the text and press Ctrl+A (Windows) or Command+A (Mac OS) to select all the text. Click on the Fill color swatch in the Control panel and choose White from the Swatches panel. This is just a temporary fix so that you can see the selected text against the dark background.

6 Press Ctrl+(plus sign) (Windows)/Command+(plus sign) (Mac OS) twice to better see the text. Highlight the first line of type in the text area (which reads, *The Benefits of Nuts)*, and in the Control panel, change the font to Myriad Pro Bold and the size to 18 pt. Now the heading, *The Benefits of Nuts*, stands out from the accompanying body text. In a later exercise, you will take these attributes and turn them into a general style for headings.

7 Click within the first full paragraph of text (which begins with, *Most people that you talk to...*), click on the Paragraph link in the Control panel, and set the alignment to Justify with last line aligned left. Set the spacing after the paragraph to 8 pt.

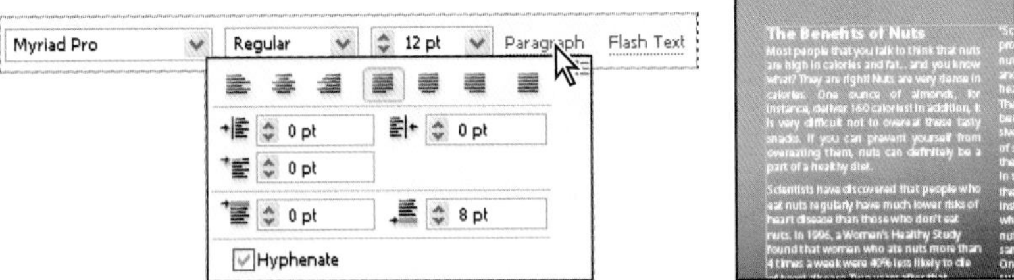

Adding space after a paragraph adds space without using an empty hard return in the copy.

8 Choose File > Save to save your work. Keep it open for the next part of the lesson.

You have now formatted some of the text. In the next section, you'll create styles to streamline the formatting of additional text in your project.

Space before and after

In the days of the typewriter, the method used to create additional space between paragraphs of text was to press the Enter or Return key twice; this was called a double-return. With a typewriter, a double-return is really the only way to accomplish this effect and may seem antiquated, but this practice is, interestingly, still in use to this day, even though there is a much better way.

You may be wondering why (and if) it matters how you add space between paragraphs. The problem with using a double-return is that doing so completely limits the control that you have over the space between paragraphs. And if you need to adjust the spacing between paragraphs for any reason, the only option you have is to manually adjust that return by changing the leading and or point size of the return. This can be very time-consuming. The solution: space before and after. Using the space before and after options allows you to add space before and/or after a paragraph without adding empty returns between paragraphs. What's more, by including that spacing in a paragraph style, you can control the space between all paragraphs in your document with just a few clicks! It's the difference between a 30-second type change and a 30-minute type change.

Paragraph and character styles

Illustrator CS4 allows you to save the formatting applied to text as a style. A style is simply a way to apply consistent formatting to text without having to do it manually. There are two types of styles that can be created in Illustrator: paragraph styles and character styles. As their names imply, paragraph styles can only be applied to an entire paragraph, while character styles can be applied to a single character or a range of characters in your text. Let's see how you can use these styles in your project.

1 With your ai0601_work.ai file still open, click once within the first line of text in the text area on the back of the box (*The Benefits of Nuts*). Choose Window > Type > Paragraph Styles to open the Paragraph Styles panel.

2 Press the panel menu button (▾≡) in the upper-right corner of the Paragraph Styles panel. Choose New Paragraph Style. In the New Paragraph Style dialog box, type **Subhead** in the Style Name text field. Press OK. The new style you created appears in the Paragraph Styles panel.

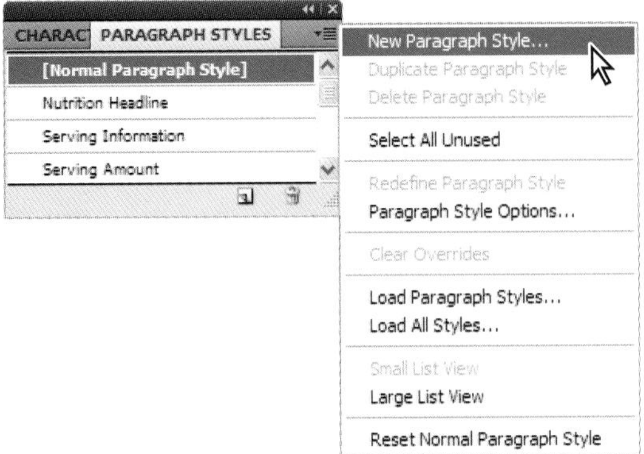

Choose New Paragraph Style from the Paragraph Styles panel menu; all the attributes of the text are automatically added to the style.

3 Highlight that first line (*The Benefits of Nuts*) with your Type tool (T), and click on Subhead in your Paragraph Styles panel to apply this style to the selected text.

4 Repeat steps 2 and 3, this time clicking inside the first full paragraph of text (beginning with *Most people...*) and naming the style **Body**. Don't forget to apply the Body style to the paragraph after you create it.

When you apply styles to text, if you see a plus sign (+) to the right of the style name, you may need to click on the name of the style once more to clear that plus sign, or Alt+click (Windows)/ Option+click (Mac OS) as you apply the style to cause your text to appear properly. A plus sign next to a style name indicates that the text contains overrides or doesn't match the definition of the style.

5 Finish styling the rest of the copy on the back of the box, applying the Body style to all the paragraphs and the Subhead style to the *Nuts Nuts Nuts* and *Only the Best!* headers.

6 Click the Character Styles tab next to the Paragraph Styles panel to reveal the Character Styles panel. Find the line in the second full paragraph (which starts with *In 2002...*) and highlight the phrase *Physician's Health Study*. In the Control panel, change the font to Myriad Pro Italic.

7 With the text still selected, press the panel menu button in the Character Styles panel, then choose New Character Style. In the New Character Styles dialog box, type **Body Italic** in the Style Name text field. Press OK.

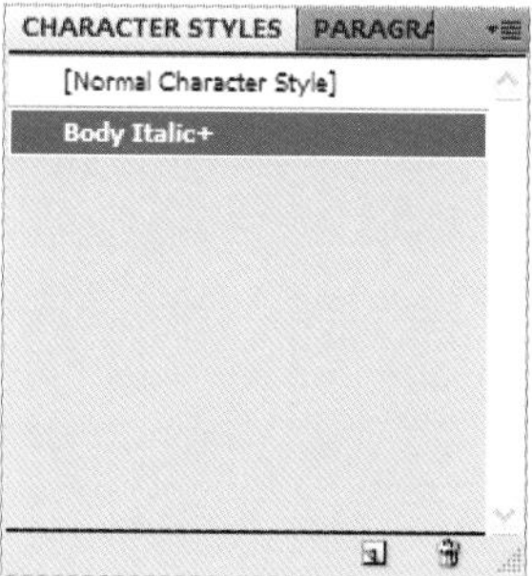

Create a new character style named Body Italic.

8 Apply the Body Italic character style to the selected text by clicking on the Body Italic entry in the Character Styles panel.

9 Now navigate to the bottom of the first column of text, highlight the word *FDA*, and apply the Body Italic character style to it as well. Repeat this process for the following sentence (which begins with *Scientific evidence...*).

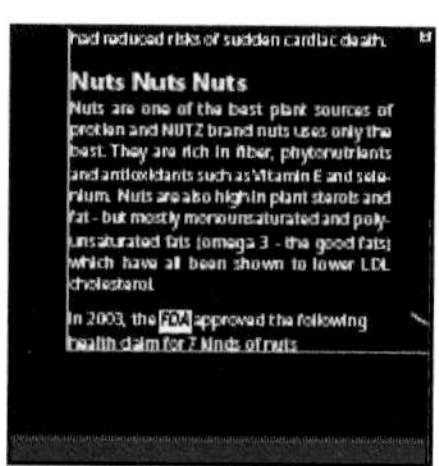

Apply the Body Italic character style.

10 Choose File > Save to save your work. Keep the file open for the next part of the lesson.

Now that your copy has been styled, maybe the subheads would look better in a different color. You could manually select each subhead and change its color, but it is much more efficient to simply edit the style, now that all the subheads have been styled using a paragraph style.

Editing styles

Styles can be edited directly from the Paragraph Styles or Character Styles panels.

1 Choose Select > Deselect, or press Shift+Ctrl+A (Windows) or Shift+Command+A (Mac OS), to deselect all the items in your document.

2 Click the Paragraph Styles tab next to the Character Styles panel to bring the Paragraph Styles panel forward. Double-click on the Subhead style in the Paragraph Styles panel.

3 In the resulting Paragraph Styles Options dialog box, make sure the *Preview* check box in the lower-left corner is checked so that you can see the changes before you press OK. Click the Character Color entry on the left side of the dialog box and select the red swatch, named Die Tracing, from the list of swatches. You may need to reposition the Paragraph Style Options dialog box so that you can see the change in your artwork. Press OK.

4 Choose Select > Deselect, or press Shift+Ctrl+A (Windows) or Shift+Command+A (Mac OS), to deselect all the items in your document.

5 Double-click on the Body style in the Paragraph Styles panel.

6 Click on the Basic Character Formats entry on the left side of the dialog box. Choose Minion Pro from the Font Family drop-down menu and Regular from the Font Style drop-down menu. Press OK. This adjusts the style settings and all the fonts throughout the document to which the style is applied.

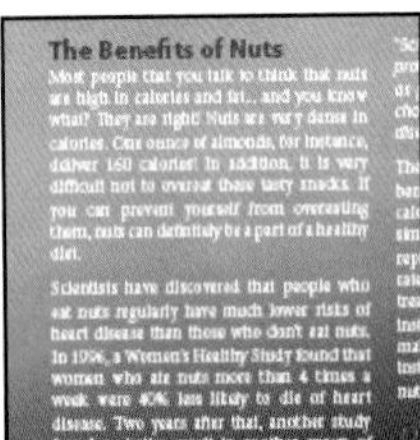

The finished styles for body and headers.

7 Press Ctrl+S (Windows) or Command+S (Mac OS) to save your work. Keep the file open.

Loading styles

Styles can also be imported from other Illustrator documents. This not only allows you to maintain consistency across multiple related documents, but also saves you the time and hassle of recreating styles manually. In the following steps, you will import a style from another Illustrator file to reuse in your project.

1 From the Paragraph Styles panel menu (▾≡), choose Load Paragraph Styles. The Select a File to Import dialog box appears. Navigate to the ai06lessons folder and select the styles.ai file. Press Open and notice that a new style, called Vitamins, has been added to the Paragraph Styles panel.

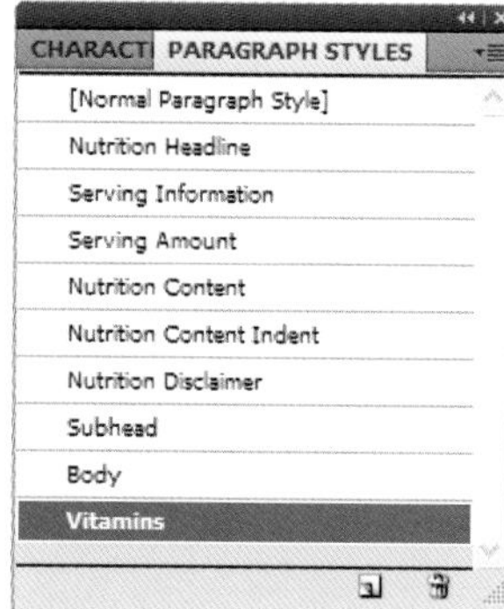

By creating a character style, you can efficiently apply character-based formatting to your text.

2 Choose View > Fit All in Window, then zoom in on the lower-left corner of the front of the Nutz box, where there are vitamins and minerals listed in white text. Apply the Subhead paragraph style to the words *Vitamins* and *Minerals*. Apply the Vitamins paragraph style to the remainder of the text. If you see a plus sign next to the style after applying the style, simply Alt+click (Windows) or Option+click (Mac OS) on the style to remove the plus sign.

3 Choose File > Save to save your work.

Text wrap

Illustrator CS4 allows your text, images, and objects to interact with each other by applying text wrap to objects, which causes the text to wrap around other objects in your Illustrator document. In the following steps, you'll apply text wrap to an image that is already in your document.

1 Press Ctrl+0 (Windows) or Command+0 (Mac OS) to fit the entire spread in the window, then press Ctrl+(minus sign) (Windows) or Command+(minus sign) (Mac OS) twice, at which point you'll see a single almond below and to the right of the spread.

When you place an image in Illustrator, it is typically a square. The almond image is being clipped using a clipping mask, which gives it the proper shape of an almond.

2 Activate the Selection tool (↖) from the Tools panel. Drag the image of the almond so that it is on top of the two-column text on the back of the box (on your right). Resize the almond to approximately 50% by dragging a corner handle while holding down the Shift key to keep its proportions intact.

3 Once the image is in the desired position and size, right-click (Windows) or Ctrl+click (Mac OS) on the almond image and choose Arrange > Bring to Front. Leave the image selected and choose Object > Text Wrap > Make. This applies text wrap to the selected image.

4 Press Ctrl+(plus sign) (Windows) or Command+(plus sign) (Mac OS) to zoom in on the almond image.

5 To adjust how closely the text wraps around the image, make sure that the image is still selected and choose Object > Text Wrap > Text Wrap Options. In the Text Wrap Options dialog box, check the *Preview* checkbox and increase the offset amount to 10 pt. Press OK.

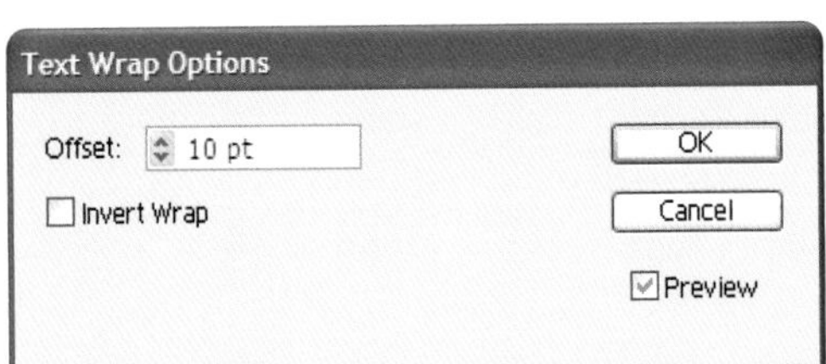

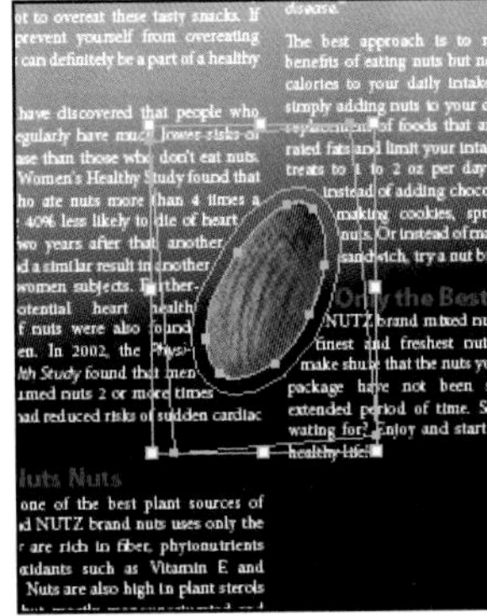

The Text Wrap Options dialog box allows you to adjust the distance that the text is offset from the edge of the image.

6 Choose File > Save. Keep the document open for the next part of the lesson.

Advanced techniques with text

Adobe Illustrator CS4 offers a variety of advanced tools for working with text. Let's explore some of those techniques now!

Text on a path

In Illustrator CS4, type can be applied to a path of just about any shape. You can use the Pen tool (✎), the Pencil tool (✐), or any of the shape tools to draw a path on which type can be applied. In the following steps, you'll add some text to a path that already exists on the box for creative effect.

1 With your ai0601_work.ai file still open, zoom in on the curved path in the lower-right corner of the back of the box.

2 Click and hold the Type tool (T) in the Tools panel and choose the Type on a Path tool (✓). Click on the far-left side of the path; this converts the existing path to a type path and allows you to enter and edit text on the path.

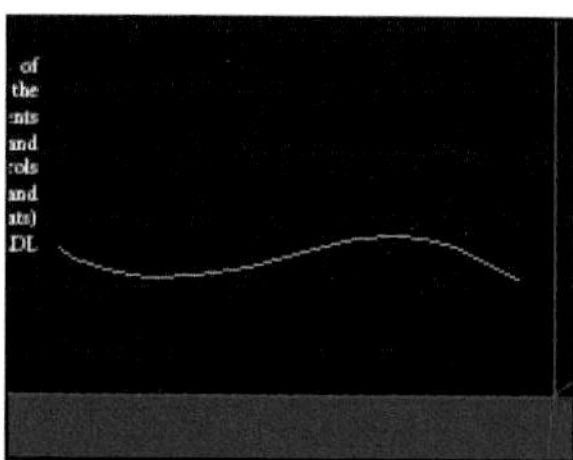

Place your Type on a Path cursor at the end of the curved line to type along it.

3 In the Control panel, click on the Fill color swatch and select the white color from the Swatches panel. Change the font to Myriad Pro Bold Condensed, then type **17** in the Size text field.

4 Type **Contains 14 Essential Vitamins and Minerals**. If the text does not fit completely on the path, choose Edit > Undo to remove the text and Edit > Undo again to remove the insertion point on the path. Repeat steps 2, 3, and 4.

The text you entered.

5 Press Ctrl+S (Windows) or Command+S (Mac OS) to save your work.

Warping text

One of the great features of Adobe Illustrator CS4 is its ability to apply effects that distort and transform type in many ways, while keeping the text editable. This is advantageous in that it makes the process of editing or modifying text very efficient. Let's apply an effect to the NUTZ logo to enhance its appearance.

1 Press Shift+Ctrl+A (Windows) or Shift+Command+A (Mac OS) to deselect all objects in your document. Choose View > Fit in Window to see the entire box. Activate the Selection tool (↖) and click on the word *NUTZ* on the front cover of the box.

2 Choose Effect > Warp > Bulge.

3 In the Warp Options dialog box, turn on the Preview checkbox so that you can see the changes to your artwork as you adjust the values in the dialog box. Make sure the *Horizontal* radio button is selected and set the Bend to 75 percent. Press OK.

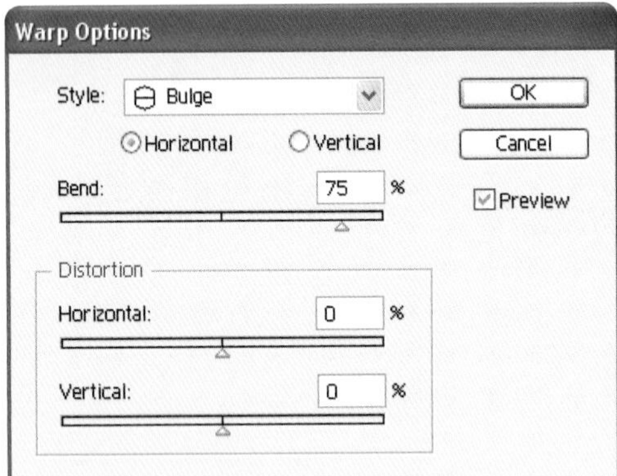

The Warp Options dialog box allows you to adjust the effect until you obtain the desired result.

Now that you've applied the effect to the logo, you will add dimension by applying an image to the text of the logo.

4 Choose File > Place. In the Place dialog box, navigate to the Links folder inside the ai06lessons folder. Select the sky.jpg image and choose Place. A small image of a sky at dusk appears on the spread.

5 Back in Illustrator, position the photo on top of the NUTZ logo and scale the photo so that it completely covers the logo. Do this by dragging one of the corner handles of the image using the Selection tool (↖) and holding down the Shift key on your keyboard. The Shift key constrains the proportions of the image so that it doesn't become stretched.

6 With the photo still selected, press Ctrl+[(Windows) or Command+[(Mac OS) several times until the image appears beneath the NUTZ logo. Ctrl+[(Windows)/Command+[(Mac OS) is the Send Backward command that can also be applied by choosing Object > Arrange > Send Backward.

7 Hold down the Shift key and click on the *NUTZ* text so that both elements are selected at the same time.

8 Press the Transparency icon (◐) in the dock on the right side of the workspace to open the Transparency panel. There is a preview of the selected items in the Transparency panel. If you do not see a preview, press the Transparency panel menu button (▾≡) and choose Show Options.

9 Press the Transparency panel menu button and choose Make Opacity Mask. The text of the logo now masks out the photo everywhere except where the type of the logo appears.

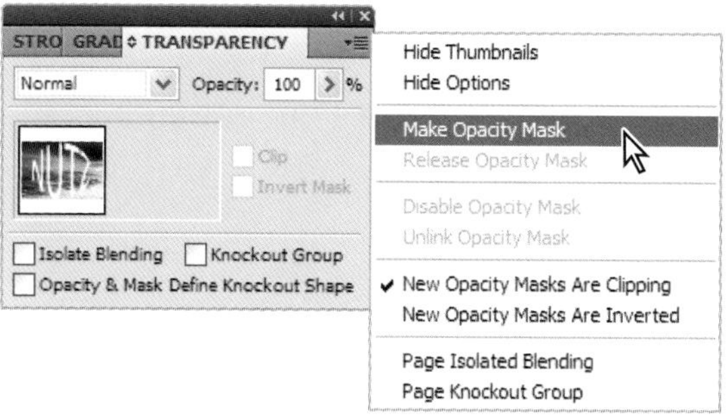

Choose Make Opacity Mask from the Transparency panel menu to make a mask out of the topmost element of your selection.

10 Select both the *NUTZ* and *Mixed* text using the Selection tool (↖) and holding down the Shift key on your keyboard. Choose Object > Group to group the elements.

11 While holding down the Alt (Windows)/Option (Mac OS) key on your keyboard, drag the grouped logo up to the top flap of the box. Holding down the Alt/Option key makes a copy of the object that you are dragging. If necessary, increase the page magnification to more clearly see the work you are performing.

12 Scale down the copied logo by holding the Shift key on your keyboard while dragging one of the logo's corner handles so that it fits on the left side of the box flap.

Scale down the copied image.

13 Choose File > Save to save your work. Keep the file open.

For more information on how to use effects in Illustrator CS4, see Lesson 9, "Using Effects and Transparency."

Text in a shape

In addition to the type features that you applied earlier in the lesson, Illustrator gives you the ability to fit type inside various shapes. In the following steps, you will place some text inside a circle on the side of the Nutz box.

1 Select the Ellipse tool by clicking and holding the Rectangle tool (□) in the Tools panel and choosing the Ellipse tool (○) from the list of options. You can also access the Ellipse tool by pressing the L key on your keyboard.

2 Navigate to the lower portion of the side panel, below the ingredients. Click and drag to draw a circle on the side panel of the box. Hold down the Shift key while you drag to keep the shape proportionate.

3 With the circle still selected, click and hold the Type tool (T) and choose the Area Type tool (T) from the list of options that appears. Click on the path at the top of the circle to convert the circle to a shape that will accommodate area type.

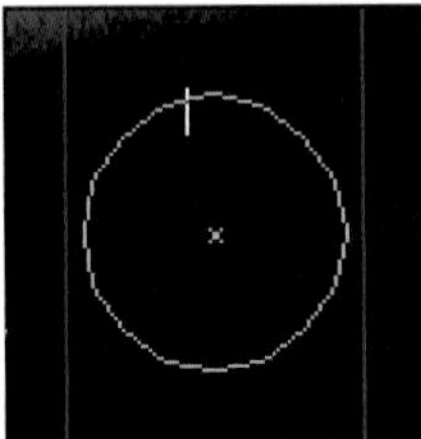

Create a circular text area using the Ellipse tool.

4 Your cursor is now inside the circle.

5 Choose File > Place and navigate to the Text folder inside the ai06lessons folder. Select the benefits.txt file and press Place. In the resulting Text Import Options dialog box, leave the settings at their defaults and press OK.

6 Press Ctrl+A (Windows) or Command+A (Mac OS) to select all the text within the circle. Change the color of the text to white and the paragraph alignment to justified.

7 At this point, you can adjust the text to fit the circle by changing the tracking values (AV) in the Character panel, as well as by adjusting the leading (A) and font size (T) of the type. Sample some of these options, experimenting with different values.

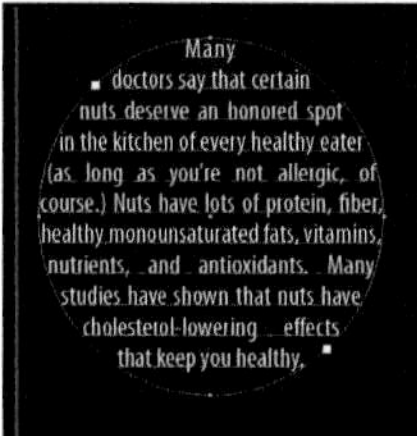

Once you have text in a shape, it can be edited at any time using the standard Type tool.

8 Once you've found a look that you like, choose File > Save to save your work. Keep the file open.

Creating outlines

You might want to modify the character shapes of type itself—you can even do this to type that you have already applied to your artwork. In these instances, you can't alter the shape of characters in live text, so you need to convert the characters to outlines. Converting type to outlines converts live text to editable paths in the shape of the original type. This is also useful when you are sending files to someone else and you don't want to include the fonts. Once type is converted to outlines, you no longer need the original font that was used to create the text. Converting text to outlines is generally not recommended with small body text, as it tends to cause the text to look slightly bolder than the original text. In the following steps, you'll see how text can be converted to outlines to create a headline on the front of the box.

1 Press Shift+Ctrl+A (Windows) or Shift+Command+A (Mac OS) to deselect all objects in your document. Activate the Type tool (T) from the Tools panel, then click in an area on the front of the box to create a point type area. If necessary, increase the magnification using the Zoom tool (🔍) so you can more clearly see your work.

2 Type **A Heart Healthy Snack!**, then press Ctrl+A (Windows) or Command+A (Mac OS) to select all the text. In the Control panel, change the font to Minion Pro Bold Italic, then type 36 into the Size text field. Click on the Fill color swatch and choose a red color from the Swatches panel.

3 Select the type using the Selection tool (↖) and choose Type > Create Outlines. This converts all the selected type to outlines (paths).

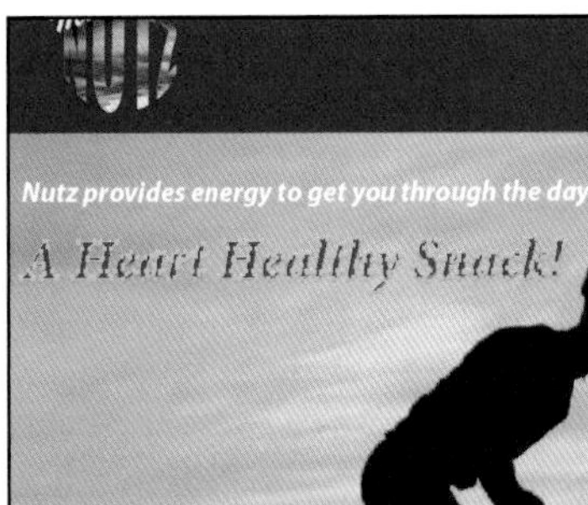

After converting the text to outlines, the text changes appearance and reveals the paths that make up the character shapes.

4 When type is converted to outlines, all the text is grouped so that it moves and adjusts as a collective unit. Ungroup the text by choosing Object > Ungroup.

5 Using the Selection tool, drag a marquee around the word *Heart* to select only that word. Press the Delete key on your keyboard to remove the word.

In the next steps, you will replace the word *Heart* with a vector drawing of a heart.

6 Choose Select > Heart from the menu at the top of your screen. In the Control panel, press the Fill color swatch and choose a red color from the swatches panel to fill the heart image.

7 Drag the drawing of the heart to the empty area of the text outlines where the word *Heart* used to be. Scale and adjust the drawing as you see fit by dragging the corner handle of the object and holding down the Shift key. You may need to zoom in on the remaining text to the right of the heart to close the space and make it look more balanced. Once you finish adjusting the headline, select the heart and the text, then group them by pressing Ctrl+G (Windows) or Command+G (Mac OS).

8 To add a finishing touch to the headline, select it and choose Effect > Stylize > Drop Shadow. In the Drop Shadow dialog box, type **5 pt** for both the X and Y offsets and **4 pt** for blur. Press OK.

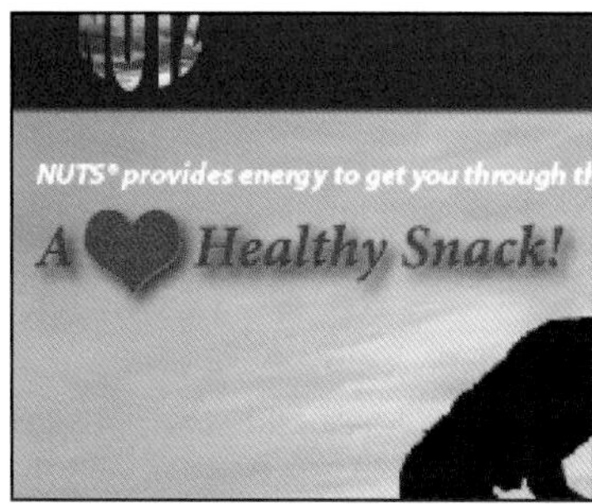

Apply a drop shadow to the headline.

Check spelling

Before you send your project to the client for approval, you should always perform a spell check to verify that there aren't any misspelled words in your document. The Check Spelling command in Adobe Illustrator CS4 compares the words in your document to a built-in dictionary and alerts you to any misspelled words. Spell check your project now.

1 Press Shift+Ctrl+A (Windows) or Shift+Command+A (Mac OS) to deselect all objects on your page. Choose Edit > Check Spelling to open the Check Spelling dialog box.

2 Click on the arrow icon in the lower-left corner of the dialog box to display additional options. Leave both checkboxes in the Find section checked, and check the boxes in the Ignore section to ignore words that are all uppercase and words with numbers. This speeds up the process, as the nutrition label contains several of these instances. Press the Start button to begin the spell checking process.

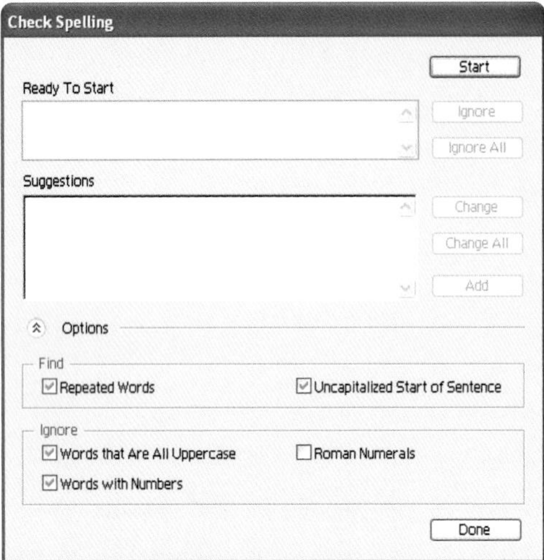

The Check Spelling dialog box allows you to define the parameters that determine what Illustrator flags as problems.

After pressing the Start button, the Check Spelling dialog box displays the errors that it finds in your document. Not all errors are necessarily spelling errors; some are repeated words and other miscellaneous errors. Some of these errors can be corrected by choosing an option offered in the Suggestions window in the middle of the dialog box. Illustrator displays the error at the top of the dialog box and also displays suggestions below it for correcting the error. You have the option of choosing Change, which changes the current error to the suggestion shown in the Suggestions window, or Ignore, which skips the currently flagged error.

3 Continue through the spell check by choosing either Change or Ignore, depending on the error. There are some misspelled words in the document, so as the spell checker flags them, change them to the correct spelling; other errors can be ignored. Make sure that when Illustrator flags the word *NUTZ*, you ignore it.

Just because a word is not found in the dictionary that Illustrator uses to spell check the document, it doesn't necessarily mean that the word is incorrect. For instance, Spell Check finds the word *Folate*. Illustrator doesn't recognize this word even though it is correct. One way to handle this situation is to click the Add button on the right side of the Check Spelling dialog box. This adds the current word to the dictionary so that Illustrator will recognize the word from now on, and will no longer flag it as an error. The Add button is useful when dealing with proper nouns and people's names, especially when they appear more than once in a document or range of documents. By adding a word to the dictionary, Illustrator no longer considers it misspelled.

4 When you have completed checking the entire document, press Done.

5 Choose File > Save to save your work.

Find and Replace

Imagine that this project is due to the client and at the last minute you realize that you omitted the ® symbol next to the NUTZ brand name, identifying it as a registered trademark. Fortunately, Illustrator provides the tool needed to fix this problem quickly. Let's see how easily this can be done.

1 Press Shift+Ctrl+A (Windows) or Shift+Command+A (Mac OS) to deselect all objects on your page. Choose Edit > Find and Replace to display the Find and Replace dialog box.

2 In the Find text field, type **NUTZ** (all caps). In the Replace With text field, type **NUTZ** (all caps) and then click on the arrow to the right of the Replace With text field. From the list of options, choose Registered Trademark Symbol. This inserts an ® next to the word *NUTZ* in the Replace With text field. This is the character equivalent that Illustrator uses for the registered trademark symbol.

3 Press the Find button once to find the first location where NUTZ appears within your project, then press the Replace All button to replace all occurrences of NUTZ with the new text, including the necessary symbol. Adobe Illustrator notifies you that it made three replacements within your document. Press OK, then press Done.

4 Choose File > Save to save your document.

Congratulations! You've finished Lesson 6, "Working with and Formatting Text."

Self study

To add a finishing touch to your document, draw a white rectangle encompassing all the text on the back of the box. Send the rectangle backward until it is behind the text. Now apply a Gaussian Blur with a radius of about 8 pixels and drop the transparency of the rectangle to about 40 percent. This is a great effect that you can use to subdue the background and allow the type to stand out a little bit.

Practice applying text to various shapes that you draw in Illustrator. Use the Pen tool (✒) or the Pencil tool (✎) to draw a path, and then use your Type on a Path tool (⤳) to add type to the shape. You can adjust how type is positioned on a path by dragging the center bracket using your Selection tool and moving it left or right along the path. You can even drag the center bracket down and flip the text to the other side of the path. In addition, draw some closed shapes and practice placing text inside them to see the different effects that you can achieve.

Add different effects to the NUTZ logo to make it stand out a little more. See Lesson 9, "Using Effects and Transparency," for more on applying effects to objects. Try adding an outer glow to the logo, or even a drop shadow with various intensities. You could also experiment with other effects options in the Effects panel. You may want to remove the existing effect first by deleting it from the Appearance panel.

Review

Questions

1 True or false: Effects can only be applied to type that has been converted to paths.

2 If you wanted to put text that wrapped inside a given area of your artwork, would you use point type or area type?

3 Which of Illustrator's features gives you the control needed to maintain consistency and control throughout a range of text in your document?

4 If a word that Illustrator's dictionary doesn't recognize appears several times in your document, how can you stop Illustrator from flagging each instance of the word?

5 Which panel in Illustrator shows you all the characters available within a given font?

Answers

1 False. Effects can be applied to live type and remain editable even after the effect has been applied.

2 You would use area type. Point type doesn't wrap within a given area. Point type only wraps if you apply a hard or soft return to the type.

3 Character and paragraph styles.

4 Add the word to the dictionary by pressing the Add button in the Check Spelling dialog box. This makes the word a recognized word and prevents Illustrator from earmarking it.

5 The Glyphs panel.

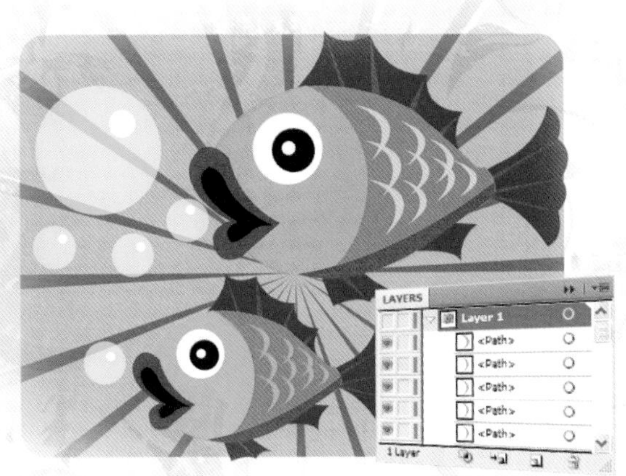

What you'll learn in this lesson:

- Selecting items on a layer
- Locking and hiding layers
- Creating new layers
- Moving items between layers
- Organizing layers

Organizing your Illustrations with Layers

Complex illustrations with many components can make it more difficult to work with and select individual components. In this lesson, you will discover how to use Illustrator CS4's Layers panel to organize and manage your illustrations.

Starting up

Before starting, make sure that your tools and panels are consistent by resetting your workspace. See "Resetting Adobe Illustrator CS4 Preferences" on page 3.

You will work with several files from the ai07lessons folder in this lesson. Make sure that you have loaded the ailessons folder onto your hard drive from the supplied DVD. See "Loading lesson files" on page 4.

See Lesson 7 in action!

Use the accompanying video to gain a better understanding of how to use some of the features shown in this lesson. The video tutorial for this lesson can be found on the included DVD.

Getting to know the Layers panel

Whether you deliberately work with layers or not, every time you create, import, or paste items in an Illustrator document, you are placing those items on a layer. The default layer that is in every new Illustrator document is called Layer 1. The order in which you add new elements to the document determines their arrangement on Layer 1. The latest additions appear on top of the earlier ones; this is called the stacking order. Just like stacking sheets of paper on your desk, the first one placed appears on the bottom of the stack and the most recent one placed is positioned on the top of the stack. The Layers panel allows you select an item or items in an illustration, change their stacking order, show or hide them, and lock them. The following exercise familiarizes you with the Layers panel.

1 Launch Adobe Illustrator CS4 if it is not already open. Choose File > Open. In the Open dialog box, navigate to the ai07lessons folder and select the ai07.ai file. Press Open.

2 Choose File > Save As. In the Save As dialog box, navigate to the ai07lessons folder and type **ai07_work.ai** in the Name text field. Press Save, then press OK when the Illustrator Options dialog box appears.

3 Press the Layers button (◈) in the dock on the right side of the workspace to open the Layers panel.

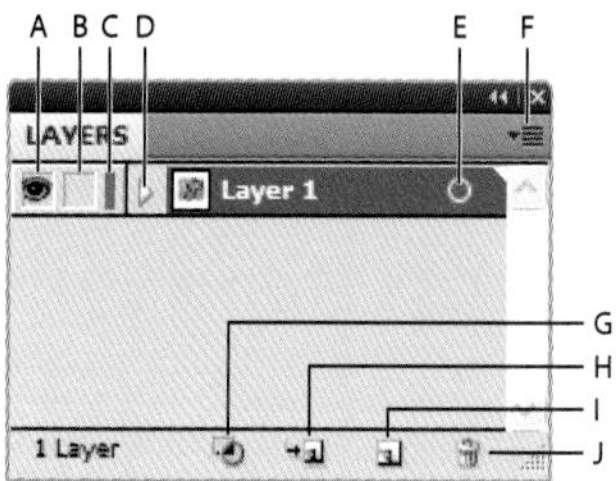

A. Visibility column. B. Edit column. C. Selection color column. D. Disclosure triangle. E. Target column. F. Panel menu. G. Make/Release Clipping Mask. H. Create New Sublayer. I. Create New Layer. J. Delete Selection.

4 Press the visibility icon (👁) in the visibility column to the left of Layer 1; all the items that reside on that layer disappear from the workspace. Click in the box once more to make the pieces visible again.

5 Press the empty box to the right of the visibility icon in the edit column of the Layers panel. The padlock icon (🔒) appears. This locks all the items on the layer, making it impossible to select or edit them. Press the padlock icon again to unlock the items on the layer.

6 To the right of the padlock icon is the Selection color column. The color listed in this column is the color assigned to identify the items on this layer. Each object on the layer will have its frame edges and bounding box appear in the layer color when the item is selected.

When new layers are created, the layer colors are assigned in sequence down the list of Adobe system colors. There are 27 named colors to choose from, or you can select Other *and specify additional color options. Layer colors can help you to visually categorize graphic elements at a glance. You can change the layer colors to fit your own visual system of organizing.*

7 To the right of the Selection color column is the disclosure triangle. Click the disclosure triangle to see all the individual and grouped items (sublayers) that make up the illustration.

Compound paths, while made up of multiple paths, show up as one item in the Layers panel. Masked items also appear as a sublayer in the Layers panel, the clipping mask and the clipped elements can be revealed by opening the disclosure triangle of the masked group.

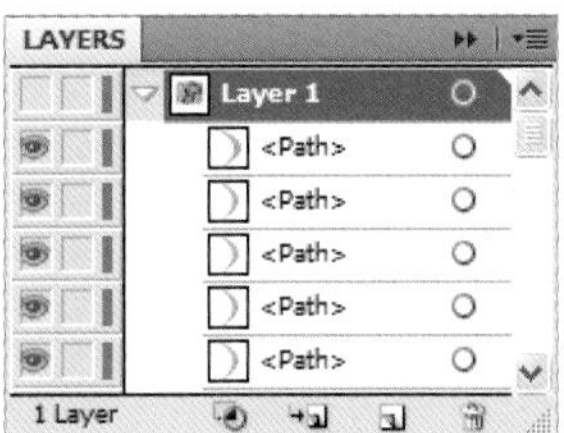

The disclosure triangle allows you to see the individual and grouped items (sublayers) that make up your illustration.

Using layers to organize your illustrations

Now that you've been introduced to the Layers panel, you'll take a look at how you can use these tools to organize the different components of your illustration. This makes it easier to edit the illustration as it becomes more complex. First you will select items, change their stacking order, and then lock, hide, group, and rename them.

1 Make sure that the disclosure triangle next to Layer 1 in the Layers panel faces downward and that all the illustration's paths are displayed. Press the Click to Target icon (○) next to any sublayer in the target column. As you click each item's target column, notice that the item is selected in your illustration. To select multiple items, hold down the Shift key on your keyboard as you click in each corresponding target column. Deselect any items you have selected by pressing Ctrl+Shift+A (Windows) or Command+Shift+A (Mac OS), and navigate to the bottom of the Layers panel.

2 Press the Click to Target icon (○) belonging to the sublayer named Bubble Group. This selects all the items on the Bubble Group sublayer and shows the items in the workspace with a light-blue bounding box. The target column allows you to select items or groups of items directly from your Layers panel. Notice that a color box (■) now appears in the active selection column to the right of the target column. This shows you that these items are selected in the Layers panel and on the artboard.

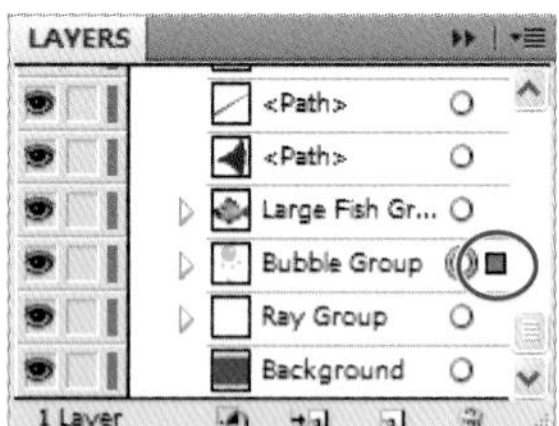

The selection color box.

3 With the Bubble Group sublayer still selected, click and drag the Bubble Group sublayer down in the Layers panel until you see a double-black line appear between the Ray Group and Background sublayers. Once you see the double line that indicates the stacking order position of the layer, release the mouse. The bubbles are now arranged beneath the rays in the illustration, but above the picture's background.

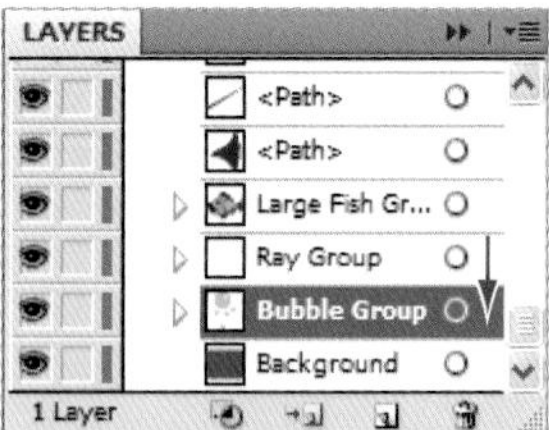

Move the bubble layer.

You have now changed the stacking order of those items in the illustration.

Double the bubbles

1. Make another copy in the same position by cloning.
2. An Alt/Option drag of a selected item on the artboard will *clone* it, leaving the original and quickly making a copy in the new position where you drag it.
3. Similarly, you can clone-drag within the Layers panel to copy an item in the same X &Y position on the artboard, leaving the original and quickly making a new copy to wherever you drag in the stacking order.
4. To efficiently duplicate an object, a clone-drag in the Layers panel is quicker than Copy / Paste in Front or Paste in Back.

Using the Layers panel to make selections

Now that you've seen how easy it is to select items in your illustration using the Layers panel target column, you will use the Edit and Visibility columns to make selections without affecting the locked or hidden sublayers.

1. In the Layers panel, click the empty boxes in the edit column of the Background, Bubble Group, and Ray Group sublayers to lock each of those layers. Press the visibility icon (👁) in the visibility column for the Large Fish Group sublayer to hide the items on that layer.
2. Choose Select > All or use the keyboard shortcut Ctrl+A (Windows) or Command+A (Mac OS). Even though you instructed Illustrator to select all the items in the illustration, none of the locked or hidden items are selected.

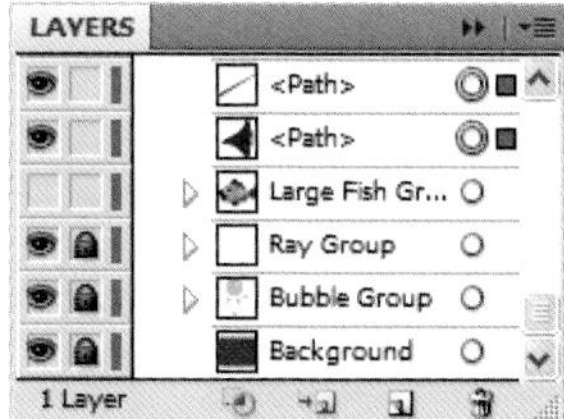

Items that are locked or hidden in the Layers panel are unaffected by the Select All action.

3. Choose Object > Group. Notice that all the selected items are now in a new sublayer in the Layers panel, named <Group>. The new Group sublayer has its own disclosure triangle that shows you all the items that make up that group.

4 Double-click on the <Group> sublayer in the Layers panel. In the Layer Options dialog box that appears, type **Small Fish Group** in the Name text field, then press OK. The Group sublayer is now named Small Fish Group in the Layers panel.

5 Press the visibility icon in the Visibility column of the Large Fish sublayer to turn on the layer's visibility, then press the padlock icons for the Background, Bubble Group, and Ray Group sublayers to unlock them.

6 Choose File > Save to save your work. Keep the file open for the next exercise.

Creating new layers and moving items between layers

Now that you have grouped all the small items in your illustration into groups, you will further organize them by creating separate layers for these grouped items. You will rename Layer 1 and create two new layers, one for each fish. You will then select the large and small fish, and then move them each to their appropriate layer.

1 Double-click on the words *Layer 1* in the Layers panel. In the Layers Options dialog box that appears, type **Background Shape** in the Name text field to rename this layer.

You can also change the layer selection color, convert the layer into a template, lock a layer, show or hide a layer, make a layer non-printing, turn off a layer's preview, or dim a layer in this dialog box.

The Print checkbox in the Layer Options dialog controls an image being included not just when output to paper, but also when exported to another file format. When this box is unchecked, the image is not included in the printout or export. In some export formats, like PDF, the layer controls are retained in the exported file. Depending on the exported file format, the non-printing graphic may be totally dropped from the resulting file. You don't want to make any changes now, so press OK.

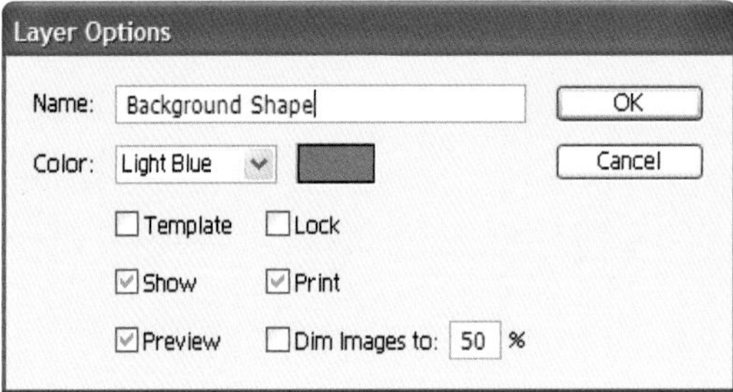

The Layer Options dialog box.

Checking/unchecking the Lock checkbox in the Layer Options dialog box has the same effect as toggling the Edit column in the Layers panel. Checking/unchecking the Show checkbox here is the same as clicking in the Visibility column in the Layers panel.

Some items should be seen and not printed

Usually, if an item is visible on the artboard it will print, and if an item is NOT visible in Illustrator, it will NOT show up on output.

So why would someone need to make a layer visible but non-printing? Unchecking the Print box in Layer Options is an opportunity to communicate to the on-screen user of the file without adding to the final artwork.

A great example would be production notes, which can be visual instructions or information about the output of the file that are not actually part of the graphic content. Perhaps there are sizing or positioning constraints established by the corporate graphic standards that should ride along with the company logo. Or, placeholder graphics can give directions about ad placement on a publication page.

2 To create a new layer, press the Create New Layer button (□) at the bottom of the Layers panel. A new layer named Layer 2 is now situated above the Background Shape layer. Change this default layer name to something more descriptive to keep your layers clearly organized. Double-click on the Layer 2 layer, and in the Layer Options dialog box, type **Large Fish** in the Name text field. Press OK.

3 You can avoid the extra step of having to change the default name of the newly-created layer by bringing up the Layer Options dialog box right away. It is more efficient to name your new layers at the same time as they are created. This time, hold down the Alt (Windows) or Option (Mac OS) key on your keyboard while you press the Create New Layer button. The Layer Options dialog box appears, allowing you to name the layer as it appears in the Layers panel. In the Layer Options dialog box, type **Small Fish** in the Name text field, then press OK. The Small Fish layer is listed above the Large Fish layer in the Layers panel.

When you draw, place or paste an object onto the Illustrator artboard, a new layer is created for it. This new object layer appears in the layer stacking order immediately above any selected layer.

Rather than create layers in an arbitrary order then have to arrange them as desired, you can build the stacking order of your graphics on-the-fly. Position new graphics and groups in the layer sequence as intended by targeting the layer immediately below where you want the new item to appear.

4 Select the Small Fish Group sublayer (listed beneath the Background Shape layer) by pressing the Click to Target icon (○) in the target column. When the color box (■) appears in the active selection column, click and drag the square to the Small Fish layer and release the mouse. Once you release the mouse, the selection square and the color of the bounding box change to green to match the selection color of the Small Fish layer.

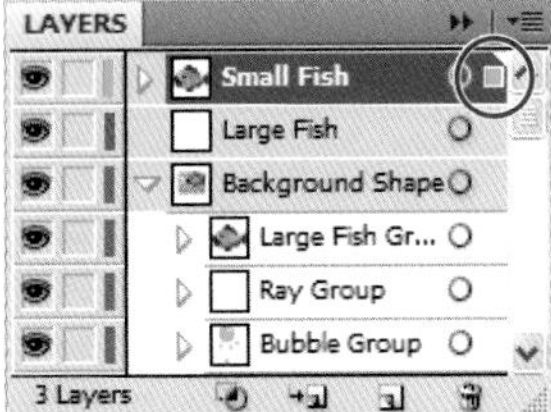

Once an item is moved from one layer to another, its active selection square and bounding box color change to the selection color of the new layer.

5 Click to target the Large Fish Group sublayer (also beneath the Background Shape layer heading), then click and drag its color box to the Large Fish layer. You have now transferred the features of one piece of a containing layer to its own separate layer.

6 Choose File > Save, then choose File > Close to close the file.

Suppressing the printing of a graphic

You can suppress the printing of a graphic in several ways:

- Hide the selected item. [Object > Hide > Selection]
- Hide the item's layer. [Click the visibility icon in the Layers panel]
- Uncheck the Print checkbox in the item's Layer Options. [Double-click on the layer, or access through the Layers panel menu]
- Choose Template in the item's Layer Options (this also dims the view to 50% by default, but can be adjusted to 100% to make item fully visible).

Using Layers for versioning

Because layers can be selectively controlled, and easily made visible or hidden, they can be utilized to make versions of your artwork.

Show or hide layers to create comps showing optional design directions, or build multi-lingual packaging using different layers per translated language over a common base of artwork.

Paste Remembers Layers

A convenient way to keep your layers organized is to use the Paste Remembers Layers option, accessed from the Layers panel menu. With this option, the clipboard holds not just the Illustrator artwork, but also information about the layer it originated on.

The Paste Remembers Layers option determines where artwork is pasted into the layer stack. When off, the pasted artwork lands on whatever layer is active. When checked on, artwork is pasted into the same layer it was copied from, no matter which layer is active in the Layers panel.

Having Illustrator keep track of the layers while you move items can let you work a little fast and loose, as you don't have to pay as much attention to the active layer while cutting and pasting items.

Where Paste Remembers Layers really gets powerful is working between documents. When pasting into a different file, artwork is automatically placed into a layer of the same name, and creates a new one of the correct name if necessary. It's a great way to transfer your carefully-named layer structure from one file to another, instead of ending up with lots of default-named layers.

Template Layers

Template layers are locked, nonprinting layers that you can use to manually trace images. Template layers can come in handy when you want to trace a raster image by hand or you want to create artwork from the scan of a mock-up design. Template layers are dimmed so that you can easily see any paths you draw over the layer. When that illustration is placed in a layout application, like InDesign or QuarkXPress, the template layer does not show or print. Template layers can be created in two ways:

The most common way to create a template layer is upon import, while placing raster artwork into Illustrator as a template. Select File > Place. In the Place dialog box, select the artwork you want to import and select the *Template* check box in the lower-left corner; then press Place. The file is placed on a locked layer and is dimmed to 50 percent by default, so that you can clearly see any paths you draw over it.

The second way to create a template layer is to convert an existing artwork layer into a template. Double-click a layer name in the Layers panel. In the Layer Options dialog box that appears, select the *Template* check box and press OK. The layers icon in the visibility column changes from the visibility icon (👁) to a template icon (△), and the layer is automatically locked. If you convert vector artwork to a template layer, it will not be dimmed.

Try converting the Large Fish layer to a template layer and trace it manually, using any combination of the path and shape drawing tools.

Congratulations! You have completed Lesson 7, "Organizing your Illustrations with Layers."

Self study

Create another layer for another sea creature. Import a raster graphic or scan as a template layer, and manually trace over it to build a multi-layered graphic contained within the sea creature layer group. Comp up another version of the undersea artwork by hiding the Large Fish layer and showing the sea creature in the same position, so that only one is visible for output.

Review

Questions

1 How do you hide a layer?

2 How do you move an item or items from one layer to another?

3 How do you change the selection color for a layer?

Answers

1 In the Layers panel, press the visibility icon (👁) corresponding to the layer you would like to hide.

2 Click or Shift+click the Click to Target icon (○) in the target column of the items you want to move. Then click and drag the layer's color box to the new layer.

3 Double-click on the layer in the Layers panel. In the Layer Options dialog box, choose a new color from the Color drop-down menu.

Lesson 8

What you'll learn in this lesson:

- Creating and editing symbols
- Importing a symbol library
- Using the symbolism tools
- Editing nested symbols
- Saving symbol libraries

Working with Symbols

Symbols make it easy to repeatedly use objects throughout an Illustrator project and even across multiple documents. Symbols can be imported, transformed, colored, and edited with the tools built into the Symbols panel, which you will discover in this lesson. Illustrator includes several symbol libraries for you to use, and also makes it easy for you to create.

Starting up

Before starting, make sure that your tools and panels are consistent by resetting your workspace. See "Resetting Adobe Illustrator CS4 Preferences" on page 3.

You will work with several files from the ai08lessons folder in this lesson. Make sure that you have loaded the ailessons folder onto your hard drive from the supplied DVD. See "Loading lesson files" on page 4.

See Lesson 8 in action!

Use the accompanying video to gain a better understanding of how to use some of the features shown in this lesson. The video tutorial for this lesson can be found on the included DVD.

Cleaning out the symbol library

When you create a new Illustrator document, the Symbols panel is automatically populated with a group of default symbols. These symbols are useful for certain applications, but not for the purposes of this lesson, so you will remove them and import a group of symbols provided in the ai08lessons folder.

1 In Adobe Illustrator CS4, choose File > Open. In the Open dialog box, navigate to the ai08lessons folder and select the ai0801.ai file. Press Open. This Illustrator file contains a logo that you will use to create and modify a group of symbols.

2 Once the file opens, press the Symbols button (♣) in the dock on the right side of the workspace to open the Symbols panel. Click to select the first symbol in the panel, a red sphere.

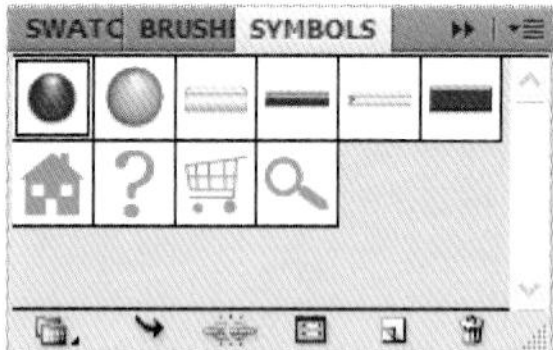

Select the first symbol in the Symbols panel.

3 While holding the Shift key, click on the last symbol listed in the panel, a magnifying glass. This also selects all the symbols between the first and last options.

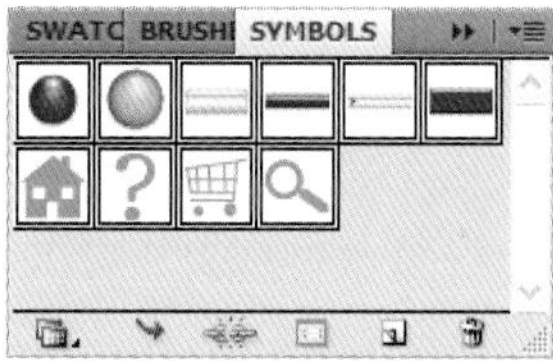

Shift+clicking the last symbol selects all the symbols between the first and last symbols.

4 Press the Delete Symbol button (🗑) in the lower-right corner of the Symbols panel to delete the default symbol library. A dialog box appears, asking you to confirm that you want to delete the selected symbols. Press Yes.

5 Choose File > Save As. In the Save As dialog box, name the file **ai0801_work.ai** and press Save. When the Illustrator Options dialog box appears, press OK. Keep the file open for the next part of the lesson.

Creating symbols

Once you have cleaned out the symbol library, you can begin to populate it with your own creations. You can make symbols from any piece of art that you create in Illustrator, and even from embedded bitmap graphics. The only limitation is that you can't use linked graphics to create symbols. You have to embed them in order to create a symbol from them.

1 Use the Selection tool (↖) to select the FlyAway logo with the double (white/black) outline in the document. Drag and drop it into the now-empty Symbols panel. The Symbol Options dialog box appears.

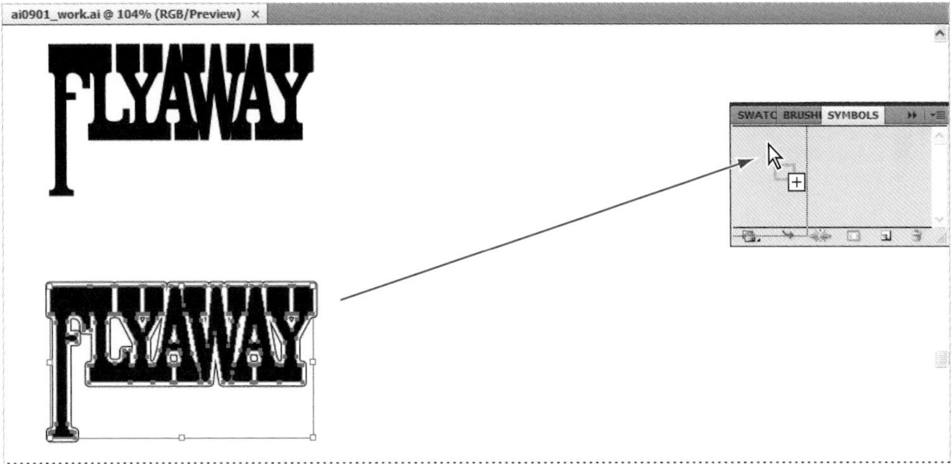

Turn the Fly Away logo into a symbol by dragging it into the Symbols panel.

2 In the Symbol Options dialog box, type **Fly Away Logo** in the Name text field. Select the Movie Clip radio button, and click on the center point of the Flash Registration bounding box. Press OK.

Symbol Options
Name: Fly Away logo OK
Type: Graphic Movie Clip Cancel
Flash Registration:
Enable Guides for 9-slice scaling

Determine the settings for the new symbol.

With the exception of the symbol name text field, the options in this dialog box deal with how the symbol will be treated if imported into Flash.

The logo is now a symbol in your library, and the occurrence of the logo on the artboard is called a symbol instance. There is a parent-child relationship between the symbol in the library and its instances on the artboard. Any change to the parent, or master, symbol in your library cascades down to the children, or instances, on your artboard.

Editing symbols

The logo symbol that you have is not bad, but it is a good idea to test out various color combinations before settling on a final one. In order to experiment with variations of the symbol you have created, you will add a new symbol instance to the artboard, make it editable, modify it, and use it to create a new symbol.

1 From the Symbols panel, drag the logo symbol onto the artboard, creating an instance somewhere away from the other graphics that are already in the document.

2 Click the Break Link button located at the top of your screen in the Control panel. This process, called *expanding*, breaks the link of the instance to the parent and makes the instance fully editable.

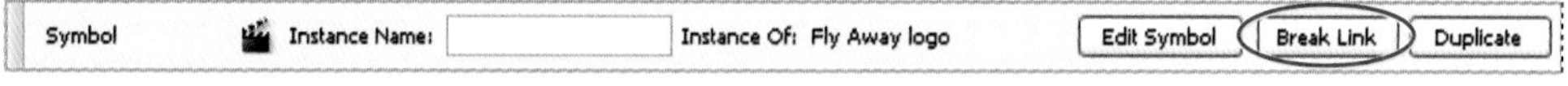

Break the symbol instance's link to the master symbol to make the instance editable.

3 With the logo still selected, choose Object > Ungroup. When the symbol was expanded, it was automatically converted to a grouped object; ungrouping it allows you to edit the strokes around the text.

4 With the logo still selected, click on the Appearance button (◉) in the dock to open the Appearance panel. The Appearance panel tells you that you are working with a compound path that has a black fill color and two strokes, one white and one black, applied to it.

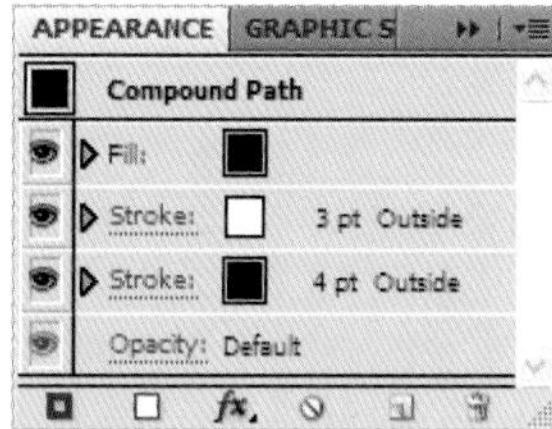

The Appearance panel details the selected symbol's components.

5 In the Appearance panel, click on the second listing, the white, 3-point outside stroke, to edit it. By selecting this listing, you've activated the color panel and stroke setting, both of which you can access and use to implement changes directly from the Appearance panel.

6 Click the Stroke color swatch next to the Stroke listing, and from the resulting Swatches panel, select the swatch named RGB Yellow.

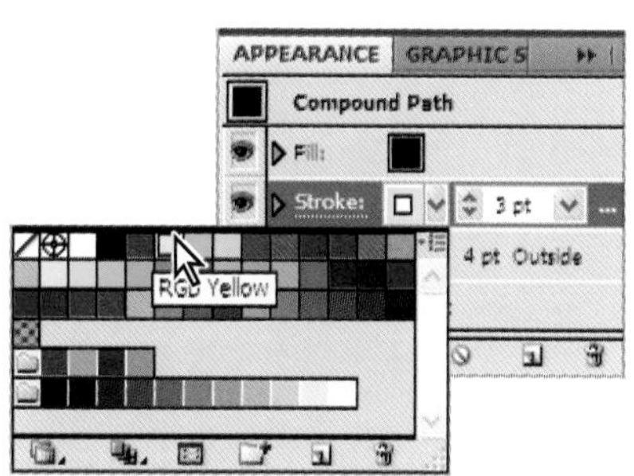

The Appearance panel updates to reflect the change in the stroke's color.

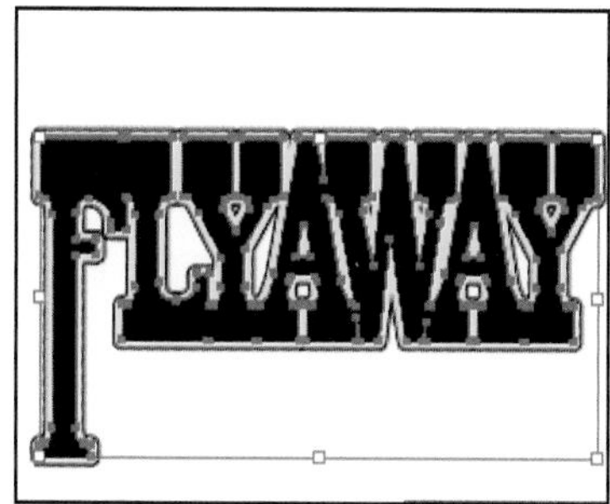

The stroke is now yellow.

7 Press the Symbols button (♣) in the dock to reopen the Symbols panel. Using the Selection tool (↖), click and drag the new logo from the artboard to the Symbols panel.

8 In the resulting Symbol Options dialog box, type **Fly Away logo yellow** in the Name text field. Choose the *Movie Clip* radio button and select the center of the Flash Registration bounding box. Press OK. You have just created another new symbol.

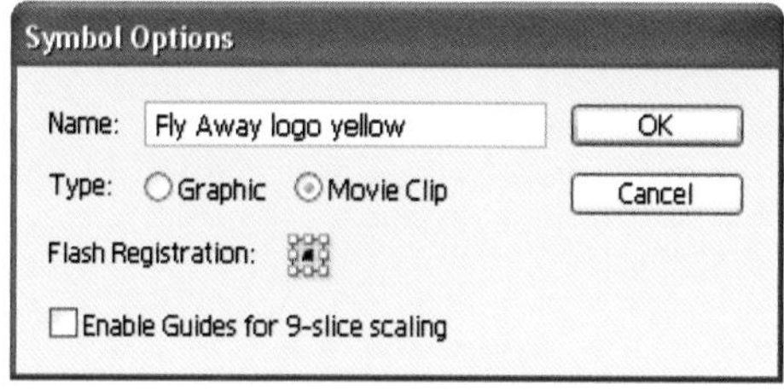

Name this symbol Fly Away logo yellow.

9 Choose File > Save to save your work.

Importing a symbol library

Symbols can be imported either from dedicated symbol libraries or regular Adobe Illustrator files. This is done from the Symbols panel menu.

1 In the upper-right corner of the Symbols panel, click on the panel menu button (▾≡). From the menu that appears, choose Open Symbol Library > Other Library.

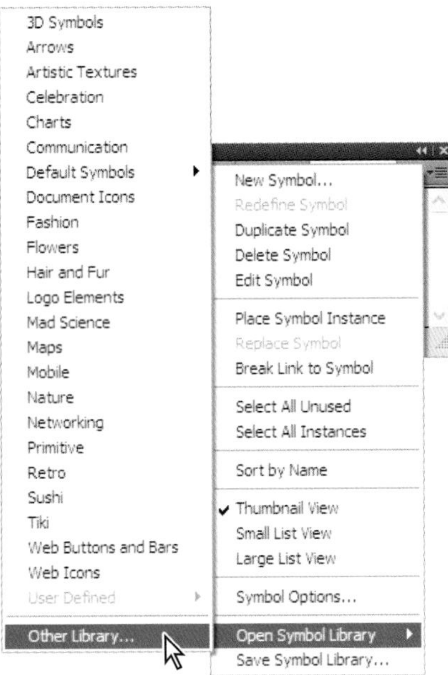

Choose Open Symbol Library > Other Library from the Symbols panel menu.

2 In the Select a Library to Open dialog box, navigate to the ai08lessons folder and select the butterflies.ai file. Press Open. A new panel named *Butterflies* appears in the workspace.

A new butterflies panel full of butterfly symbols appears in your document.

Symbol libraries are saved in the native .ai format. If you want to edit a library, all you need to do is open the file, add or remove content there, then resave the file over itself. External libraries like the one you just imported are not editable in your local document. For this reason, you must move the library contents into your Symbols panel.

3 Make sure that both the Butterflies Library panel and the Symbols panel are visible at the same time. In the Butterflies Library panel, Shift+click the first and last butterflies to select the panel's entire contents.

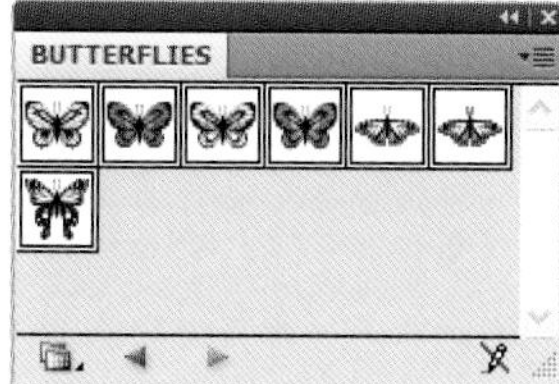

Select all the butterflies in the library.

4 Drag the selected contents from the butterflies library to the Symbols panel. Once they are in the Symbols panel, they are treated exactly like the symbols you created locally.

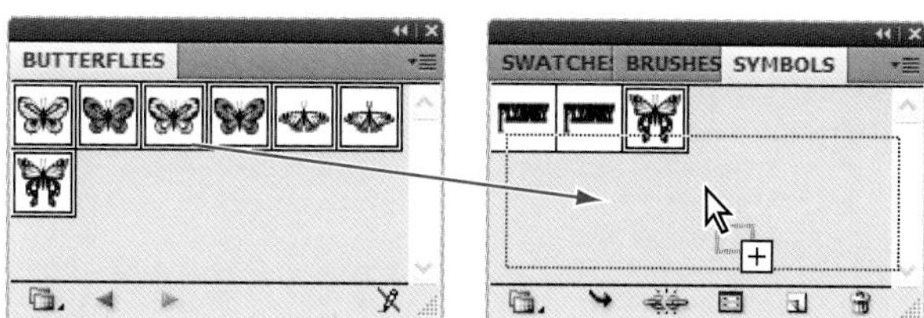

Drag the symbols from the butterflies panel to the Symbols panel.

5 Close the butterflies library, then choose File > Save to save your work.

Using the symbolism tools

As you have already seen, you can work with symbols by manually dragging them from the Symbols panel. Once they are on your artboard, you can move, rotate, and scale them individually using tools designed specifically for working with symbols. Now you will use these tools to add and manipulate symbols to create a new logo.

The symbolism tools allow you to create sets of symbol instances and then transform and edit them.

ICON	TOOL NAME	USE
	Symbol Sprayer	The Symbol Sprayer tool can place multiple symbol instances, also known as a symbol set, on the artboard at once in a fashion like that of a spray paint can. You can edit symbol sets using the other symbolism tools.
	Symbol Shifter	The Symbol Shifter tool moves symbol instances.
	Symbol Scruncher	The Symbol Scruncher tool moves instances in a symbol set closer together or farther apart.
	Symbol Sizer	The Symbol Sizer tool makes symbols in a set larger or smaller.
	Symbol Spinner	The Symbol Spinner tool rotates symbols in a set.
	Symbol Stainer	The Symbol Stainer tool colorizes symbols in a set.
	Symbol Screener	The Symbol Screener tool adjusts the opacity of symbols.
	Symbol Styler	The Symbol Styler tool is used to apply a style from the Graphic Styles panel to symbol instances.

1 Open the Layers panel by choosing Window > Layers, or pressing the Layers button ( ) in the dock on the right side of the workspace.

2 So far in this lesson, you have been working on Layer 1, the default layer. Press the Create New Layer button ( ) at the bottom of the Layers panel. This creates Layer 2.

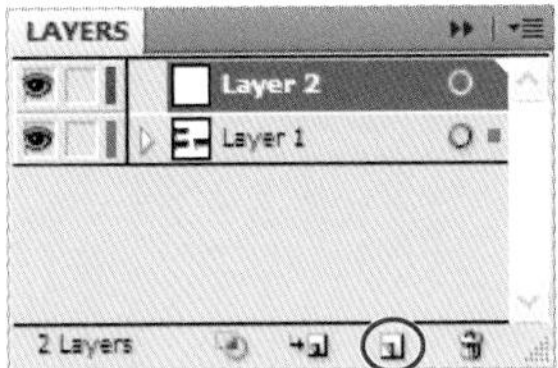

Create a new layer in the Layers panel.

3 Double-click Layer 2 in the Layers panel to open the Layer Options dialog box. In the Name field, type **Logo**. Leave all the other settings at their defaults and press OK.

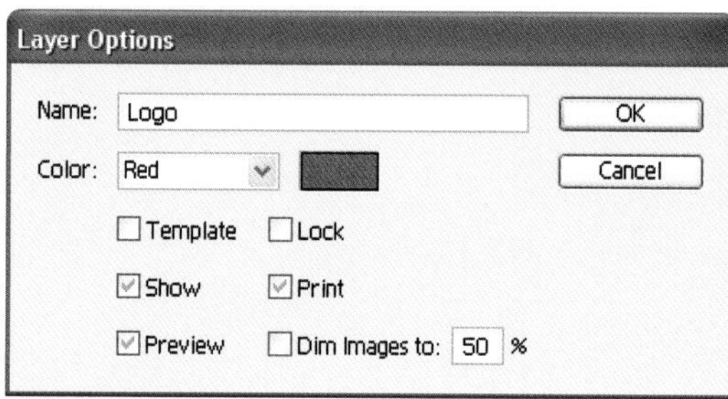

Rename the layer.

4 Click on the Visibility icon (👁) to the left of Layer 1 in the Layers panel to toggle off the layer's visibility. The document appears to be empty.

5 Open the Symbols panel by clicking on its icon (♣) in the dock. Drag an instance of the Fly Away logo yellow symbol onto your artboard, then press Shift+Ctrl+A (Windows) or Shift+Command+A (Mac OS) to deselect the symbol instance.

If you are not sure which symbol listed in the Symbols panel is the yellow logo, hold your cursor over each symbol and a tooltip appears with the symbol's name.

6 Click and hold the Symbol Sprayer button ( ) in the Tools panel to view all eight available symbolism tools. To the right of the list of symbolism tools is a small black arrow. Click on the arrow to tear off these tools and turn them into a floating Symbolism Tools panel.

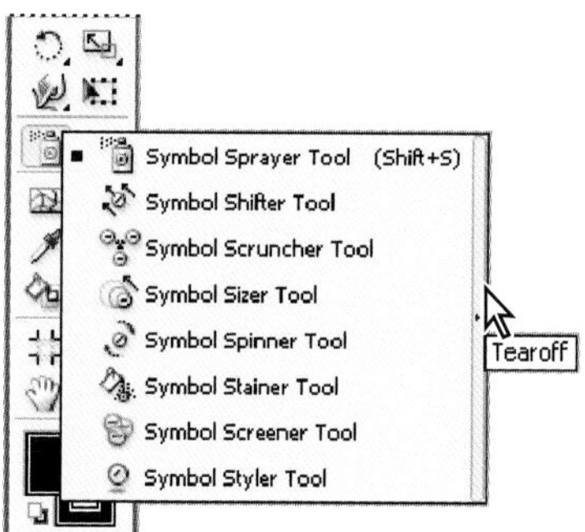

Click on the black arrow to the right of the list of symbol tools to turn them into their own floating panel.

7 Double-click the Symbol Sprayer tool in the floating panel; this opens the Symbolism Tool Options dialog box. Change the intensity value to 3, either by typing **3** into the text field or clicking the arrow to the right of the text field and adjusting the slider to 3. The intensity value specifies the rate at which the symbol sprayer creates symbols. Leave all other values at their defaults and press OK.

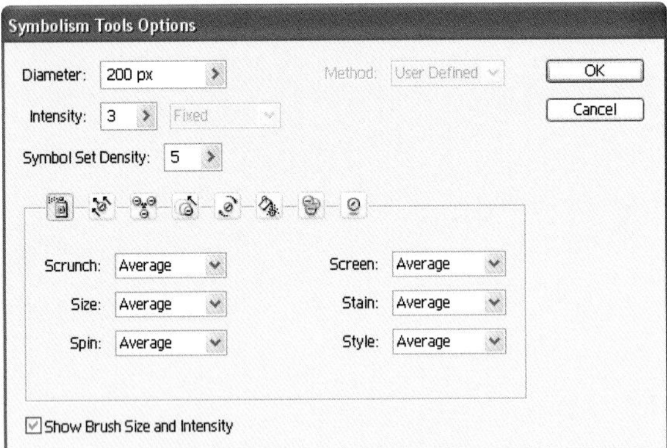

Use the Symbol Sprayer tool to create a butterfly symbol set.

The symbolism tools all share a common options dialog box. The area at the top of the dialog box allows you to change the overall parameters of the brush that the tools use, while the field at the bottom of the dialog box allows you to view and edit the parameters of each individual tool.

8 In the Symbols panel, select the butterfly symbol named butterfly_03. Move your cursor, which now resembles a miniature spray paint can with a circular perimeter surrounding it. Click and drag from above and to the left of the logo symbol in a sweeping circle around it. This creates a symbol set of multiple butterflies.

Use the Symbol Sprayer tool to create a butterfly symbol set.

Depending on how long you hold down your mouse, you may end up with more or fewer symbol instances than you see in the figure above. You can add symbol instances to the artboard by single-clicking where you'd like to add individual instances.

9 Double-click on the Symbol Shifter tool (![]) in the floating Symbolism Tools panel. In the Symbolism Tool Options dialog box, type **8** in the intensity value text field. This increases the strength of the tool and allows you to move the symbol instances more easily. Press OK.

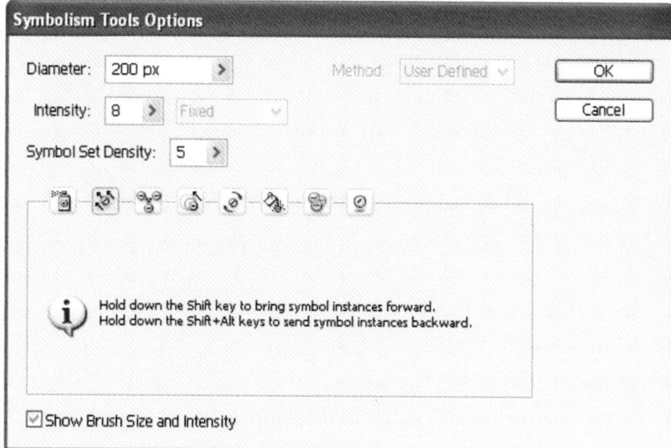

Set the intensity of the Symbol Shifter tool to 8.

10 Use the Symbol Shifter tool to click and drag on the individual symbol instances, positioning the butterflies around the logo.

Position the butterflies around the logo.

11 Click on the Symbol Sizer tool ( ) in the floating Symbolism Tools panel. Hold down Alt (Windows) or Option (Mac OS) and click on some of the butterflies to reduce their size. Keep some of the butterflies big and make some of them small so that each is a different size. The butterflies' size variations can add to the overall appearance of the logo.

Use the Symbol Sizer tool to adjust the butterflies' sizes.

12 Click on the Symbol Spinner tool ( ) in the floating Symbolism Tools panel. Click on one of the butterflies. A red arrow appears along its body, demonstrating the angle and direction of the butterfly's readjustment. When you're happy with the butterfly's position, release the mouse. Do the same for the remaining butterflies, positioning them around the logo so that they appear as if they are all flying along the same path around the logo.

Use the Symbol Spinner tool to set the butterflies flying on the same path around the logo.

13 Activate the Symbol Shifter tool again. Click and drag each symbol instance to move all the butterflies closer together. Don't worry if the butterflies overlap the logo.

Move the butterflies closer together.

14 With the Symbol set selected, choose Object > Arrange > Send to Back. This positions the butterflies behind the logo.

15 Activate the Selection tool (↖) from the Tools panel and choose Select > All, or use the keyboard shortcut Ctrl+A (Windows) or Command+A (Mac OS).

16 Click and drag the selected logo and symbol set into the Symbols panel. In the Symbol Options dialog box, type **logo & butterflies** into the Name text field and set the center anchor as the Flash registration point. Press OK. This creates a new symbol. This symbol is a bit different from the ones you have worked with previously, in that it has other symbols nested inside it.

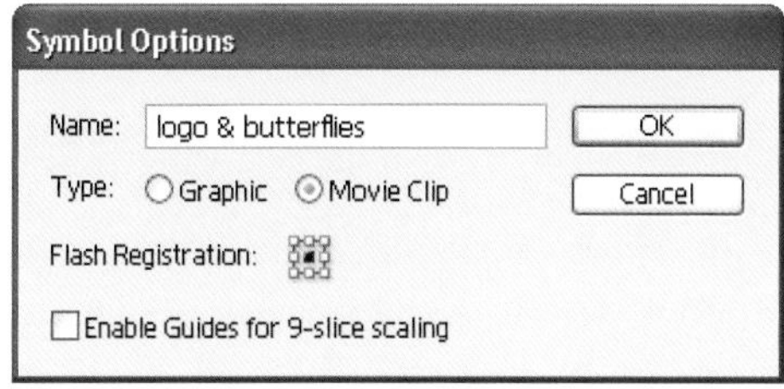

Edit the symbol options for the logo.

17 Choose File > Save to save your work. Keep the file open.

Editing nested symbols

Nested symbols form whenever you create a symbol using other symbol instances as components, as you did in the previous exercise.

1 Double-click on the *butterfly_03* symbol in the Symbols panel. This places a temporary instance of the symbol on the artboard.

2 Click the Fill color swatch in the Control panel and choose RGB Yellow, the same color you used to create an alternate version of the logo at the beginning of this lesson.

3 Select the Eyedropper tool (✐) from the Tools panel. The Eyedropper tool can sample appearance attributes and apply them to other objects.

The keyboard shortcut for the Eyedropper tool is I.

4 Alt+click (Windows) or Option+click (Mac OS) on all the gray-tinted interior parts of the butterfly wings.

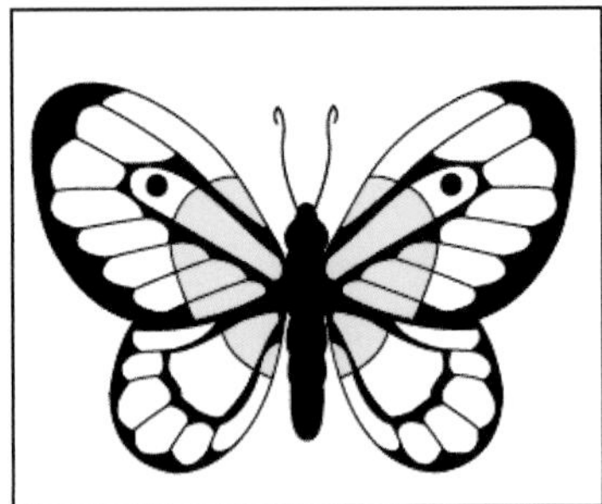

Color part of the butterfly yellow.

5 Click on the Exit Isolated Group button (◈) in the gray area above the artboard to return to the main artboard area. The butterflies are now also yellow, reflecting the change you just made to the parent symbol.

6 Choose File > Save to save your work.

Replacing symbols

Another of Illustrator CS4's cool symbol features is the ability to swap an onstage symbol instance with another instance from the Symbols panel.

1 Switch to the Selection tool (↖) and double-click on the instance of the logo & butterflies symbol on your artboard. A warning message appears, notifying you that you are about to edit the symbol, thus affecting all the symbol's instances as well. Press OK.

2 You are now in isolation mode. This mode exists to make it easier to edit the content of symbols and groups. Select the Fly Away logo on your artboard.

3 On the right side of the Control panel is a Replace drop-down menu. Select the first Fly Away logo from the menu. The original Fly Away logo replaces the yellow-bordered symbol instance on the artboard.

4 This is a variation of the butterflies symbol in the library that might fit a little better with this new logo. Using the Selection tool, click on the butterflies symbol set on the artboard.

Replace the yellow Flyaway logo with the original one.

5 Select the butterfly_04 symbol in the Symbols panel.

6 From the Symbols panel menu, select Replace Symbol.

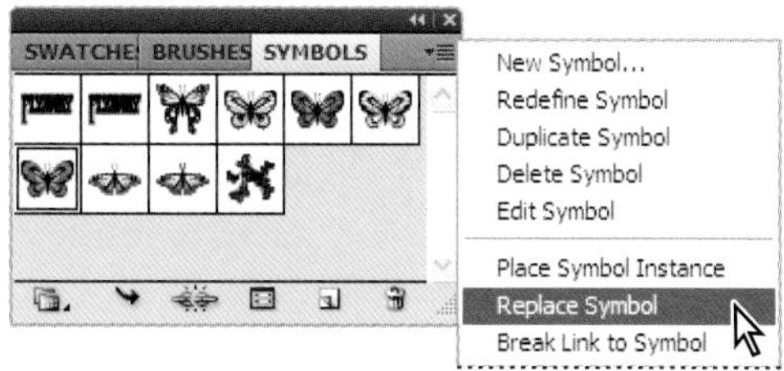

Replace the yellow butterfly you've used in the logo with another from the Symbols panel.

7 The new symbol replaces the instances of the original butterfly. All transformations that had been made to the original symbols in your set carry over to the new symbol instances. Click the Exit Isolation Mode button (◈) in the upper-left corner of your screen then save the file by choosing File > Save.

The new butterflies & logo symbol.

Saving symbol libraries

You can save symbol libraries for later use in other documents.

1 Click on the panel menu button (-≡) in the upper-right corner of the Symbols panel. Select Save Symbol Library from the Symbols panel menu.

2 In the Save Symbols as Library dialog box, navigate to the ai08lessons folder and type **MySymbols.ai** into the Save As text field.

3 Press Save to save the symbol library.

4 Choose File > Save to save your work.

Congratulations! You have completed Lesson 8, "Working with Symbols."

Self study

Open a new file and import the butterflies.ai symbol library into it. Practice editing symbols from the library and creating new symbols from them.

Open the cartoonbot.ai file included in the ai08lessons folder. This is a robot character that has been divided into segments—arms, legs, a head, and so on. Practice creating symbols by converting each segment into a symbol.

Review

Questions

1 What types of objects can you convert into symbols?

2 Explain the relationship that exists between symbols in the Symbols panel and their symbol instances on the artboard.

3 In what two places on the Illustrator interface do you have the option to replace one symbol on your artboard with another from the Symbols panel?

Answers

1 You can convert almost all Illustrator objects—shapes, groups, even embedded bitmap graphics—into symbols. The only limitation is that you can't use linked graphics.

2 There is a parent-child relationship between the symbols in the Symbols panel and the symbol instances on the artboard. Any changes made to the parent object, either by editing it directly in the Symbols panel or by entering isolation mode for the instance on the artboard, results in a change to the symbol instance on the artboard.

3 **a.** When a symbol is selected, the Replace option appears in the Control panel.

b. When a symbol is highlighted and you click on a new parent symbol in the Symbols panel, the *Replace Symbol* option is available in the Symbol panel menu.

What you'll learn in this lesson:

- Applying effects using the Appearance panel
- Learning how to edit effects
- Saving graphic styles
- Applying a graphic style to a symbol
- Working with blending modes and opacity

Using Effects and Transparency

You can separate an object's pieces and control its appearance, including fills, strokes, effects, and transparency, all while maintaining the structure of an object. Properties that define the appearance of an object can be saved as graphic styles and then applied to other objects, making your artwork more consistent and providing an efficient workflow.

Starting up

Before starting, make sure that your tools and panels are consistent by resetting your workspace. See "Resetting Adobe Illustrator CS4 Preferences" on page 3.

You will work with several files from the ai09lessons folder in this lesson. Make sure that you have loaded the ailessons folder onto your hard drive from the supplied DVD. See "Loading lesson files" on page 4.

See Lesson 9 in action!

Use the accompanying video to gain a better understanding of how to use some of the features shown in this lesson. The video tutorial for this lesson can be found on the included DVD.

Working with the Appearance panel and effects

In this exercise, you will work with a series of text logos for the masthead of an imaginary magazine called *Vector Magazine*. You will explore various looks for this logo using Illustrator's effects and working with the Appearance panel and graphic styles.

1 Open Adobe Illustrator CS4, if it is not already open. You will work with a pre-existing file in this exercise.

2 Choose File > Open. In the Open dialog box, navigate to the ai09lessons folder and select the ai0901.ai file. Press Open.

3 Choose File > Save As. In the Save As dialog box, navigate to the ai09lessons folder and type **ai0901_work.ai** in the Name text field. Press Save. The Illustrator Options dialog box appears. Leave the settings at their defaults and press OK.

   You will be applying different effects to the same text in order to compare the results.

The file contains a few example logos.

4 Choose Window > Appearance or press the Appearance button (◉) in the dock on the right side of the workspace to open the Appearance panel. The Appearance panel allows you to determine what the attributes of an object, group, or layer are. As your files become more complex, the Appearance panel becomes increasingly useful.

5 Choose the Direct Selection tool (↖) from the Tools panel and select the blue and yellow hexagon to the left of the *Vector Magazine* text at the top of the page. When you select an object, group, or layer, the selection's attributes are listed in the Appearance panel. There are currently three attributes for this object: Stroke, Fill, and Default Transparency.

Attributes affect the look or style of an object but they do not affect the structure. Attributes in Illustrator are strokes, fills, transparency, and effects. The order in which the appearance attributes appear in the panel affects the appearance of the object. For an overview of the Appearance panel, review Lesson 1, "Adobe Illustrator CS4 Jumpstart."

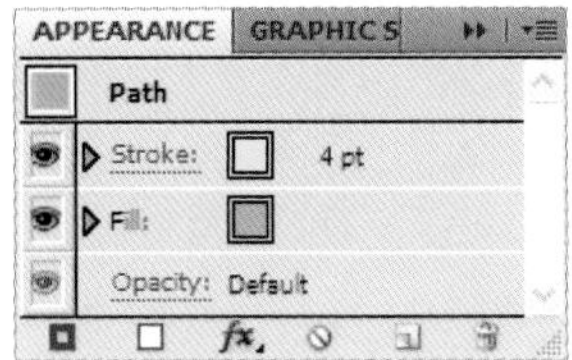

The attributes of the object in the Appearance panel.

6 Select the text to the right of the object. The appearance attributes for the text object are Characters and Default opacity.

7 Double-click on the Characters attribute in the Appearance panel. Stroke and Fill attributes now appear listed in the panel, indicating that they are nested inside.

8 Select the Type: No Appearance attribute at the top of the Appearance panel to return to the default view.

Applying effects

As you have seen from the last exercise, the Appearance panel is a convenient location to view and modify the fill and stroke of an object. When you add an effect to an object, the effect name is listed in the Appearance panel and you are able to modify the effect by double-clicking it.

1 Choose the Selection tool (↖) from the Tools panel and select the blue and yellow hexagon, if it is not already selected. You will now add an effect to the entire object.

2 Choose the Effect menu at the top of the workspace, and in the Illustrator Effects portion of the drop-down menu, choose Stylize > Scribble. The Scribble Options dialog box appears. Click and drag the window to the side, if necessary, in order to see the original object.

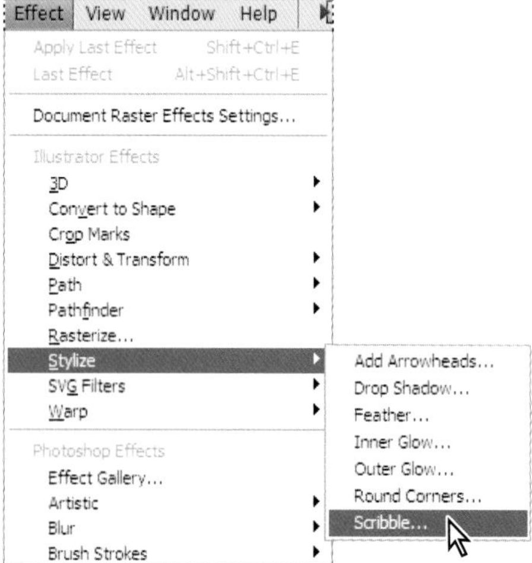

Open the Scribble Options dialog box by choosing Stylize > Scribble from the Edit menu.

3 Make sure the Preview checkbox on the right side of the dialog box is selected in order to view any applied effect in real time. The default scribble effect is visible and is currently being applied to the entire object.

4 Choose Loose from the Settings drop-down menu. The appearance of the shape changes, based on the values of this preset. Press OK.

In the Appearance panel, note the order of the attributes. The top of the panel reads *Path* (which is the path of the hexagon), and indented below are Stroke, Fill, and Scribble. These three attributes apply to the path. You will now apply the Scribble effect to the fill only.

5 In the Appearance panel, click the Scribble effect and drag it on top of the Fill. When you see two black arrows on either side of the Fill, release the mouse to apply the effect.

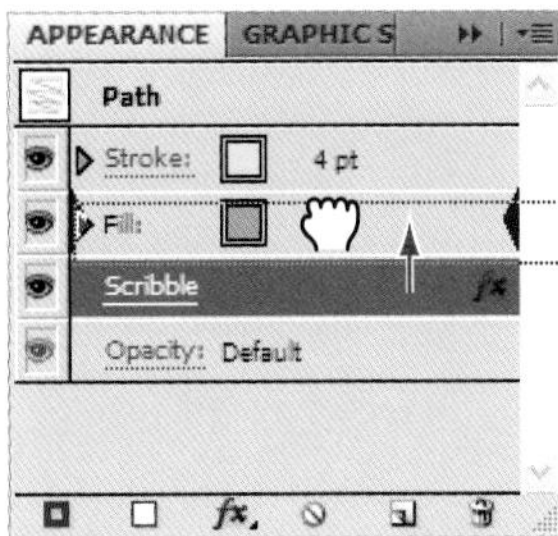

Move the Scribble attribute onto the Fill attribute.

The Scribble effect is now nested inside the Fill attribute (with the Color attribute) and the stroke is unaffected.

6 Click the arrow next to the Fill attribute to collapse it. When an effect is applied to either a fill or stroke, the attribute expands by default. You may find that collapsing these nested attributes makes it easier to understand the hierarchy within the Appearance panel.

7 Select the Stroke attribute in the Appearance panel. Press the Swatches button (▦) that appears next to the Stroke attribute and select the None swatch (☒) to remove the 4 pt yellow stroke.

In a later exercise, you will learn how reordering effect attributes allows you to create more complex effects.

8 Choose File > Save to save your work.

Editing effects

Once you have added an effect, it is fairly easy to modify it through the Appearance panel.

1 Press the Appearance button (◉) in the dock or click on the Appearance tab to open the Appearance panel, and click the arrow to the left of the Fill attribute to expand it.

2 Double-click on the Scribble effect, and the Scribble Options dialog box appears. Any visible effect in the Appearance panel can be modified directly from within the Appearance panel.

It is important to distinguish between effects and filters. Effects are live; you can add an effect to an object and modify it at a later point. Filters change the shape of the object and cannot be modified at a later point.

3 Choose Sketch from the Settings drop-down menu.

4 Move the Path Overlap slider to the right, or type **7 pt** into the Path Overlap field. This demonstrates how the shape's original structure, including the anchor points, is constant; only the shape's appearance has been modified. Notice also that when you change one of the values in the Scribble Options dialog box, the Setting drop-down menu changes to Custom.

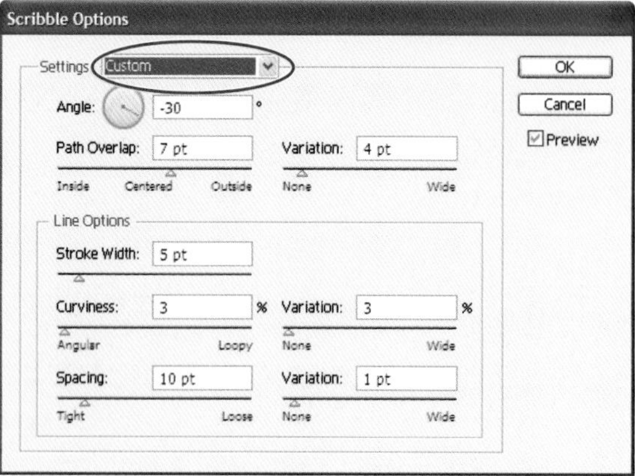

The Setting drop-down menu changes to Custom once you modify a setting in the Scribble Options dialog box.

5 Press OK to close the dialog box and modify the effect.

Scribble Options

Angle controls the direction of the scribble lines. You can click any point on the angle icon, drag the angle line around the angle icon, or enter a value between –179 and 180 in the box. If you enter a value that's outside that range, the value is translated to its equivalent in-range value.

Path Overlap controls the amount the scribble lines stay within or extend beyond the path boundaries. A negative value constrains the scribble lines within the path boundary, and a positive value extends the scribble lines beyond the path boundary.

Path Overlap Variation controls the lengths of the difference in scribble line lengths relative to each other.

Stroke Width controls the width of the scribble lines.

Curviness controls the amount the scribble lines curve before they reverse direction.

Curviness Variation controls how the different scribble line curves are relative to each other.

Spacing controls the amount of space between scribble line folds.

Spacing Variation controls the amount of space between scribble line folds.

Using graphic styles

In the previous exercise, you created and modified an effect; what if you wanted to apply this same effect to different objects? For example, what if you were creating multiple headers in the same style as the first? Or perhaps you would like to use the same effect in another project. In all these cases you would use Illustrator CS4's graphic styles feature.

Graphic styles allow you to reuse common styles within a single document or between documents. In this exercise, you will add a preset graphic style and then create and save your own.

1 Using the Selection tool (↖), select the second *Vector Magazine* headline located above the title *Using Graphic Styles* (it's the second heading from the top of the document).

2 Press the Graphic Styles button in the dock or choose Window > Graphic Styles to open the Graphic Styles panel.

3 Press the panel menu button (▾≡) in the upper-right corner of the Graphic Styles panel and select Open Graphic Style Library; then choose Type Effects. The Type Effects panel appears with a series of thumbnails representing the various type styles. Illustrator CS4 comes pre-installed with a number of Graphic Style Libraries.

4 Press the panel menu button of the Type Effects panel and choose Large List View. This allows you to view the names of the graphic styles, as well as the styles' corresponding thumbnails.

5 Select the Shadow style, and the appearance of the type changes to a white fill with a gray shadow. This is an example of a graphic style preset. The original orange color of your text has been overwritten, as the graphic style's fill color was saved as white. Close the Type Effects panel.

6 Press the Appearance button (◉) in the dock or click on the Appearance tab to open the Appearance panel, and scroll down to see the two fill colors and the Shadow effects that make up the Shadow text style. While many of the preset styles in Illustrator are fairly sophisticated, they often will not match your project. While it is possible to modify graphic styles, it is usually more efficient to create your own. You will now do just that.

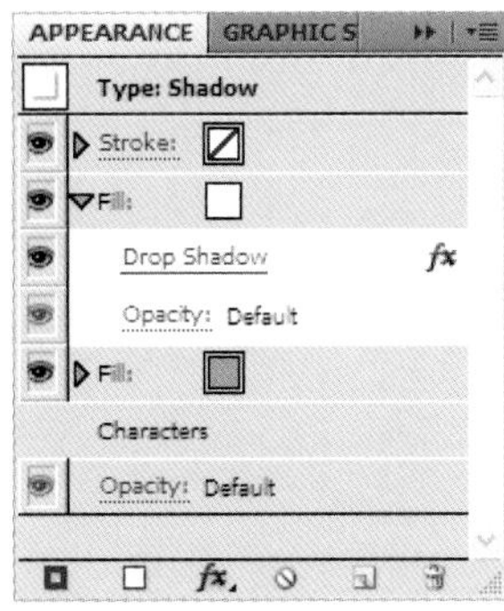

The Appearance panel with updated attributes.

Creating and saving graphic styles

Creating your own graphic styles gives you the most flexibility and allows you to easily reuse your own assets. In this exercise, you will add an extra fill and the transform effect to create a custom outline style for your logo.

1 Select the third *Vector Magazine* headline (the one above the *Creating and Saving Graphic Styles* title).

2 Press the panel menu button (-≡) in the Appearance panel and choose Add New Fill. By default, the fill is black. Because this new fill is located above the content, it overrides the original orange color. You will now reorder the attributes, placing the new fill below the Characters attribute. Note that there is also a Stroke attribute of *None* that was automatically added in the last step. When you add a new fill, a stroke is necessary as well.

3 Click and drag the black fill so that it is below the Characters attribute and the headline's fill reverts to orange. Reordering appearance attributes is very similar to the way you reorder layers in Illustrator. The attributes closer to the top are displayed first. You will now add an effect to this new fill to create an outlined appearance.

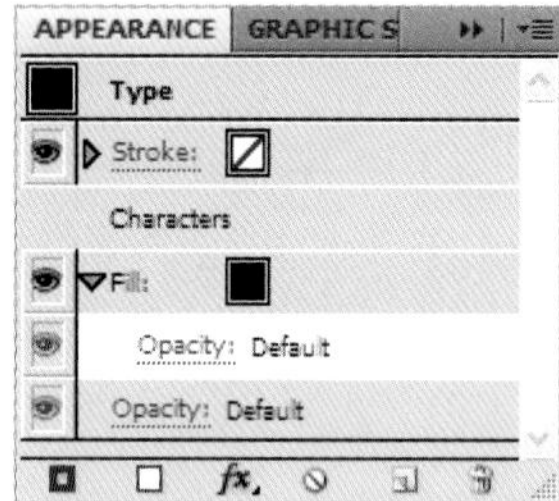

Re-order the attributes in the Appearance panel.

4 Click on either side of the new black fill to select it. Choose Effect > Path > Offset Path. The Offset Path dialog box appears. The value for the Offset should be 10 pt (which is the default). If it is not, type **10** in the Offset text field. Select the Preview checkbox to see the effect.

5 Choose Round from the Joins drop-down menu and press OK.

6 In the Appearance panel, notice the Offset Path effect listed under the Fill attribute. Select the Fill attribute and click on the built-in color swatch to see the color options. Select the yellow swatch in the top row.

7 Press the Graphic Styles button in the dock to open the Graphic Styles panel. Alt+click (Windows) or Option+click (Mac OS) the New Graphic Style button (![]) at the bottom of the panel. When the Graphic Style Options dialog box appears, type **VM Style Yellow Outline** in the Style Name text field and press OK.

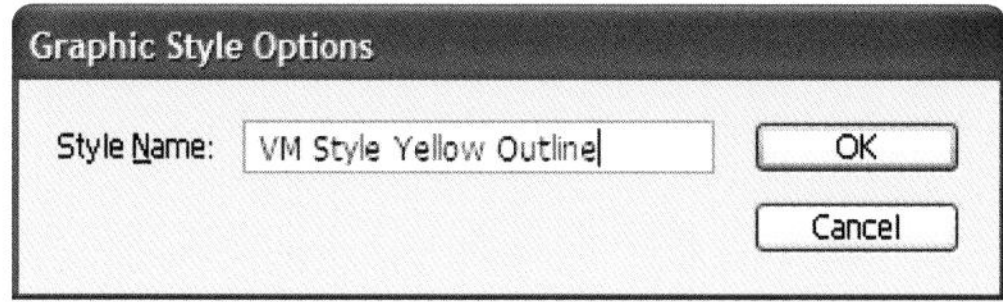

The Graphic Style Options dialog box

8 Notice the last thumbnail in the Graphic Styles panel. The style you just created is listed last and is ready to be used on other objects.

Applying and modifying graphic styles

Now that you have created a graphic style, you can apply that style to objects, groups, and even entire layers. Additionally, you can share graphic styles between documents.

1 Select the smaller *Vector Magazine* headline, located at the bottom of the document. You will now apply and modify the graphic style you created in the last exercise.

2 Select the *VM Style Yellow Outline* style in the Graphic Styles panel. For obvious reasons, the effect doesn't work when applied to a smaller object. However, it's easy to modify the size using the Appearance panel.

3 Press the Appearance button (◉) in the dock, or click on the Appearance tab, if necessary, to open the Appearance panel. Click the arrow to the left of the Fill attribute and double-click on the Offset Path effect to open the Offset Path dialog box. Highlight the value in the Offset text field, then type **2 pt**.

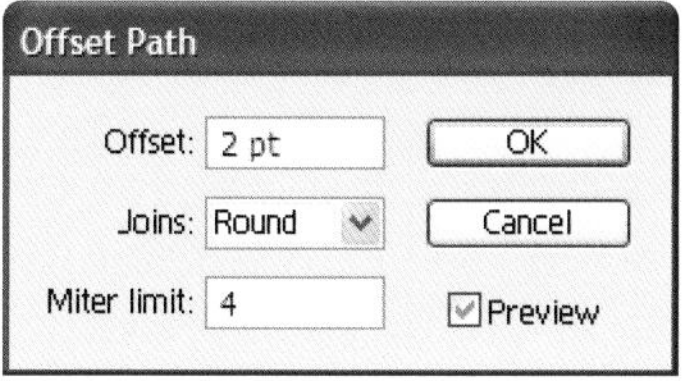

The Offset Path dialog box.

4 Press OK to apply the change.

5 Choose File > Save to save your work.

Working with object transparency

If you have worked with Illustrator or other image editing applications in the past, you may have worked with transparency (also called opacity). Objects in Illustrator are 100 percent opaque by default, meaning that the fill and stroke of an object cover underlying objects. Reducing the opacity of an object reveals the underlying objects and can be used to create interesting layered effects. As you have seen in this chapter, objects in Illustrator can have multiple attributes in the Appearance panel, such as the extra Fill attributes and the Offset Path effect in the previous exercise. These attributes can be selected and their transparencies independently controlled using the Appearance panel. For this exercise, it may be useful to expand both the Appearance and Transparency panels so they are easily accessible.

1 Select the *VM* logo at the very bottom of the document. Press the Graphic Styles button ( ) in the dock to open the Graphic Styles panel.

2 Select the *VM Style Yellow Outline* graphic style you created in the previous exercise to apply it to the *VM* logo.

3 Press the Appearance button (◉) in the dock or click on the Appearance tab to open the Appearance panel. The attributes from your graphic style have been applied.

4 Choose Window > Transparency or press the Transparency button ( ) in the dock to open the Transparency panel. The opacity value is 100 percent.

5 Highlight the value in the Opacity text field, type **30**, then press Enter (Windows) or Return (Mac OS). The entire object is now set to 30 percent opacity. Notice that the colored square behind the type now shows through. Additionally, the opacity value of 30 percent is visible in the Appearance panel.

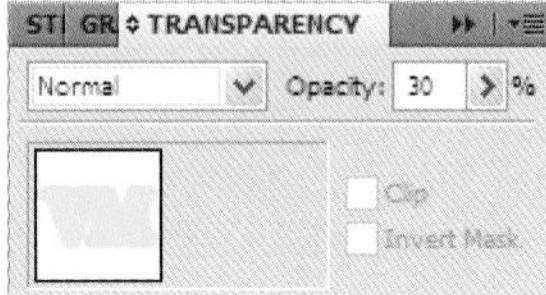

Change the opacity in the Transparency panel.

6 Click inside the Opacity text field and press the up arrow on your keyboard. The opacity value begins to increase by 1 percent increments. Stop when you reach 50 percent. Press and hold down the Shift key and press the up arrow; the value now increases by 10 percent. Stop increasing the value when you get to 100 percent, the original opacity.

Working with multiple opacity

You can also control each of an object's many attributes independently, which gives you precise control over the object's appearance.

1 Select the *VM* logo, if it is not already selected. Open the Appearance panel and double-click the Characters attribute. This expands the characters, allowing you to view and modify the fill and stroke of the text object. Set the fill color of the text to the first orange swatch in the second row of the Swatches panel.

Text is different from other Illustrator objects such as shapes. Because a single word is composed of multiple characters, Illustrator nests the Fill, Stroke, and Transparency attributes inside the Characters attribute.

2 Double-click the Opacity: Default attribute at the bottom of the Appearance panel and in the Transparency panel, click inside the Opacity field. Press and hold the Shift key and press the down arrow until the value is 50 percent. Press Enter (Windows) or Return (Mac OS).

3 Reopen the Appearance panel and select the Type attribute listed at the top to return to the standard attribute list. The orange fill of the text is set to 50 percent but the yellow fill still has its original 100 percent opacity.

4 Select the Fill attribute in the Appearance panel. Open the Transparency panel, highlight the value in the Opacity text field, type **20**, then press Enter (Windows) or Return (Mac OS). This fades the yellow fill and the offset effect to 20 percent, while the fill of the characters remains at 50 percent.

5 In the Appearance panel, click the arrow to the left of the Fill attribute and scroll down if necessary; notice the opacity is set to 20 percent. Click the arrow again to hide the Fill attributes.

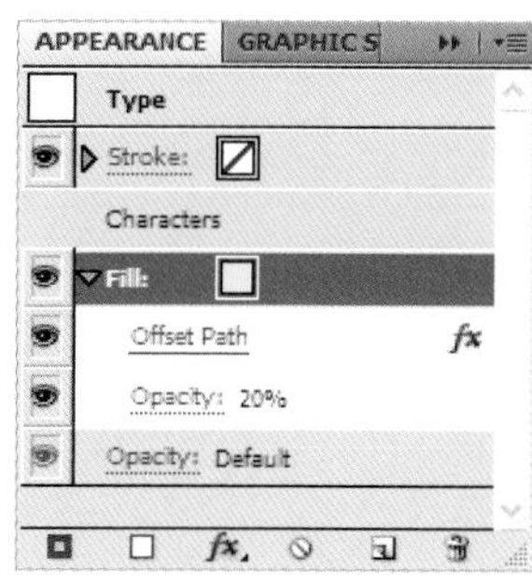

The Appearance panel reflects the opacity that was set.

6 Double-click the Opacity: Default setting at the bottom of the Appearance panel. Note that this is still set to 100 percent. Click and drag the opacity slider to the left to 75 percent. Press Enter (Windows) or Return (Mac OS). The entire object now fades out. There are three levels of opacity in this object: the opacity of the characters themselves, the opacity of the separate yellow fill and effect, and the opacity of the entire object.

7 Choose File > Save to save your work.

Working with blending modes

Blending modes are another feature you may be familiar with from other applications, particularly Photoshop. Blending modes let you change the ways in which the objects' colors blend with the colors of underlying objects. When a blending mode is applied to an object, the effect of the blending mode is seen on any objects that lie beneath the object's layer or group. Like opacity, you can control the blending modes of the separate attributes in an object.

1 Select the blue and yellow object in the bottom-right corner of the document. Open the Appearance panel. This object has a yellow stroke of 4 points and a blue fill. You will now apply a blending mode to this object. First you will magnify your view of the object. This will help you to better understand blending modes.

2 Select the Zoom tool (🔍) from the Tools panel and click on the object until the magnification is 300 percent. The magnification value is listed in a drop-down menu in the lower-left corner of the workspace.

3 Press the Transparency button (◐) to open the Transparency panel. Choose Darken from the Blending mode drop-down menu. The hexagon blends with the background behind it.

Choose Darken from the Blending mode drop-down menu.

Understanding blending modes is easier when you use the following terminology: the *blend color* is the original color of an object, in this case, the yellow stroke and blue fill. The *base color* refers to the underlying color(s), in this case, the maroon and gray. The *resulting color* is how it appears to the eye.

For specific details on the various blending modes, refer to the Transparency and Blending Modes section in the Painting section of the Illustrator CS4 Help Viewer.

4 Choose Normal from the Blending mode drop-down menu in the Transparency panel to return the object to its original state.

5 Return to the Appearance panel and select the Stroke attribute. Open the Transparency panel again and choose Multiply from the drop-down menu. Notice how the stroke now interacts with not only its background, but also the fill color. This is because it is located above the fill in the hierarchy of the Appearance panel.

6 In the Appearance panel, click and drag the Stroke attribute to below the Fill listing and notice the change in the hexagon's coloring. Because the stroke is now below the fill, it is only blending with the underlying colors.

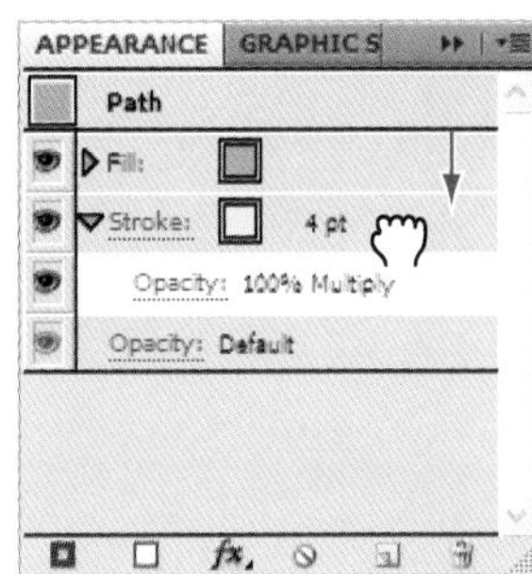

Move the Stroke attribute to beneath the Fill attribute.

7 Select the Fill attribute and in the Transparency panel, choose Overlay from the Blending Mode drop-down menu. Because the fill is above both the stroke and the underlying colors, it blends with both.

Saving and importing graphic styles

Earlier in the lesson, you created the *VM Style Yellow Outline* graphic style. You can apply that style to objects, groups, and even entire layers. You will apply the style to groups and layers shortly, but first you will learn how to share graphic styles between documents.

1 Press Shift+Ctrl+A (Windows) or Shift+Command+A (Mac OS) to deselect everything in the document.

2 Open the Graphic Styles panel. Ctrl+click (Windows) or Command+click (Mac OS) on all the default graphic styles except the *VM Style Yellow Outline* style.

3 With the default styles selected, press the Delete Graphic Style button (🗑) at the bottom of the Graphic Styles panel. When the Delete the Style Selection warning message appears, press OK (Windows) or Yes (Mac OS). You are deleting these styles because you do not want them to be saved as part of your new Graphic Style library.

4 Press the panel menu button (-≡) in the upper-right corner of the Graphic Styles panel and choose Save Graphic Style Library.

The Save Graphic Styles as Library dialog box appears. Normally, you are directed to save libraries in your system folder. For this exercise, navigate to the ai09lessons folder. In the Name text field, type **ai0901_styles.ai** and press Save.

5 Choose File > Save to save your work, then choose File > Close.

6 Choose File > Open. In the Open dialog box, navigate to the ai09lessons folder and select the ai0902.ai file. Press Open.

7 Choose File > Save As. In the Save As dialog box, navigate to the ai09lessons folder and type **ai0902_work.ai** in the Name text field. Press Save. When the Illustrator Options dialog box appears, leave the settings at their defaults and press OK. You will now import the Graphic Style library you just saved.

8 Press the Graphic Styles button in the dock (▭) to open the Graphic Styles panel. Press the panel menu button and choose Open Graphic Style Library > Other Library. The Select Library dialog box appears. Navigate to the ai09lessons folder, select the ai0901_styles.ai file, then press OK. The ai0901_styles.ai graphic styles open in a separate panel.

Applying graphic styles to layers and symbols

In addition to applying graphic styles to a single object, you can also apply them to all objects in a layer. In this example, there are three different logo types, and you are interested in seeing how the same effect looks on each of them.

1 Press the Layers button (◈) in the dock to open the Layers panel. Select the Click to Target button (○) to the right of the *Three logos* layer name to target the entire layer. All three objects on the artboard are on the same layer and are automatically selected.

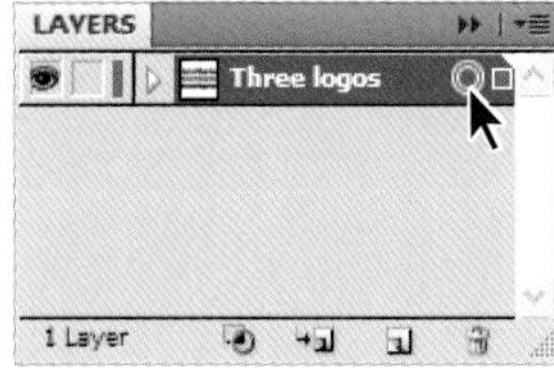

Press the Click to Target button to target and thus apply attributes to the entire layer.

2 Select the VM Style Yellow Outline style from the ai0901_styles panel. All three objects now have the same style applied to them.

3 Choose Window > Symbols or press the Symbols button (♣) in the dock to open the Symbols panel. From the default group of symbols, click and drag the Cloud symbol onto the artboard. Notice that the graphic style is automatically applied to the cloud symbol instance you just added to the document. Since you targeted the entire layer, all objects on the layer with a graphic style applied inherit the style's properties.

If you want to add a new object without the graphic style, the best idea is to place it on a new layer. In this case, you will remove the graphic style from the layer and then reapply it to the three logos as a group.

4 Open the Appearance panel and select the Layer:VM Style Yellow Outline attribute at the top of the panel to select all the objects on your artboard. At the bottom of the Appearance panel, press the Clear Appearance button (⊘) to remove the graphic style.

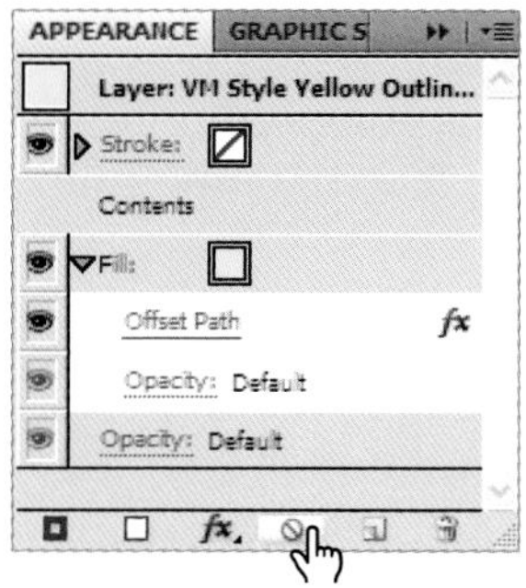

Press the Clear Appearance button.

5 Click anywhere in the background of the document to deselect the objects. Place your cursor above the three logos and click, drag downwards, and release to select them (but not the cloud illustration).

6 Click on the Yellow Outline Graphic Style in the ai0901_styles panel to apply it to the group of three logos.

7 Choose File > Save to save your work, then choose File > Close.

Congratulations! You have finished Lesson 9, "Using Effects and Transparency."

Self study

You can create unique graphic styles for your projects by combining combinations of effects, fills, strokes, and transparencies. Experiment with the following combinations; when you find ones that you like, be sure to save them into a library for reuse.

1 Open a new Graphic Style library in the Graphic Style panel. The Image Effects and Artistic Effects libraries are good places to start. Apply a complex graphic style preset to an object and break down the way it was created by looking at the order and properties of the attributes in the Appearance panel. Reverse-engineering the Illustrator CS4 presets is an excellent way to learn useful combinations for your own projects.

2 Create a graphic style that uses a gradient as a fill color. Applying this graphic style to rectangles or circles will allow you to make buttons for the Web, for example. Also try applying gradients to text for interesting effects, being sure to save the graphic style.

3 Create a bull's-eye graphic. Use a basic circle shape with a large stroke. Add multiple strokes using the Appearance panel and apply the Transform effect, increasing the horizontal and vertical scale as necessary.

Review

Questions

1 What are the attributes of an object and where are they located in Illustrator?

2 After you add an effect to an object, what are the steps you need to take to modify the effect?

3 What are graphic styles? Name at least one advantage and disadvantage to using preset graphic styles.

4 True or False: The attributes of an object in Illustrator can have multiple levels of transparency.

5 How are graphic styles shared between documents?

Answers

1 The attributes of an object can be broken down into four categories: Fill attributes, Stroke attributes, Transparency attributes, and Effects attributes. These attributes are editable and are located in the Appearance panel, where they can also be modified.

2 You can edit an effect by double-clicking on the effect name in the Appearance panel. Double-clicking the effect name opens an effect dialog box, allowing you to make changes.

3 Graphic styles are combinations of attributes that have been saved into a library. An advantage of graphic styles is the ability to quickly apply a complex style to an object or multiple objects. A disadvantage to using preset styles is that the style may not match the design of your project.

4 True. An object in Illustrator, such as a circle, might have attribute such as a stroke, a fill, and an applied effect. The transparency of these attributes can be controlled independently of each other. Additionally, each of the attributes has a blending mode that can be controlled.

5 After you create a custom graphic style, you can save it by pressing the panel menu button in the Graphic Styles panel and choosing Save Graphic Style Library. In another document, choose Open Graphic Style Library > Other Library from the Graphic Styles panel menu and select the custom library. Once this library is available in the new document, you can use the graphic styles.

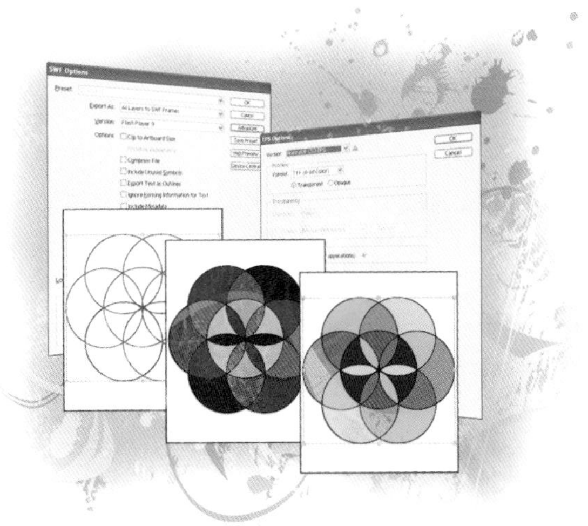

What you'll learn in this lesson:

- Saving native Illustrator files
- Saving a file as an EPS format for use in layout applications
- Saving a file as a PDF for distribution or review
- Saving a file for use on the Web

Exporting and Saving Files

In this lesson, you will re-create a logo and then save and export the logo in a variety of different ways for use in print and on-line. You will save it as an Illustrator file, a PDF, and as a Flash animation.

Starting up

Before starting, make sure that your tools and panels are consistent by resetting your workspace. See "Resetting Adobe Illustrator CS4 Preferences" on page 3.

You will work with several files from the ai10lessons folder in this lesson. Make sure that you have loaded the ailessons folder onto your hard drive from the supplied DVD. See "Loading lesson files" on page 4.

See Lesson 10 in action!

Use the accompanying video to gain a better understanding of how to use some of the features shown in this lesson. The video tutorial for this lesson can be found on the included DVD.

Saving using the AI file format

The default Adobe Illustrator file format saves all the data needed to edit and work with your Illustrator documents. Layers, symbols, swatches, and graphic styles are all included when you save a file in the .ai format, and the file's contents remain fully editable.

1 In Illustrator CS4, choose File > Open. In the Open dialog box, navigate to the ai10lessons folder and select ai1001.jpg. Press Open. The file that opens is a low resolution JPEG that you will be re-creating. The first thing you should do is save it as a native .ai file, then you can start to modify it.

2 Choose File > Save As. In the Save As dialog box, navigate to the ai10lessons folder and type **ai1001_work.ai** in the Name text field. Press Save. The Illustrator Options dialog box appears.

   The dialog box is divided into four editable sections: Version, Fonts, Options, and Transparency. Make sure that the Version drop-down menu is set to Illustrator CS4. This menu allows you to set the version of Illustrator with which your files are compatible. Choosing an older version of Illustrator from this drop-down menu is called saving a legacy file. It is important to remember that legacy files do not support all the features of the current version of Illustrator.

3 Make sure that the Fonts text field is set to 100%. The Fonts area specifies when to embed the entire font as opposed to only the characters that are used in your document. If a font has 1000 characters and you only use 20 of them in your file, it is usually not worth using up the extra file space to include the entire font in your document. This file does not use any text except the logo, which has been converted to a graphic; leave this option unchanged.

4 Leave the checkboxes in the Options section at their defaults.

ADJUSTMENT	USE
Create PDF Compatible File	Saves a PDF representation of the document in the Illustrator file. This option is used to make Illustrator compatible with other Adobe applications.
Include Linked Files	Embeds files that are linked to the artwork. If your document does not use any linked files then this option is grayed out.
Embed ICC Profiles	Embeds the color profile that Illustrator was using when your file was created and creates a color-managed document.
Use Compression	Uses lossless compression to compress the data in the Illustrator file, shrinking the Illustrator file size without sacrificing image quality.

By default, in a new document the Create PDF compatible File, Embed ICC Profiles, and Use Compression options will be selected.

The transparency field is grayed out unless you are saving to a version of Illustrator prior to Illustrator 9. When active, this area allows you to determine whether transparent areas of your document are discarded (to preserve the edibility of document paths) or maintained (to preserve the document's appearance).

5 Press OK to save your new Illustrator file. Keep it open for the next part of the lesson.

Saving an illustration with layers

In this exercise, you will create a logo using the transform effect, then you will make three different versions of the logo on separate layers. Later on, you will generate a PDF that contains layers that you email to a fictitious client.

Make a template layer

The first thing you will do is make it a template layer. A template layer automatically locks the layer, and dims the image to 50%. This makes it easier for you to rebuild a new logo over it, because of the color difference and the fact that the layer is locked means that you can't select the logo and move it by accident.

1 Open the Layers panel by choosing Window > Layers or by pressing the Layers button () in the dock on the right side of the workspace.

2 Double-click the text *Layer 1* in the Layers panel. The Layer Options dialog box appears. In the Name text field, type **template** to rename the layer, then select the Template checkbox to automatically convert this layer to a template layer. Press OK.

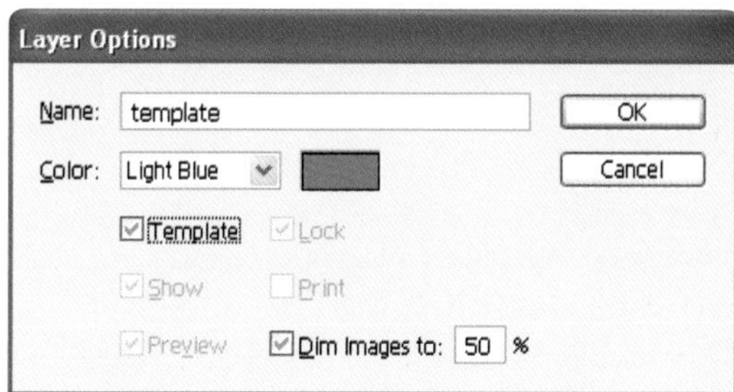

Converting a layer into a template layer.

You can now make a new layer on which you can work.

3 In the Layers panel, press the panel menu button (▾≡) and select New Layer from the list. When the Layer Options dialog box appears, type **working** in the Name text field and press OK.

4 From the Tools panel, select the Ellipse tool (○). The Ellipse tool may be hidden under the Rectangle tool (□). If this is the case, click and hold the Rectangle tool to reveal the other hidden tools and choose the Ellipse tool.

The first circle you will draw is the bottom left circle. You will then use the Transform Effect to make all the other circles.

5 In the Control panel at the top of the workspace, choose None (⧄) from the Fill drop-down menu and make sure that the Stroke is set to black.

6 Start by holding down the Alt (Windows) or Option (Mac OS) key to make your reference point centered, then click in the center of the bottom left circle and drag down and to the right to make the circle bigger. Don't let go of the mouse.

7 Press and hold the Shift key. This will make your ellipse a perfect circle.

8 If the circle is not aligned, you can hold down the spacebar to move the object you are drawing. You may need to ask a colleague to help you hold down a few keys!

9 Now you can let go of the mouse. If necessary, use the Selection tool (↖) from the Tools panel to move the circle into place.

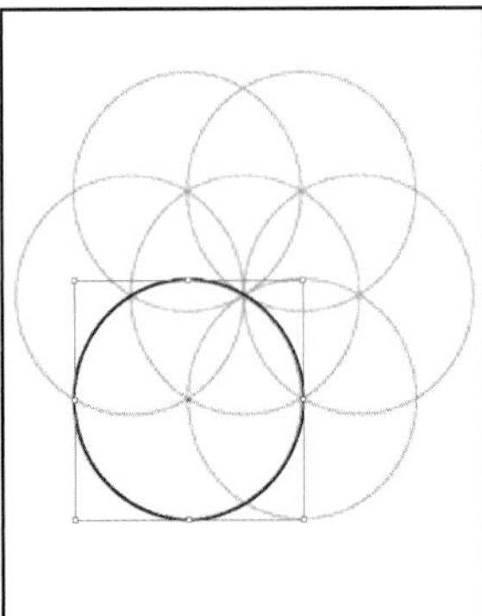

Drawing the first circle

Using the Transform Effect

Instead of copying and pasting this circle, then manually positioning it, you will use the Transform Effect to do the work for you. The Transform Effect allows you to move, scale, and rotate, while making copies of any given object.

1 Make sure the circle is still selected. If necessary, click the circle using the Selection tool (↖).

2 Open the Appearance panel by choosing Window > Appearance or by pressing the Appearance button (◉) in the dock on the right side of the workspace. In the Appearance panel, select the stroke.

3 Press the Add New Effect button (*fx*) and choose Distort & Transform > Transform.

   The Transform Effects dialog box opens. You need to have six circles around the center circle that you have not yet defined. Since you already have 1 circle, you will need 5 more that rotate around the center circle

4 In the copies text field, type **5**.

5 Under Rotate, type **60** in the Angle text field.

6 Make sure Preview is checked and drag the Move Horizontal slider to the right. You can start seeing the effect take place. Now type **43 pt** in the Horizontal text field. Press OK.

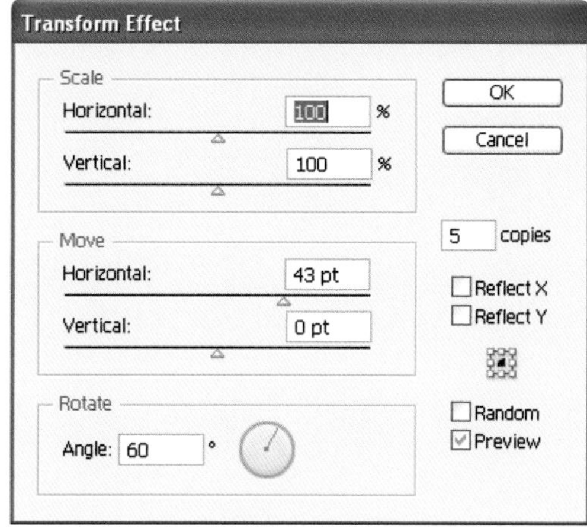

Choosing the correct settings for the transform.

Duplicating a Stroke

You will now duplicate a stroke, to make the center circle.

1 Make sure the Stroke is selected in the Transform panel and press the Duplicate Selected Item button (⊒).

2 Now that you have a duplicate Stroke, you will change the Transform options for your top Stroke. Press the arrow next to the top Stroke, and click the *Transform* text that appears.

3 The Transform Effect dialog box appears. In the copies text field, change the number to **1**. In the Move section, change the Horizontal text field to **21 pt**. and in the Vertical text field type **38**. Select the Preview checkbox to view the change. You should now have the center circle. Press OK.

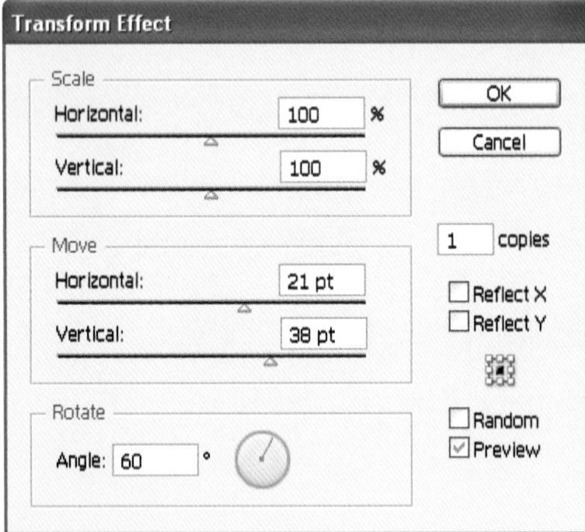

The settings for the second transform.

Now that you have the logo completed, you will get the file ready to be made into a layered PDF.

4 Choose File > Save to save your work.

Saving different versions of the logo onto separate layers

Now that you have made the logo, it is time to save it onto different layers and colorize it.

Expanding appearance

The logo itself is just two strokes with Transform applied to each stroke. In order for you to colorize the logo, you will need to reduce the logo down to paths.

1 Choose View > Outline. Notice that your illustration is just one path.

2 Choose View > Outline, again. This takes you back into Preview mode.

Saving as a graphic style

By saving this illustration as a graphic style, you can create another circle, then apply the graphic style to get this same sort of effect. This effect was based on the size of the original circle, so results may vary, if you draw a circle of the same size you can get this exact effect with one click. Try it with a square, or any object and it will apply the same stroke and transform options to the object. See Lesson 9, "Using Effects and Transparency," for more info on graphic styles.

3 Choose Select > All to make sure your artwork is selected, then choose Object > Expand Appearance.

4 Choose View > Outline. Notice that the entire illustration appears as paths.

5 Choose View > Outline, again. This takes you back into Preview mode.

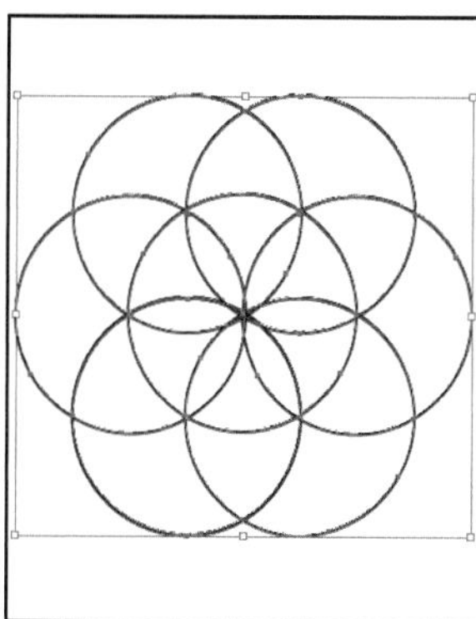

The artwork expanded.

Save the first version

Now for a little layer management.

1 Open the Layers panel by choosing Window > Layers or by pressing the Layers button (◈) in the dock.

2 Select the template layer and drag the layer to the Delete Selection button (🗑) at the bottom of the panel. You no longer need the template layer.

   If a dialog box appears stating that the template layer contains artwork and asks if you want to delete it, choose Yes.

3 Double-click the text *working* in the Layers panel. In the Layer Options dialog box that appears, type **Version 1** in the Name text field and press OK.

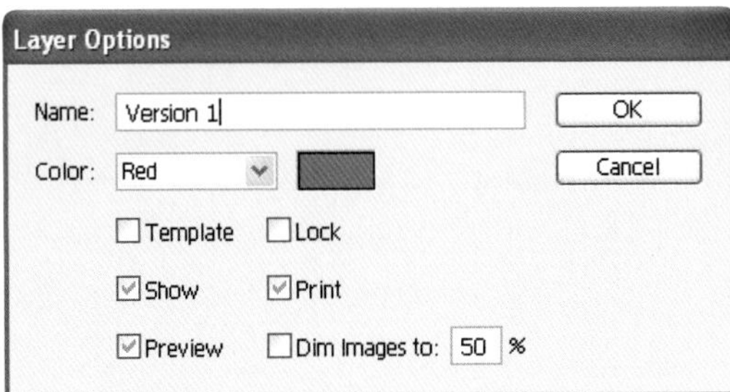

Renaming layers.

4 Press the Layers panel menu button (▾≡) and choose Duplicate 'Version 1'.

5 Double-click the *Version 1 copy* layer and in the Layer Options dialog box, type **Version 2** in the Name text field and press OK.

6 Click the visibility icon (👁) to the left of the Version 1 layer to hide the layer. Now that Version 1 is on its own hidden layer, you can change the look of Version 2.

7 Choose File > Save.

Using Live Paint

The easiest way to colorize all the individual pieces of this logo is to make this logo a Live Paint Group. You will then be able to colorize this logo with the Live Paint Bucket tool.

1 Make sure the logo is still selected. If necessary choose Select > All. Select the Version 2 layer to make sure you are working on it.

2 Choose Object > Live Paint > Make.

3 From the Tools panel, choose the Live Paint Bucket tool (🪣).

4 Double-click the Fill color in the Tools panel and choose any color from the Color Picker dialog box, then press OK.

5 Randomly click the Live Paint Bucket tool in any section of the logo any way you like. You may want to color the object symmetrically the same on corresponding sides for a better overall look.

Using the Color Guide panel

Since you created this document from a jpeg, there are no colors in the Swatches panel. You will use the color guide to pick colors that are in harmony with your current color, then you can add them to your Swatches panel.

1 Choose Window > Color Guide or press the Color Guide button (◭) in the dock to open the Color Guide panel.

2 Click on the Harmony Rules drop-down menu at the top of the panel to view all the Harmony Rules for the initial color you picked. Choose any Harmony Rule from the list.

3 Press the Color Guide panel menu button (▾≡) and choose Save Colors as Swatches. The colors are added to the Swatches panel as a color group.

4 Make sure the image is deselected by choosing Select > Deselect, then open the Swatches panel by pressing the Swatches button (▦) in the dock. Choose a color from the new color group created in the last step.

5 Now you can use your left and right arrows on the keyboard, with the Live Paint Bucket tool selected and colorize the artwork any way you would like.

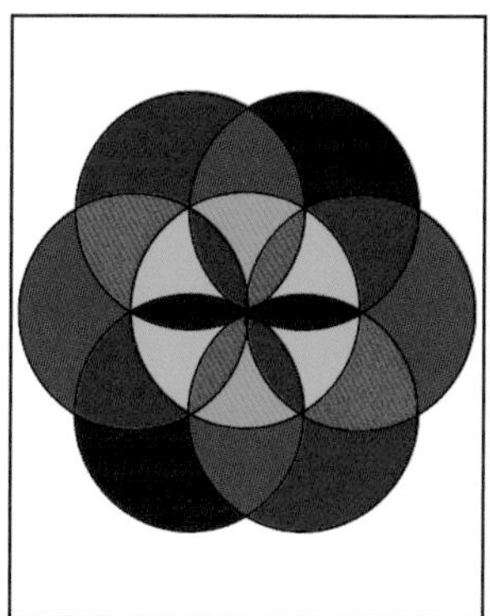

Your finished Version 2 should look something like this.

Saving the third version

1 With the Version 2 layer still selected, open the Layers panel. Press the Layers panel menu button (▾≡) and choose Duplicate 'Version 2.'

2 Double-click the *Version 2 copy* layer and in the Layer Options dialog box, type **Version 3** in the Name text field and press OK.

3 Click the visibility icon ( ) to the left of the Version 2 layer to hide the layer. Now that Version 2 is on its own hidden layer, you can change the look of Version 3.

Your layers should look something like this.

4 Choose File > Save.

Using Recolor Artwork

You want one more option to send off to a client. You will now use Recolor Artwork to change the color.

1 Select the Version 3 layer in the Layers panel and choose Select > All.

2 Open the Color Guide panel by pressing the Color Guide button ( ) in the dock. In the Color Guide panel, press the Color Guide panel menu button ( ) and choose Recolor Artwork.

3 At the top of the dialog box, choose any harmony rule from the drop-down menu. Make sure that recolor art is checked in the bottom left of the dialog box. Press OK when you find a color scheme you like and save any changes to the swatch group.

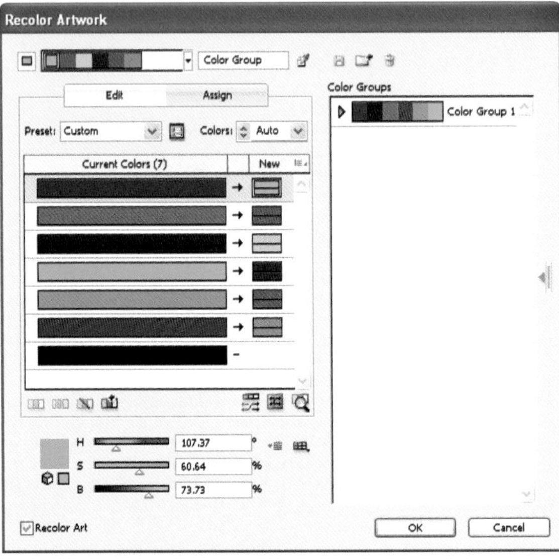

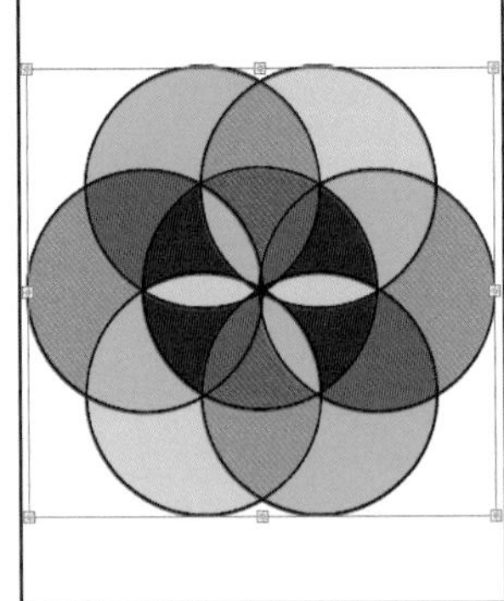

Recoloring Artwork for the third version.

4 Choose File > Save.

Saving a layered PDF

Adobe created the Portable Document Format (PDF) as a universal document distribution format. PDF has become the *de facto* standard for the distribution and exchange of forms and electronic documents around the world. Since you created a file with multiple layers, you can export this PDF so that a client can look through the layers within the PDF and choose which illustration they like best.

1 Choose File > Save As. In the Save As dialog box, select Adobe PDF (.pdf) from the Format drop-down menu. The Name text field automatically adds the .pdf extension to the existing file name. Press Save. The Save Adobe PDF dialog box appears.

2 Choose [High Quality Print] from the Preset drop-down menu. This changes the PDF settings to create a file that is optimized for printing on a desktop printer. Unless you have a specific reason for altering the settings of the PDF, it is best to work with one of the provided presets.

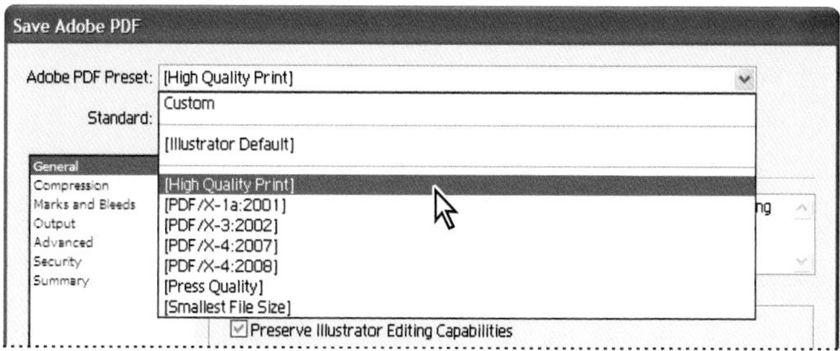

Choose [High Quality Print] from the Preset drop-down menu.

3 Choose Acrobat 7 (PDF 1.6) from the Compatibility drop-down menu. The Create Acrobat Layers from Top-Level Layers checkbox becomes active. Click the checkbox to enable this option, which allows the PDF file to create PDF layers from your top-most Illustrator layers.

A practical application of creating PDF layers from Illustrator would be in a situation where different illustration variations were saved on different layers. You are using it to view separate illustrations. The PDF viewer could then view the different project versions by turning layers on and off.

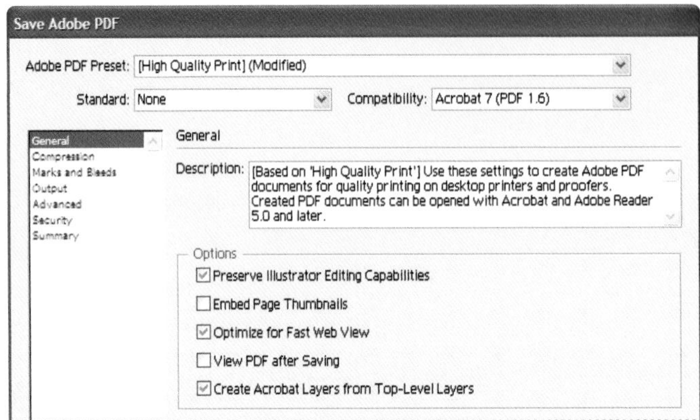

Choose Acrobat 7 (PDF 1.6) from the Compatibility drop-down menu.

Additional PDF options

The Adobe PDF options are divided into categories. Changing any option will cause the name of the preset to change to Custom. The categories are listed on the left side of the Save Adobe PDF dialog box, with the exception of the Standard and Compatibility options, which are at the top of the dialog box.

Standard is used to specify a PDF standard for the file.

Compatibility specifies with which version of Adobe Acrobat the PDF file will be compatible.

General specifies basic file options, such as Illustrator's ability to edit the created PDF file and whether PDF layers are created.

Compression specifies whether bitmap artwork should be compressed.

Marks and Bleeds specifies printer's marks and the bleed and slug areas.

Output controls how colors and PDF/X output intent profiles are saved in the PDF file.

Advanced controls how fonts, overprinting, and transparency are saved in the PDF file.

Security is used to add security (passwords) to the created PDF file.

Summary displays a summary of the current PDF settings.

4 Press Save PDF to save your changes and create your PDF file. Choose File > Close.

Now when the client opens the PDF they can view the different layers, even if they only have the free Adobe Reader.

Integration with other applications

One of the Adobe Creative Suite's greatest strengths is the integration between the individual applications.

Exporting for Photoshop

Illustrator has two ways of integrating with Adobe Photoshop. The first is Illustrator's ability to export files in the Adobe Photoshop (.psd) format. The second is Photoshop's ability to open and place the native Illustrator file format.

Integrating with InDesign

There are two ways in which you can use Adobe Illustrator files in Adobe InDesign: Illustrator files can be copied in Illustrator and pasted directly into InDesign. When brought into InDesign in this fashion, Illustrator files remain completely editable. InDesign also has the ability to import Illustrator files using the Place command.

Integrating with Flash

Illustrator can export files in the Adobe Flash .swf format for publishing on the Web. Also, Illustrator artwork can be imported or pasted into the Flash authoring environment.

Integrating with Premiere and After Effects

If you are working with the applications of the Adobe Production Studio or Creative Suite 3 Production Premium you can easily import native Illustrator files into both After Effects and Premiere for use in motion graphics and video projects.

Saving as EPS

Next you will save this logo as an EPS, as if you needed to import this logo into an older version of QuarkXPress. You can view any one of the three layer versions you like for this exercise.

The Encapsulated Post Script (EPS) file format is an image format used primarily in the print industry. The EPS format supports both bitmap and vector information and is ideal for situations in which you have to take artwork from Illustrator into applications, such as Quark, that don't support native Illustrator file import. Virtually all graphic and word processing programs accept imported EPS artwork. Two important facts to note about EPS files: because they are based on the Postscript language, they can contain both bitmap and vector graphics; and they do not support transparency.

1 Choose File > Open. In the Open dialog box, navigate to the ai10lessons folder and select ai1001_work.ai. Press Open.

2 Choose File > Save As. In the Save As dialog box, select Illustrator EPS (.eps) from the Format drop-down menu. The Name text field automatically adds the .eps extension to the existing file name. Press Save; the EPS Options dialog box opens.

3 Set the Version to Illustrator CS3 EPS. The Version option allows you to specify the version of Illustrator with which you want your new EPS file to be compatible. When you save the EPS file to a legacy version you lose some editing features.

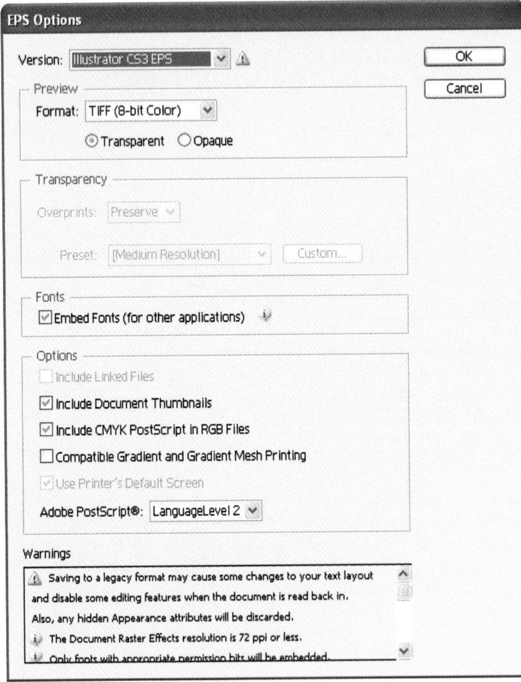

The EPS Options dialog box.

4 Leave the Format section at its defaults. The format settings determine the appearance of the preview image that is saved with your EPS file. Preview images are used in applications that cannot display EPS files.

5 Leave all other settings at their defaults. Press OK to save your EPS file. Keep it open.

A warning dialog will appear informing you that saving to a legacy format (CS3 or earlier) may cause some changes in the document. This warning appears whenever you save an illustrator file to a legacy format. Press OK or Yes to continue.

The settings in the Save As dialog box are reset to the default configuration every time a new file is created. When a file is opened and re-saved, the settings in the dialog box are based on the previously set options for that file.

Additional EPS options

Embed Fonts (For Other Applications) Embedding fonts ensures that the original font is displayed and printed if the file is placed into another application, such as Adobe InDesign. Selecting the Embed Fonts option increases the size of your EPS file.

Include Linked Files embeds files that are linked to the artwork. This option is grayed out if Illustrator does not detect a linked file.

Include Document Thumbnails creates a thumbnail image of the artwork. The thumbnail is displayed in the Illustrator Open and Place dialog boxes. Activating this option increases the file size minutely.

Include CMYK PostScript In RGB Files allows RGB color documents to be printed from applications that do not support RGB output.

Compatible Gradient And Gradient Mesh Printing enables older printers and PostScript devices to print gradients and gradient meshes by rasterizing gradient objects.

Adobe PostScript determines the level of PostScript used to save the artwork.

Save for Web & Devices

Illustrator's Save for Web & Devices functionality allows you to optimize Illustrator artwork for the Web and mobile devices. Because of the nature of web browsers, only a few file formats can be displayed on the Internet. While you always want to keep your working files in the native Illustrator format, you have to optimize your images before they can be displayed on the Web. In this exercise, you will save a file in the .gif format, which is a good format for limited color artwork like logos and motifs. And because the .gif format supports transparency, which means you won't get a white box around your logo like you would with a .jpeg

1 With the ai1001_work file open, choose File > Save for Web & Devices to open the Save for Web & Devices dialog box. You can view any one of the three layer versions you like for this exercise.

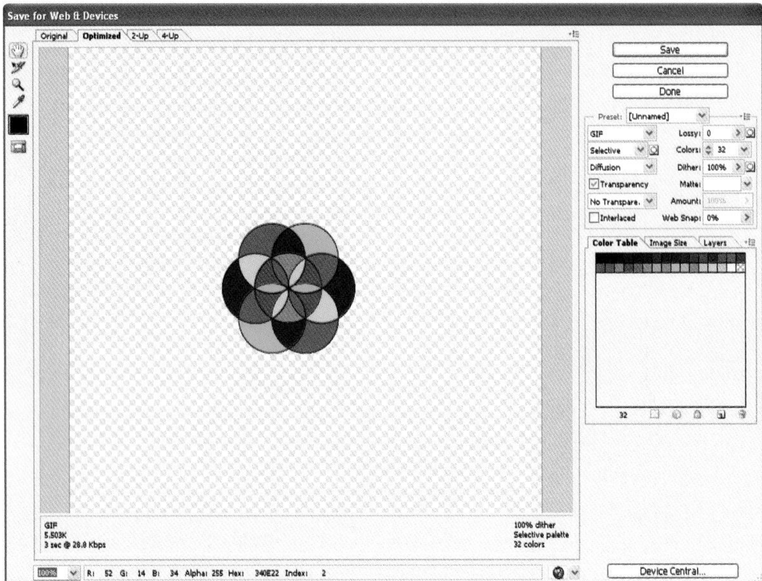

The Save for Web and Devices dialog box.

2 Select GIF from the Optimized file format drop-down menu in the preset area on the right of the dialog box.

3 In the Colors drop-down menu, select 32. The GIF format allow the image to contain a maximum of 256 colors, which is what makes it unsuitable for saving photographs and other imagery with continuous tones of color. The logo in this example contains a smaller number of colors so saving the additional color information only adds to the file size without providing any improvement in the appearance of the image. Note that even though the logo contains only 6 colors, if we restrict the GIF too much, the edges of the image will appear blocky and unattractive.

4 Make sure that the Transparency checkbox is selected. This will allow your GIF image to have transparent areas. Leave all other settings at their defaults.

5 Press Save. In the Save dialog box, navigate to the ai10lessons folder and press Save to complete the process.

Web image formats

GIF is an acronym for Graphic Interchange File, the GIF format is usually used on the Web to display logos, motifs, and other limited tone imagery. The GIF format supports a maximum of 256 colors as well as transparency, and is the only one of the three formats listed here that supports built-in animation.

JPEG is an acronym for Joint Photographic Experts Group, the JPEG file format has found wide acceptance on the Web as the main format for displaying photographs and other continuous tone imagery. The JPEG format supports a range of millions of colors allowing for the accurate display of a wide range of artwork.

PNG is an acronym for Portable Network Graphics. PNG files come in two different varieties: PNG-8 files can support as many as 256 colors (like the GIF format); PNG-24 files can support millions of colors (like the JPEG format). Both PNG varieties can support transparency and in an improvement on the GIF format PNG-24 images can actually support varying degrees of transparency.

Making a Flash animation

You can make basic flash animations right out of Adobe Illustrator. In this next exercise, you will make your logo rotate around, then save it as a Flash .swf file. Illustrator does not have a timeline, so to animate an object, you need to either do it by layers or by using blends. You will use layers to convert the layers into SWF frames.

1 Make sure you still have the ai1001_work file open. You can animate any version you like, just make sure none of the other layers are visible. (Non-visible layers will not be animated.)

2 Choose the Selection tool (↖) from the Tools panel and select the image.

3 Double-click the Rotate tool (↻) in the Tools panel. In the Rotate dialog box that appears, type 20 in the Angle text field, then press Copy.

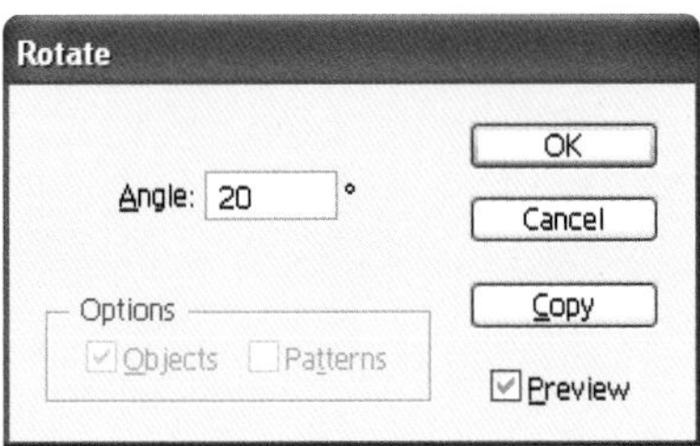

Rotate the illustration 20 degrees.

4 Now you have two copies of the illustration. To animate the rotation 360 degrees you will need 16 more copies. (18 illustrations X 20 degrees = 360 degrees).

5 Instead of using the Rotate tool 16 more times, Hold down the Ctrl key (Windows) or the Command key (Mac OS) and press the D key 16 times. This shortcut accesses Object > Transform > Transform Again.

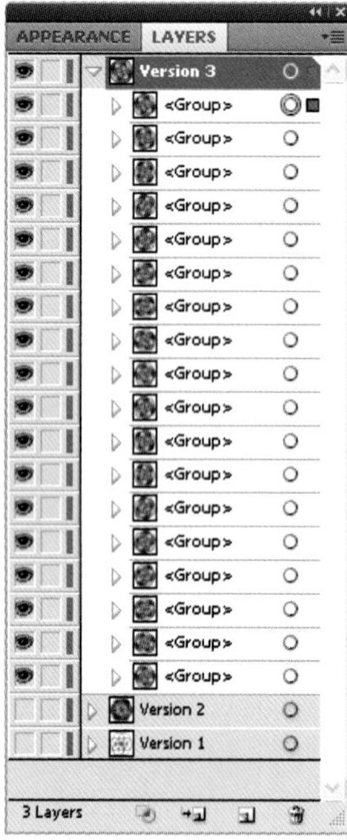

This is what your layers should look like.

Because Illustrator can animate only top-level layers, you need to release the sublayers in sequence, so that they become their own layers. Then you will drag them above the top layer, because that layer is really just a holder for all the sublayers. You will then delete that holder layer, and you will be ready to animate.

6 Select all the sublayers in the Version 3 sublayer by clicking on the circle to the immediate right of the Version 3 layer.

7 Press the Layers panel menu button (▾≡) and choose Release to Layers (Sequence).

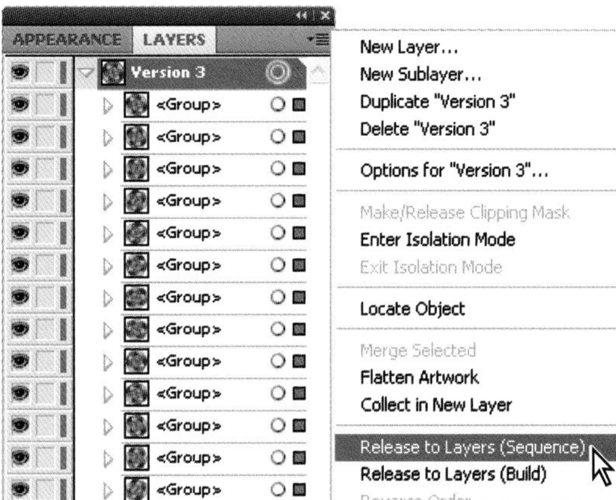

Releasing Layers to a sequence.

Now that the layers are released, they should be numbered 4-21. This means you have all 18 versions you need.

8 Select Layer 4 through Layer 21 by clicking on the first one, holding Shift, then clicking on the last one. Drag these layers above the Version 3 layer.

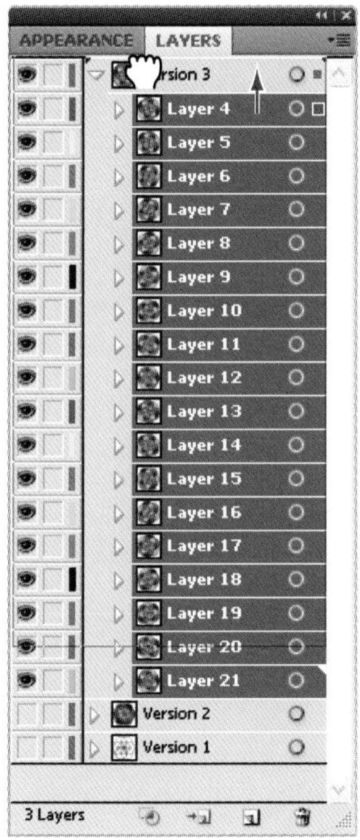

Moving the sublayers to top-level layers.

9 You can now select the Version 3 layer and press the Delete Selection button (🗑) to delete the layer. The Version 3 layer was a holder layer which is not needed after you released the layers to sequence.

Now you're ready to animate the illustration.

Exporting a Flash animation

1 Choose File > Export.

2 In the Export dialog box, choose Flash (*.SWF) from the Save as type drop-down menu. Navigate to the ai10lessons folder and press Save.

3 In the SWF Options dialog box, choose AI Layers to SWF Frames from the Export As drop-down menu.

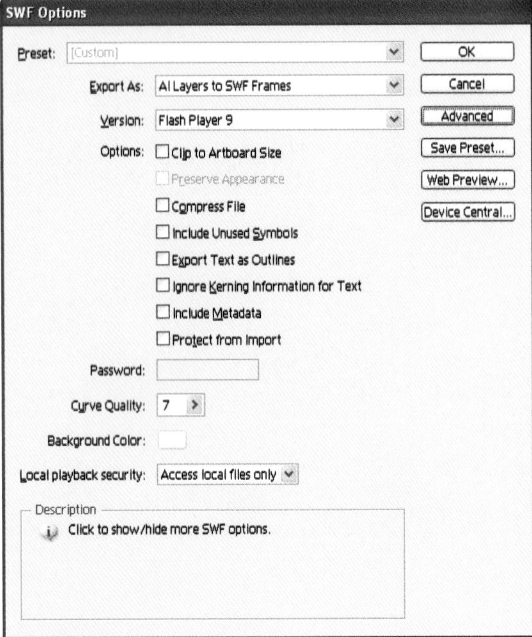

The Basic SWF Options.

4 Press the Advanced button on the right side of the dialog box and select the Looping checkbox. This will rotate your logo for infinity.

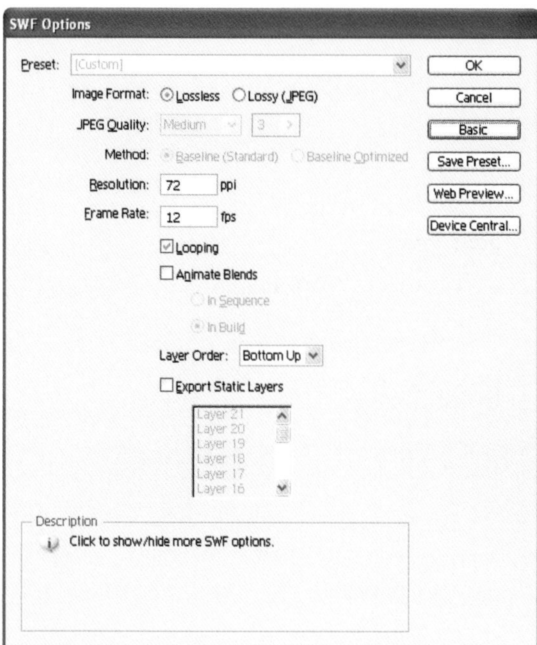

The Advanced SWF Options.

5 Press OK. Now you can open your animation by double clicking it if you have Flash Player; if not, you should be able to open it in any Browser window such as Safari or Internet Explorer to see your animation.

6 Choose File > Close. If asked to save the file, choose No.

Congratulations! You have finished Lesson 10, "Exporting and Saving Files."

FILE FORMAT	NAME	DESCRIPTION	EXPORT COMMAND
AI	Adobe Illustrator	Illustrator native format, used for representing single-page vector-based drawings. Also available in AIT (Template) format.	File > Save
PDF	Portable Document Format	Captures formatting information from a variety of applications, making it possible to send formatted documents and have them appear on the recipient's monitor or printer as they were intended.	File > Save
EPS	Encapsulated PostScript	Standard file format for importing and exporting PostScript files.	File > Save
FXG	Flash XML Graphics	Format based on a subset of MXML, the XML-based programming language used by the FLEX framework.	File > Save
SVG	Scalable Vector Graphics	Vector format that produces high-quality, interactive web graphics. Also offers SVGZ (Compressed) format.	File > Save, File > Save for Web & Devices
DWG	AutoCAD Drawing	Standard file format for saving vector graphics created in AutoCAD.	File > Export
DXF	AutoCAD Interchange File	Drawing interchange format for exporting AutoCAD drawings to or importing drawings from other applications.	File > Export
(W)BMP	Bitmap Picture	Standard Windows image format for low-resolution printing and Web applications.	File > Export, File > Save for Web & Devices
EMF	Enhanced Metafile	Windows interchange format for exporting vector graphics data.	File > Export
JPEG	Joint Photographic Experts Group	Standard format for displaying photographic images over the Web.	File > Export, File > Save for Web & Devices
PICT	(Macintosh) Picture	Used with Mac OS graphics and page-layout applications to transfer images between applications.	File > Export
SWF	ShockWave Flash	Vector-based graphics format for creating interactive, animated web graphics.	File > Export, File > Save for Web & Devices
PSD	Photoshop Document	Standard (native) Photoshop export format.	File > Export

FILE FORMAT	NAME	DESCRIPTION	EXPORT COMMAND
PNG	Portable Network Graphics	Lossless compression and display of images on the Web in 8- or 24-bit formats.	File > Export, File > Save for Web & Devices
TGA	Targa	For use on systems that use the Truevision® video board.	File > Export
TXT	Text Format	Exports text in an illustration to a text file.	File > Export
TIFF	Tagged-Image File Format	Flexible bitmap image format supported by most paint, image-editing, and page-layout applications.	File > Export
WMF	Windows Metafile	Exchanges files from 16-bit Windows drawing and layout programs.	File > Export
GIF	Graphics Interchange Format	Used for web graphics that allow an image to reference a palette of up to 256 colors from the 24-bit RGB color space.	File > Save for Web & Devices

Self study

Open one of the Illustrator files you saved from one of the other lessons and practice saving it as a PDF and EPS file.Try re-coloring the artwork on a saved copy layer.Then view the layers in the PDF.

Review

Questions

1 What does the Create PDF Compatible File in the Save As Illustrator Options dialog box do?

2 What does EPS stand for and where is it primarily used?

3 Which web graphics format is best for saving an image with continuous tones of color, without transparency and is compatible with most web browsers?

4 Can you create a Flash animation in Illustrator?

Answers

1 Saves a PDF representation of the document in the Illustrator file.This option is used to make Illustrator compatible with other Adobe applications.

2 EPS stands for Encapsulated Post Script. It is a legacy file format used primarily in the print industry.

3 The JPEG format is best for continuous tone imagery, does not support transparency and is compatible with the majority of common web browsers.

4 Yes, you can export layer or blend based .SWF files from Illustrator.

Lesson 11

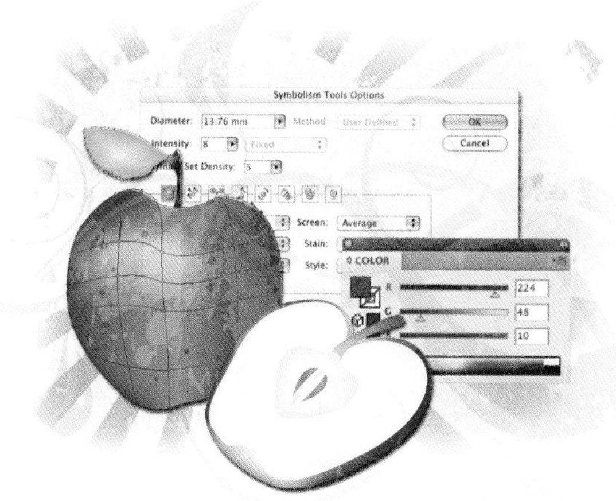

What you'll learn in this lesson:

- Combining objects using the Blend tool
- Applying a gradient mesh
- Creating symbols
- Using the symbolism tools

Advanced Blending Techniques

In this lesson, you will explore methods to blend objects to create realistic appearances and artistic effects. You will use the Blend tool and create advanced gradients using the gradient mesh options, and use symbols to create a surface texture.

Starting up

Before starting, make sure that your tools and panels are consistent by resetting your workspace. See "Resetting Adobe Illustrator CS4 Preferences" on page 3.

You will work with several files from the ai11lessons folder in this lesson. Make sure that you have loaded the ailessons folder onto your hard drive from the supplied DVD. See "Loading lesson files" on page 4.

See Lesson 11 in action!

Use the accompanying video to gain a better understanding of how to use some of the features shown in this lesson. The video tutorial for this lesson can be found on the included DVD.

Using the Blend Tool

The Blend tool and Make Blend command allow you to create a blend, which is basically a transition of color between two or more selected images. Blends are often desirable when there are images overlapping each other that you may want to have a more combined look instead of images that appear more separated, and just kind of sitting on top of one another. To see the blending in action, you'll start by working on the seeds of the apple.

1 In Illustrator CS4, choose File > Open. When the Open dialog box appears, navigate to the ai11lessons folder and select the ai1101.ai file. Press Open.

2 Select the Zoom tool from the Tools panel (🔍), then click and drag a marquee around the area of the seeds to zoom in more closely.

Zoom in on the inner parts of the apple.

3 Choose the Selection tool (↖) and click on the innermost portion of the seed on the upper left. To see your selected area with more detail, you might want to view the edges of the selected image. To do so, choose View > Show Edges. If you find that you don't like the edges, simply choose View > Hide Edges.

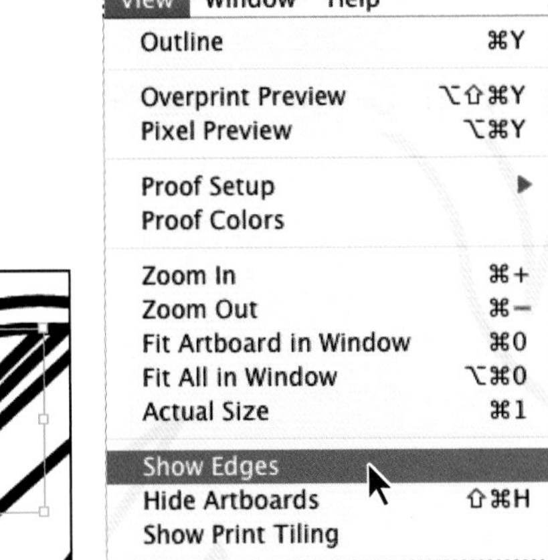

Select the inner part of the apple's seed, then show the edges.

4 With the inner portion of the seed selected, make the sure the fill is active in the Tools panel. Open the Swatches panel by pressing the Swatches button (▦) in the dock on the right side of the workspace. Press the Swatches panel menu button (-≡) in the upper right corner of the panel and choose Small List View, so that you can see the swatch names to apply as you explore this lesson. Choose the swatch *Inner Seed* from the Swatches panel to apply it to the fill of the seed. All the Swatch colors you need are in descending order. Next, you will remove the stroke color.

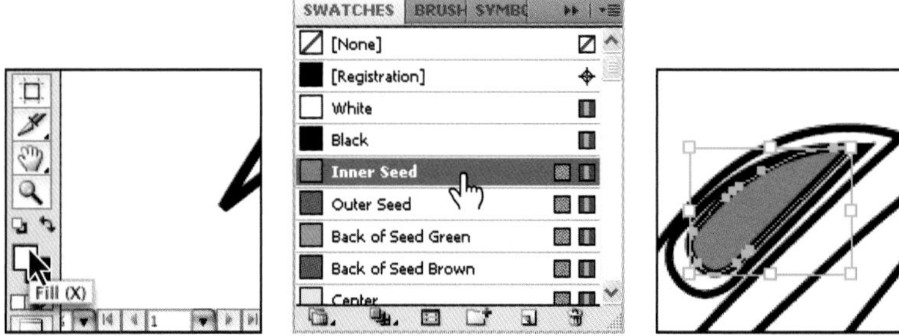

Make sure the fill is active, then select a color from the Swatches panel to color the seed.

5 To remove the stroke, select the Stroke icon (⧉) in the Tools panel. Just below the Stroke icon, press the None button (⧄) to remove the stroke from the seed. Removing the stroke eliminates an adverse effect that can occur on the blend when you combine both objects together depending on the look you're trying to achieve. In the case of the seeds, you want a smooth blending of color rather than harsh edges that the stroke would create.

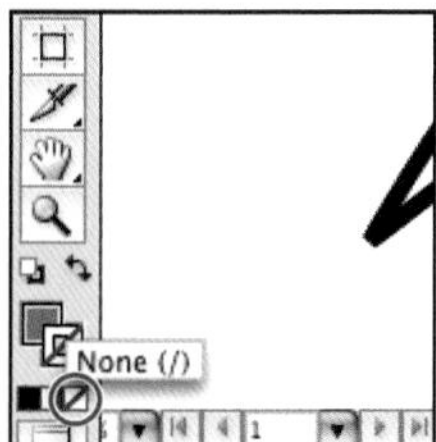

Remove the stroke.

Next you will color the part of the seed located below the area you filled with color and then finish by blending the two together to complete the fill process.

6 Using the Selection tool, select the part of the seed just below the area you just filled.

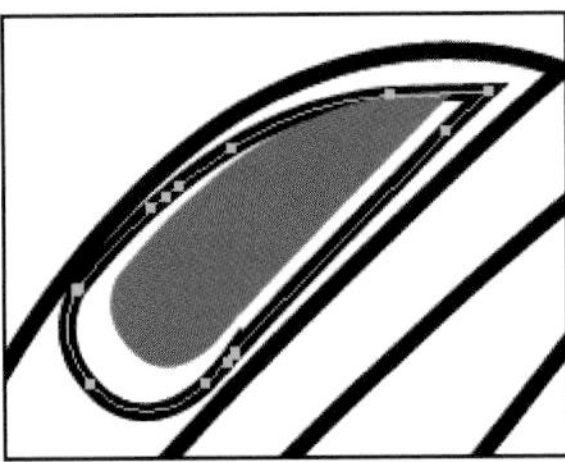

Select the outer part of the seed.

7 Make sure the fill is active in the Tools panel and choose the *Outer Seed* swatch from the Swatches panel to apply it to the fill. Once the dark brown is applied, remove the stroke by selecting the Stroke icon, then pressing the None button below it.

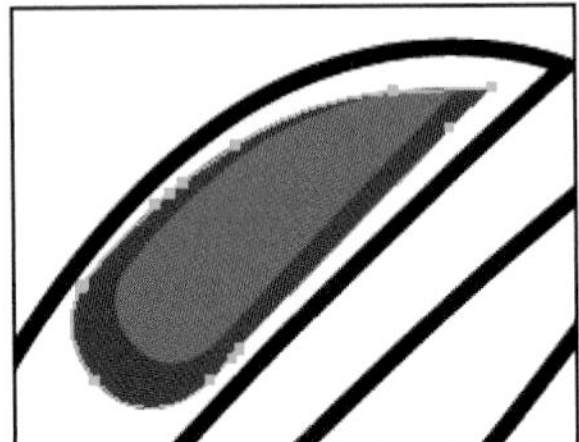

Color the outer part of the seed.

Next, you will blend the two together to create a smooth transition of color between both objects.

8 Keeping the bottom part of the seed selected, hold down the Shift key on your keyboard and click on the light brown part of the seed with the Selection tool so both parts of the seed are now selected.

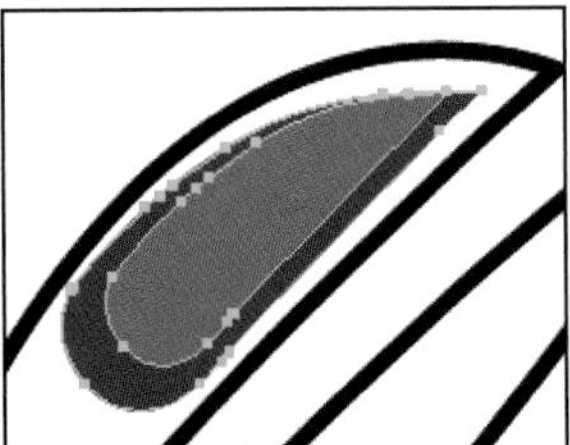

Select both the inner and outer part of the seed.

9 With both images selected, choose Object > Blend > Make or use the keyboard shortcut, Ctrl+Alt+B (Windows) or Command+Option+B (Mac OS).

10 Deselect both images by choosing Select > Deselect and take note of the transition of color between both objects.

Repeat steps 2-9 for the next seed to the lower right. You'll come back to more blend options with the Blend tool shortly.

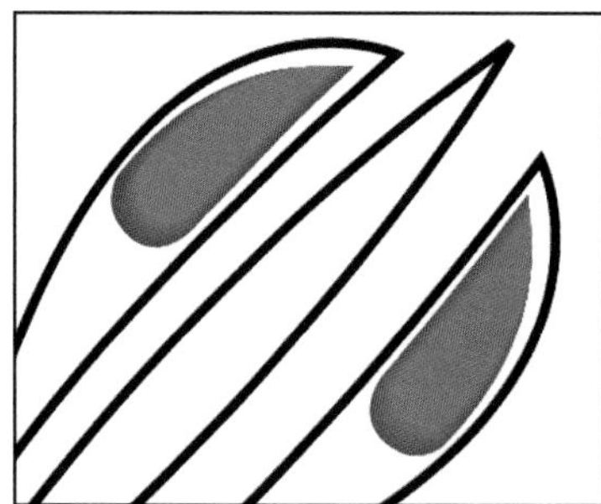

The colored seeds.

11 Choose File > Save As. When the Save As dialog box appears, navigate to the ai11lessons folder and type **ai1101_work.ai** into the Name text field, then press Save. The Illustrator Options dialog box appears, Press OK to continue.

Applying a gradient

Next, you will be applying some gradients to fill in the other shapes that make up the various components of the sliced apple.

1 Select the cutout area just below the top left seed.

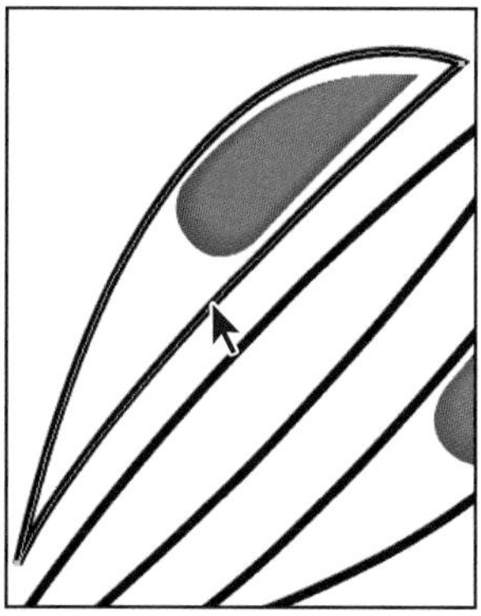

Select the hollow part of the apple.

2 At the bottom of the Tools panel, make sure the fill is active and select the Gradient button to apply a gradient fill to the cutout.

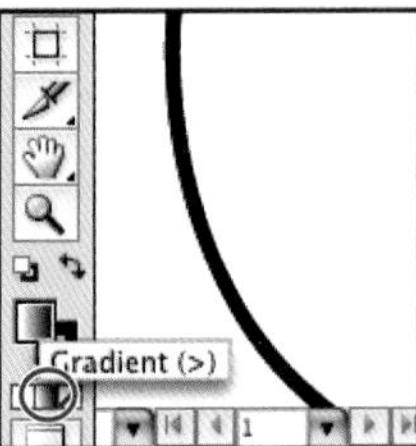

Press the Gradient button to fill the hollow section.

3 Select the Stroke icon in the Tools panel, then press the None button. Next, you'll change the colors of the gradient to more realistic colors.

4 Open the Gradient panel by choosing Window > Gradient or by pressing the Gradient button in the dock on the right side of the workspace.

5 In the Gradient panel, undock the panel by clicking and dragging the tab of the panel where the name is off to the left to separate it from the dock. For more information on altering the workspace, please take a look at Lesson 2, "Getting to Know the Workspace." This makes it easier to use both the Gradient and Color panels consecutively.

6 Choose Window > Swatches to open the Swatches panel or press the Swatches button in the dock.

7 With the cutout of the apple still selected, make sure the fill is active in the Tools panel so you can change the gradient color values of the image.

8 In the Gradient panel, you'll notice a color ramp at the bottom of the panel and two Gradient Sliders. The Gradient panel has more options that appear in the panel, if you can't see the other options, press the panel menu button in the upper-right corner of the panel and choose Show Options from the menu that appears.

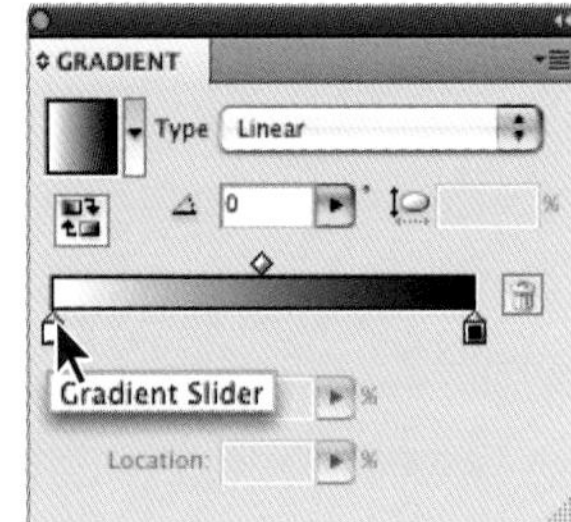

Expand the options of the Gradient panel.

When the gradient is first applied, the colors are set to black-and-white by default. You will be changing the colors in the gradient by using the Gradient panel and the Swatches panel.

9 Start by clicking on the white Gradient Slider on the left to select it.

10 From the Swatches panel menu, you will drag and drop swatches over the color stops in the Gradient panel to create the gradient. Click and hold the swatch *Back of Seed Green* and drop it directly over the White color stop in the Gradient panel.

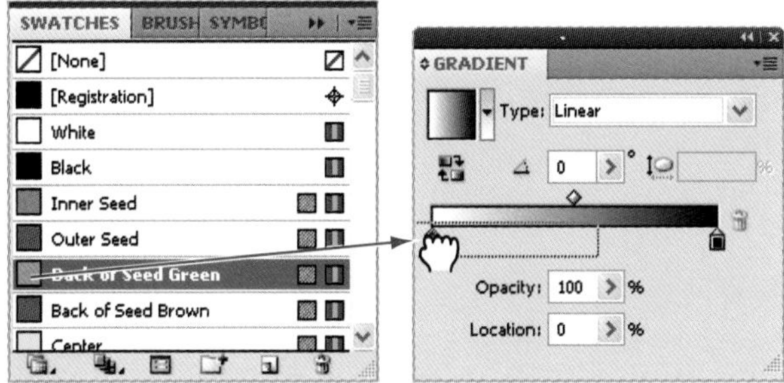

Drag the color swatch from the Swatches panel onto the Gradient panel.

11 Now click and drag the *Back of Seed Brown* swatch from the Swatches panel over the Black color stop in the Gradient panel.

To create the gradient in the next cutout, you will use a shortcut method with the Eyedropper tool.

12 Select the cutout to the bottom right. With the cutout selected, choose the Eyedropper tool (✐) from the Tools panel.

13 Using the Eyedropper, click on the fill of the first cutout, the second cutout should inherit all the color properties from the first one.

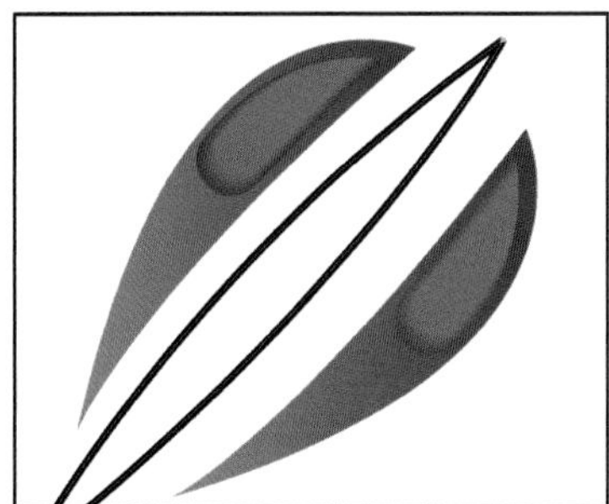

Use the Eyedropper tool to copy the gradient of the first hollow area to the second.

The slit in the apple between the seed cutouts will be where you will apply the next gradation.

Applying Radial Gradients

You'll now apply a radial gradient instead of the default linear gradient. You can change gradient patterns easily in the Gradient panel.

1 Choose the Selection tool (↖) from the Tools panel and select the slit between the cutouts.

2 Apply a gradient fill like you did in step 2 of the last exercise. You'll notice that it applies the gradient using the same color values from the previous gradient that was applied. You will change the colors just like you did before, only this time you'll also change the gradient pattern.

To add another slider, just click below the color ramp in the Gradient panel. To remove a slider, click and drag down on the slider and it just disappears!

3 Click and drag the *White* color swatch over the left color stop.

4 Click and drag the *Center* color swatch over the right color stop.

5 To change the pattern of the gradient, choose Radial from the Type drop-down menu just above the color ramp.

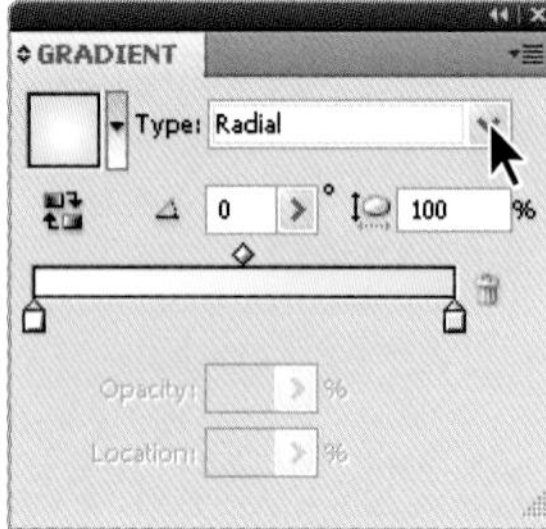

Change the type of gradient to Radial.

6 Finish the process by setting the stroke value of the object to None. When finished, the image should look similar to the figure below.

The finished seeds.

As you can see, there are some nice color and shading options using gradients. For more information about standard gradients, refer to Lesson 4, "Adding Color."

7 Choose File > Save to save your work.

Applying gradients using Illustrator's Gradient Mesh options

While standard gradients are really nice for shading, they don't offer the flexibility you may need for more-complex shading alternatives. With the Gradient Mesh options that are available in Illustrator, you'll find that you can get much more detailed with the shading and color placement of the gradient. You will start by modifying the apple core area with a gradient mesh.

1 Using the Selection tool (↖), select the apple core area just below the seed cutouts and the slit in the middle. If necessary, choose the Zoom tool (🔍) and zoom out to view the apple core area.

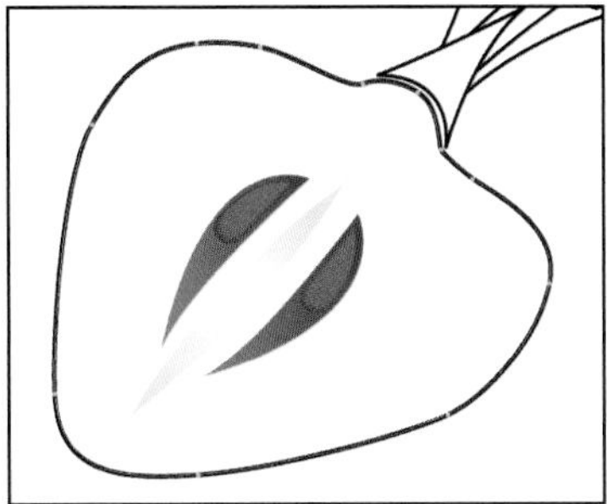

Select the core of the apple.

2 Choose Object > Create Gradient Mesh.

3 In the Create Gradient Mesh dialog box, type **3** into the Rows text field and **2** in the Columns text field. Choose Flat from the Appearance drop-down menu and type **100** in the Highlight text field. Select the Preview checkbox to see the results, then press OK.

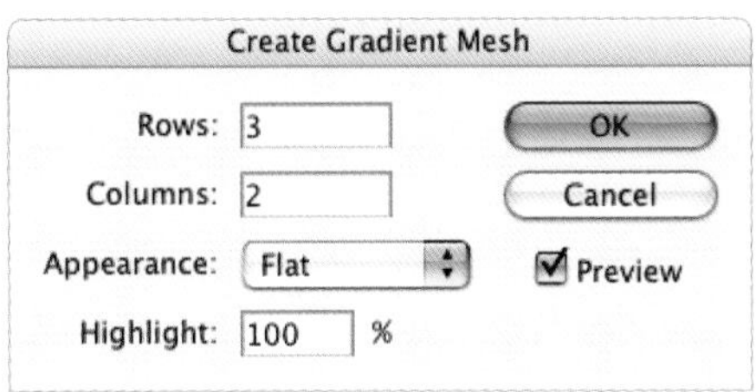

Gradient Mesh settings.

Once the mesh has been established, you can use different tools to modify it including the Mesh tool and the Direct Selection tool.

4 Choose the Direct Selection tool ( ) from the Tools panel. You'll notice anchor points on the mesh, click the anchor point at the top of the middle division line. You'll also see that handles for the anchor points appear when you select it with the Direct Selection tool.

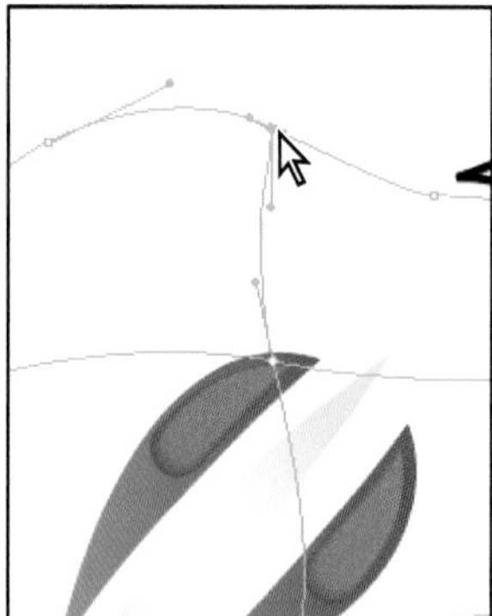

Select the anchor point to reveal its handles.

5 With the anchor point selected, make sure the Fill icon ( ) is active in the Tools panel and the Swatches panel is visible. Choose *Inner Apple 1* from the Swatches panel for the Fill color.

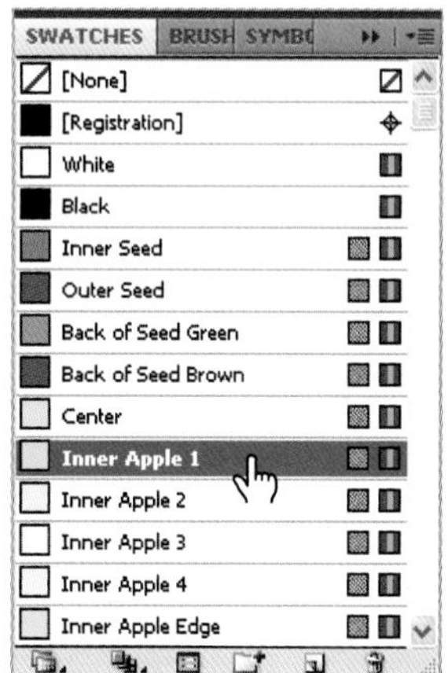

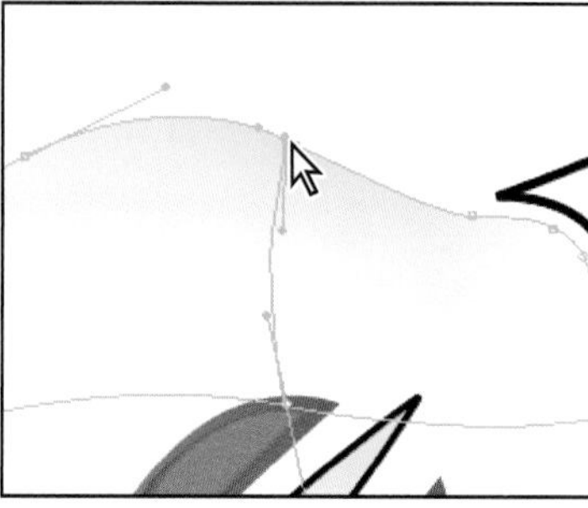

Select Inner Apple 1 *from the Swatches panel to apply to the anchor point of the apple.*

You can see how the gradient spreads and diffuses from the point of selection. Next, you'll add some more colors to see how they blend together.

6 Click on the next anchor point below the top one and select *Inner Apple 2* from the Swatches panel.

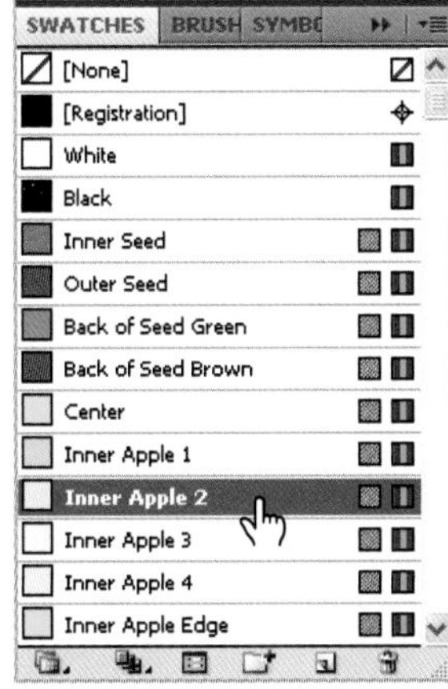

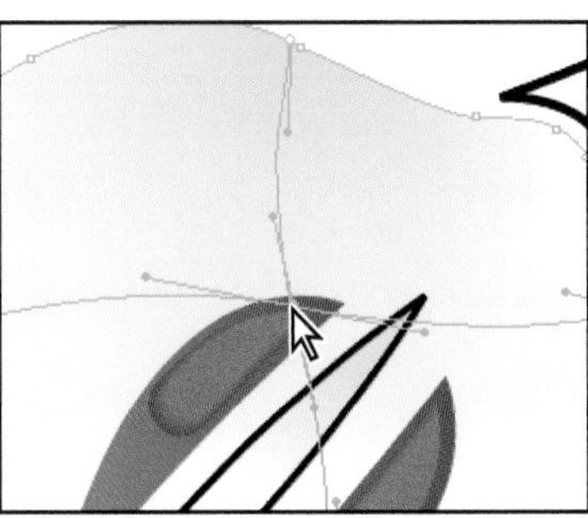

Select another anchor point in the gradient mesh and choose Inner Apple 2 *from the Swatches panel.*

7 Select the next anchor point down and select *Inner Apple 3* from the Swatches panel.

If you're having trouble selecting the anchor points on the mesh, zoom in more closely with your Zoom tool (), as anchor points can be tricky to select at times.

8 Select the bottom anchor point at the base of the line and choose *Inner Apple 4*.

Clicking one point at a time can take awhile. Sometimes you'll want to apply the same color to multiple points (such as at the edge of the image). You can select multiple points by holding Shift on your keyboard and clicking the different points using the Selection tool. Another alternative is to use the Lasso tool to click and drag a marquee around the points you'd like to select.

9 Select the Lasso tool () from the Tools Panel.

10 Click and drag a marquee around the anchor points on the lower right portion of the apple core. Choose *Inner Apple Edge* from the Swatches panel.

11 Using the methods you've just discovered, apply *Inner Apple Edge* to the remaining anchor points of the apple core to finish coloring it.

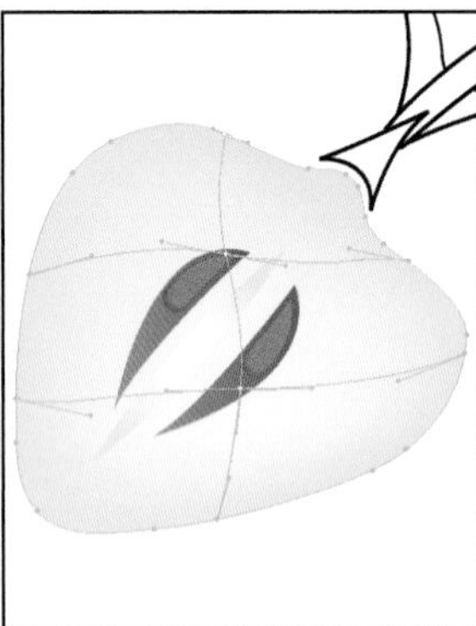

Add more color to the anchor points of the apple.

Adjusting the Mesh

Once you've applied the mesh, you can keep adjusting it to your liking. Simply use the Direct Selection tool or the Lasso tool to select the points you want and update the color. You can also grab the points and move them to adjust the spread of color.

1 Using the Direct Selection tool (), select the second anchor point on the middle division line. Choose a different shade of color and then drag the anchor point to move it. Notice how the color updates immediately and how the spread of the gradient is affected by moving the anchor point.

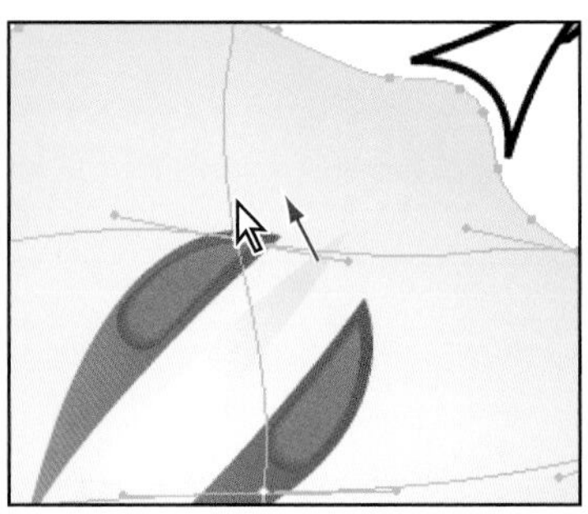

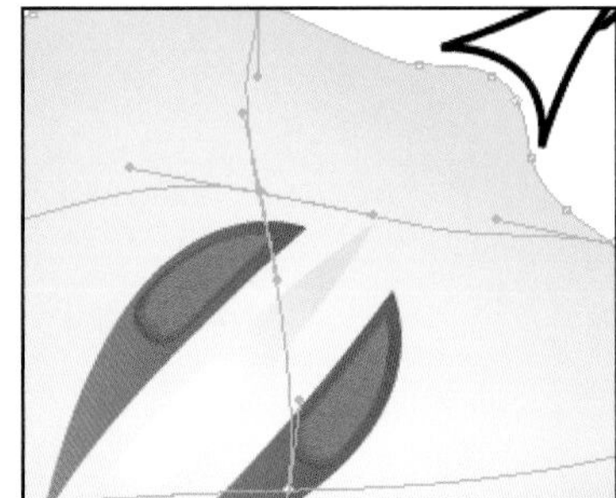

Select an anchor point and watch as the color updates when you move the anchor point.

2 Choose File > Save to save the file.

Revisiting Blend Options

You started the process working with the Blend options, next you'll explore how you can control the transition of color between the blended objects using specified steps or smooth color options to help expand the choices you'll have during the process.

1 Choose the Selection tool (↖) from the Tools panel and select the triangular shape just above the apple core. From the Swatches panel, choose the *Triangle* swatch for the fill and set the stroke value to None.

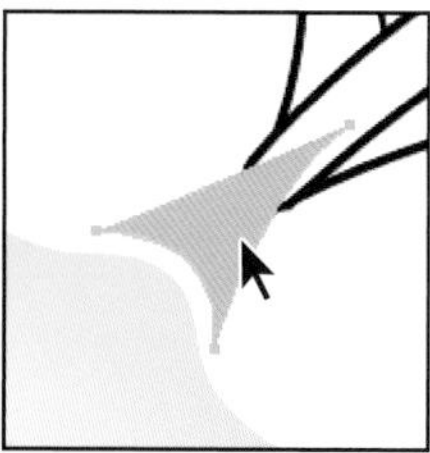

Select then color the triangle object above the apple's core.

2 Make sure the fill is active and select the stem above the triangle shape. From the Swatches panel, choose the *Stem* swatch. Set the stroke to None.

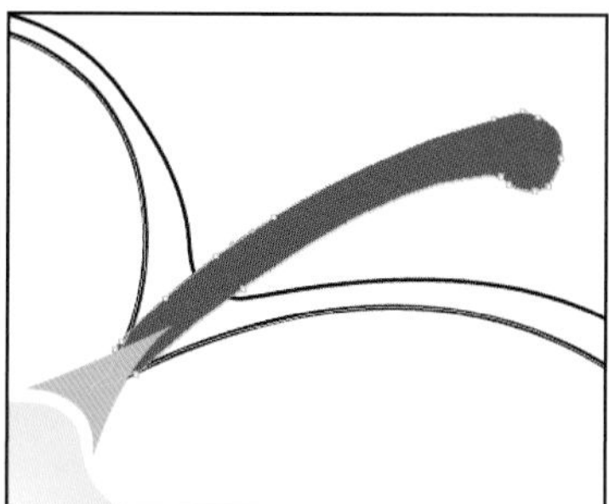

Select then color the apple's stem.

3 Choose Select > Deselect.

Last time you used the menu to create the blend; this time you will use the Blend tool and investigate some of the other options available to you.

4 Choose the Blend tool ( ) from the Tools panel.

With the Blend tool selected, double-click the tool in the Tools panel. The Blend Options dialog box appears.

5 From the Spacing drop-down menu, choose Specified Steps and leave the steps set to the default of 8. Press OK.

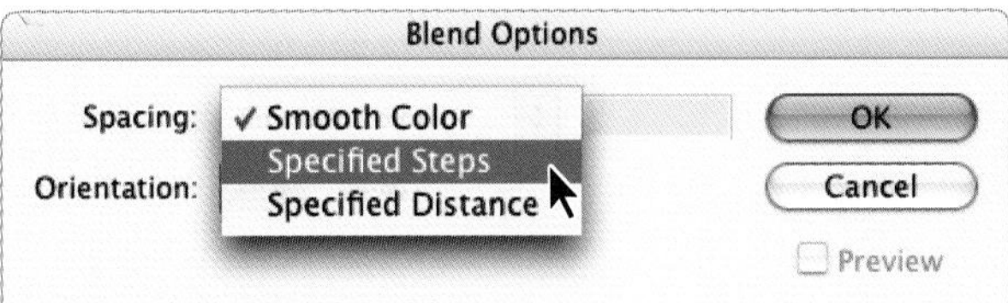

Blend Options.

6 Click once on the triangular shape, then click once on the stem and notice the results of the blend.

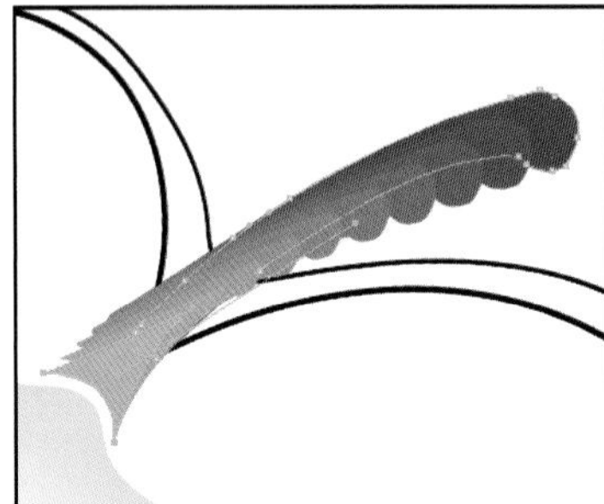

The blend between the two objects.

You can see the effect of the specified steps gives the appearance of the blend a kind of morphing effect between the shapes. While this creates a pretty cool and funky way of tranisitioning between the shapes, this isn't really the desired effect for the apple. Now you'll try this using a smooth color transition.

7 Choose Edit > Undo Make Blend.

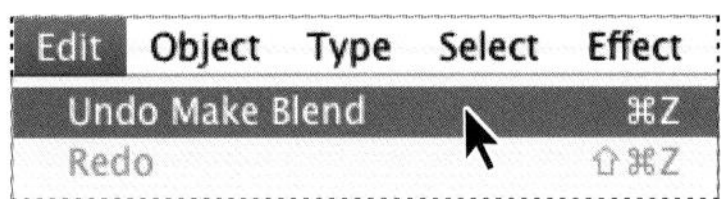

Choose Edit > Undo Make Blend.

8 Double-click on the Blend tool in the Tools panel to open the Blend Options dialog box. Set the Spacing value back to Smooth Color and press OK.

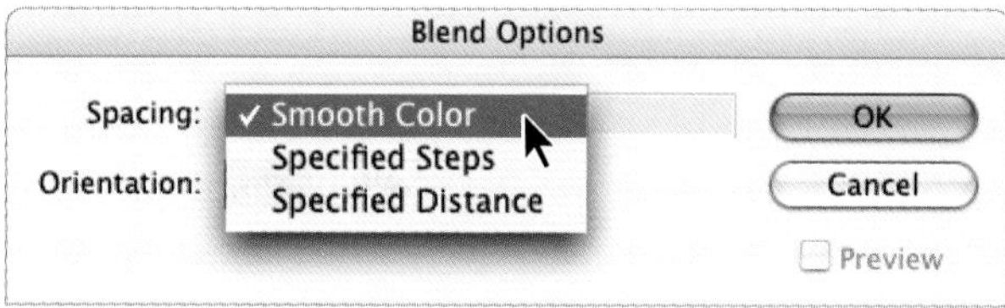

Choose Smooth Color from Spacing drop-down menu.

9 Click once on the triangular shape and then click once on the stem and take note of the difference. You are back to that smooth transition of color again. Another thing you'll see is the way the blend affects the nature of each image where the images widen a bit to blend the underlying framework of each shape together to form one overall merged image.

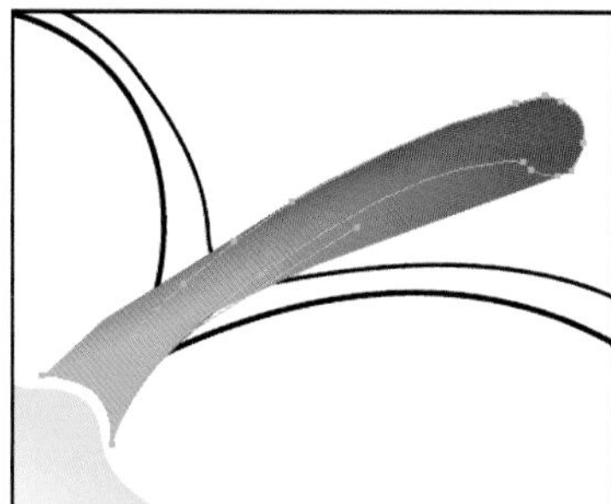

The two objects blended together.

Keep in mind that the Blend tool can distort the underlying framework of the images you're blending. This may have an impact on how you're drawing images that you're considering blending together.

As you have seen, the Blend tool create smooth color transitions, it can create new shapes! You'll finish the sliced apple with a bit more gradient mesh work.

More mesh work

You'll apply another gradient mesh and continue to adjust the mesh by selecting multiple points on the grid at the same time.

1 Start by selecting the inner part of the sliced apple with the Selection tool (↖).

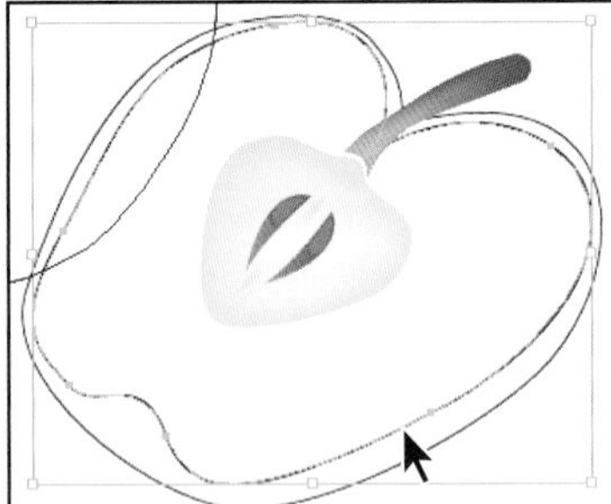

Select the inner part of the sliced apple.

2 Choose Object > Create Gradient Mesh. In the Create Gradient Mesh dialog box, type **3** in the Rows text field and **3** in the Columns text field. Leave the other settings at their defaults and press OK.

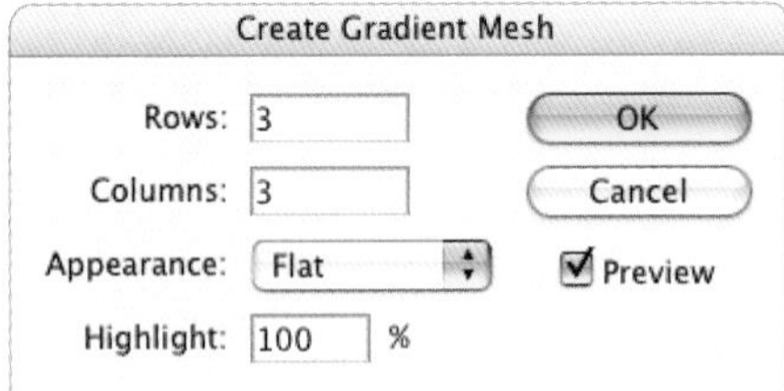

Set the Rows and Columns for the Gradient Mesh.

3 With the grid still active, choose the Direct Selection tool (↖) from the Tools panel.

4 Using the Direct Selection tool, click on one of the anchor points that's on the outside edge of the gradient mesh grid. You'll see handles appear on the point once you select it.

5 Hold down the Shift key and continue to select the rest of the anchor points on the outside edge of the grid until all the anchor points on the outside edge of the grid are selected.

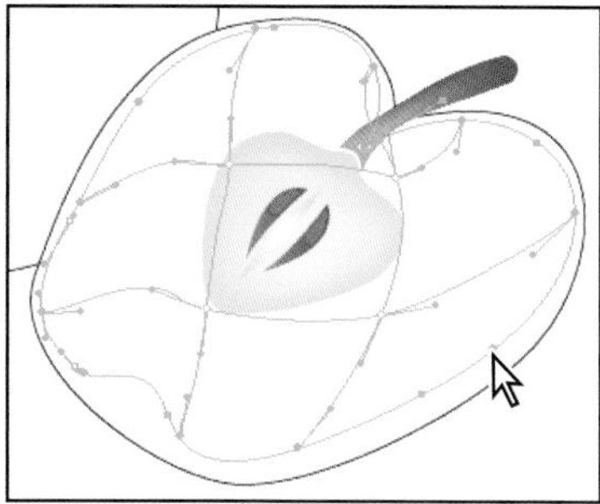

Select the outer anchor points of the gradient mesh.

6 Once they're all selected, select *Middle Apple* from the Swatches panel.

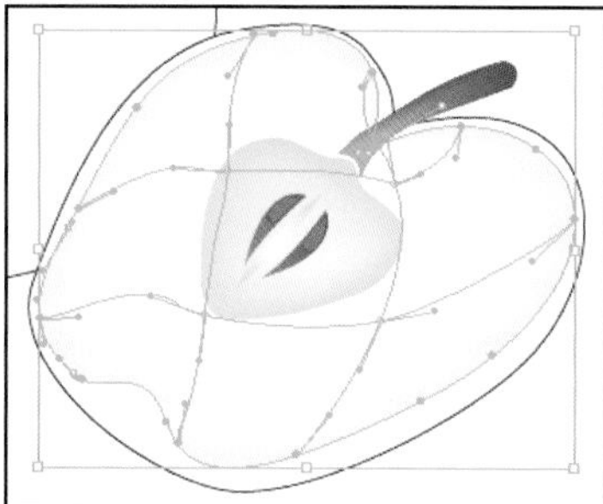

Select Middle Apple *from the Swatches panel to color the apple.*

7 Choose File > Save to save your work.

Leave the center of the sliced apple on white for the color; the overall effect of the gradient works well to create some depth. Next you will wrap up the sliced apple by finishing the outside framework.

Overlapping images

Overlapping images can make the selection process very difficult when it comes to working with multiple gradient mesh objects. You'll start out this time by locking the inner part of the apple shape.

1 Choose the Selection tool (↖) from the Tools panel and click on the inner part of the sliced apple (the part of the apple you just finished with the last grid). Shift+click the apple core, the seeds, and the stem work.

2 Choose Object > Lock > Selection. Now the inner part of the apple is locked in place, which is going to make the selection process for the next grid a lot easier for us.

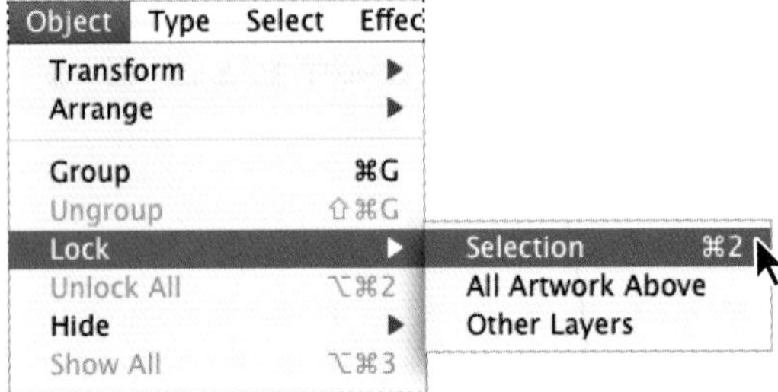

Lock the selection.

3 Using the Selection tool, click on the outer framework of the sliced apple.

4 Choose Object > Create Gradient Mesh. In the Create Gradient Mesh dialog box, type **6** into the Rows text field and **3** into the Columns text field. Leave the other settings at their defaults and press OK.

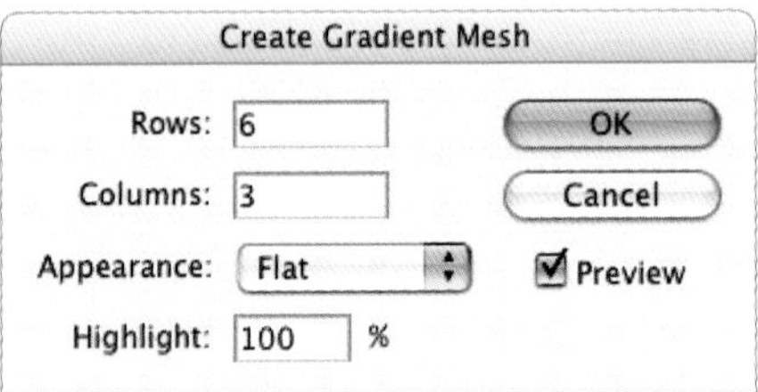

Set the Gradient Mesh options.

5 Choose the Direct Selection tool (↖) from the Tools panel. Select the anchor points on the right side of the apple's outer framework by Shift+clicking each anchor point as you did before.

6 Choose *Outer Apple Right* from the Swatches panel.

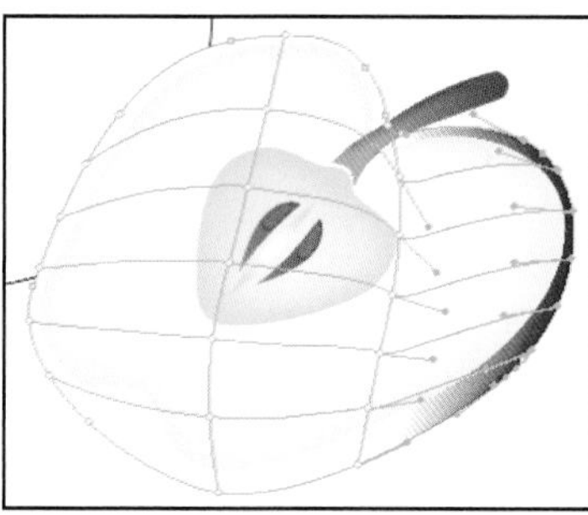

Choose Outer Apple Right *from the Swatches panel to color the outer part of the apple.*

7 Using the Direct Selection tool, select the anchor points at the bottom of the shape.

8 Choose *Outer Apple Bottom* from the Swatches panel.

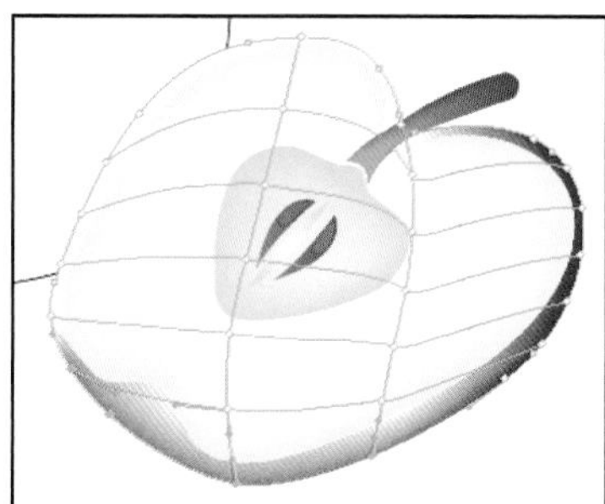

Choose Outer Apple Bottom *from the Swatches panel to color the outer part of the apple.*

9 Select the anchor points on the left side of the apple shape. Choose *Outer Apple Left* from the Swatches panel.

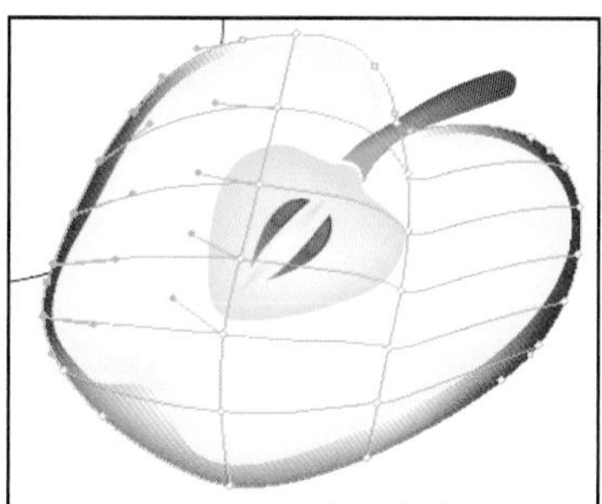

Choose Outer Apple Left *from the Swatches panel to color the outer part of the apple.*

10 Select the remaining anchor points at the top of the apple shape and choose *Outer Apple Top* from the Swatches panel.

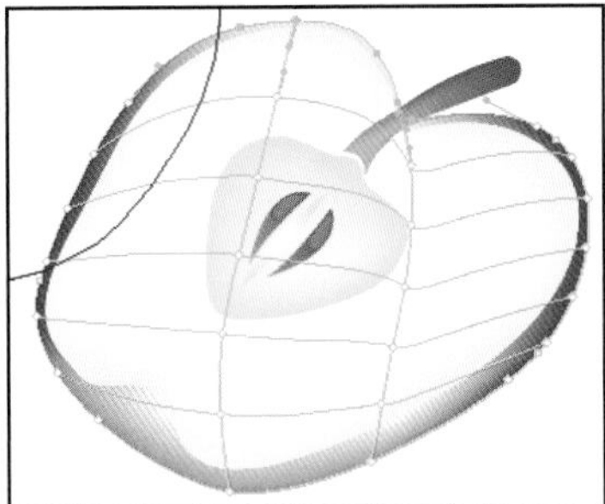

Choose Outer Apple Top *from the Swatches panel to color the outer part of the apple.*

11 Choose Select > Deselect, then choose File > Save to save your work.

Applying a gradient mesh using the Mesh tool

In addition to applying a gradient mesh through the Object menu, there's a more visual way of pointing and clicking to apply the mesh, add grid segments and choose colors using just one tool.

Again, when there are overlapping images that each have grids, it can make the selection and application process a bit tricky. You can temporarily hide images to get them out of your way to ease the process. That's what you'll do to get things rolling—you'll hide the sliced apple and then continue from there.

1 From the Object menu, choose Object > Unlock All to unlock the components of the apple that you locked earlier so you can re-select them.

You can't select a locked object again unless you unlock it first.

2 Choose the Selection tool (↖) from the Tools panel and Shift+click the remaining parts of the sliced apple that you completed earlier.

3 Choose Object > Hide > Selection.

You can reveal a hidden object at any time by choosing Object > Show All.

Now that the sliced apple is out of the way, you can turn your attention to the next apple. The last time you applied the gradient mesh, you went through the Object menu, this time, you'll go for the Mesh tool.

4 Select the Mesh tool (▦) from the Tool panel.

5 Using the Mesh tool, move over the body of the apple and click on it. A grid appears the moment you click with the Mesh tool using the last color used as a fill. If the Gradient Mesh appears with a color, Undo this step, press the **D** key on the keyboard to get your default fill of white, then click with the Gradient Mesh tool again.

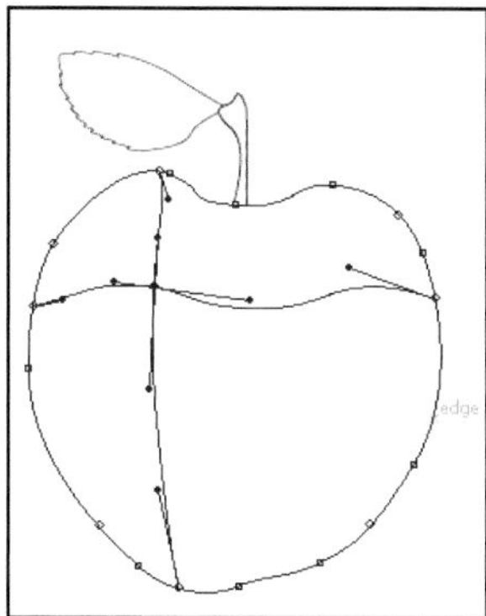

Use the Mesh tool on the whole apple.

6 Click to the right and a little higher from where you clicked the first time and then to the left and a little lower. You add new segments to the grid each time you click.

7 Go to the center grid line and click on the line itself toward the bottom of it. Take note that you added a horizontal segment to the existing vertical segment.

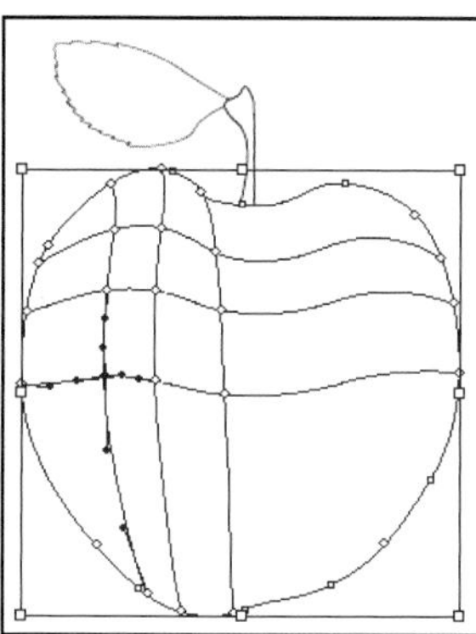

Add more segments to the apple using the Mesh tool.

To remove a line segment, hold down the Alt Key (Windows) or Option (Mac OS) and click on the segment you want to remove when you see the minus sign next to the Mesh tool.

Unfortunately, you cannot select multiple anchor points with the Mesh tool to apply color to multiple points at once. You will use something else this time instead of the Direct Selection tool.

8 To select multiple points this time, select the Lasso tool (⟡) in the Tool panel.

9 Using the Lasso tool, click and drag a marquee around the anchor points on the right side of the grid.

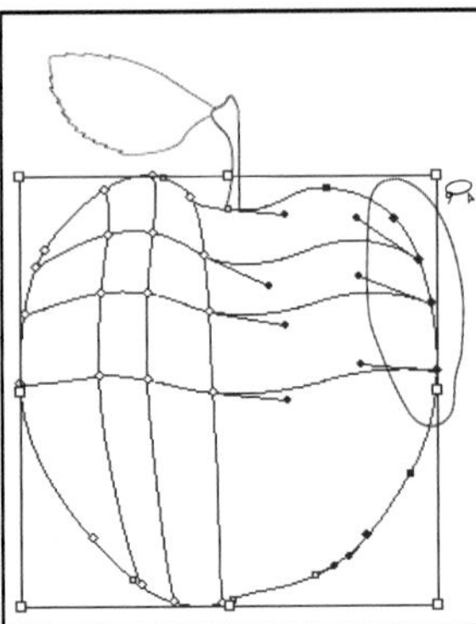

Make a selection on the right side of the apple.

10 Select *Apple Right* from the Swatches panel. Continue to make selections using the Lasso tool on the bottom, left and top of the apple, and apply the correct swatches; *Apple Bottom 1*, *Apple Bottom 2*, *Apple Left*, and *Apple Top*. Remember to include the inner anchor points.

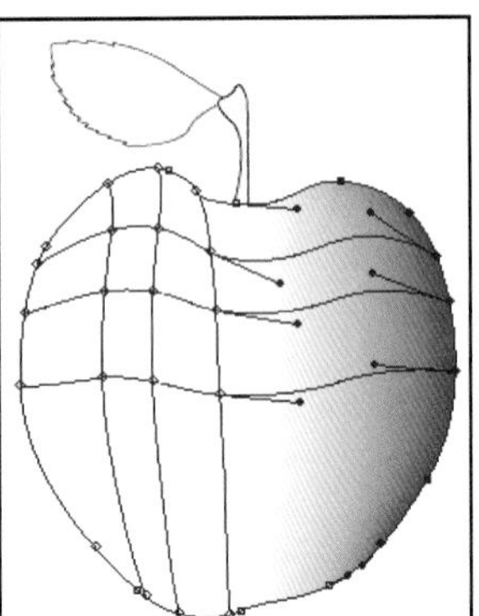

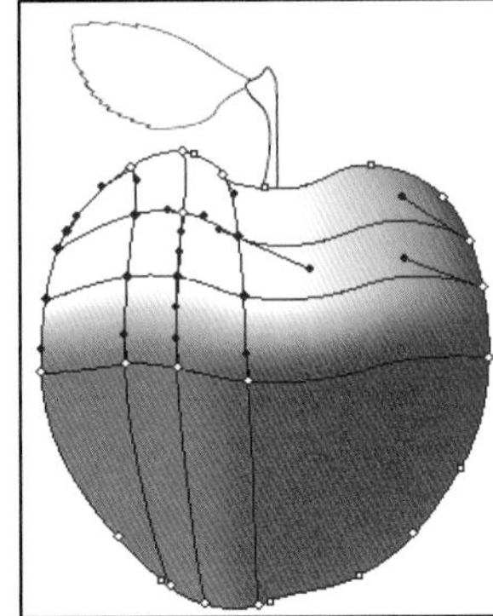

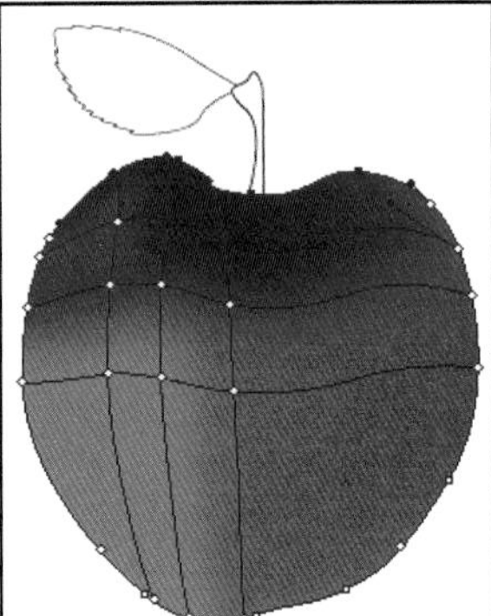

Apply the swatches to the remainder of the apple.

11 Choose File > Save to save your work.

Next you will fine-tune the gradient mesh with the Mesh tool to modify the shading.

12 Select the Mesh tool (▦) from the Tools panel. With the tool selected, click one of the anchor points toward the left side of the grid and select *Apple Highlight 1*.

Be careful when making your selection, it's easy to accidentally add a new segment to your grid.

13 Now click the anchor point to the right of the one you just selected and choose *Apple Highlight 2* from the Swatches panel.

14 With the Mesh tool still selected, click and drag on the point that you have currently selected. Notice how you can move the point to adjust the spread of the resulting gradient!

15 Continue to add additional shading on the apple and use the Mesh tool to click and drag the points until you're happy with the shading.

16 Choose Select > Deselect to take a look at your shading.

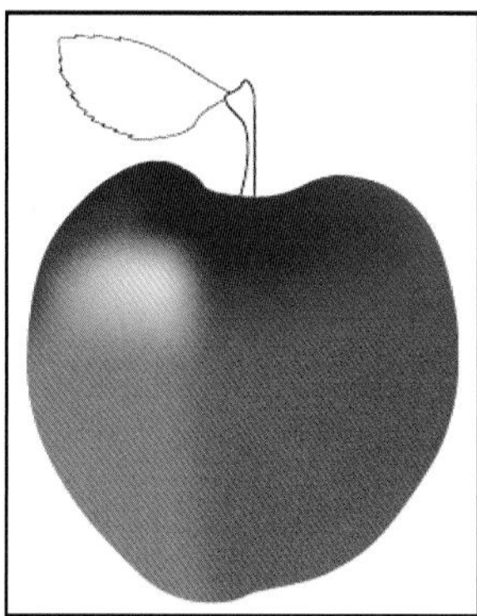

Finish adding shading to the apple.

17 To make further changes to a grid once it's been de-selected, choose the Direct Selection tool (↖) from the Tool panel and click on the object with the grid. The Direct Selection tool will reactivate the grid.

18 Choose File > Save to save your work.

Finishing up with the Mesh tool and automatically adding a Highlight

You'll continue to shade the remaining parts of the apple with the Mesh tool.

1 Select the Zoom tool (🔍) and zoom in on the area of the stem of the apple.

2 Choose the Mesh tool from the Tool panel and then click on the stem of the apple to apply a mesh.

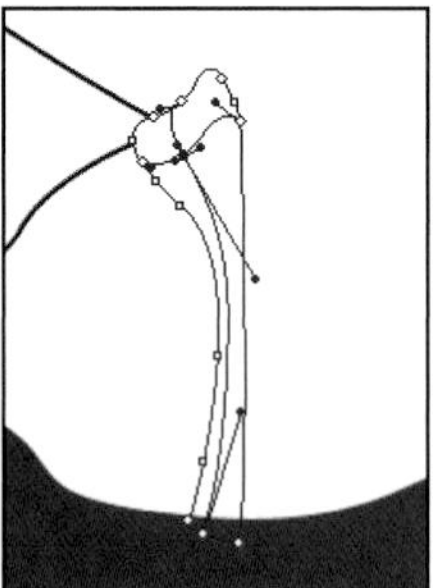

Apply a mesh to the apple stem.

3 Using the same methods as you used for the body of the apple, apply the *Stem 2* swatch from the Swatches panel to different anchor points on the stem until you have the stem shaded as you like.

Don't forget to zoom in and out to make selecting the points on the grid easier to select. Staying zoomed out can make the selection process with the grid much more difficult.

4 Choose Select > Deselect when finished to take a look at your work.

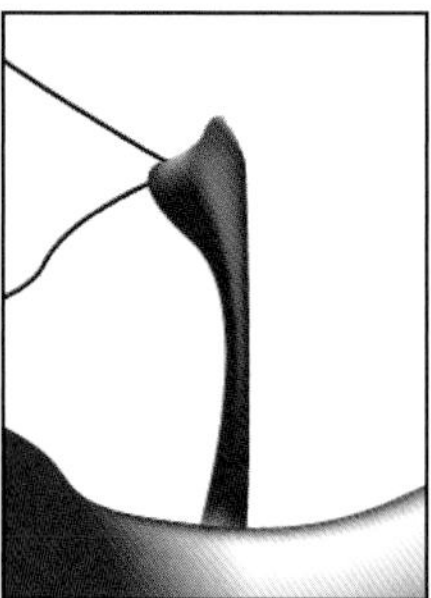

The shaded stem.

To finish the shading process, you'll apply the mesh to the leaf of the apple. This time you'll add one more touch by adding a highlight to the mesh as you apply the gradient mesh.

5 Choose the Selection tool (↖) from the Tools panel and select the leaf of the apple. Before applying the mesh this time, you'll first fill in the leaf with the *Leaf* swatch.

6 With the leaf selected, select the *Leaf* swatch from the Swatches panel. You'll go back to the menu to apply the mesh this time.

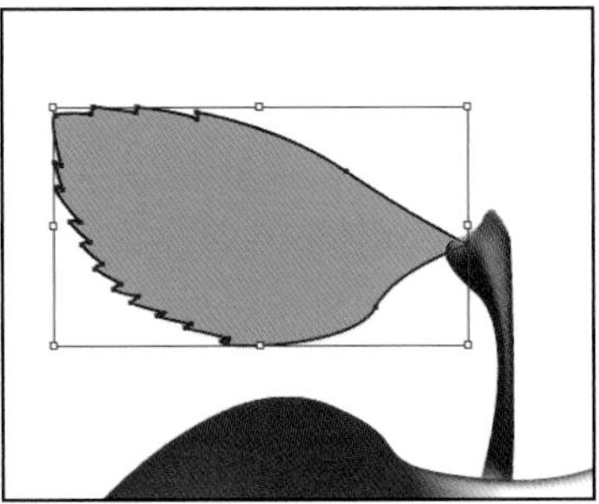

Set the color of the leaf in the Swatches panel.

7 Choose Object > Create Gradient Mesh. In the Create Gradient Mesh dialog box, type **8** in both the Rows and Columns text fields.

8 Choose To Center from the Appearance drop-down menu and set the Highlight value to 75%. Press OK.

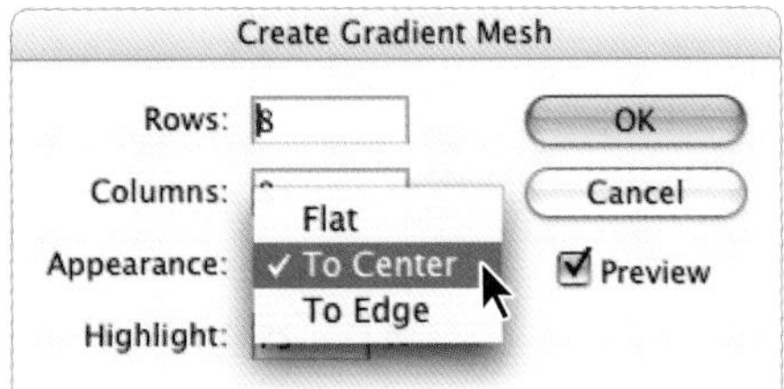

Set the Gradient Mesh options.

9 Choose Select > Deselect and then save your work.

To apply a highlight while creating a gradient mesh, you must first fill the object with a fill color other than white before choosing the Highlight option in the Create Gradient Mesh dialog box.

The apple's shading is done, and you're almost finished! You'll be finishing by stylizing the apple's surface a bit using the Symbol tools.

Using the Symbol tools

Symbols are essentially reuseable art objects that are built into Illustrator. Think of them as your own personal clip art library that comes with the program. You can either use the symbols in Illustrator or you can create your own that can be saved within the program to be used later on. In addition to the symbols themselves, they come with a series of tools that can be used to apply the symbols to your project as well as modify properties of the symbols such as their size, color, position, rotation, and more.

For more information about symbols, see Lesson 8, "Working with Symbols."

You'll start the process by creating the object you want to convert into a symbol and then you'll start to incorporate the symbol tools to apply and modify the symbol to the artwork.

1 Choose the Ellipse tool (○) from the Tool panel. If necessary, click and hold the Rectangle tool (□) to reveal the hidden Ellipse tool.

2 Using the Ellipse tool, draw a small circle next to the apple (holding Shift while you draw will produce a perfect circle).

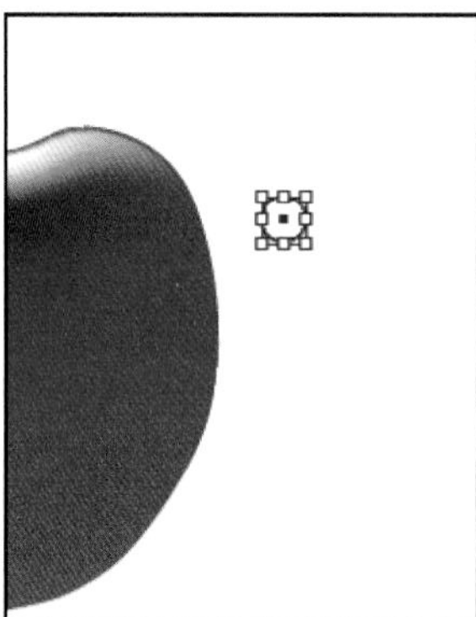

Using the Ellipse tool, create a small circle next to the apple.

3 Fill the circle with a gradient by pressing the Gradient button (■) from the bottom of the Tool panel.

4 The Gradient panel should have opened for you when you applied it to the circle, if not choose Window > Gradient to open it.

You can change the colors of the gradient in the gradient panel by double-clicking the color stop to open its color properties.

5 Double-click the white color stop.

6 Once the Gradient Slider panel appears, press the panel menu button (▾≡) in the upper right corner and choose RGB for the color mode. Type a value of **255, 100, 46** respectively in the R, G, and B text fields.

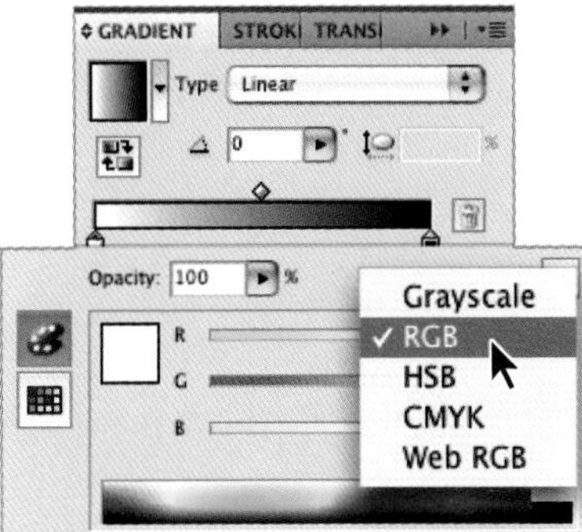

Gradient Slider color settings.

7 Click back on the Gradient panel to close the Gradient Slider panel. Double-click the black Gradient Slider and type a value of **158, 0, 0** in the R, G, and B text fields using the same procedure as listed in the previous step.

8 In the Gradient panel, choose Radial for the pattern of the gradient.

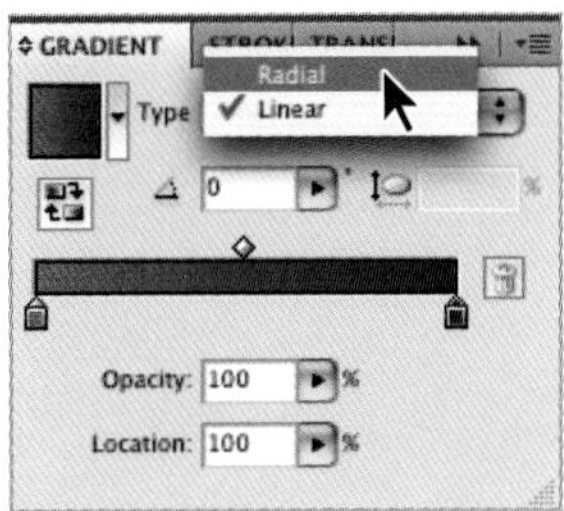

Set the gradient to Radial.

Next you will adjust the gradient a bit to stylize the radial gradient.

9 Using the Zoom tool (🔍), zoom in on the gradient and then slide the diamond-shaped Gradient Slider (the one above the other two in the panel) to the left a bit to collapse the radial gradient a little.

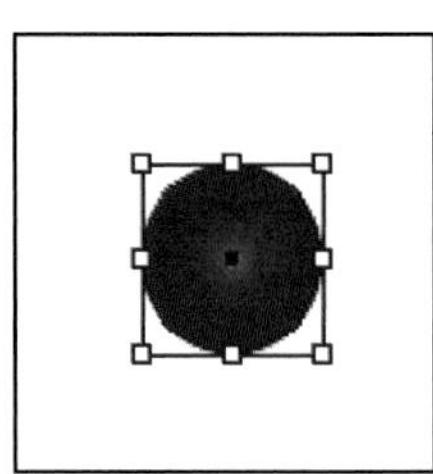
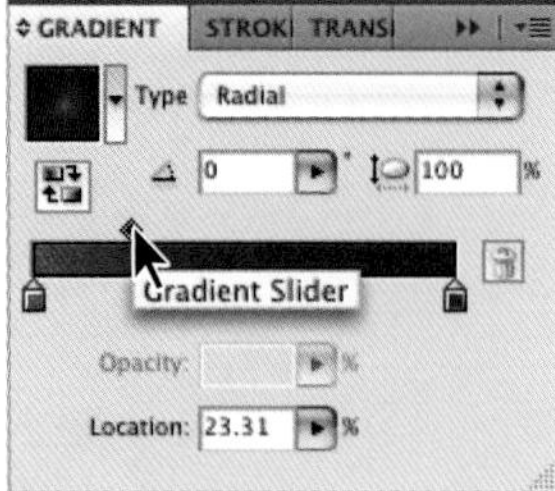

Edit the gradient.

10 Finish the image by setting the Stroke value to None.

Creating a symbol

Next you'll make the image a symbol, and then start to use it on the artwork to create a texture on the apple.

1 Choose Window > Symbols to open the Symbols panel.

2 Once the panel is open, choose the Selection tool (↖) from the Tool panel and then select the gradient circle and drag it into the Symbols panel.

3 In the Symbol Options dialog box, type Gradient Circle in the Name text field. Leave the other settings at their defaults and press OK.

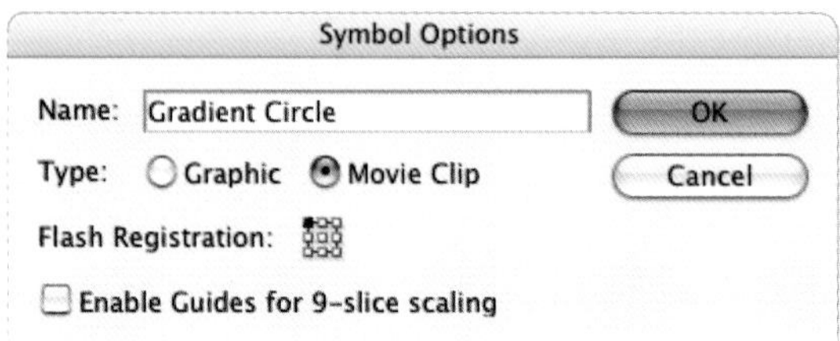

A Symbol Options dialog box appears when creating a new symbol.

Once you've created a symbol, you can then save it to use in other projects. To do so, press the panel menu button (▾≡) in the upper-right corner of the Symbols panel and choose Save Symbol Library and then name the library. To use the library with your symbols in other projects, choose Open Symbol Library from the panel menu and then simply navigate to the place where your library is saved to open it.

4 With the Selection tool (↖), click on the gradient circle on the artboard and delete it, you'll be reapplying it to the artwork in a different way.

5 Zoom out a bit so you can see the whole apple.

6 Select the Symbol Sprayer tool (🔘) from the Tool panel.

Before you apply the symbol, you'll adjust the Symbol Sprayer tool settings.

7 Double-click the Symbol Sprayer tool to open the Symbolism Tools Options dialog box. Set the Diameter value to approximately 13mm and press OK.

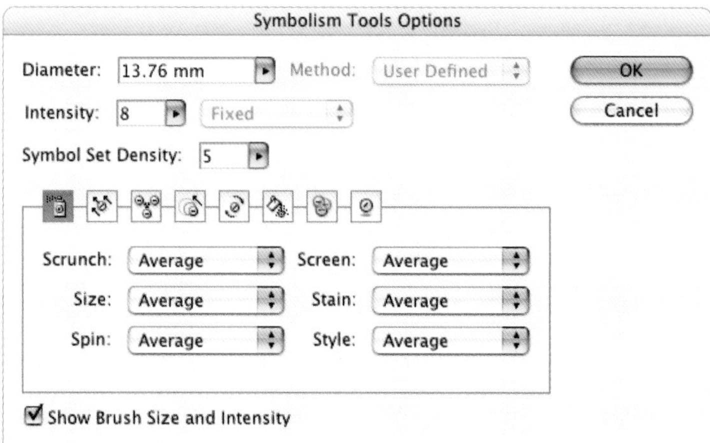

Symbolism Tools Options.

8 Make sure the Gradient Circle is selected in the Symbols panel (you must select the symbol) and then click and drag with the Symbol Sprayer over the surface of the apple to paint the symbol on top of the apple.

The more you click and drag, the more instances of the symbol are created. Each copy of the symbol on the artboard is referred to as an instance.

Paint the Gradient Circle symbols over the apple.

9 Choose File > Save to save your work.

Modifying a Symbol's appearance

Next, you'll use a few more symbol tools to adjust the symbol's appearance. You'll find a number of tools that can be used to alter the symbol; you will use tools that will affect size and transparency.

1 Using the Zoom tool (🔍), zoom in on the apple, then choose the Symbol Sizer tool ( ) from the Tool panel. If necessary, click and hold the Symbol Sprayer tool ( ) to reveal the hidden Symbolism tools.

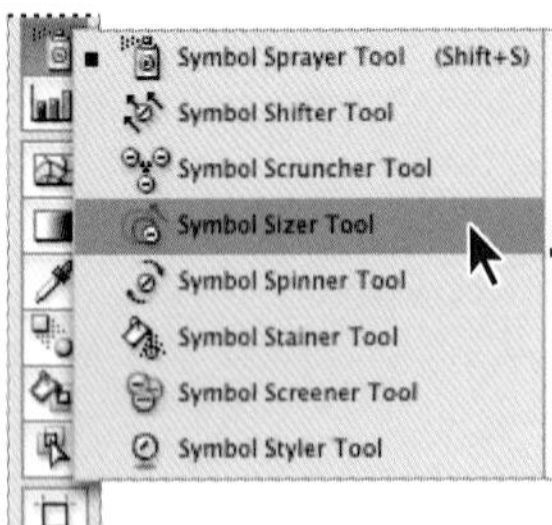

Select the Symbol Sizer tool from the Tools panel.

If you click and hold on any of the gradient circle symbol instances on the apple, they'll start to enlarge.

2 Hold the Alt key (Windows) or Option (Mac OS) and then click and hold on one of the gradient circles on the apple to adjust its size. Let go of the mouse when you're satisfied with size.

3 Keep re-sizing various instances of the gradient circles to adjust the look of them to your liking.

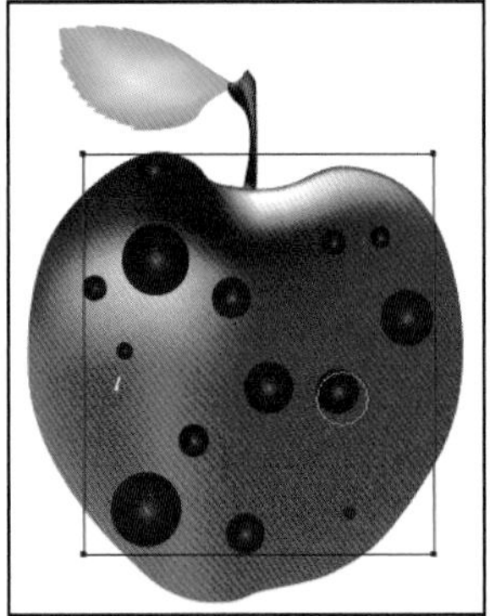

Resize the symbols.

Now you'll work on the transparency a bit.

4 Select the Symbol Screener tool () from the Tool panel.

The more you click and hold with the Symbol Screener, the more transparent the image becomes.

5 Click and hold on the different instances of the gradient circle instances on the apple to adjust them to varying degrees of transparency.

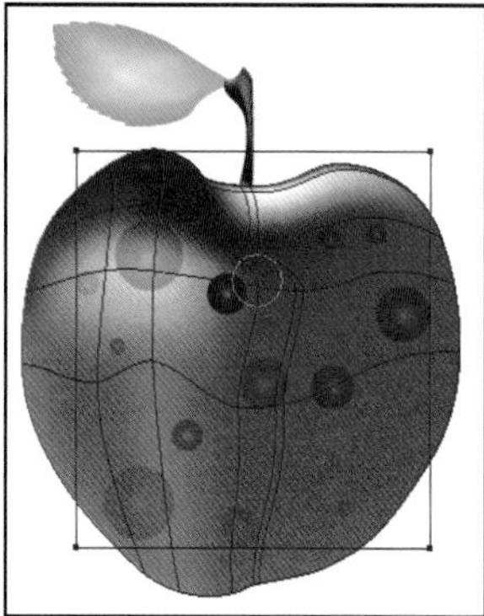

Add transparency to the symbols.

Let's finish up by taking a look at everything together.

6 Choose Select > Deselect to deactivate the selected symbols.

7 Zoom out a bit. To reveal the hidden images, choose Object > Show All.

8 Choose File > Save to save your work.

The finished image.

Excellent! Now you've got the circles to blend in a bit with the apple itself, giving the images a more natural combined appearance.

Congratulations! You've finished Lesson 11, "Advanced Blending Techniques."

Self study

Continue experimenting with the Blend tool by drawing two different objects that are two different colors. Select the Blend tool and try blending them together in different ways. Try this with different shapes, different colors, and different positioning each time.

Review

Questions

1 How do you access the blend options for the Blend tool?

2 How can you apply a gradient mesh?

3 How do you save an image that you've created as a symbol?

Answers

1 Double-click on the Blend tool.

2 By using the Mesh tool from the Tool panel or by selecting an image and choosing Object > Create Gradient Mesh.

3 Select the image with the Selection tool and then drag it into the Symbols panel.

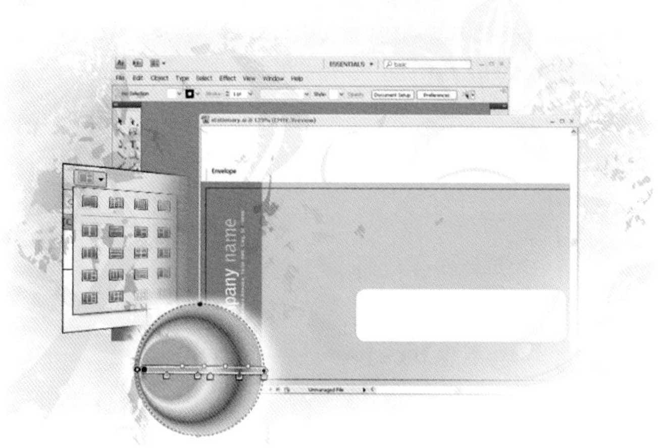

What you'll learn in this lesson:

- Understanding the Application Bar and Application Frame
- Arranging documents using Tabs and Groups
- Switching Screen Modes
- Using the enhanced Gradient tool

Illustrator CS4 New Features

This lesson provides an overview of the features added or enhanced in Illustrator CS4. From the more prominent changes, such as multiple artboards in a single document, to the more subtle improvements, like the Smart Guides feature, Illustrator CS4 includes a number of changes that benefit users familiar with older versions of Adobe Illustrator.

Starting up

This lesson provides an overview of the new or modified features in Illustrator CS4 and does not require any lesson files.

See Lesson 12 in action!

Use the accompanying video to gain a better understanding of how to use some of the features shown in this lesson. The video tutorial for this lesson can be found on the included DVD.

The new user interface

The new user interface inside Adobe Illustrator CS4 has made navigating documents a lot easier. This new interface allows users to tab between documents by clicking on tabs that exist on the top of each document when multiple documents are open. You can also group tabs into multiple document windows, and arrange them any way you like. This makes the behavior of document windows more like the way panels behave. You will also notice the brand-new Application bar that has replaced the title bar and menus. In this section, you will explore some of the new features that are related to Illustrator CS4's new interface.

Application bar

The Application bar inside Illustrator CS4 replaces the title bar and menus that were in previous versions of Illustrator. It still contains the File, Edit, Object, Type, Select, Effect, View, Window, and Help menus. Filter has now been removed, as Filters were not dynamic; once a filter was applied, there was no way to turn it on or off. Effects are dynamic, and all the features that were under Filters can be found in the Effects menu. The shortcut to Bridge (Br) has been added, as well as a drop-down menu () for arranging documents, which you will explore later on in this lesson. There is now a workspace drop-down menu as well, so that you can now quickly access your workspaces. And finally, a Search for Help box has been added that allows you to search the Help menu. Having things like the Search for Help box makes getting to know Illustrator easier.

This is the new Application bar in Illustrator CS4.

Application Frame

The Application Frame inside of Illustrator CS4 provides a frame in which the program resides. This makes it easier to view and shuffle documents. This is enabled by default in Windows. MacOS users can choose Window > Application Frame to take advantage of the new tabbed interface.

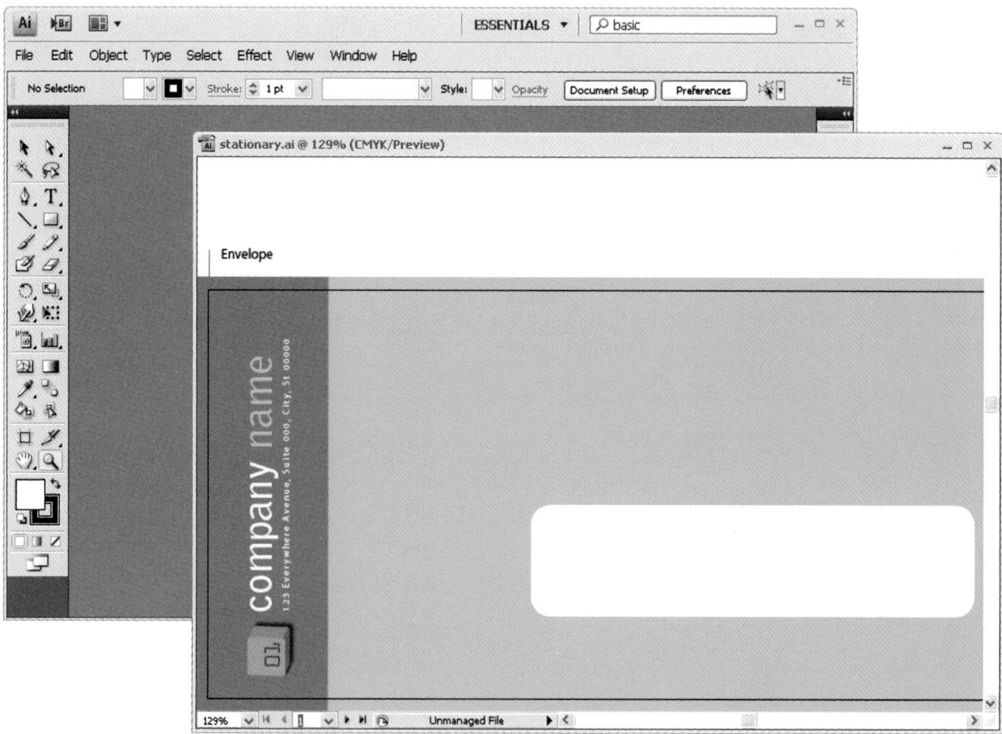

This is the new Application Frame in Illustrator CS4.

This means that when a window is floating, you can now drag the top grey title bar of the window and it will snap back into the Application Frame.

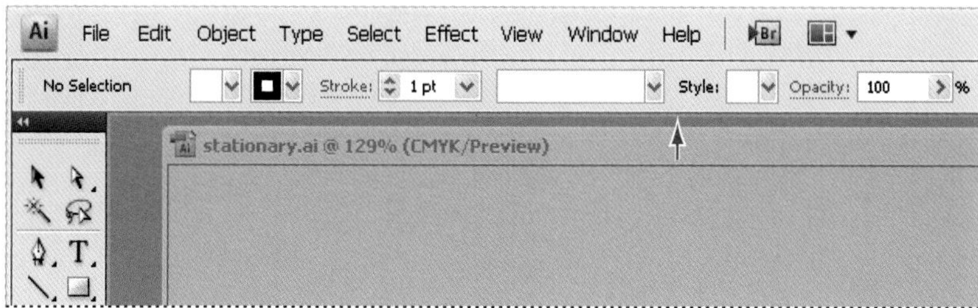

Dragging a document window back into the Application Frame.

Document tabs

When a document is first opened, it is part of the Application Frame. At the top-left corner of the document, you can see the name of the document, the view percentage, and what color mode you are previewing it in. This information resides in a tab. To move the document away from the application window, you drag the tab away from its docked position.

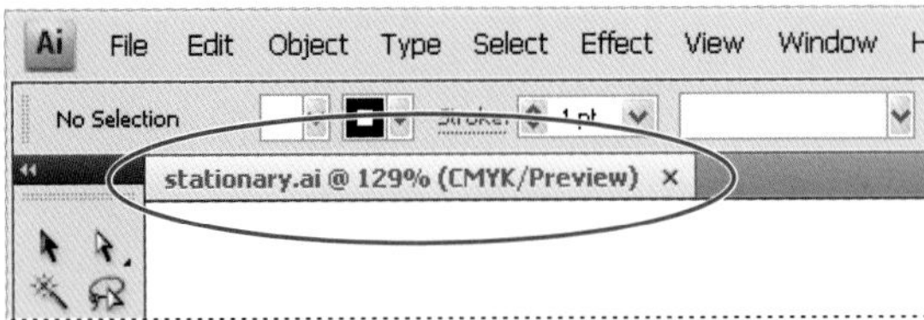

This is a single document represented by one tab.

If you have multiple documents open, you will see a tab for each new document you open or create.

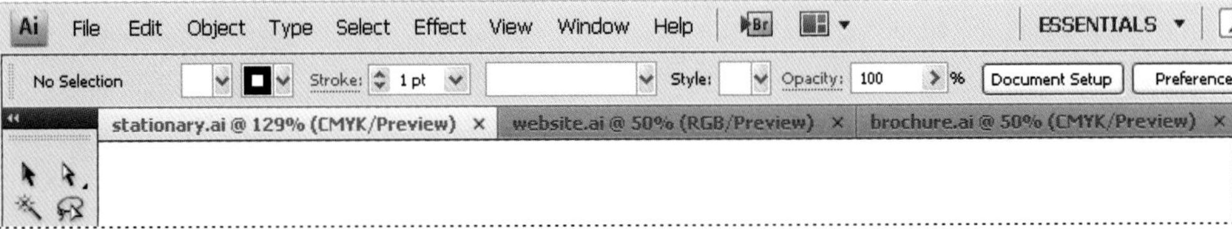

Multiple tabs representing a group of your open documents.

To navigate from one document to the next, simply click on the tab for that document. You can also re-order the tabs by dragging them. You can turn this tab function off by selecting Preferences > User Interface > Open documents as Tabs.

Document groups

Because documents can exist as tabs at the top-left corner of a document window, you can have different groups of files stacked as tabs. Just like you can have different groups of panels stacked and grouped individually, you can now do so with documents. This is especially useful if you have more than one monitor. If you drag out a tab, the document becomes its own free-floating window. To put another document with that document and create a group, you can drag another document either from the tab, or if it is free-floating, from the top title bar, under the top title bar of the first document. You now see a blue outline appear around the inner edge of your document. When you release the mouse, you have two tabs, and you have created a document group.

Two different document groups.

Arranging documents

For users who also need to see two layouts at once or even multiple views of the same document, you can now move documents or document groups into different arrangements. There are even several built-in arrangements for documents. To drag a document or document group into a specific spot—top, bottom, left, or right—of another document, click on the title bar of that document, and drag it to the corresponding area you would like it to appear—top, bottom, left, or right. You now have a different arrangement of your documents.

You can make an endless number of arrangements, to view multiple documents in one arranged window. You can also choose Window > New Window to set up two views of the same document. For example, you can zoom in on one document window to make changes, but view the other window at 100 percent; this allows you to see how your small changes affect the whole document.

You also have the ability to choose from pre-existing arrangements of documents by clicking on the Arrange Documents button (▦) in the Application bar. This changes your current selected arrangements to new arrangements.

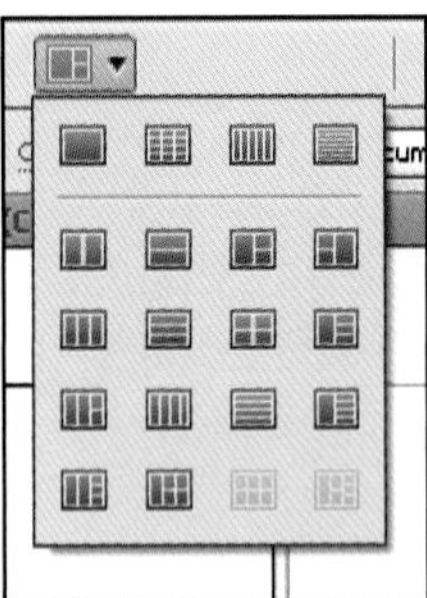

Choose from the pre-existing document arrangements in the Application bar.

Screen modes

New to Illustrator CS4 is the reduction of screen modes. The Normal Screen Mode in CS4 is the Maximize Screen Mode of CS3. This means that as you expand panels in CS4 in Normal Mode, your document size updates accordingly. The only real change is that Standard Screen Mode has been removed. This allows the user to work with the Tabs feature, as well as document groups with multiple documents open. You can still work as if you were in the old Standard Mode (free-floating panels) by just dragging out a tab, or turning off the preference for opening tabs in the Preferences window.

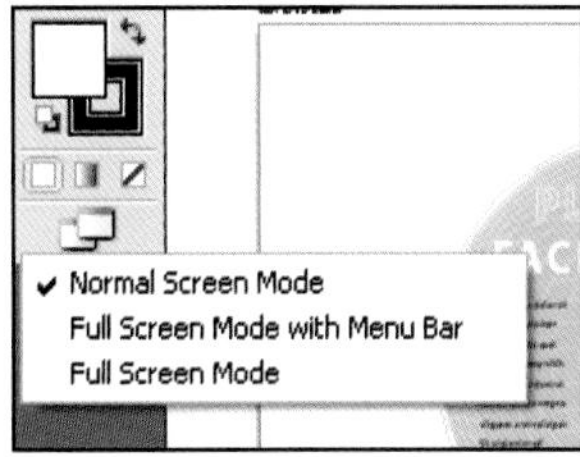

Choosing a Screen Mode in the Tools panel.

Smart Guides

The second you start using Illustrator CS4, you're going to notice the Smart Guides feature, which has been greatly enhanced. Guides should speed up your workflow and make your illustrations more accurate; they shouldn't get in your way as you design. What Adobe has done in this release of Illustrator is to really make guides smart! They are turned on by default when you open a new document. The way Smart Guides worked previously was that when you positioned your cursor, guides would appear based on the point your mouse was hovering over. Now guides appear based on the object edges and anchor points. This means that you can select an object or group and snap it to another object based on the other object's shape. For instance, if you would like to line up the centers of two objects, Illustrator shows you when the two centers are intersecting, making guides that much more useful to your workflows.

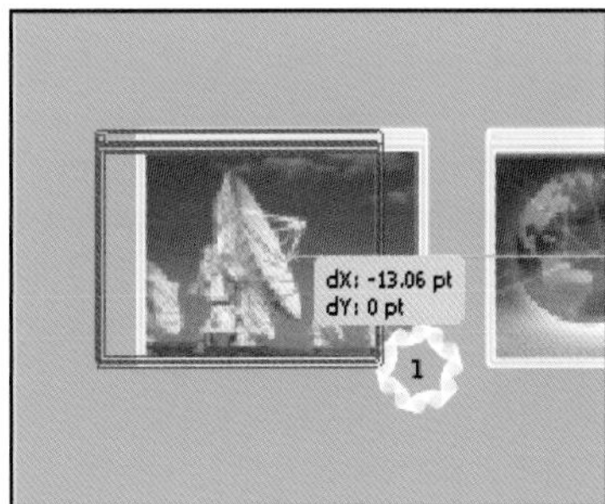

Smart Guides show the intersecting points between two objects.

Another big change to the Smart Guides feature is that the alignment guides are not drawn across the entire page, but across relevant locations, such as two objects.

Smart Guides also work with bounding box transformations, as well as your transforming tools, such as Reflect, Rotate, Scale, Shear, and Free Transform. For instance, when you begin to rotate an object, the cursor now displays the angle at which you are rotating the object. This visual indicator should make your transformations that much easier, as you no longer need the Transform panel to complete an accurate transform. Now you will see information such as percentage and rotation angle while performing the transformation.

Smart Guides also work with the transforming tools.

You will also notice that the Smart Guides feature has been given its own Preference panel where you can turn these functions on or off as necessary. You can also change the color of the Smart Guides, unlike previous versions. The new default color for Smart Guides is green, to be more consistent with other Adobe applications.

Multiple artboards

Finally! You can have more than one artboard in a document in Illustrator CS4. It is important to realize that a pages panel was not added, or the artboards are not referred to as pages in CS4. Multiple-page layout is still the job of InDesign. The word *artboard* is important because you can draw wherever you want on an artboard. When you print, it prints to the size of the artboard, but if you are bringing this Illustrator document into another program, you can clip the image to the artwork bounds, and the rest of the artboard size is irrelevant.

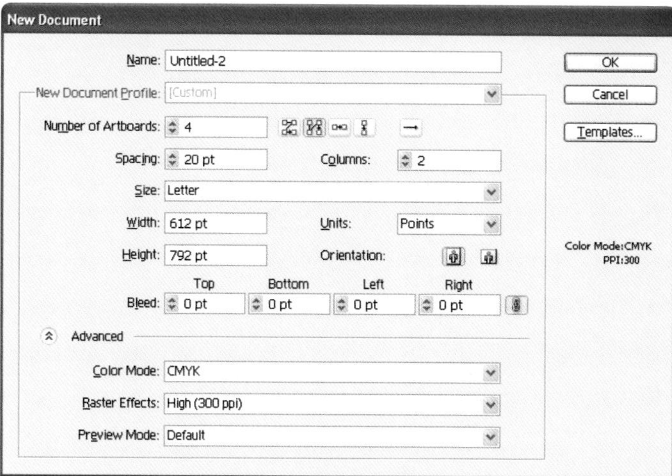

Choosing multiple artboards in the New Document dialog box.

The first place you'll notice the new artboard settings is in the New Document dialog box. You can choose up to 100 artboards; their arrangement by Row, Column, or Grid; the spacing between artboards; and the number of columns. You will also notice that the Bleed feature has been added to the New Document dialog box so that you no longer have to add a bleed at print time, but can view a bleed right on a page as you design within Illustrator CS4.

New Artboard tool

The new Artboard tool replaces the former Crop tool. With the new Artboard tool, you can resize documents, and move them to different locations in your layout. You will notice that Smart Guides also works with this feature. This means that you can finally have multiple artboards in a document, and that all those artboards can be different sizes. Imagine having a letterhead, an envelope, and a poster in one document for a client, instead of in three different documents.

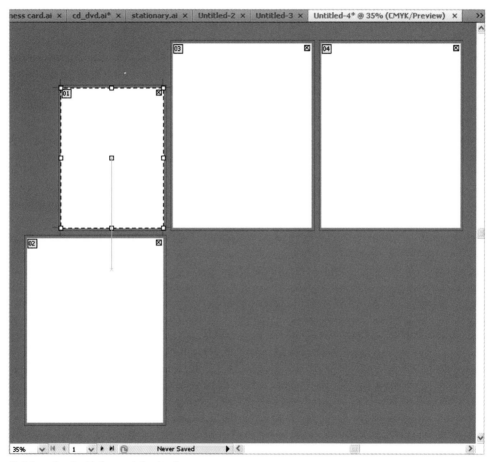

Resizing artboards with the new Artboard tool.

Printing and PDFs with artboards

When you print an Illustrator CS4 document, you can now choose which artboards you would like to print; you can also reverse the order, or skip blank artboards. You can also turn off the Artboard feature altogether by selecting Ignore Artboards. You will notice that you can now preview artboards individually in the Preview panel as well.

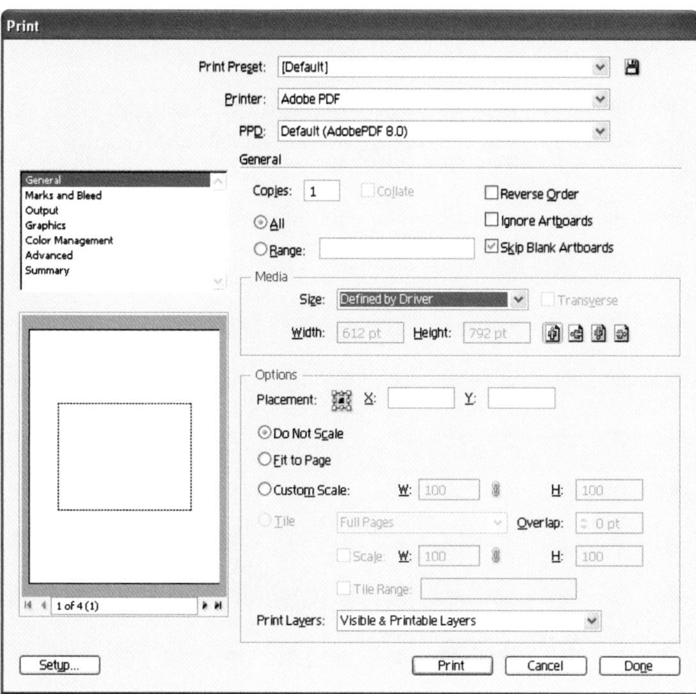

Choosing artboard printing options.

When you save to PDF, there are also choices for which artboards you would like to save as a PDF.

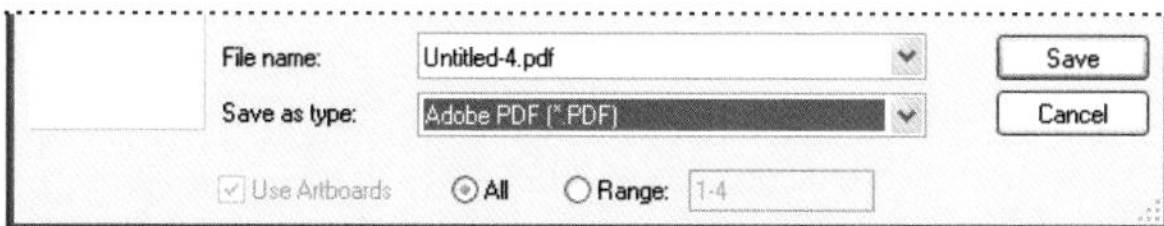

Choose which pages you want to save to the PDF format.

The new Appearance panel

New to CS4 is the ability to control the visibility of everything in the Appearance panel. Previously, items such as Stroke and Fill did not have an visibility icon (👁) to the left of them in the Appearance panel. You now have more control than ever! Even when you apply a Graphic Style, you can now control the visibility of Fills, Strokes, Transparency, and Effects. This is for both top-level items and nested items, such as an effect applied to a specific stroke.

When you save artwork to previous versions of Illustrator, the visual appearance is preserved, while hidden attributes are removed. The hidden attributes are also removed when you print, export, or save to a PDF, unless the *Preserve Illustrator Editing Capabilities* option is checked.

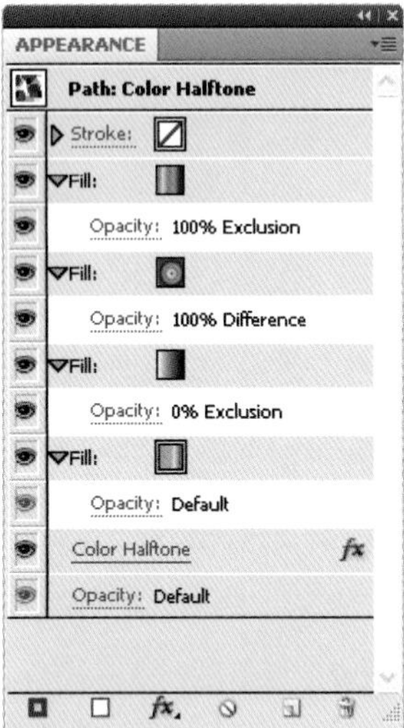

You can now control the visibility of attributes inside the Appearance panel.

Enhanced Gradient tool

The new Gradient tool is more intuitive than ever. Instead of having to use the Gradient panel to control color stops in a gradient, you can now select the Gradient tool (▣), hover over the object, and get gradient information as you mouse over. You can control the start and end points of a gradient, by dragging on either side of the line. The smaller, first black circle on the left, with a white center, lets you control the length and orientation of the gradient; the larger black circle with a white center, lets you move the whole gradient; the diamond on the end lets you resize the whole gradient proportionally. If you double-click one of the color stops, the Color panel appears, where you can control the color and—new in CS4—the transparency of a color. This means that you can finally make vignette-like gradients over images or objects. (Gradients that contain transparency were not possible prior to CS4.) If you need to make a new color stop, just Alt-drag (Windows) or Option-drag (Mac OS) a color stop.

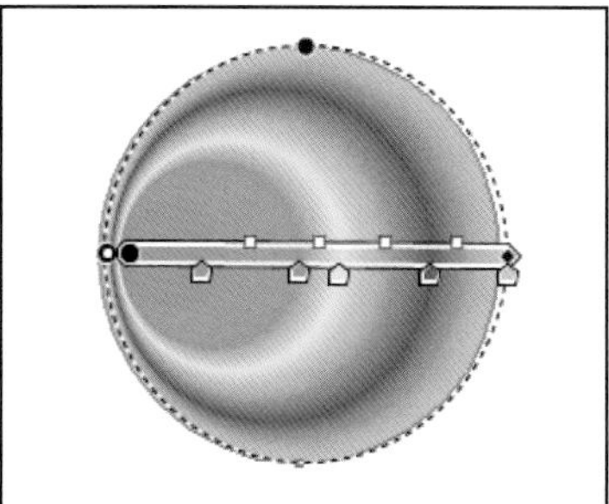

Changing a gradient right on the object with CS4.

CS4's new Gradient tool ends the old issue of multiple panel management. You no longer need both the Gradient panel and the Color panel to create and edit a gradient; you can now edit the gradient right on an object!

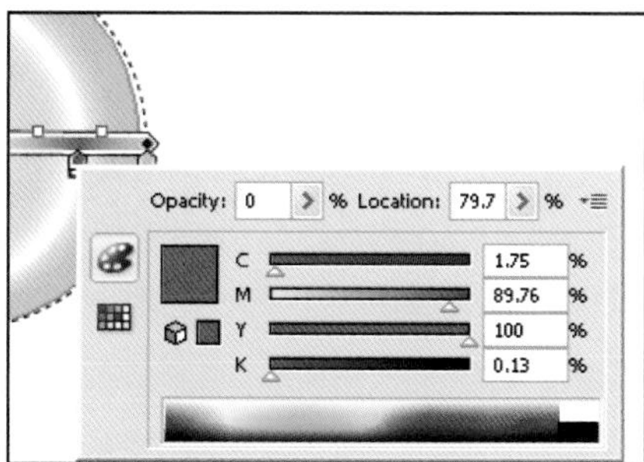

Double-click a color stop to change both the color and transparency of a gradient color stop.

You will find additional new features introduced throughout the book. Some, like the new features introduced in this lesson, will have a significant impact on how you create artwork in Adobe Illustrator, and some will just make working in Adobe Illustrator a little easier and a lot more comfortable.

Index

Numerics

A

B

C

D

E

F

G

H

M

R

S

T

U

V

W

Y

Z

Wiley Publishing, Inc.
End-User License Agreement

READ THIS. You should carefully read these terms and conditions before opening the software packet(s) included with this book "Book". This is a license agreement "Agreement" between you and Wiley Publishing, Inc. "WPI". By opening the accompanying software packet(s), you acknowledge that you have read and accept the following terms and conditions. If you do not agree and do not want to be bound by such terms and conditions, promptly return the Book and the unopened software packet(s) to the place you obtained them for a full refund.

1. **License Grant.** WPI grants to you (either an individual or entity) a nonexclusive license to use one copy of the enclosed software program(s) (collectively, the "Software") solely for your own personal or business purposes on a single computer (whether a standard computer or a workstation component of a multi-user network). The Software is in use on a computer when it is loaded into temporary memory (RAM) or installed into permanent memory (hard disk, CD-ROM, or other storage device). WPI reserves all rights not expressly granted herein.

2. **Ownership.** WPI is the owner of all right, title, and interest, including copyright, in and to the compilation of the Software recorded on the physical packet included with this Book "Software Media". Copyright to the individual programs recorded on the Software Media is owned by the author or other authorized copyright owner of each program. Ownership of the Software and all proprietary rights relating thereto remain with WPI and its licensers.

3. **Restrictions on Use and Transfer.**

   (a) You may only (i) make one copy of the Software for backup or archival purposes, or (ii) transfer the Software to a single hard disk, provided that you keep the original for backup or archival purposes. You may not (i) rent or lease the Software, (ii) copy or reproduce the Software through a LAN or other network system or through any computer subscriber system or bulletin-board system, or (iii) modify, adapt, or create derivative works based on the Software.

   (b) You may not reverse engineer, decompile, or disassemble the Software. You may transfer the Software and user documentation on a permanent basis, provided that the transferee agrees to accept the terms and conditions of this Agreement and you retain no copies. If the Software is an update or has been updated, any transfer must include the most recent update and all prior versions.

4. **Restrictions on Use of Individual Programs.** You must follow the individual requirements and restrictions detailed for each individual program in the "About the CD" appendix of this Book or on the Software Media. These limitations are also contained in the individual license agreements recorded on the Software Media. These limitations may include a requirement that after using the program for a specified period of time, the user must pay a registration fee or discontinue use. By opening the Software packet(s), you agree to abide by the licenses and restrictions for these individual programs that are detailed in the "About the CD" appendix and/or on the Software Media. None of the material on this Software Media or listed in this Book may ever be redistributed, in original or modified form, for commercial purposes.

5. **Limited Warranty.**

   (a) WPI warrants that the Software and Software Media are free from defects in materials and workmanship under normal use for a period of sixty (60) days from the date of purchase of this Book. If WPI receives notification within the warranty period of defects in materials or workmanship, WPI will replace the defective Software Media.

- **(b)** WPI AND THE AUTHOR(S) OF THE BOOK DISCLAIM ALL OTHER WARRANTIES, EXPRESS OR IMPLIED, INCLUDING WITHOUT LIMITATION IMPLIED WARRANTIES OF MERCHANTABILITY AND FITNESS FOR A PARTICULAR PURPOSE, WITH RESPECT TO THE SOFTWARE, THE PROGRAMS, THE SOURCE CODE CONTAINED THEREIN, AND/OR THE TECHNIQUES DESCRIBED IN THIS BOOK. WPI DOES NOT WARRANT THAT THE FUNCTIONS CONTAINED IN THE SOFTWARE WILL MEET YOUR REQUIREMENTS OR THAT THE OPERATION OF THE SOFTWARE WILL BE ERROR FREE.
- **(c)** This limited warranty gives you specific legal rights, and you may have other rights that vary from jurisdiction to jurisdiction.

6. Remedies.

- **(a)** WPI's entire liability and your exclusive remedy for defects in materials and workmanship shall be limited to replacement of the Software Media, which may be returned to WPI with a copy of your receipt at the following address: Software Media Fulfillment Department, Attn.: *Adobe Illustrator CS4 Digital Classroom*, Wiley Publishing, Inc., 10475 Crosspoint Blvd., Indianapolis, IN 46256, or call 1-800-762-2974. Please allow four to six weeks for delivery. This Limited Warranty is void if failure of the Software Media has resulted from accident, abuse, or misapplication. Any replacement Software Media will be warranted for the remainder of the original warranty period or thirty (30) days, whichever is longer.
- **(b)** In no event shall WPI or the author be liable for any damages whatsoever (including without limitation damages for loss of business profits, business interruption, loss of business information, or any other pecuniary loss) arising from the use of or inability to use the Book or the Software, even if WPI has been advised of the possibility of such damages.
- **(c)** Because some jurisdictions do not allow the exclusion or limitation of liability for consequential or incidental damages, the above limitation or exclusion may not apply to you.

7. U.S. Government Restricted Rights. Use, duplication, or disclosure of the Software for or on behalf of the United States of America, its agencies and/or instrumentalities "U.S. Government" is subject to restrictions as stated in paragraph (c)(1)(ii) of the Rights in Technical Data and Computer Software clause of DFARS 252.227-7013, or subparagraphs (c) (1) and (2) of the Commercial Computer Software - Restricted Rights clause at FAR 52.227-19, and in similar clauses in the NASA FAR supplement, as applicable.

8. General. This Agreement constitutes the entire understanding of the parties and revokes and supersedes all prior agreements, oral or written, between them and may not be modified or amended except in a writing signed by both parties hereto that specifically refers to this Agreement. This Agreement shall take precedence over any other documents that may be in conflict herewith. If any one or more provisions contained in this Agreement are held by any court or tribunal to be invalid, illegal, or otherwise unenforceable, each and every other provision shall remain in full force and effect.